CHINA SINCE 1644

A History Through Primary Sources

Edited by the Curriculum Specialists at
Primary Source, Inc.

Foreword by Dr. Ezra Vogel
Introductory essay by Dr. William Kirby

Cheng & Tsui Company
Boston

Second Edition
First Edition published as *China in the World: A History Since 1644*

19 18 17 16 15 14 13   2 3 4 5 6 7 8 9 10

Published by
Cheng & Tsui Company, Inc.
25 West Street
Boston, MA 02111-1213 USA
Fax (617) 426-3669
www.cheng-tsui.com
"Bringing Asia to the World"™

ISBN 978-0-88727-996-6

Cover art: Shanghai skyline © iStockphoto/Robert Churchill. Used by permission. "Factory site, Guangzhou," 1865 M20567.A (detail). Courtesy of the Peabody Essex Museum, Salem, Massachusetts. Girl with Red Book. Used by permission of Sally & Richard Greenhill. "Emperor Qianlong on Horseback" (detail). Used by permission of Arthur M Sackler Gallery, Smithsonian Institution, Washington, D.C.: Purchase-Smithsonian Collections Acquisition Program, and partial gift of Richard G. Pritzlaff, S1991.60.

Acknowledgements and copyrights can be found at the back of the book on pages 382–383, which constitute an extension of the copyright page.

Printed in the United States of America

Companion Website Downloads

Users of this textbook have access to full versions of the primary sources, color images, slideshows, and other resources on the free companion website at **www.chinasince1644.com**. Primary sources in this book which have fuller versions available on the companion website are indicated by ⬚. To access these resources, you simply need to answer a question about this book. For example:

Question:
What is the first word in the paragraph under Activity 6 on page 83?

Answer:
Read

Instructions for Accessing Companion Website Resources

1. Visit the companion website at **http://www.chinasince1644.com**.

2. On the home page, there will be a prompt asking a question about the book.

3. Using your book, answer the question.

4. After entering your answer, you will have full access to all the materials on the site. As long as you have cookies enabled, you will not have to answer another question.

5. For technical support, please contact **support@cheng-tsui.com** or call 1-800-554-1963.

Companion Website Content

- Full versions of primary source documents in PDF format, including additional background information

- Larger versions of all images, including full-color versions when available

- Chapter Supplementary Materials

- Links to Activity-specific Websites

- Film clips

- Full-color maps

- Slideshows with additional background information and full-color photographs

- Suggested Resources with websites updated annually

- Introduction for Teachers

- Teaching Strategies

- Support for Common Core State Standards

- Resource Guides

- Online search tips

- Indexes of images and slideshows

- Glossary

Table of Contents

Primary Source dedicates
China Since 1644: A History Through Primary Sources to
The Freeman Foundation
which has so generously supported our work.

Acknowledgments

Primary Source is deeply indebted to the scholars who freely shared their expertise, helped us shape the book, so patiently answered our many questions, and later reviewed the content. We apologize for any errors that remain; they are the sole responsibility of the author.

Dr. Kenneth Hammond, New Mexico State University

Dr. Stephen R. Platt, University of Massachusetts, Amherst

Dr. Caroline Reeves, Associate in Research, Harvard University Fairbank Center

Dr. John Watt, Fairbank Center, Harvard University

Dr. Shiping Zheng, Bentley College

These scholars provided substantial revisions for the second edition:

Dr. Joseph Fewsmith, Boston University

Dr. Caroline Reeves, Associate in Research, Harvard University Fairbank Center

Dr. Ronald Suleski, Suffolk University

Zachary Scarlett, Doctoral Candidate, Northeastern University

Dr. Shiping Zheng, Bentley University

In addition, a number of scholars and educators provided valuable advice:

Dr. Dorothy V. Borei, Guilford College (retired)

Robert Daly, co-director of Nanjing-Hopkins Center, Nanjing, China

Dr. Christina Gilmartin, Northeastern University

Hong Zheng, principal, Dandelion School, Beijing, China

Dr. Anne Watt, co-founder, Primary Source

Dr. Weili Ye, University of Massachusetts, Boston

Dr. Fang Zhu, Fudan University, Shanghai, China

Yongbiao Zhang, English teacher, officer in the Ministry of Education, China

We thank the teacher-authors who contributed chapters to the book. They spent countless hours tracking down the most engaging primary sources, researching and writing the introductory essays, and developing tried and true activities. Without them, there would be no book.

Cara Abraham, formerly of Brookfield High School, CT

Michael Abraham, New Milford High School, CT

Ryan Bradeen, formerly of Bangor High School, ME and Primary Source

Philip Gambone, Boston University Academy and Harvard Extension School

Dr. Rachel Zucker Gould, Burlington High School, MA

David Green, Acton-Boxborough Regional High School, MA

Kongli Liu, Bryant University and formerly Primary Source

Shirley Moore Huettig, formerly of Concord Academy

Jamie Moore, Newton North High School, MA

Todd Whitten, Social Studies Department Chair, Burlington High School, MA

Nan Ye, formerly of Bangor High School, ME

A number of additional educators offered guidance and materials. We thank you.

Marilyn Day, Marblehead Public Schools, MA

Rachel Eio, Brookline High School

Margaret Harvey, Winchester Public Schools, MA

Seth Kirby, Social Studies Chairperson, Boston College High School

Nicholas Krippendorf, Academy of Pacific Rim, Boston

Chris Kurhajetz, Winchester High School, MA

Richard Meegan, Masconomet Regional High School, MA

Carolyn Platt, formerly of Carlisle Public Schools, MA

Mark Quinones, Somerville High School, MA

David Walsh, Masconomet Regional High School, MA

David Wang, China Youthology, Beijing, China

For their photographs, we thank:

Michael Abraham, Ryan Bradeen, James Brown, Christiane Corcelle-Lippeveld, Renee Covalucci, Abby Detweiler, Sarah Dorer, Eugene Dorgan, Liz Gray, Jennifer Hanson, Margaret Harvey, Wanli Hu, Elizabeth Lewis, Kongli Liu, Lee McCanne, Liz Nelson, Julie Newport, Carolyn Platt, and Anne Watt

Primary Source Staff

Several staff members were key to the creation of this sourcebook
(titled *China in the World: A History Since 1644* in the first edition of 2009):

Liz Nelson, Editor

Kathleen M. Ennis, Executive Director

Ryan Bradeen, Program Director

Peter Gilmartin, Program Director

Wanli Hu, Program Director

Kongli Liu, Program Coordinator

Renee Covalucci, Program Coordinator

For revisions to the second edition, *China Since 1644*:

Dr. Deborah Cunningham, Senior Program Director, Co-Editor

Carolyn Platt, Consultant, Co-Editor

Julia de la Torre, Executive Director (from 2010)

Jennifer Hanson, Librarian

Peter Gilmartin, Program Director

Contributing staff members to one or both editions of this book:

Abby Detweiler, Director of Program Operations

Mark Lyons, Finance Administrator

Sinie Huang, Program Coordinator

We thank Eve Lehmann for serving as Permissions Editor for both editions of this book.

Foreword

There is tremendous dynamism in China, and it is unlikely that anything will stop the continued rise of China. Perhaps nothing is more important in maintaining peace between two great powers, the United States and China, than better understanding between the people of the two nations.

The world is also becoming a smaller place. Over 20 percent of the world's population is Chinese, and Chinese people will play a larger role in affairs around the world in every arena—politics, business, art, music and sports—and in dealing with issues like managing the environment, aiding the poor people of the world, coping with disease, and responding to terrorism.

People around the world may use the same cell phones and the same computers, but the people behind those cell phones and computers have a very different culture, a very different history, a very different way of thinking. It is important for all Americans to be prepared for a world in which they will be interacting with Chinese people.

China Since 1644: A History Through Primary Sources combines knowledge from specialists in the field and the curricular expertise of classroom teachers. It is a timely contribution to helping prepare Americans for the world of the twenty-first century. It is well rounded, covering many different topics from geography to history to society. We should all be thankful to the dedicated teachers who have put together this wonderful sourcebook.

Jump in.

Ezra F. Vogel

Henry Ford II Professor Emeritus,
Harvard University

Lessons of China's Modern History:
A Nation Engaged with the World

By William C. Kirby, Geisinger Professor of History and Director, Fairbank Center for Chinese Studies, Harvard University

It is a pleasure to introduce this extraordinary volume, *China Since 1644: A History Through Primary Sources*. By exploring the texts and images of the past few centuries, the voices of Chinese people become more real and vivid, less distant and abstract. This important approach, of making Chinese perspectives closer and more accessible, mirrors a key shift in our understanding of China's history more broadly: China is not a land apart; it cannot be studied in isolation. China has been shaped by the wider world and the world by China. The sources in this volume extend and illustrate this theme, raising rich questions as they reshape our understanding.

Until recently, scholarship on China (and indeed *in* China) emphasized China's insularity vis-à-vis other cultures. There are to be sure, both symbols and monuments of Chinese defensiveness, such as the Great Wall, built mostly as an anti-Mongol defense perimeter during the Ming era (1368–1644). But for the large majority of the imperial era, China-based empires crossed (often loosely defined) borders routinely, and for good reason: to engage in trade; to adjudicate diplomatic disputes; and to fight wars—that most common of human "international relations."

Particularly in the twentieth century, foreign relations became, quite simply, all penetrating, all permeating, all prevailing—*durchdringend*, as the Germans say—ultimately forcing their way into every part of Chinese society. In the realm of high diplomacy, Chinese statecraft delineated and protected the borders of the new nation-state to which all Chinese (and not a few non-Chinese) were now said to belong. China's modern economic development was founded in turn on an unprecedented opening to international economic influences. The early decades of the last century witnessed the first "golden age" of Chinese capitalism (we are now in the second) as well as the birth of modern state capitalism, neither of which could have existed without foreign partners. Patterns of dress and consumption would be influenced by international models, from the Sun Yat-sen (or "Mao") jacket, a military tunic adopted from Japan, to the nationwide addiction to nicotine, aided by the British-American Tobacco Company. Most striking of all in the twentieth century was the self-conscious attempt to overhaul Chinese culture, particularly political culture, according to international categories. Every government sought legitimacy in the context of one or another internationally authenticated "ism," from constitutionalism to communism.

What lessons might we draw from China's modern international history? Let us start, a bit more than a century ago, in the mad summer of 1900.

On June 21, 1900, the Great Qing Empire declared war on eight countries, including the United States. The Qing—the Manchu dynasty that had ruled China since 1644—besieged the legations of the foreign powers in Beijing. During the "Fifty-Five Days in Peking," as Hollywood would later film it, a small band of foreigners held out against great odds before an international expeditionary force could rescue it. This 20,000-man force then subdued an empire of 450 million subjects, making quick work of the Qing armies and the "Boxer" irregulars who joined them. The Western forces sacked and plundered Beijing, occupied its ancient palaces, and extracted an enormous indemnity. The humiliation of the Qing was complete. Eleven years later it collapsed, ending an imperial tradition of more than 2,000 years.

How the world changes. Little more than a century earlier, at the time of the American Revolution, the Qing dynasty presided over the strongest, richest, and most sophisticated civilization on the planet. It was supremely self-confident. It ruled China, and dominated East Asia, by a combination of power and cultural prestige. Through the famous examination system, it recruited the most learned men in the realm to government service. It did not want or need contact with the West. By 1895, however, China had been invaded, defeated, and degraded by first the Western nations and then Japan. Such was the sudden, overwhelming power of the industrial revolution and the aggressive militarism of the imperialist age. The Boxer Uprising was a final, futile act of resistance by a government, and indeed an entire system of governance, that would be blown away. Today, more than a century after the Boxer Uprising, China is again formidable. It is an industrial power, a military power, and a growing economic power. It has become a great power because of, not despite, its relations with the rest of the world. Yet its power is at once shaped and constrained by its modern history.

China is an ancient civilization, but it is really a very young country. "China" as a political entity did not exist until 1912, when the Republic of China—Asia's first republic—was proclaimed as the successor to Manchu rule. The questions posed at that time are the dominant ones for Chinese history in this century. What would be China's physical domain? How would China interact with the outside world? What kind of government would replace that of the old empire? Let us discuss these questions, briefly, as a prelude to allowing the primary sources in this volume to speak for themselves.

China's Borders

The government that succeeded the empire in 1912 inherited not what one might call "historical China" but the vast Qing Empire, a multinational and multicultural expanse that included Manchuria, Mongolia, Eastern Turkestan, and Tibet, among other areas. No *Chinese* empire had ever been so big for so long as the Qing realm of the Manchus. The amazing fact of the twentieth century is that this space had not only been redefined, as "Chinese" and as the sacred soil of China, but also defended diplomatically to such a degree that the borders of the People's Republic of China today are essentially those of the Qing, minus only Outer Mongolia. The Qing fell but the empire remained.

These borders have enjoyed international diplomatic recognition since 1912, because the great powers of the day believed—rightly—that a divided China would be a source of international instability. But it was the job of Chinese governments to defend these borders, often from a position of great weakness, relying on a diplomacy that was hard-pressed, often creative, and always obstinate.

For example, Chiang Kai-shek's Nationalist government, which ruled the Chinese mainland from 1927 to 1949, held on to at least nominal title to areas that the Manchus had governed but where the new Republic had little power: in Tibet, for example, where the Nationalists, like the Communists after them, would aim to undermine a stubbornly autonomous Dalai Lama by playing up the authority of a (China-friendly) Panchen Lama; or in the Muslim region of Xinjiang (Eastern Turkestan), in the far northwest, where Chinese rule was finally reasserted in the mid-1940s after a period of Soviet occupation. In each instance China used forms of what we would call the non-recognition doctrine: refusing to recognize anyone else's sovereignty until matters could be settled in China's favor. The non-recognition of unpleasant realities was carried to an art form in the case of

Manchuria, which Japan occupied in 1931. It speaks volumes about the power of modern Chinese nationalism that China would mobilize for war—as it did in the 1930s—in defense of the *Manchu* homeland into which Chinese settlement had been legally permitted only since 1907. And it convinced the rest of the world not to legitimize Japan's conquest. If the case of Outer Mongolia turned out differently, this was because the Mongolians enjoyed powerful foreign support. In any event, this was the one part of the old Qing Empire where people actually got to vote whether they would be part of the Chinese nation. Mongolians ratified their independence in the Stalinesque plebiscite of October 1945. With the Russians counting, the vote was 487,000 to *nothing*.

This agenda of national unification is still very much alive. After the Nationalists lost the mainland to the Communists in 1949, and retreated to Taiwan, official maps in Taipei still showed Outer Mongolia as part of the Republic of China. The return of Hong Kong to China was something on which both Nationalists and Communists could agree.

Curiously enough, for most of the first half of the twentieth century Taiwan was not *terra irredenta*, like Manchuria, but quite literally off China's map. Taiwan was not part of the old Manchu empire when it collapsed, because it had been ceded to Japan as the victor in the Sino-Japanese War of 1894–1895. The Republican government failed to challenge Japan's right to Taiwan until 1943, when Japan's defeat in World War II seemed likely. Taiwan became part of the Republic of China in 1945. When the Nationalists made it their last bastion in 1949, and when the United States intervened to protect them in 1950, Taiwan's "liberation" became a national cause on the Chinese mainland.

Now it is the last remaining cause of China's "reunification." It promises to be the most difficult cause. Taiwan's inhabitants, although culturally Chinese, were Japanese subjects from 1895 to 1945, and were largely removed from the growth of Chinese nationalism on the mainland. Many of them resented, and some resisted, Nationalist Chinese control after 1945. Taiwan's first reunification with the mainland did not go well. Taiwan's Democratic Progressive Party had its origins in Taiwanese resistance to Chinese mainland domination. Now even the old Nationalist party, which for decades aimed to make (anticommunist) Chinese patriots out of the people of Taiwan, has itself become largely "Taiwanized." Gradually but surely, a separate, Taiwanese political identity is evolving on this island, even as its economic and cultural relations with the mainland deepen, and even as it retains the historic name of the Republic of China.

Meanwhile, on the other side of the Strait, the tenacity, obduracy, and overall *success* of China's twentieth-century diplomacy, which made the most distant regions of the Manchu realm part of "China," helps to explain the People's Republic of China's (PRC's) unyielding determination to "recover" Taiwan, historically part of China though never governed by the PRC.

China's Internationalization

The demarcation of China's borders took place in a century of onrushing, inescapable, internationalization at home. There is a great misperception that China "opened its doors" only in the last thirty years. This is not true. Rather, the years of isolationism (ca. 1960–1972) are the great exception to the rule of China's international engagement in modern times.

Engagement was essential, for example, if China was to rid itself of the humiliations of the imperialist era. At the beginning of the twentieth century, foreigners in China enjoyed extraordinary privileges, extracted at gunpoint and by treaty. Through tough, relentless negotiations, by the mid-1940s China had regained full control of its "inner borders," that is, over the territorial concessions, monopolies, and special legal rights once held by foreigners.

China's commercial and industrial development in the twentieth century is unthinkable without internationalization, for it was founded on an unprecedented opening to international economic influences. The 1910s and 1920s witnessed the creation of a distinctly Chinese class of entrepreneurs, combining inherited and imported business cultures in a powerful way. Although the Communist revolution would force Chinese capitalism into temporary exile on China's periphery, its return to China after 1978, in the form of investments from Chinese in Hong Kong, Taiwan, and Southeast Asia, would be the driving force in the great boom of the 1980s and 1990s. The growth of modern state capitalism from the 1930s onward was similarly dependent on foreign investment. In the late twentieth century, as Chinese state industries rusted and decayed, foreign capital was found to reinvent them through "corporatization."

Chinese higher education has similarly been shaped by the world at large. Beijing University, China's most venerable, is little more than a century old, and resides on the campus of the old Yenching University, which began as a missionary college. American, European, and Soviet models of higher education have each had their impact on the training of modern Chinese intellectuals. And waves of Chinese students have studied abroad: in Japan in the 1900s; in the United States in the 1910s and 1920s; in Germany in the 1930s; in the Soviet Union and Eastern Europe in the 1950s; and again, on a massive scale, in the United States in the 1980s and beyond. Only in the last case can one speak of a "brain drain" from China; and to judge from the case of Taiwan, which sent thousands of students to the United States beginning in the 1950s, it will prove a temporary phenomenon.

Political partnership with foreign powers was vital to China's very survival in the middle decades of the twentieth century. In the 1930s and 1940s, China entered into alignments with three of the world's most powerful countries—Germany, the Soviet Union, and the United States—in order to defend itself against the fourth, Japan. From 1942 to 1960 China sought security through formal alliances with two "superpowers," first with the United States, and then, after the Communist revolution, with the Soviet Union, in part to defend China *from* the United States.

Although from an American perspective China was "isolated" in the 1950s, China was never so deeply incorporated into an international system as it was in the hottest years of the Cold War. The Sino-Soviet alliance was the most fully articulated military alliance in China's history. It was an intense cultural and educational alliance, confirmed by the thousands of Chinese who studied in the Soviet Union and the thousands of Russians who taught in China. It was an economic alliance of greater depth and complexity than any of modern China's foreign economic relationships. And it was an alliance based on an initially shared vision as to how a country should be governed.

Governing China

It is ironic but inevitable that modern China, in seeking to be master of its own fate, has so consistently looked abroad for its models of government. No government believed that China's twentieth-century crises could be solved by a return to the Qing state. There were certainly no clear precedents in Chinese political history for the task of integrating a new set of social groups—among them a bourgeoisie, a proletariat, an intelligentsia, and a permanent, professional military—into the altogether new structure of a nation-state. Therefore the last century was one of continual experimentation with political forms, not one of which was indigenous in origin: the parliamentary republic of 1912–1913, the military dictatorship of 1913–1916, the attempt at constitutional monarchy in 1916, the "Confucian fascism" of Chiang Kai-shek, and the several forms of communism under Mao Zedong and his successors.

Since the 1920s this experimentation has taken place within the framework of one enduring institution, the Leninist Party-State, of which there have been two incarnations—Nationalist and Communist. The Party-State is a *one*-party state. Sun Yat-sen, the father of the Nationalist state, defined the mission of the ruling Guomindang (Nationalist Party) as that of tutoring the Chinese people for democracy. "Tutelage" was to last six years. For Chinese under Nationalist rule on the mainland and on Taiwan, it lasted sixty. And when the Nationalists were ousted from the mainland in 1949, they were replaced by the other Chinese Party-State, of the Communists, in an intensification of Party-State rule that has survived until the present day.

The Party's purpose was not only to lead the government, but also to remake the Chinese people, to forge a citizenry for the new nation-state. Chiang Kai-shek's New Life Movement of the mid-1930's aimed to discipline an undisciplined populace, to give it a sense of obligation to the nation. Mao Zedong would take this transformative effort in a much different direction in his "Great Proletarian Cultural Revolution" of the 1960s.

The Party-State was a developmental state. It aimed to mobilize and industrialize China from the top down. Sun Yat-sen's famous work, *The International Development of China* (1921) was the first attempt to plot out the integrated economic development of a reunified China. It remains the most audacious and—still today, many Three-, Four-, Five-, and Ten-Year Plans later—the most memorable of national development programs. Sun's faith that international capital could be mobilized to construct Chinese socialism would be shared widely by Nationalist and Communist leaders. Sun's more concrete plans also left their mark. His two-paragraph proposal to "improve the upper Yangzi" with an enormous dam spawned seventy-five years of effort and debate before work on the great Three Gorges Dam finally began in the mid-1990s.

The Party-State was also a military state. Both the Nationalists and the Communists fought their way to power in the first half of the twentieth century, when China had more men under arms than any other part of the world. Western militarism (in its Soviet, German, and U.S. national forms) was undoubtedly the single most successful cultural export from the West to China. Militarily defeated on the mainland, the Nationalists governed Taiwan on the formal basis of martial law until 1987. It was under Communist rule, however, that militarization would be taken furthest. Whereas the Nationalist military took oaths to defend the nation, the People's Liberation Army swore to uphold the rule of the Chinese Communist Party. This they did in the Tiananmen Incident of 1989. Through the 1990s, a significant part of the state sector of the economy (no one knows for sure how much) was owned and operated directly by the military.

The Party-State had a Leader. The formal titles given first to Sun Yat-sen, Chiang Kai-shek, or Mao Zedong hardly captured the spirit and scope of their domination over their followers. Until very recently, both the Nationalist and Communist Party-States were led by a series of leadership cliques that are understood better as conspiratorial brotherhoods rather than as political factions. In short, for much of the twentieth century China was ruled by a very small group of men (one to two dozen) under one Leader. Whether as a continuation of monarchical political culture or as an example of Soviet and fascist influence, the Chinese Party-State demanded a single head, a *yuanshou*—as the term *Führer* used to be translated into Chinese. Whether the Party-State can survive political competition (as in Taiwan) or collective leadership (in the PRC) remains to be seen.

Lessons

The emphasis on personal leadership reveals the greatest weakness of the Party-State: its inability to work together with civilian elites to erect an enduring, self-replicating, system of government. Civilians could serve the Party-State, but could not govern separately from it. Like the Nationalist Party-State that preceded it (and the Manchu conquerors that preceded it) the People's Republic began as a military conquest regime. But as the old political wisdom goes: one conquers from horseback, but one cannot rule from horseback. Unlike the Manchus, who ruled China for 267 years, and unlike every other successful ruling house in Chinese history, by the early part of the twenty-first century the Chinese Communist Party had yet to show that its power could be transferred to, or even shared with, civilian political and legal institutions with enduring legitimacy. The Nationalists on Taiwan, by contrast, learned to cohabit with the sober-minded, authoritarian technocrats who guided Taiwan's economic miracle. But even these elites never exercised political power independent of the Party-State and never fundamentally challenged it. Even after the end of Party "tutelage" on Taiwan in 1987, certain habits of the Party-State died hard: in the late 1990s, after a decade of democratic reforms, the Guomindang's Central Executive Committee still met every Wednesday to set the agenda for the government Cabinet meetings on Thursday.

Pressures for Taiwan's eventual democratization would come from other quarters, above all from the Taiwanese majority who had long chafed under Nationalist Chinese rule. Is this a portent for other regions? Will ethnic challenges lead the process of political change in China itself? It is too early to say. But the evolution of a democratic, autonomous Taiwan in the past decade allows us to recast the question of China's "reunification." From the perspective of history, we may ask not how soon will Taiwan become enfolded in the arms of the motherland, but how long can China hold on to non-Chinese areas that were captured as part of the old empire, like Tibet or Xinjiang? In the short run, the Chinese state is surely strong enough to retain these regions. But from a longer, historical perspective, we must remember that no Chinese empire, ever, has been so big, for so long, as the empire of the Great Qing and its Chinese successors. If the People's Republic is ultimately to get smaller, like all Chinese dynasties that preceded it, or simply "looser"—the Qing's great genius was to rule these territories with a "loose rein"—how it does so, and if it can do so peaceably, will be of enormous importance both to China and to the wider world.

Ultimately the key to China's future lies in the great, unresolved question of the last century: what kind of political system will, in the long run, take the place of the old empire? Chinese governments have been much more successful in defending territory and sovereignty than they have been in erecting stable political systems. Save for the 1990s, every decade in the twentieth century witnessed a major political upheaval. If twentieth-century history is any guide, when political change comes in China, it will be closely related to international political and intellectual currents.

For the present, as the immediate successor in our century to the old imperial system, the Chinese Party-State has shown that it can do many things better. It can organize. It can industrialize. And it can militarize. But unlike that system that disappeared in 1912, it has not yet shown that it can *civilize*. One may use that term in two senses: first, to re-establish a lasting system of *civil* service, and indeed to institutionalize civilian rule, using the great talent of the Chinese people; and, second, to stand for something enduring in human values, for a civilization that goes beyond political control, material development, and martial strength. This was the great strength of the old empire, for all its limitations. This was how its influence radiated throughout East Asia. Perhaps this will be the quest of political structures still unformed, once the Party-State has finally had its day.

Introduction for Students

In his book *Arts of China*, Michael Sullivan writes, "The Chinese painter deliberately avoids a complete statement because he knows that we can never know everything… All he can do is to liberate the imagination and set it wandering… His landscape is not a final statement, but a starting point. Not an end, but the opening of a door." That is precisely how we view our book, *China Since 1644: A History Through Primary Sources*. Our goal is to introduce you to events that occurred in China and people who lived through them. In addition, in the final section, we take a look at contemporary China. Through essays, primary source documents, and student activities, our book provides a starting point for understanding the complex, vibrant, and sometimes tumultuous recent history of a people with the longest continuous civilization in the world.

"In 1600, the empire of China was the largest and most sophisticated of all the unified realms on earth," writes Jonathan Spence in his seminal work *The Search for Modern China* (p. 7). By 1800, the empire was not only still the most sophisticated state on earth, but had more than doubled in size. Why then, at the dawn of the twenty-first century, did we talk about China *becoming* one of the global superpowers? What happened in the intervening centuries?

Who Are We?

Primary Source is a non-profit global education organization dedicated to helping you prepare for the challenges and complexities of today's interconnected world. In partnership with teachers, scholars, and the broader community, Primary Source strives to equip you with the skills, knowledge, and resources necessary for global literacy. Primary Source is guided by a commitment to affect the way you learn history and understand culture such that your knowledge base is broad, your thinking flexible and given to inquiry, and your attitudes about peoples of the world open and inclusive.

Using Primary Sources

Primary Source, the organization, takes its name from the same term used by historians to distinguish original, uninterpreted material from second- or third-hand accounts. Thus a photograph, a memoir, or a letter is a primary source, while an essay interpreting the photograph or memoir is usually, though not always, a secondary source.

China Since 1644 utilizes a range of primary sources, some of which have never previously appeared in print. We include letters from American traders in Guangzhou (formerly Canton), writings of missionaries, treaties, imperial writing, propaganda posters, poetry, short stories, photographs, and more. All Chinese text has been translated, making it, arguably, no longer a primary source. We have selected translations by eminent scholars to ensure the most accurate reading possible.

While it is imperative to read secondary sources, including textbooks, in order to understand context and background, access to "the real stuff" (albeit some in translation) offers opportunities for you to make discoveries independently. Original source material provides rich opportunities for inquiry, and the chance to move from concrete to abstract thinking.

How to Use This Book

The Organization of *China Since 1644*

The first two chapters in the book introduce information helpful to understanding all the chapters that follow. Chapter 1 looks at China's geography and diverse population of today, and provides a sense of how the vast majority of China's people—the rural population—lived in much of the twentieth century and before. Chapter 2 steps back into the sixteenth century, the last century of China's Ming dynasty, to showcase the cities and capture the lives of the elite who contributed to making the empire "the most sophisticated on earth."

The remaining chapters are arranged chronologically and clustered in units. Each unit begins with an overview and most also include a timeline that lists the events in China in the context of related events in regional and world history.

Each chapter contains:

- Chapter Contents
- Key Idea
- Guiding Questions
- Terms to Know
- Essay
- Primary Sources
- Activities
- Suggested Resources
- A Closer Look

Together, the **context essay by Dr. Kirby** at the beginning of the book, the **unit overviews**, and the **introductory essays** to individual chapters provide background information necessary for understanding the primary sources and engaging in the activities. The book is designed so that chapters can be used independently of each other. *We strongly recommend that you read a unit overview before reading an isolated chapter.*

Terms to Know are included, and the words are defined in the **glossary** (The glossary is in the book and on the companion website at **www.chinasince1664.com**).

Each chapter includes a variety of **activities** from which to choose. Each activity is based on one or more **primary sources**. Together they are designed to stimulate critical and creative thinking. Excerpts of the primary sources appear in the book; in most cases, longer versions are included on the companion website. *It is important to understand that in order to complete any of the activities, you must read the full text of the document on the companion website.* Suggested activities include study and analysis of primary sources, mapping, research and writing, debating, and creative responses.

A list of **Suggested Resources** (websites, books, and films) is provided in each chapter in the book, and on the companion website. While every effort has been made to ensure that reputable websites are current and stable, material on the Internet does change. Be sure to carefully evaluate information found online, always considering who the author is, who sponsors the site, and what biases might be present.

Wherever applicable, chapters include the special feature **A Closer Look**. This feature gives the reader a more in-depth look at men and women who played key roles in events explored in the chapter.

The Companion Website

A wealth of chapter, supplementary, and additional materials to support learning can be found at **www.chinasince1644.com**, including:

- Materials for **Chapters** include primary source documents and images, suggested resources (websites updated annually), and links to websites for specific activities. Many of the documents on the companion website include background introductions not found in the text.
- **Additional Resources** include essays on the histories of Taiwan, Tibet, and Xinjiang, a glossary, online search tips, maps, and indexes of all slides and slide shows.

A Note on the Text

In 1859, Sir Thomas Francis Wade, professor of Chinese at Cambridge University, created a system for the Romanization of Chinese characters. His successor Herbert Giles revised it in 1892, establishing the Wade-Giles system, which served as the primary English-language method of writing Chinese in the Roman alphabet until the middle of the twentieth century. In 1953, the People's Republic of China devised its own system of Romanization, called *pinyin*. Most older transliterations use the Wade-Giles spelling of Chinese words, while recent publications have increasingly adopted pinyin as the standard. We use pinyin throughout *China Since 1644*, with just a few exceptions. The names of Chiang Kai-shek and Sun Yat-sen appear in their older Romanized forms because those spellings are most familiar to the majority of readers.

Note that for Chinese names in the Suggested Resources, we have followed the ordering of first and last names that the author uses in publishing his or her work. Chinese authors using the Chinese convention appear last name then first name with no comma separating the two. This also applies to Chinese who are well-known in the West by the Chinese form of their name (Deng Xiaoping or Ding Ling). Chinese authors using the Western convention appear last name, first name with a comma between the two.

In the introductory essays, the first time that historically significant words or phrases appear, we have included the word written in *pinyin* and simplified Chinese characters. Sometimes the terms are already in *pinyin*, so only characters are included in the parentheses that follow.

All monetary figures cited in the book are given according to the currency of the time; they have not been converted into present-day rates.

Finally, many of the English primary source documents written in the eighteenth and nineteenth centuries include spelling, capitalization, and syntax typical for the period. We have left those unchanged. In a few letters, we did add periods where sentences end and capital letters where new ones begin for clarity.

CHINA SINCE 1644
A History Through Primary Sources

CHAPTER RESOURCES

Primary Sources

DOCUMENT 1.1: Slide show "The Rural Landscape of China," 2000–2007

DOCUMENT 1.2: Excerpts from *Peasant Life in China* by Fei Xiaotong, 1938

DOCUMENT 1.3: Excerpts from *The Good Earth* by Pearl S. Buck, 1931

DOCUMENT 1.4: Excerpts from memoir by Li Xiuwen (1890–1992), describing life in the village where she grew up, early 20th century

DOCUMENT 1.5: Excerpts from "The Village With No Name," in *Daughter of Heaven* by Leslie Li, 2005

DOCUMENT 1.6: Slide show "Among the Peoples of China," 2006

DOCUMENT 1.7: Excerpts related to minority peoples from "The Common Program of the Chinese People's Political Consultative Conference," September 29, 1949

Supplementary Materials

ITEM 1.A: Outline map of the world

ITEM 1.B: Outline map of China

ITEM 1.C: Map of China's provinces, autonomous regions, and municipalities

ITEM 1.D: "Han Diversity and Unity," an essay

ITEM 1.E: China's national minorities and major areas of distribution

 Excerpts of these primary source documents appear in this chapter. Go to **www.chinasince1644.com** for the full version of these documents and for the Supplementary Materials.

CHAPTER 1

China's Geography and Political Divisions

By Liz Nelson and Primary Source staff

Chapter Contents

Key Idea

The People's Republic of China is a nation with a highly diverse landscape, climate, and population, all of which both enrich the country and pose challenges.

Guiding Questions

What are China's most important topographical features?

How are China's topography and climate related to population density?

Which regions of China are likely to be the most difficult to cultivate? Why?

Which borders do you think have been the most troublesome for China's government in the past 250 years? Which are likely to be the cause of the most concern for China's government today? Why?

When and why were the autonomous regions established? In what ways are the regions "autonomous"?

When and why were the "municipalities" established?

Are the relationships between each of China's minority peoples and the central government the same? If not, how and why are the relationships different?

What were the characteristics of agrarian life in China before the founding of the People's Republic of China in 1949? How has rural life changed since that time?

Terms to Know

jia	monsoon
loess	province

Essay

China (*Zhongguo* 中国) is a country of enormous diversity. Over 60 percent of its land is more than a mile above sea level and includes some of the highest mountains in the world. Most of the uplands, however, are hills and plateaus. The country's climate ranges from tropical in the South to sub-arctic in the far North. The population is predominantly Han (汉) Chinese,[1] but China also includes fifty-five distinct minority nationalities, whose languages and cultures differ significantly from those of the Han.

As for any other country, China's location, landforms, rivers, and climate play a crucial role in its history and culture. Since ancient times, Chinese men and women have been changing their environment through great cooperative human effort. They have built terraces on hills, drained marshes, created huge new waterways by building canals, and contained rivers by building massive dikes. Even level areas, such as plains and banks of rivers, have been modified by human action. Twenty-first century projects, such as the Three Gorges Dam (*San Xia Daba* 三峡大坝) and the diversion of water from the South to the North, though they may be controversial, are in keeping with this tradition spanning millennia.

Administrative Units

Today more than 1.3 billion people live in China—roughly one out of five people on our earth. The present-day People's Republic of China (*Zhonghua Renmin Gongheguo* 中华人民共和国) encompasses essentially the same land area that was controlled by the Qing (清) dynasty after 1750.[2] The country is divided into twenty-three provinces, four "Municipalities,"[3] five Autonomous Regions,[4] and two Special Administrative Regions.[5] Chinese people identify strongly with their native provinces, several of which are larger than Germany, the biggest country in Europe.

Ethnic Minorities

Before World War II, the Chinese (Guomindang) government recognized four ethnic groups other than the Han Chinese: Manchus, Mongolians, Tibetans, and Chinese Muslims. After the People's Republic of China (PRC) was founded in 1949, the government began an inventory and identification of the many other minority peoples (*shaoshu minzu* 少数民族). According to the Common Program of 1949 and the subsequent 1954 constitution, the rights of all Chinese citizens are guaranteed, including those of ethnic minorities. In regions where a substantial proportion of the population includes minority nationalities, the PRC has established autonomous counties and provinces

---

[1] More than 90 percent; however, given the size of China's population, the minority nationalities together comprise approximately 106 million people.

[2] Over the course of the first century of their rule, Qing dynasty (1644–1911) emperors greatly increased the size of China (see Chapter 3).

[3] Beijing, Shanghai, Tianjin, and Chongqing. The "municipalities" stand alone like provinces.

[4] Guangxi Zhuang, Xizang (Tibet), Xinjiang Uyghur, Ningxia Hui, and Nei Mongol. See Resources on the companion website for additional information about Tibet and Xinjiang.

[5] Hong Kong and Macao (see Chapter 17).

with the stated goal of ensuring the minority peoples' autonomy.[6] Different laws and regulations apply to people designated as members of a minority. For example, they are permitted to have more than one child, and affirmative action programs help them enter universities. However, the "autonomous" regions are not independent in any political sense, and groups of activists the central government sees as potentially troublesome (such as those among the Uyghurs or Tibetans) are repressed, sometimes with great force.

While the land area of China is essentially the same size as that of the United States, only about 15 percent of its land is suitable for growing crops. (Approximately 40 percent of U. S. land could be cultivated.) As a result, 90 percent of China's population is concentrated in the eastern third of the country, where thriving cities and arable land lie.

The Rivers

Two major rivers are China's most prominent geographic features. From their sources in the western highlands, the Huang He and Chang Jiang flow for thousands of kilometers across the land to empty into the Pacific Ocean. The northernmost river is the Huang He (黄河) or Yellow River. The 5,464-kilometer-long[7] river gets its name from the amount of yellow earth—*loess* (*huangtu* 黄土)—in the water. Loess is the fine, yellow wind-blown soil found in northern China, which blows in from the Gobi Desert and provides a wonderful base for agriculture. Vast quantities of loess are eroded by rainfall, carried into streams, and then into the Huang He as a dense sediment. In the lower reaches of the Huang He, the deposits of the eroded sediment constantly raise the riverbed's level. In some areas, because of natural and manmade banks along the river, the river itself actually flows above the level of the fields.

When the river breaks through its banks, floods devastate the surrounding countryside and ruin the crops and livelihood of many farmers who live along it. As a result, the Huang He has earned the name "China's sorrow." However, the water and loess it carries have also made agriculture possible for millennia. In recent decades, the flow of the river has decreased substantially in the lower reaches of the Huang He, so that instead of a flood there is now only the trickle of a stream (see Chapter 20). Indeed, it is in the rich soil of the river's bottom that farmers now till their fields.

Another major river system is called the Chang Jiang (长江), also known in the West as the Yangzi River. It is the longest river in China and one of the five longest rivers in the world. It flows 6,380 kilometers[8] down through central China to the coast at Shanghai. Fed by snowmelt and heavy rain, this river and its tributaries (more than 3,000) provide the major transportation system for all of central China. Approximately 40 percent of China's grain production and 70 percent of its rice production occur in the river's huge basin. For these reasons, many of China's important cities have developed here.

Climate

China has great climatic differences resulting from the size of the country, the variety of its natural features, and the monsoon-like wind system that controls precipitation. Although China does not experience the prominent monsoons of South Asia, there is a monsoon-like seasonal reversal of winds in East Asia. This is especially true throughout the winter, when winds blow out from central Asia, carrying cold, dry air toward the sea in North China, extending even into some areas of southern China. From late spring to early fall, on the other hand, moist and hot air blows inland from the southeast seacoast and leads to substantial rainfall when the air rises over the hills and mountains. Because of these monsoon-like seasonal reversals of winds, more rain falls in

[6] Ma Yin, ed., *China's Minority Nationalities* (Beijing: Foreign Languages Press, 1994) 25.

[7] 3,395 miles

[8] 3,965 miles

summer than in winter throughout China. Most parts of the country receive more than 80 percent of their rainfall from May to October. Moreover, far more rain falls on Southeast China than on North China, making it possible for farmers in the southeast to have two or even three harvests in a year. In the North, rainfall occurs mostly in the summer months, but it is unpredictable and varies from year to year, often creating problems of either drought or flooding.

Temperatures in China vary greatly from region to region. Northern and western China have cold and long winters like those in the north central United States. In South China winters are usually mild. Summer temperatures average about 26–32° Celsius[9] throughout much of China, but in southeastern China summers are also extremely humid.

[9] 80–90 degrees Fahrenheit

Land formation and climate in China determine which crops are grown in different regions. This has, in turn, dictated people's diet. The staple foods in the North are noodles and dumplings made of wheat and other hardy grains such as millet and sorghum; even steamed bread is commonly eaten. In southeastern and eastern China, on the other hand, people generally eat rice, which can be made into noodles and dumplings in addition to being steamed. Poultry and pork are preferred meats because raising these animals requires little land, unlike the grazing of cattle. China's environment has influenced every aspect of its history and culture, from the location of major cities to innovative farming practices to the food people eat.

Note: For information about China's environmental challenges, see Chapter 20.

Primary Sources

DOCUMENT 1.1: Photographs from the slide show "The Rural Landscape of China," 2000–2007

Yaks grazing; en route between Lhasa and Yamdrok-tso Lake, Xizang Autonomous Region (Tibet), 2005

(Photo by Abby Detweiler)

Harvested rice in the foreground, rice paddies in the center, and tea bushes in the background, Huangcun, Anhui Province, 2007

(Photo by Ryan Bradeen)

 Go to **www.chinasince1644.com** for the slide show "The Rural Landscape of China," **Document 1.1**.

DOCUMENT 1.2:
Excerpts from *Peasant Life in China* by Fei Xiaotong, 1938
....

The main purpose of marriage, in the village, is to secure the continuity of descent.... Beliefs connected with the relation of living descendants to the spirits of their ancestors are not clearly and systematically formulated among the people. The general view is that the spirits live in a world very similar to ours, but that economically they are partially dependent on the contributions of their descendents, which are made by periodically burning paper money, paper clothes, and paper articles. Therefore it is essential to have someone to look after one's well-being in the after-world....

The desire to have children is backed up by a two-fold motive; it ensures, in the first place, the continuity of the line of descent; and, in the second place, it is a concrete expression of filial piety by the future father towards his ancestors....[10]

SOURCE: Fei Xiaotong, *Peasant Life in China: A Field Study of Country Life in the Yangzi Valley* (New York: Oxford University Press, 1946) 30–31.

 Go to **www.chinasince1644.com** for the full text of **Document 1.2**.

---

[10] Traditionally men, not women, conduct the ancestor worship rites.

DOCUMENT 1.3:
Excerpts from *The Good Earth* by Pearl S. Buck, 1931

[W]hen he had gone in the morning, [his wife] took the bamboo rake and a length of rope and with these she roamed the countryside, reaping here a bit of grass and there a twig or a handful of leaves, returning at noon with enough to cook the dinner. It pleased the man that they need buy no more fuel.

In the afternoon, she took a hoe and a basket and with these upon her shoulder she went to the main road leading into the city where mules and donkeys and horses carried burdens to and fro, and there she picked the droppings from the animals and carried it home and piled the manure in the dooryard for fertilizer for the fields....

And she took their ragged clothes and with thread she herself spun on a bamboo spindle from a wad of cotton, she mended and contrived to cover the rents in their winter clothes.... Day after day she did one thing after another, until the three rooms seemed clean and almost prosperous....

Source: Pearl S. Buck, *The Good Earth* (New York: Washington Square Press, 1994 edition) 27–28.

 Go to **www.chinasince1644.com** for the full text of **Document 1.3**.

DOCUMENT 1.4: Excerpts from memoir by Li Xiuwen (1890–1992), describing life in the village where she grew up, early 20th century

Usually farmers ate rice cooked with sweet potatoes or white potatoes with one dish of home-grown vegetables three times a day. Meat, mixed with vegetables, appeared at the table only on the New Year. People thought of eating melon or vegetables as producing cold in the body, so they ate hot peppers to counteract it. Therefore each family had a hot pepper stone grinding bowl in the house. Some nights, the farmers, after their hard day's work, went out to the river to catch fish, shrimp, and frogs. They would eat the frogs, and dry the fish, to save for meals in later days. In the busy farming season, farmers usually ate a little better. At dinner, they added a dish of fried soybeans, cooked dried fish, vegetables, and they might even drink some rice wine. Only the male workers drank rice wine, not female workers. Usually the men and women ate separately. The men's table had better food than the women's table.

Source: Li Xiuwen, unpublished memoir.

 Go to **www.chinasince1644.com** for the full text of **Document 1.4**.

DOCUMENT 1.5: Excerpts from "The Village With No Name," in *Daughter of Heaven* by Leslie Li, 2005

The village was enclosed, strangled really, by a high stone wall, which blocked out not only the sun's debilitating heat but also its life-giving light. Within this tight embrace, each lane—flanked by the outer stone walls of the two-story houses themselves—was narrow and labyrinthine, its flagstones smeared with animal dung. Lanes led, torturously, to different family compounds, all in a sad state of disrepair and disuse. I peered inside the various gates at the wooden houses and open courtyards. Clucking hens wandered in and out of the rooms. A dirty, half-naked child played with a plastic rice bowl and a knotted piece of rope. A woman appeared in one doorway and stared at me with undisguised suspicion, then disappeared inside. A man in a stained tunic, smoking a pipe, studied me with grave indifference and held his ground…. There was no electricity, no plumbing here, not even an open sewer to flush away waste…. I was appalled by the poverty, the squalid living conditions….

SOURCE: Leslie Li, *Daughter of Heaven: A Memoir With Earthly Recipes* (New York: Arcade, 2005) 222–225.

Go to **www.chinasince1644.com** for the full text of **Document 1.5**.

DOCUMENT 1.6: Photograph from the slide show "Among the Peoples of China," 2006

A Yi woman wearing a traditional
headdress
(Photo by Michael Abraham)

Go to **www.chinasince1644.com** for the slide show "Among the Peoples of China,"
Document 1.6.

DOCUMENT 1.7: Excerpts related to minority peoples from "The Common Program of the Chinese People's Political Consultative Conference," September 29, 1949

Article 50. All nationalities within the boundaries of the People's Republic of China are equal. They shall establish unity and mutual aid among themselves, and shall oppose imperialism and their own public enemies, so that the People's Republic of China will become a big fraternal and co-operative family composed of all its nationalities. Greater Nationalism and chauvinism shall be opposed. Acts involving discrimination, oppression and splitting of the unity of the various nationalities shall be prohibited.

Article 51. Regional autonomy shall be exercised in areas where national minorities are concentrated and various kinds of autonomy organizations of the different nationalities shall be set up according to the size of the respective populations and regions. In places where different nationalities live together and in the autonomous areas of the national minorities, the different nationalities shall each have an appropriate number of representatives in the local organs of political power....

SOURCE: The Important Documents of the First Plenary Session of the Chinese People's Political Consultative Conference (Beijing: Foreign Languages Press, 1949).

Go to **www.chinasince1644.com** for the full text of Document 1.7.

Activities

ACTIVITY 1: Before Reading

Part 1: Collaborate

Before reading the essay, work independently or in small groups to assess what you know.

1. List the names of the countries you think border China.
2. On individual copies of a blank world map (Item 1.A on the companion website), draw in China. Compare maps and vote on which one the group thinks is most accurate.
3. How does China compare in size to Europe, Russia, Australia, Canada, Mexico, Brazil, and the United States?
4. How large is China's population? How does it compare to the populations of these other countries?
5. What kind of climate does China have?

Part 2: Use Primary Sources

Look at the slide show showing photographs taken since 2000 in the rural areas of various Chinese provinces (1.1). Please note that you are not seeing photographs of China's cities. For a look at urban China, see the slide show in Chapter 18.

1. What is most striking about the photographs?
2. What surprises you?
3. What can you conclude about China's landscape based on these photographs?
4. What can you conclude about farming practices?
5. Why might Chinese farmers terrace hillsides?
6. What crops do you see growing?

Read the introductory essay; using what you've learned from the slides, atlases, and online resources listed at the end of the lesson, find the correct answers to the questions in Part 1. Compare the accurate answers to your earlier guesses. What had you been relying on as sources for your first set of answers? If your initial answers were very different from the facts, what can you conclude from the ways in which you thought about China's location, population, and topography?

ACTIVITY 2: Creating Big Maps

Part 1: Research

Project an outline map of China (Item 1.B) onto a large piece of paper. Follow the instructions for making a Big Map provided by your teacher. Working in a small group, using atlases and online resources, create a map showing one of the following topics. Establish map keys and a color code. The goal is for members of each group to become experts on their topic.

1. Topography with basic land formations—rivers, river basins, mountain ranges, lowlands, plateaus, deserts
2. Population density
3. Climate, including rainfall
4. Agricultural regions and crops
5. Autonomous regions
6. Major cities and municipalities
7. Bordering countries and the provinces or autonomous regions that lie on those borders

Part 2: Ask Questions

After the map is finished, as a group, create six questions related to your map for classmates to answer. Place all the maps, with the questions attached, around the room. Examine all the maps and answer the related questions.

Part 3: Present

Each group should briefly present its map and explain what group members discovered. The group should then elicit answers to the questions and clarify any misconceptions.

Part 4: Use Digital Media

View the slide show (1.1) again. Create a tour on Google Earth, inserting the photos provided on the appropriate provinces. Alternatively, either on a Big Map or on individual copies of a map that shows China's provinces (Item 1.C), match the slides to the region and add the information you've learned.

ACTIVITY 3: Understanding Agrarian Life

To better understand China and the appeal of the Chinese Communist Party to rural Chinese, it is helpful to examine how peasants lived prior to Liberation in 1949. The majority of the population of pre-1949 China could be called peasants. In Chinese, the word used is *nongmin*, which literally translated means "agriculture person." In addition, a look at the life of China's rural citizens today helps put future challenges in perspective.

Part 1: Before Reading

Before coming to class, read excerpts from *Peasant Life in China* by one of China's renowned social scientists, Fei Xiaotong (1.2). Take notes on the topics addressed: the village site, the *jia*, population control, parents and children, and rural education.

Part 2: Collaborate

Jigsaw: In class, you will be assigned one of the Documents 1.3–1.5 to read in a small group, so that each group is reading one account. Discuss the details in your group and add to your notes on peasant life. Reconvene in new groups that include individuals who have read different documents. Report on your reading to the new group and, as you hear new information, add to your notes.

Part 3: Discuss

Prepare to discuss in class:

1. What is most striking about these descriptions of rural China?
2. Note one feature that is similar to something you have seen or read about.
3. Which aspects of peasant life appear to be distinctly Chinese?
4. Which aspects of peasant life appear to lend themselves to reform efforts, and which ones do you suspect would be difficult to change?

Creative Extension:

Write a travel essay, a short story, or an illustrated children's book incorporating as many details of rural life in China as you can. Alternatively, working with a partner, create an electronic presentation to depict rural life in China.

ACTIVITY 4: Responding to Peasant Life in Film

View any one of the films or documentaries listed under Suggested Resources at the end of the chapter that are either set in rural China in the past thirty years or specifically examine village life. Compare what you learned from the readings to the visual depictions. What has changed? What hasn't? What challenges remain and how might they best be addressed?

NOTE: For information about rural education, see Chapter 19.

ACTIVITY 5: Researching China's Diverse Peoples

Part 1: Discuss

Begin by reading the essay about Han Chinese (Item 1.D), who make up more than 90 percent of China's population. Prepare to discuss in class:

1. What unifies the Han Chinese?
2. What is the origin of the name "Han" Chinese? How far back does it date?
3. What are the differences among Han Chinese people? Give several specific examples.

Part 2: Research

Together, China's ethnic minorities add up to more than 100 million people, ranging from the Zhuang, who number more than 16 million, to the De'ang, who number around 18,000. Look at the slide show of a number of minority peoples in China (1.6). Discuss your first impressions of the photographs. (For example, consider the people's appearances, surroundings, relations with the camera, and so on.)

Read the excerpts from the Common Program (1.7). What rights did this document guarantee?

Look at the list of minority groups, as the Chinese government identifies them (Item 1.E). Working independently or with a partner, choose one minority people you wish to learn about. (The larger groups have an asterisk.) Conduct research using the suggested online sources and create a presentation to share with the class (posters with captions, or a digital presentation). Your presentation should include a map of China showing where the people live, ethnic identity (do they identify with a larger group?), economic life, customs, language, religion(s), dress, food, housing, etc., as well as challenges they may face.

ACTIVITY 6: Concluding Discussion on Ethnic Minorities

After everyone has shared information about an ethnic group with the class, be prepared to discuss:

1. How does the Chinese government define a minority nationality?

2. What is the purpose of this process?

3. How does it benefit a people?

4. How might it be detrimental?

5. Do other countries create similar categories? Which ones? For what purposes?

6. What is striking about *where* China's ethnic minorities live? What is the relationship between the regions where minority nationalities live and government policies toward them? (The class may want to create a Big Map showing the locations of all the minority nationalities they researched.)

7. Based on your research, what are the biggest challenges Chinese minority nationalities face in the twenty-first century?

8. How do these challenges compare to those faced by minorities in other countries? Consider, for example, the Sioux nation in the United States, Maori people in New Zealand, Muslims in a western European country, Asian Australians or any other minority people.

Suggested Resources

Note: For Chinese names, we have followed the ordering of first and last names that the author uses in publishing his or her work.

Books

Atlas of China: An Expansive Portrait of China Today with More Than 400 Maps and Illustrations. Washington, DC: National Geographic, 2008. Maps ranging from contemporary ones related to trade or tourism to historic ones. Includes maps of key cities.

Bailey, Alison et al., eds. *China: People Place Culture History.* New York: DK Publishing, 2007. Stunning photographs and succinct information.

Benewick, Robert and Stephanie McDonald. *The State of China Atlas: Mapping the World's Fastest-Growing Economy.* Berkeley: University of California Press, 2009.

Buck, Pearl S. *The Good Earth.* New York: Washington Square Press, 2004. A novel about a farmer and his family confronted by new practices that threaten to wash away old traditions. It includes themes of women's rights, family, class conflict, spiritual and moral trials, and hardships of the modern world. Buck won the Pulitzer Prize for this work, and in 1938, won the Nobel Prize for Literature.

Lipman, Jonathan Neaman. *Familiar Strangers: A History of Muslims in Northwest China.* Seattle: University of Washington Press, 1997.

Ma Yan. *The Diary of Ma Yan: The Struggles and Hopes of a Chinese Schoolgirl.* New York: HarperCollins, 2005.

Mullaney, Thomas S. *Coming to Terms with the Nation: Ethnic Classification in Modern China.* Berkeley: University of California Press, 2011.

Primary Source. *The Enduring Legacy of Ancient China: Primary Source Lessons for Teachers and Students.* Boston: Cheng & Tsui, 2006.

See, Lisa. *Snow Flower and the Secret Fan: A Novel*. New York: Random House, 2005.
Set in Hunan county in the nineteenth century, young Lily is matched with a *laotong*, "old same." The two women exchange messages using *nu shu*, a unique, secretive language.

Starr, S. Frederick. *Xinjiang: China's Muslim Borderland*. Armonk, NY: M.E. Sharpe, 2004.

Websites

China Country Profile, Asia Society
http://asiasociety.org/countries/country-profiles/china
Map and statistics about China.

China from the Inside, PBS
http://www.pbs.org/kqed/chinainside/
Includes an interactive soundscape map of China.

East Asia in Geographic Perspective, Asia for Educators
http://afe.easia.columbia.edu/geography/
Includes maps and activities on places and regions, physical systems, and environment and society.

Google Earth
http://earth.google.com
Free download allows for "flying" from place to place on Earth and exploring geographic details of a country or city.

Perry-Castañeda Library Map Collection, University of Texas at Austin
http://www.lib.utexas.edu/maps/china.html
City, country, thematic, and historical maps. Includes ethnolinguistic maps.

A Visual Sourcebook of Chinese Civilization: Geography
http://depts.washington.edu/chinaciv/geo/geo.htm
A site by Patricia Buckley Ebrey that includes information about China's geography, autonomous regions, and minority populations.

World Panoramic Photography: 360Cities
http://www.360cities.net/map
View dozens of panoramic tours of cities and sites in China by selecting locations on the 360Cities world map.

Films

All Under Heaven (58 mins; 1986)
Part of the *One Village in China* series, this documentary, directed and produced by Carma Hinton and Richard Gordon, captures the various ways in which the Communist Party of China has tackled the challenge of land reform and gives insight into rural traditions.

Not One Less (106 mins; 1999)
In Mandarin with subtitles. The film tells the true story of Wei Minzhi, a fourteen-year-old girl who is ordered to a remote impoverished village in Hebei province to work as the substitute teacher for a month. Clueless when it comes to teaching, she is, however, extraordinarily determined to keep the class intact.

One Day in Ping Wei (30 mins, 2004);
New Year in Ping Wei (30 mins; 2005);
Return to Ping Wei (30 mins; 2007)
Filmed entirely on location in Ping Wei, a small village on the banks of the Huai He River within the city limits of Huainan. Follow Liu Yen Twin from age ten to fourteen as she goes to school, celebrates Chinese New Year with her family, and participates in the village's spring harvest.

The Road Home (89 mins; 2000)
In Mandarin with subtitles. This film gives insight into life in rural China.

Small Happiness (58 mins; 1984)
Produced and directed by Carma Hinton and Richard Gordon. Another film in the three-part documentary series *One Village in China*, examining life in Long Bow, a rural community 400 miles southwest of Beijing. This segment looks at the lives of women in the village.

To Taste a Hundred Herbs (58 mins; 1986)
Produced and directed by Carma Hinton and Richard Gordon. The third of the three-part documentary series *One Village in China*, this segment looks at the role of traditions and traditional Chinese medicine, and the lives of Chinese Catholics in the village.

Up the Yangtze (93 mins; 2008)
As the Three Gorges Dam is completed, families living along the Yangtze River are affected in various ways. This film documents the struggles of one family as their daughter takes a job on one of the Yangtze River "Farewell Cruises" and the family is forced to leave their home for higher ground.

CHAPTER RESOURCES

Primary Sources

DOCUMENTS 2.1, 2.2, AND 2.4: Excerpts from *The Journals of Matthew Ricci, 1583–1610* (not available on the companion website)

DOCUMENT 2.3: Annual calendar of festival-related activities, 1635

DOCUMENT 2.5: "A Visit to High Beam Bridge" by Yuan Hongdao (1568–1610)

DOCUMENT 2.6: "Inscribed on the Doors of My Bookshelves," a poem by Yang Xunji (1456–1544)

DOCUMENT 2.7: Excerpt from *The Craft of Gardens* by Ji Cheng, 1630s

DOCUMENT 2.8: Slide show "A Nearby Journey Into Nature" on traditional Chinese gardens

DOCUMENT 2.9: Excerpts from the "Biography of Gentleman Wang," by Wang Daokun (1525–1593) (not available on the companion website)

DOCUMENT 2.10: Excerpt from "On Merchants," essay by Zhang Han

DOCUMENT 2.11: Poems written by women during the Ming dynasty (1368–1644)

DOCUMENT 2.12: Excerpts describing severe hardship in the lives of peasants during the latter part of the Ming dynasty

Supplementary Materials

ITEM 2.A: Additional information related to *The Journals of Matthew Ricci*

 Excerpts of these primary source documents appear in this chapter. Go to **www.chinasince1644.com** for the full version of these documents and for the Supplementary Materials.

CHAPTER 2

An Introduction to Sixteenth-Century China

By Philip Gambone

Chapter Contents

Scholar-Officials

Literati

Merchants

Educated Women

Peasants

Key Idea

After the emperor, scholar-officials comprised the top level of China's hierarchical society. They, together with a thriving merchant class, created a vibrant urban culture in sixteenth-century China. Although in many ways a time of cultural and social continuation, the sixteenth century also ushered in an era of profound political and economic transformation that made China highly vulnerable to Western encroachment in the nineteenth century.

Guiding Questions

What was the traditional social hierarchy in China?

What characterized the lives of scholar-officials?

What was life like for educated Chinese women in the sixteenth century?

What was life like in the cities?

What challenges did peasants face?

What factors made China vulnerable to Western imperialism in the nineteenth century?

Terms to Know

Confucius	literati
connoisseur	magistrate
dynasty	Ming dynasty (1368–1644)
eunuch	scholar-official
Jesuit	*simin*

Essay

For centuries, a child born in China grew up in a rigid social hierarchy. The so-called "four categories of the people" (*simin* 四民) reflected ancient Confucian beliefs and allowed for few opportunities to change one's social class. The traditional Confucian hierarchy placed scholar-officials at the top of society, followed by the peasants, then by artisans, then, at the bottom, merchants. Yet in the increasingly wealthy sixteenth century, merchants flourished, and their actual role in society far outstripped their place in the traditional social hierarchy. Their new wealth opened opportunities for them within the scholar-official classes, as well.

Civil Service Examinations

Over the course of its long history, Chinese leaders had administered the country in various ways. Ming dynasty emperors, who ruled the country from 1368 to 1644, divided the country into fifteen major provinces, which were run by a hierarchy of government officials from provincial governors to local magistrates. In order to be assigned to a government position, a man had to pass the second in a series of increasingly difficult civil service exams (*shengyuan* 生员, *juren* 举人, and *jinshi* 进士).[1] The exams were based on memorization of four Chinese classics.[2] The examination questions allowed each candidate to demonstrate his literary skills, and the top candidates were also expected to write policy recommendations on government issues for the emperor.

The intent was to have only men educated and invested in Confucian ethics serving the people in government positions. However, Chinese official records, literature, and folktales are full of examples of corrupt, disengaged, or immoral officials, which suggests the system was far from perfect.

Scholar-Officials

Passing the first of the three exams gave a man social standing as one of the educated in the community. Passing the provincial *juren* exam would make him eligible for a government position, which would enable him to increase the family income. A comfortable income allowed a family to educate its sons, who would then be able to pass the civil service exams and ensure the family's prosperity. (While there were sons from poor families who managed to pass the civil service exams, this happened rarely because there was no free public education.) Scholar-officials generally earned their wealth from landownership, but they usually lived in larger towns and thus managed their properties as absentee landlords.

A scholar-official was expected to know history, classical literature, and art. As the ethical and cultural elite, scholar-officials not only ran the government bureaucracy and performed important ceremonial functions but also set the standard for moral behavior and artistic taste. Many were intellectuals, who cultivated intellectual friendships with other scholar-officials with whom they would enjoy conversation, poetry contests, and outings into the countryside. Aesthetic gardens graced their traditional courtyard homes (*siheyuan* 四合院). Connoisseurship—of painting, calligraphy, tea, porcelain, laquerwork, and even spider fighting!—was among their highest pleasures.

The Literati

As highly educated individuals, the literati were also among China's elite. Also educated in the classics, they were men who perhaps had failed one or more of the civil service exams and did not serve in the government, but rather dedicated their lives to scholarship, poetry, and one or all of

---

[1] A form of these exams had been in place for approximately 1,500 years.

[2] The four texts upon which the exams were based during the Ming dynasty were the *Analects of Confucius, Mencius, Doctrine of the Mean*, and *Great Learning*.

the four accomplishments—music, chess, calligraphy and painting. Members of the literati were not necessarily wealthy, but enriched their lives in the same ways as scholar-officials.

Women

The traditional Confucian view of women held that they were to be subservient to men. At the same time, during the Ming dynasty, women (at least those in the elite echelon of society) enjoyed greater literacy and freedom of expression than in earlier periods. An unprecedented number of female poets wrote during the Ming dynasty.

Commerce at Home and Abroad

Despite the traditional Confucian scorn for merchants, who were seen as profiting unfairly from the hard labor of the peasants, the fifteenth and sixteenth centuries in China were a time of enormously successful commercial activity. Small market towns thrived across the country, and regions became known for their agricultural and mercantile specialties. For example, cotton and silk came from the Yangzi River Delta, while in coastal Fujian Province, farmers grew tobacco and sugar cane. Jingdezhen in Jiangxi Province became famous for its porcelain.

At the start of the Ming Dynasty, China had been actively engaged in overseas trade and exploration. Private foreign trade was prohibited, but the Imperial court sponsored and encouraged overseas expeditions as a way of increasing China's imperial presence around the world and thus attracting more vassal states (Zheng He's early fifteenth-century missions are the most famous of these voyages). But as the Ming treasury began to feel the pinch of expanding responsibilities both at home and to its vassals, such as funding costly military expeditions to defend Vietnam's ruling Tran dynasty (1407) and battle Japan over Korea's sovereignty (1592–1598), these missions ceased. Although not all Ming officials agreed with this approach (see Zhang Han's essay, Document 2.10), the Ming government began to think defensively, constructing its famous wall to keep Mongol invaders out and imposing a harsh military cordon on its maritime frontiers. Much of China's bourgeoning Indian Ocean trade was forced into "piracy" to avoid these restrictions. Nonetheless, as the rest of the world began to seek out China's unparalleled goods, China could not defend itself from an increasingly intrusive foreign presence.

Early European Presence

European traders and missionaries began to visit China and Southeast Asia in increasing numbers at this time, bringing with them new ideas, religious movements, and inventions—often based on Chinese technologies. The Ming government slightly relaxed the previously imposed maritime trade restrictions, and in 1577, the Portuguese established a trading post at Macao. The Spanish, Dutch, and English ships that soon followed brought new products—potatoes, peppers, sweet potatoes, maize, and peanuts from their new New World outposts, food products that radically changed the Chinese diet and added sufficient calories to ultimately effect a rise in the birth rate. Silk and porcelain were the principal export commodities of the Chinese. Largely as a result of the Spanish discoveries of silver in South and Central America, huge quantities of silver poured into China in payment for the exports. This created new wealth at all levels of Chinese society and a corresponding desire for luxuries. As the Ming dynasty wore on, the well-to-do classes tended to cultivate their private lives at the expense of public service. Indeed, the elite enjoyed a higher standard of living than perhaps any of their contemporaries in the rest of the world. With the elite, China's lower classes also experienced increasing commercialization, urbanization, and growing sense of cohesion as a Chinese polity.

This period set the stage for early modern China. On the one hand, it represented economic expansion and the renewed development of the great artistic and cultural tradition of ancient China. On the other hand, rapid population growth, foreigners' interest in China, and economic disparity would lead to social turmoil in the eighteenth and nineteenth centuries.

Primary Sources

DOCUMENT 2.1: Excerpts from *The Journals of Matthew Ricci, 1583–1610* in which he describes Nanjing, ca. 1600

By the Ming dynasty, China had already been an urbanized culture for almost a thousand years. Cities like Nanjing, Xi'an, and Beijing were crowded, lively, and cosmopolitan centers of activity. As far back as Marco Polo's account in the thirteenth century, Westerners had commented on the marvels and sophistication of city life in China. The Chinese, too, recognized their capital (with a population of approximately one million people) as a splendid one. Several guidebooks were published during the Ming. And like urbanites today, city dwellers during the Ming complained of the congestion, the dirt, and the noise that were part of urban life.

Matteo (Matthew) Ricci, the author of this excerpt, was an Italian Jesuit missionary to China from 1582 until his death in Beijing in 1610. He targeted the literati class for Christian education, a "top-down" approach to conversion. Ricci became fluent in Chinese and wrote and translated several works into his adopted language.

In the judgment of the Chinese this city [Nanjing] surpasses all other cities in the world in beauty and in grandeur, and in this respect there are probably very few others superior or equal to it. It is literally filled with palaces and temples and towers and bridges, and these are scarcely surpassed by similar structures in Europe.... The climate is mild and the soil is fertile. There is a gaiety of spirit among the people, who are well mannered and nicely spoken, and the dense population is made up of all classes; of hoi-polloi, of the lettered aristocracy and the Magistrates [high-level scholar-officials]. These latter are equal in number and in dignity to those of Beijing, but due to the fact that the king does not reside here, the local Magistrates are not rated as equal with those of the Capital City. Yet in the whole kingdom of China and in all bordering countries, Nanjing is rated as the first city.

It is surrounded by three circles of walls. The first and innermost of these, and also the most decorative, contains the palace of the king. The palace, in turn, is surrounded by a triple wall of arches, and of circling moats, filled with circulating water.... The second wall, encircling the inner one, which contains the king's palace, encloses the greater and the more important part of the city. It has twelve gates, which are covered with iron plates and fortified by cannon from within....The third and exterior wall is not continuous. At places that were judged to be danger spots, they scientifically added to natural fortifications. It is difficult to determine the full length of the circuit of this particular wall. The natives here tell a story of two men who started from opposite sides of the city, riding on horses toward each other, and it took a whole day before they came together.

This city was once the capital of the entire realm and the ancient abode of kings through many centuries, and though the king changed his residence to Beijing, in the north [in the early fifteenth century]... Nanjing lost none of its splendor or its reputation.

SOURCE: Louis J. Gallagher, *China in the Sixteenth Century: The Journals of Matthew Ricci, 1583–1610* (New York: Random House, 1953) 268–270.

DOCUMENT 2.2: **Excerpts from *The Journals of Matthew Ricci, 1583–1610* in which he describes Beijing, ca. 1601**

[Beijing] is closed in on the south by two high, thick walls, wide enough for twelve horses to run along the tops of them without interference. These walls are built mostly of brick. At the foundations they are sustained by stones of tremendous dimensions, and the interiors are filled with prepared earth. They are not higher than city walls seen in Europe. On the north, the city is protected by a single wall. At night, all these walls are guarded by a host of soldiers, as numerous as if a war were raging. During the day, the city gates are guarded by the palace eunuchs, or at least they are supposed to be guarded, but these eunuchs are too busy taking tolls, something that is never done in other cities. The royal palace[3] is built into the southern wall, like an entrance to the city, and it extends clear to the northern wall, the entire length of the city and right through the middle of it. The rest of the town is spread on either side of the palace....

Very few of the streets in Beijing are paved with brick or stone, and it is difficult to say which season of the year is more objectionable for walking. The mud in the winter and the dust in the summer are equally obnoxious and fatiguing. As it seldom rains in this province, the surface earth dissolves into a coating of dust, which even a slight wind raises, blowing it into the houses, where it covers and soils nearly everything. In order to overcome this dust nuisance, they have introduced a custom which is probably unknown anywhere else. During the dust season here, nobody of any class would think of going out, either on foot or in conveyance, without wearing a long veil, falling in front from the hat, and thus sheltering the face. The material of the veil is fine enough to see through but no dust can penetrate it....

We have already noted that there is an abundance of everything in Beijing, most of which is brought into the city, but despite this fact, living in Beijing is difficult, save for such as are wealthy and do not have to retrench. Firewood is always lacking here, but this shortage is made up for by a bituminous substance, which for want of a better name, we shall call asphalt or mineral pitch.[4] It is a sort of fossil tar, dug out of the earth... The Chinese use it for cooking and also for heating their houses during the extreme cold of winter... The abundance of this material makes up nicely for the lack of firewood. The beds here are built up with bricks with a hollow space underneath, through which pipes from a fireplace are passed, creating a heat chamber beneath the bed. One does not have to keep the heat on during the night because the chamber stays hot for a long time. This kind of bed is in common use through all the northern provinces. The northern Chinese are more warlike and courageous than those from the south but less alert mentally. Such is the balance of human nature, that some are superior in one respect and some in another.

SOURCE: Louis J. Gallagher, *China in the Sixteenth Century: The Journals of Matthew Ricci, 1583–1610* (New York: Random House, 1953) 309–311.

---

[3] The Forbidden City; see Chapter 3.

[4] Coal was used in China long before it was known in the West.

DOCUMENT 2.3: Annual calendar of festival-related activities, 1635

Date	Activity
Lichun	Prefect and elites "welcome spring" in the eastern suburbs.
1/1–15[5]	Lunar New Year. Families celebrate the new year at home and call on relatives and friends over the next weeks. Visit certain temples.
1/8–18	Lantern market. Buy, display, and view lanterns on city streets.
1/15	Lantern festival. Everyone can stroll the streets and stay out all night.
1/25	Cook and eat a huge meal of special cakes, called "filling up the granaries."
2/2	Clear out insects and eat special foods associated with the "dragon raising his head."
Qingming	Commemorate deceased ancestors by visiting family graveyards.
3/28	Birthday of the god of the Eastern Peak, celebrated in his temple.
4/8	Birthday of Shakyamuni, celebrated in Buddhist monasteries
4/18	Birthday of Bixia Yuanjun, celebrated in various temples
5/5	Visit scenic spots. Take prophylactic measures to "avoid poisons" thought to be in the air.
5/13	Birthday of Guan Yu, celebrated at his temples
6/6	Air books and clothing, at homes and in temples.

SOURCE: *Dijing jingwu lue* ("Description of the Scenery of the Imperial Capital"), 1635. Quoted in Susan Naquin, *Peking: Temples and City Life, 1400–1900* (Berkeley: University of California Press, 2000) 275.

Go to **www.chinasince1644.com** for the text of **Document 2.3**.

DOCUMENT 2.4: Excerpts from *The Journals of Matthew Ricci, 1583–1610* in which he describes the literati

The sect of the Literati is proper to China and is most ancient in the kingdom. They rule the country, have an extensive literature, and are far more celebrated than the others…. Confucius is their Prince of Philosophers, and according to them, it was he who discovered the art of philosophy. They do not believe in idol worship. In fact they have no idols. They do, however, believe in one deity who preserves and governs all things on earth. Other spirits they admit, but these are of less restricted domination and receive only minor honors. The real Literati teach nothing relative to the time, the manner, or the author of the creation of the world….

The ancients scarcely seem to doubt about the immortality of the soul because, for a long time after death, they make frequent reference to the departed as dwelling in heaven. They say nothing, however, about punishment for the wicked in hell. The more recent Literati teach that the soul ceases to exist when the body does, or a

---

[5] The 1/1–15 does *not* correspond to the Western New Year, January 1, but rather to the months of the traditional Chinese lunar calendar. The Chinese New Year falls on the eve of the second new moon following the winter solstice.

short time after it.... [T]his school teaches that only the souls of the just survive. They say that the soul of a man is strengthened by virtue and solidified to endure, and since this is not true of the wicked, their souls vanish, like thin smoke, immediately after leaving the body....

Although the Literati, as they are called, do recognize one supreme deity, they erect no temples in his honor. No special places are assigned for his worship.... Neither are there any public or private prayers or hymns to be said or sung in honor of a supreme deity. The duty of sacrifice and the rites of worship for this supreme being belong to the imperial majesty alone. This is so true that if anyone else should offer such a sacrifice in usurpation of this right, he would be punished as an intruder upon the duty of the emperor and as a public enemy....

The most common ceremony practiced by all the Literati, from the emperor down to the very lowest of them, is that of the annual funeral rites.... As they themselves say, they consider this ceremony as an honor bestowed upon their departed ancestors... They do not really believe that the dead actually need the victuals which are placed upon their graves, but they say that they observe the custom of placing them there because it seems to be the best way of testifying their love for their dear departed.... [I]t was [also] hoped that children, and unlearned adults as well, might learn how to respect and to support their parents who were living, when they saw that parents departed were so highly honored by those who were educated and prominent....

The Temple of Confucius is really the cathedral of...the Literati. The law demands that a temple be built to the Prince of Chinese Philosophers in every city.... In the most conspicuous place in the temple there will be a statue of Confucius, or if not a statue, a plaque with his name carved in large letters of gold....

The ultimate purpose and the general intention of...the Literati is public peace and order in the kingdom. They likewise look toward the economic security of the family and the virtuous training of the individual....Their writings explain at length the second precept of charity: "Do not do unto others what you would not wish others to do unto you." It really is remarkable how highly they esteem the respect and obedience of children toward parents, the fidelity of servants to a master, and devotion of the young to their elders.

SOURCE: Louis J. Gallagher, *China in the Sixteenth Century: The Journals of Matthew Ricci, 1583–1610* (New York: Random House, 1953) 94–97.

DOCUMENT 2.5:
"A Visit to High Beam Bridge" by Yuan Hongdao (1568–1610)

[The bridge] has the best view in the capital area. The embankment lies in the middle of water. Weeping willows extend for more than three miles. The river flows rapidly. The water is so clear that even the fins and scales of the fish at the bottom of the river can be seen. Buddhist temples dot the scene like pieces on a chessboard. Crimson towers and pearly pagodas beam among green trees. The Western Hills seem to be right within one's reach, enchanting tourists with their colors from morning till night. In the height of spring, gentlemen and ladies from the city gather there, and the crowd is thick as clouds. No government official would ever refrain from making a trip there unless he were extremely busy.

On the first day of the third month, I had an outing with Wang Changfu and the Buddhist monk Jizi. A fresh green was sprouting at the tip of the willow branches. The hills shone from behind a thin mist. The river water rose up almost to the level of the embankment, and musicians were playing on their strings and pipes along both banks. Squatting on the root of an old tree, we drank some tea in place of wine, and, to accompany our drink, we looked at the patterns of ripples and the shade of trees and watched, like a stage performance, the birds in the air, the fish in the water, and the people who walked back and forth.

SOURCE: Yang Ye, ed. and trans., *Vignettes from the Late Ming: A Hsiao-p'in Anthology* (Seattle: University of Washington Press, 1999) 50–51.

Go to **www.chinasince1644.com** for the full text of **Document 2.5**.

DOCUMENT 2.6: "Inscribed on the Doors of My Bookshelves," a poem by Yang Xunji (1456–1544)

When angry, I read and become happy;
When sick, I read and am cured.
Piled helter-skelter in front of me
Books have become my life.
The people of the past who wrote these tomes,
If not sages, were certainly men of great wisdom.
Even without opening their pages,
Joy comes to me just fondling them.

SOURCE: Yang Hsün-chi, "Inscribed on the Doors of My Bookshelves," trans. John Timothy Wixted, *The Columbia Anthology of Traditional Chinese Literature*, ed. Victor H. Mair (New York: Columbia University Press, 1994) 273.

Go to **www.chinasince1644.com** for the full text of **Document 2.6**.

DOCUMENT 2.7:
Excerpt from *The Craft of Gardens* by Ji Cheng, 1630s

Generally, in the construction of gardens, whether in the countryside or on the outskirts of a city, a secluded location is the best. In clearing woodland one should select and prune the tangled undergrowth; where a fine piece of natural scenery occurs one should make the most of it. Where there is a mountain torrent one may cultivate orchids and angelica together. Paths should be lined with the "three auspicious things"[6] whose property it is to symbolize eternity. The surrounding wall should be concealed under creepers, and rooftops should emerge here and there above the tops

---

[6] Pine, bamboo, and flowering plum; or rocks, bamboo, and flowering plum.

of the trees. If you climb a tower on a hill-top to gaze into the distance, nothing but beauty will meet your eye; if you seek a secluded spot among the banks of bamboo, intoxication will flood your heart. The pillars of your verandah should be tall and widely spaced; your windows and doors should give an unimpeded view.

SOURCE: Ji Cheng, *The Craft of Gardens,* trans. Alison Hardie (New Haven: Yale University Press, 1988) 43.

 Go to **www.chinasince1644.com** for the full text of Document 2.7.

DOCUMENT 2.8: Slide Show "A Nearby Journey into Nature"

Go to **www.chinasince1644.com** for the slide show of Document 2.8.

DOCUMENT 2.9: Excerpts from the *Biography of Gentleman Wang* by Wang Daokun (1525–1593)

This biography written by a Ming scholar-official, Wang Daokun, gives us a portrait of a successful merchant during the late Ming dynasty. Wang is a common Chinese surname. The author and the subject of the biography are not related.

Even at his great age [of ninety] Mr. Wang is a man of the highest integrity; therefore I now extol his deeds in order to show my respect for virtuous old men…. Mr. Wang lives in Shanghai. Even as a teenager, he was famous for his skill in making money. Being open and confident, he has attracted the respect of many capable and prosperous people who compete to attach themselves to him. At first, Mr. Wang's capital was no greater than the average person's. Later, as he grew more prosperous every day, the number of his associates also steadily increased. To accommodate his apprentices, Mr. Wang built buildings with doors on four sides. Whenever customers came, they could be taken care of from all four directions; thus, no one ever had to wait long.

Mr. Wang set up the following guidelines for his associates: do not let anyone who lives in another county control the banking; when lending money, never harass law-abiding people unnecessarily or give them less than they need; charge low interest on loans; do not aim at high profit and do not ask for daily interest. These principles led customers to throng to him, even ones from neighboring towns and provinces. Within a short time, Mr. Wang accumulated great wealth; in fact, of all the rich people in that area he became the richest.

Mr. Wang liked to help people and to give assistance to the poor. If anyone among his kinsmen could not afford a funeral for his parents, Mr. Wang would always buy some land and build a tomb for him. As soon as he heard someone could not make ends meet, he would buy land to rent to him. Whenever he was out traveling and met some unburied spirit, he would bid his servants bury it and present some offering.

The biography goes on to describe how Mr. Wang gave advice on how to distribute grain during a drought. He gave money to repair a bridge and an ancestral temple.

Later, when Mr. Zhu set up dikes, a dispute occurred which involved thousands of people. The official tried to straighten out the merits of the case, but still it could not be resolved. Therefore the official asked Mr. Wang to take a hand in the matter. He successfully mediated the dispute merely by sending out a long letter. Later he was singled out to promote good community relations in Linhe and resolved all the quarrels there. Thus everybody praised him, saying, "Mr. Wang is capable of mediating disputes. He has the manner of a gentleman of national stature, and even the gentlemen of antiquity were not his equals."

SOURCE: Patricia Buckley Ebrey, ed., *Chinese Civilization and Society: A Sourcebook* (New York: Free Press, first edition 1981) 159–160.

DOCUMENT 2.10: Excerpt from "On Merchants," essay by Zhang Han

As to the foreigners in the southeast, their goods are useful to us just as ours are to them. To use what one has to exchange for what one does not have is what trade is all about. Moreover, these foreigners trade with China under the name of tributary contributions. That means China's authority is established and the foreigners are submissive. Even if the gifts we grant them are great and the tribute they send us is small, our expense is still less than one ten-thousandth of the benefit we gain from trading with them. Moreover, the southeast sea foreigners are more concerned with trading with China than with gaining gifts from China. Even if they send a large tribute offering only to receive small gifts in return, they will still be content. In addition, trading with them can enrich our people. So why should we refrain from the trade?

Some people may say that the southeast sea foreigners have invaded us several times so they are not the kind of people with whom we should trade. But they should realize that the southeast sea foreigners need Chinese goods and the Chinese need their goods. If we prohibit the natural flow of this merchandise, how can we prevent them from invading us? I believe that if the sea trade were opened, the trouble with foreign pirates would cease. These southeast sea foreigners are simple people, not to be compared to the unpredictable northeast sea foreigners. Moreover, China's exports in the northwest trade come from the national treasury. Whereas the northwest foreign trade ensures only harm, the sea trade provides us with only gain. How could those in charge of the government fail to realize the distinction?

SOURCE: Ebrey, Patricia Buckley ed., "Zhang Han's Essay on Merchants," *Chinese Civilization: A Sourcebook* (New York: The Free Press, 1993) 217–218.

Go to **www.chinasince1644.com** for the full text of **Document 2.10**.

DOCUMENT 2.11:
Poems written by women during the Ming dynasty (1368–1644)

"Hardships of the Road," by Lu Qingzi

With orchid and musk tapestried quilts perfumed;
Behind silk screens breezes of spring still cold.
When I bound up my hair and became your bride
We were always together like a bundle tied:
You were my heart's beloved.

We were lacquer and glue; who could come between?
We were metal and stone, enduring to the end.
Then a mere word, by chance caused the ruin of all my hopes;
Your angry glance was the first sign of ill will.

The lady's beauty gradually faded away;
The shining mirror took leave of the soaring phoenix.
I mounted the carriage, went out the gate and left.
The knot of our bond for a thousand miles unraveled.

When I was young, I enjoyed your loving favor;
Who could know then my road would be hard to travel?
Though it hasn't been long they speak of someone new;
Your generous love for me is truly already spent!

Source: Kang-I Sun Chang and Haun Saussy, eds., *Women Writers of Traditional China: An Anthology of Poetry and Criticism* (Stanford, CA: Stanford University Press, 1999) 256.

Go to **www.chinasince1644.com** for additional poems in **Document 2.11**.

DOCUMENT 2.12: Excerpts describing severe hardship in the lives of peasants during the latter part of the Ming dynasty

Excerpt A: "Letter to a Friend" by Wang Wenlu, 1545

The drought in Haiyan county began in 1538 when a tidal wave crossed the sea wall in the south, inundating the fields with saltwater, and then flowed north and attacked the crops. What with the blazing autumn sun and no sources of fresh water to irrigate, the rice put forth ears that did not turn to seed, or produced seed that then rotted. Growing plants shrank and turned to weeds, the fields yellowed: as far as you looked it was a scene of desolation. The officials did not report this to the throne. The stricken were excused from paying taxes, yet the prosperous were so pressed that they also became impoverished. Paddy rice did not come on the market and the price of rice went even higher. People fed themselves first on chaff and bean pods, then on tree bark and weeds. In 1539 and 1544 we suffered virulent epidemics. Both in the country villages and in the towns, nine out of ten houses stood empty. In any village, half the girls and boys were sold off. Now it is spring, and as we wait for the end of the summer growing season, the corpses of the starved lie everywhere—beside the monasteries, below the fords, within the suburban gates, in the middle of the roads—and everywhere the sound of wailing pierces our ears.

SOURCE: Qtd. in Timothy Brook, *The Confusions of Pleasure: Commerce and Culture in Ming China* (Berkeley: University of California Press, 1998) 105–106.

Go to **www.chinasince1644.com** for the full text of **Document 2.12**.

Activities

ACTIVITY 1: Analyzing Life in the Cities

Documents 2.1–2.3 provide glimpses into the daily life of urban citizens in the early 1600s. After reading them, be prepared to discuss in class:

1. What are your impressions of Matteo Ricci's accounts of Nanjing and Beijing?

2. How do his descriptions compare to your sense of how China's cities once looked?

3. How did China's cities of 1600 compare to cities elsewhere in the world during the same era?

Select one or more of the following activities and be prepared to share with the class:

1. Using the documents as evidence, imagine you are a European merchant or missionary. Write a letter home, describing life in the city that you are visiting. Alternately, create a travel poster.

2. Ricci describes "a bituminous substance"—coal—that the residents of Beijing used as fuel. Research the history of coal. What did people in Europe and other parts of the world use for fuel at this time? When did Europeans first encounter coal? Did they discover its use as a fuel independently or did the Chinese introduce it to them?

3. Research several key festivals listed in the "Annual Calendar, 1635" (2.3). What religions and beliefs are reflected in this calendar? What values does this list of celebrations reflect?

Extended Research:

Working with a partner or in a small group, compare these Chinese celebrations to ones celebrated elsewhere in the world in the seventeenth century (e.g., France, Mexico, England, Brazil, Puritan Massachusetts, Virginia, Japan, India, etc.). The class could make a chart comparing and contrasting festivals around the world.

NOTE: For more information about Chinese festivals, see Lesson 9 in *The Enduring Legacy of Ancient China* (Cheng & Tsui, 2006).

ACTIVITY 2:
Examining the Lives of Scholar-Officials and Literati

Part 1: Write or Draw

Documents 2.4–2.6 give a taste for what the lives of scholar-officials and the literati were like. After reading the selections, choose from among the following activities:

1. What is Ricci's understanding of the literati's spiritual beliefs (2.4)? Who is at the center of the beliefs? How was Ricci's understanding of the spiritual beliefs of the literati affected by his own goals? According to Matteo Ricci, what do members of this class value?

2. Describe the differences between an outing into the countryside on which you might go and the one described by Yuan Hongdao in "A Visit to High Beam Bridge" (2.5).

3. Illustrate the setting in Yuan's description.

4. What differences between the scholar-officials and the merchant class does the poem "Inscribed on the Doors of My Bookshelves" (2.6) emphasize? Describe the tone of the poem and how the poet views himself.

5. Write a script about an event in the daily life of a scholar-official. Make sure you account for various roles: official, amateur artist, and connoisseur. Act it out for the class.

NOTE: For a deeper understanding of the values of scholar-officials and the literati, read the lessons on the Four Accomplishments—calligraphy, chess, painting, and music—in *The Enduring Legacy of Ancient China* (Cheng & Tsui, 2006).

Part 2: Discuss

Read the excerpt from Ji Cheng's book (2.7) and look at the slide show of classical Chinese gardens (2.8). Prepare to discuss:

1. What stands out for you in the description and the images of the gardens?

2. What appear to be consistent features?

3. Given the values of scholar-officials and the newly wealthy merchant class, do you think that the gardens of the scholar-officials served purposes that were similar to or different from those of the merchants? Explain.

Creative Extensions:

- Draw or paint a Ming dynasty garden based on Ji's description and the photos. Alternatively, using these sources and additional information from books and websites, sketch a plan for a small Chinese garden.

- Other important crafts during the Ming dynasty included furniture making and the manufacture of blue-and-white porcelain. Work with a partner or in a small group to create a presentation on either of these.

Extended Research:

- The "three auspicious things" Ji mentions (in 2.7) may be pine, bamboo and flowering plum (*Prunus mume*), also known as the "three friends in winter," or rock, bamboo and flowering plum. Find out why these would be considered the "three auspicious things."

- Why did garden design rise to become such an art in China? Research Daoism and/or read some Chinese landscape poetry to further your understanding.

- Some cities outside of Asia have small Chinese (or Japanese) gardens, either within the city's park system or at a museum. If there is a Chinese or Japanese garden near you, visit it. What are the differences and similarities between Chinese and Japanese gardens? Compare these gardens to city parks and/or other gardens with which you are familiar.

ACTIVITY 3:
Comparing the Life of a Merchant with Businesspeople Today

Read the *Biography of Gentleman Wang* (2.9) and make a list of the qualities that helped make Mr. Wang a successful businessman. Are these the same qualities we would find in successful businesspeople today? Why or why not?

1. What prejudices against merchants come through in this short biography?

2. Review Mr. Wang's four guidelines. Why were they so effective in generating business? Would these guidelines work today? Why or why not?

3. Compare Mr. Wang's examples of philanthropy with the philanthropic activity of today's successful businesspeople like Bill Gates.

4. The author of this biography calls Mr. Wang "virtuous." Would you agree? What do you think a scholar-official of the Ming dynasty would have to say about businessmen such as Mr. Wang?

ACTIVITY 4: Analyzing a Ming Official's Position on the Value of Merchants and Trade

Read Zhang Han's essay "On Merchants" (2.10).

1. As you read, consider these questions:
   a. What clues can you find in the text about who Zhang Han is and what his family background is?
   b. How does Zhang Han establish his credibility for writing about the topic of trade and how merchants should be treated?
   c. What clues can you find about who his intended readers are? Consider the topics and "expert opinions" he chooses to include.
   d. What is the central point or purpose of this essay?

2. Zhang Han's essay includes many statements of opinion. Read the essay closely and highlight phrases or sentences where he is giving his own view on a subject.

Then review the list, and choose one opinion to illustrate in the form of a single-panel political cartoon that captures his view on a certain issue. (Note that cartoons did not exist in China at the time.)

3. Your teacher will post the whole class's cartoons, in the order that their topics appear in the essay, around the room. You will do a "gallery walk" to see the range and complexity of opinions represented in the essay.

4. Debrief: What did Zhang Han believe about merchants, trade, and foreign trade? Reading his essay, would you find his ideas convincing?

ACTIVITY 5: **Examining the Lives of Women**

After reading the selections of poetry (2.11), be prepared to discuss:

1. What are the subjects of these poems?

2. What were these women's joys? What were their sorrows?

3. What values are reflected in the poems?

4. One poem is by a concubine; the others are not. How are they similar and different?

5. What is the picture of the lives of Ming dynasty women that comes through in these poems? What assumptions do the women make about their lives?

The preface to one anthology of Chinese women poets, written late in the Ming dynasty, says, "Men must travel to all the corners of the earth in order to know the world....But women never have to do that. They have country villages right on their pillows and mountain passes in their dreams, all because they are so pure.... Alas! How far in their skillfulness men fall behind women!"[7] Do you agree? What prejudices are embedded in this statement?

NOTE: To deepen understanding of the lives of educated women during the sixteenth century, read more of their poems in *Women Writers of Traditional China* (see Suggested Resources).

Creative Extension:

Write a poem in the voice of a Ming dynasty woman. Or write a pair of poems: one in the voice of a Ming dynasty woman and the other in which a present-day individual responds to her words. With a partner, be prepared to read the pair of poems to the class.

---

[7] qtd. in Chang and Saussy, *Women Writers in Traditional China*, 9–10.

ACTIVITY 6:
Writing and Researching about the Life of the Peasantry

Read Document 2.12, which includes four selections describing conditions for the vast majority of the people in the 1500s, the last century of the Ming dynasty. (Refer to Chapter 1 for additional primary sources describing rural life.) Then choose from among the following activities:

1. In these accounts, we get various glimpses of government officials. (Liu in excerpt C is also an official.) Make a Venn diagram to compare and contrast the qualities of a good government official, today and in Ming dynasty times. (You might want to do research to find out how Confucius thought a good government official should behave.)

2. In these accounts, the starving peasants resort to dire measures in order to survive—selling one's wife, selling one's children, cannibalism. What do these things tell us about the power of hunger? Where else have you heard of individuals having to make unbearable choices? You might want to research the peasant revolts that occurred toward the end of the Ming dynasty and report to the class.

3. There are places in the world today where conditions exist similar to the ones described in these documents. Research a region in the world afflicted by droughts, floods, or other conditions that hinder good farming. Create a blog about the situation. Be sure to address the following questions: Is the present situation exactly like that of the sixteenth-century peasants? If not, how is it different? What is being done to help the people affected by catastrophic conditions? Is one form of government better able to address the problems of farmers than another? Why?

EXTENDED RESEARCH:

To get a deeper understanding of various aspects of life in sixteenth-century China, explore any one of these topics:

- The life of Matteo Ricci, Jesuit living in China
- The bed "built up with bricks" (Document 2.2) is called a *kang* 炕 in Chinese. Research this and other aspects of courtyard homes (*siheyuan* 四合院).
- Research a topic such as calligraphy, the tea ceremony, or Ming dynasty poetry.
- Learn about the Confucian examination system through which all scholar-officials had to pass before they could serve in the government. Be prepared to debate the merits and liabilities of such a system.
- Read the historical novel *The Examination* by Malcolm Bosse (see Suggested Resources) and report on what you learn about Ming dynasty China from the book.

Suggested Resources

Books

Bosse, Malcolm. *The Examination*. New York: Farrar, Straus, & Giroux, 1994.
This historical novel gives a sense of the civil service examination system and secret societies.

Brook, Timothy. *The Confusions of Pleasure: Commerce and Culture in Ming China*. Berkeley: University of California Press, 1998.

Chang, Kang-I Sun, and Haun Saussy, eds. *Women Writers of Traditional China: An Anthology of Poetry and Criticism*. Stanford: Stanford University Press, 1999.

Clunas, Craig. *Fruitful Sites: Garden Culture in Ming Dynasty China*. Durham, NC: Duke University Press, 1996.

Crosby, Alfred W. "New World Foods and Old World Demography." *The Columbian Exchange: Biological and Cultural Consequences of 1492*. Westport, CT: Praeger, 2003.

Dreyer, Edward L. *Zheng He: China and the Oceans in the Early Ming Dynasty*, 1405–1433. New York: Pearson Longman, 2007.

Huang, Ray. *1587, A Year of No Significance: The Ming Dynasty in Decline*. New Haven: Yale University Press, 1981.

Idema, Wilt Lukas, and Beata Grant. *The Red Brush: Writing Women of Imperial China*. Cambridge: Harvard University Asia Center, 2004.

Knapp, Ronald, Jonathan Spence, and A. Chester Ong. *Chinese Houses: The Architectural Heritage of a Nation*. Rutland, VT: Tuttle Publishing, 2005.

Levathes, Louise. *When China Ruled the Seas: The Treasure Fleet of the Dragon Throne, 1405–1433*. New York: Simon & Schuster, 1994.

Roberts, J.A.G. "The Early Modern Period: The Ming and Early Qing." *A Concise History of China*. Cambridge: Harvard University Press, 1999.

Spence, Jonathan D. *The Memory Palace of Matteo Ricci*. New York: Viking, 1984.

Tsai, Shih-shan Henry. *The Eunuchs in the Ming Dynasty*. Albany: State University of New York Press, 1996.

Websites

Amazing Facts About the Secret World of the Forbidden City, Oakland Museum of California **http://museumca.org/exhibit/exhib_fc2.html**

Asia for Educators **http://afe.easia.columbia.edu** Select the 1450–1750 time period to explore primary sources and information about the relationship between China, Japan, and Korea.

Chinese Gardens and Collectors' Rocks, Thematic Essay from the Heilbrunn Timeline of Art History, The Metropolitan Museum of Art **http://www.metmuseum.org/toah/hd/cgrk/hd_cgrk.htm**

The Columbian Exchange by Alfred Crosby, History Now, The Gilder Lehrman Institute of American History **http://www.gilderlehrman.org/history-by-era/american-indians/essays/columbian-exchange** Exchange between East and West brought new imports, such as potatoes and peppers, to China while China's exports of silk and porcelain were traded around the world.

Discovery Atlas China Revealed: The Forbidden City **http://dsc.discovery.com/videos/discovery-atlas-china-revealed-chinese-architecture.html** An excerpt about the Forbidden City from the Discovery Channel's documentary about China.

Forbidden City Unlocked, National Geographic **http://traveler.nationalgeographic.com/2008/11/insiders-map/beijing-interactive** This interactive map of the Forbidden City provides an overview of sections of the Beijing palace.

Ming Dynasty (1368–1644), Thematic Essay from the Heilbrunn Timeline of Art History, The Metropolitan Museum of Art **http://www.metmuseum.org/toah/hd/ming/hd_ming.htm**

Films

The Emperor's Eye (58 mins; 1990)
This documentary captures the preeminence of the arts in Chinese culture.

UNIT TWO

The Qing Dynasty
(1644–1911)

UNIT OVERVIEW

By Liz Nelson

The words highlighted in this overview are key people, concepts, or movements that appear in the chapters that follow.

After the last Ming emperor to rule from Beijing hanged himself in 1644, the Manchu people swept down from the northeast and gradually took control of China. They established the **Qing dynasty**. Throughout Chinese history northern peoples had often ruled part of China, sometimes for several hundred years at a time. The Mongol Yuan dynasty from 1279 to 1368 was one of these. But the Qing dynasty of the Manchu people was the largest and most successful of all the dynasties controlled by northern peoples. Over the course of the next century, Qing forces expanded and solidified China's borders, creating an immense continental power.

Under the reigns of **three powerful emperors: Kangxi, Yongzheng, and Qianlong**, China enjoyed more than a century of peace during which culture and commerce flourished. These three rulers and their successors incorporated Chinese values and aesthetics into Manchu court life, while at the same time keeping a firm grasp on military power. Chinese scholar-officials continued to be appointed to government positions, ensuring their support. By the 1700s, Chinese culture and society under the Manchus was at one of its zenith points. A huge "civil service" of bureaucrats and officials governed the country, woodblock-printed books were in wide circulation, refined poetry was being composed, and material luxuries of all sorts were produced in great numbers.

The Chinese had had experience interacting with peoples beyond their borders for centuries. For example, Chinese merchants were engaged in trade over the Silk Routes for extended periods of time, first during the Han dynasty (206 B.C.E.–220 C.E.) and again during the Tang dynasty (618 C.E.–907 C.E.). During the latter period, Xi'an,[1] the start of the trade route, was the most cosmopolitan city in the world. By the thirteenth century, the Chinese had developed the most reliable ocean-going vessels in the world, with watertight bulkheads and moveable rudders. This advanced technology allowed them, 200 years later, to launch an enormous fleet of 300 vessels on tributary missions in South and Southeast Asia, the Persian Gulf, and East Africa.

Each dynasty conducted its relations with non-Chinese-speaking peoples (regarded as "barbarians") with the understanding that China was the Middle Kingdom, the direct

---

[1] Formerly known as Chang'an

TIMELINE

Elsewhere in the world as the Manchus founded the Qing dynasty:

- The Ottoman Empire, founded in 1288 and ruled from present-day Istanbul, spanned southeastern Europe, the Middle East, and North Africa. At its height, it stretched from the Strait of Gibraltar to the Caspian Sea.

- Africa knew this as the period of Great African Kingdoms (e.g. Dahomey, Great Zimbabwe, and Axum).

- The Mughal Empire, in existence from the early 1500s, stretched across the Indian subcontinent.

- In Korea, the Joseon dynasty began rule in 1392.

- In Japan, during the Tokugawa or Edo period, the country was unified under a military government, beginning in 1600.

- In Vietnam, the Le dynasty had ruled since 1428.

1600

1602: Dutch East India Company established

1644: Qing dynasty established

1648: Taj Mahal completed in India

1650: Dutch East India Company brings tea to New Amsterdam (later New York City)

1652–1654: The English begin to drink tea

1661: The first of two 17th-century civil wars in Vietnam between Trinh in the North and Nguyen in the South (the second civil war begins in1672)

1662: Kangxi Emperor begins his reign (1662–1722)

1670: England's King Charles II expands powers of British East India Company

1683: Qing annex Taiwan

1689: Peter the Great becomes emperor of Russia

1689: Treaty of Nerchinsk signed with Russia

1697: Qing conquer western Mongolia

---

translation of its name, *Zhongguo*. (In much the same way, "Mediterranean" means "middle of the earth," with Rome at the center.) The emperor was the Son of Heaven and all foreign rulers owed him allegiance as heads of what the Chinese rulers considered **tributary states**.

In the late 1700s, the emperors of the Qing dynasty continued to focus on their immediate neighbors and had little knowledge of or interest in **European imperial powers**. When they had to, they dealt with them as they had with other nations—as unequal parties. But with the Industrial Revolution underway in the West, China was up against a new kind of "barbarian," and China's lack of knowledge cost the Chinese

dearly. Western imperial powers, followed by Japan later in the nineteenth century, were transforming themselves from agrarian into industrial nations with new kinds of weaponry and territorial ambitions. Their merchant fleets traded all over the world, and their citizens eagerly purchased the tea, silk, and porcelain from China that ships brought home. China, however, had no interest in Western products and restricted Western traders to Guangzhou[2] in what was known as the **Canton System**. The Chinese government also demanded payment in silver, supplies of which were plummeting

---

[2] Formerly known as Canton

1700

1700s: Age of Enlightenment in Europe

1700: As Mughal authority weakens, regional powers rise in India

1711: East India Company establishes trading post in Guangzhou

1715: Chinese Rites Controversy

1720: Tibet becomes Qing protectorate

1723: Emperor Yongzheng begins his reign (1723–1736)

1729: Opium smoking prohibited in China

1736: The reign of Qianlong, China's longest-ruling emperor, begins (1736–1795)

1750: Population of China 177.5 million

of Europe 140 million

of the 13 North American colonies 1.3 million

1757: Battle of Plassey, victory gives East India Company control of Bengal, beginning expansion of British rule in India

1759: Qing annex Xinjiang

1770: Bengal Famine kills an estimated 10 million people, one third of the population in the affected area

1771: The Tay Son Revolt topples the Le dynasty in Vietnam

1773: British Parliament passes the Tea Act, sparking protests in Boston, Massachusetts

1775–1783: American War for Independence

1784: The vessel *Empress of China* opens trade between the United States and China

End of 18th century: Industrial Revolution begins in Great Britain

1789–1799: French Revolution

1793: The Macartney embassy meets with Emperor Qianlong

1793–1815: Napoleonic Wars; end with Napoleon's defeat at Waterloo

1796–1805/06: White Lotus uprising

---

in the West. British and American merchants began to import opium into China, and after Qing officials banned its production, use, and importation, Western vessels smuggled the drug in via Chinese middlemen. The Western nations also demanded rights of trade, travel, and residence in China that traditionally had not been granted to foreigners.

Tension between China and the West escalated until in 1839, the British government used its state-of-the-art weaponry and highly trained soldiers to conduct "gunboat diplomacy." China lost both what became known as **Opium Wars** and the Manchus were coerced into signing a series of **unequal treaties**, thus

ushering in what the Chinese refer to as their "century of humiliation."

At the same time that Qing leaders were coping with pressure from the West, various factors contributed to **social unrest** in many areas of the country. The population of China had tripled from 143 million in 1741 to 430 million in 1850, but arable land had only increased by about 35%, exacerbating hardship for peasants. The ever-growing smuggling of opium had now reversed the trade balance: more silver was leaving China than entering. As a result, the price of silver rose sharply, and members of the working class, who were paid in copper coins, found it increasingly difficult to

1800

1800: Dutch East India Company dissolved

1802: Nguyen dynasty founded in Vietnam

1807: British Atlantic slave trade ends

1810–1820: The majority of Latin American countries declare independence from Spain and Portugal

1811: Population of China 358.5 million

1812–1815: War of 1812 fought between United States and Great Britain

1813: Opium smoking banned in China

1819: The British establish Singapore as a colony

1826: Cholera pandemic begins in India and spreads from Russia to Central Europe to Scotland by 1832

1839–1842: Opium War fought between Britain and China ending with the Treaty of Nanjing, the first of the "unequal treaties"

1849: First Chinese immigrants arrive in Peru

1850: Emperor Xianfeng begins his rule

1848–1858: California Gold Rush; first Chinese immigrants begin to arrive in the United States

1851: Population of China 431.9 million

1850s: First Chinese immigrants arrive in Australia

1851–1854: Taiping Rebellion led by Hong Xiuquan

1851–1868: Nian Rebellion led by Zhang Luoxing

1853–1856: Crimean War between Britain, France, the Ottoman Empire, and Russia

1854: Convention of Kanagawa negotiated by Commodore Matthew Perry ends Japanese isolation policy

1858: Treaty of Tianjin

1858: British East India Company's rule ends, and direct British rule begins in India

1861–1865: United States Civil War

1862: Treaty of Saigon is the first unequal treaty between France and Vietnam

pay taxes in silver currency as the government required. In the 1840s and 1850s, millions also suffered from such natural disasters as droughts and floods. The educated elite had trouble finding employment. Some who did have government positions had bought them rather than having passed the traditional examinations, and corruption was widespread. In addition, the army was in dismal shape: poorly equipped and, like all other segments of society, riddled with opium addicts. Four major rebellions rocked the Qing dynasty mid-century, the most significant of which was the **Taiping Rebellion** (1851–1864).

The combination of internal strife and external pressure greatly damaged the Qing dynasty. While a number of prominent Chinese scholar-officials launched many thoughtful plans to reform China, their **self-strengthening efforts** were up against an entrenched bureaucracy and a dynasty desperate to hang onto power. Chinese students studied abroad, and foreign language schools and armories were established at home, but no multi-faceted program took hold. China lagged decades behind the industrial strength of the West and Japan rather than forging ahead as it had in the past.

1862: Six-year-old Tongzhi becomes emperor; Cixi acts as Empress Dowager; Tongzhi Restoration

1863: Cambodia becomes a protectorate of France

1868–1912: Meiji Period in Japan begins, launching the Meiji Restoration

1875: Tongzhi dies; three-year-old Guangxu appointed emperor; Empress Dowager Cixi continues to rule

1882: Chinese Exclusion Act passed in the United States

1887: French create the Indochinese Union (ICU), which includes Cochinchina (southern Vietnam) as a colony and Annam (central Vietnam), Tonkin (northern Vietnam), and Cambodia as protectorates; Laos added as a protectorate in 1893

1894–1895: Sino-Japanese War. Treaty of Shimonoseki cedes Taiwan to Japan and gives Japan control of Korea

1897–1910: Emperor Gojong proclaims the Republic ot Korea

1898–1901: Boxer Uprising

1900

1900: Commonwealth of Australia established

1901: Australia passes the Immigration Restriction Act, also known as the "White Australia Policy"

1904–1905: Russo-Japanese War won by Japan; Treaty of Portsmouth ends hostilities

1905: Abolition of traditional Confucian examination system

1906: Great Earthquake of San Francisco

1908: Empress Dowager Cixi dies; Puyi becomes emperor

1910: Japanese colonial rule in Korea begins

1910: Slavery abolished in China

1911: Qing dynasty falls to revolutionary forces led by Sun Yat-sen

Merchants from Britain, France, Portugal, the United States, and Russia set aside segments of China's port cities, such as Shanghai and Tianjin, as their own "concessions," where *their* legal systems applied instead of China's. Now they traded freely with inland China, too. Thousands of Protestant and Catholic **missionaries** proselytized and established schools and hospitals across the country. Much of their social work improved the lives of countless Chinese men, women, and children. But increasing hardships for the Chinese peasantry made foreigners an easy target for mistrust, and violence broke out a number of times, culminating in North China in the **Boxer Uprising** of 1900.

As increasing numbers of upper-class Chinese men and women studied abroad (especially in Japan), they became keenly aware of the disparities between industrialized nations and China. Expatriates, such as **Dr. Sun Yat-sen**, gathered supporters and funds, eager to end imperial rule and establish a republic in China. Several revolts failed, but eventually one that began by accident in Wuhan spread rapidly. The formal **abdication** by the child-emperor Puyi on February 12, 1912 marked the end of more than two millennia of dynastic rule in China.

CHAPTER RESOURCES

Excerpts of these primary source documents appear in this chapter. Go to **www.chinasince1644.com** for the full version of these documents and for the Supplementary Materials.

CHAPTER 3

Three Manchu Emperors

By Jamie Moore

Chapter Contents

The Manchu Invasion
Qing Dynasty Expansion
Manchu and Chinese Cultures Integrate

Key Idea

The Manchu were an ethnically non-Han people who in the seventeenth and eighteenth centuries controlled the largest territory that China had ever possessed in one of the country's most prosperous periods. Qing rulers kept their own Manchu identity, while at the same time incorporating and preserving Chinese culture and values.

Guiding Questions

What were the effects of foreign, Manchu rule on China?

What were the challenges and benefits of territorial expansion for the Qing dynasty?

In what ways did Qing rulers preserve Chinese values? What did they emphasize? What did they control?

Terms to Know

civil service examination system	Manchu
Confucianism	maxim
courtesan	Mongols
dynasty	Qing
edict	queue
eunuch	treaty
Han Chinese	

Essay

The Manchu Invasion

In the early 1600s, the Manchus (*Manzu* 满族), who lived in the northeast in what are now Liaoning (辽宁), Heilongjiang (黑龙江), and Jilin (吉林) provinces, began to consolidate their forces north of the Great Wall. They took advantage of the declining Ming (明) dynasty (1368–1644) to begin their gradual conquest of China. In the twelfth century, their ancestors had ruled northern China as the Jin (晋) dynasty. The Manchus used this historical connection as a justification for the legitimacy of their rule.

Nurhaci (*Nuerhachi* 努尔哈赤) (1559–1626), the *khan* or ruler of the Manchus, organized his military forces into eight units known as "banners" that consisted of soldiers and their family members. This was an efficient way to keep track of people and plan strong military advances. As the *khan* conquered Chinese territory, he encouraged the Chinese to join him by giving them powerful leadership positions. After Nurhaci's death, his sons pushed for the complete defeat of the Ming, and in 1636, Huangtaiji (皇太极) (r.1626–1643) officially named the new dynasty "Qing" (清), meaning "pure" or "clear." After an uneasy first forty years, the dynasty's early history was one of relative stability, unity, and success. This can be attributed to the rule of three powerful Qing emperors: Kangxi (康熙), Yongzheng (雍正), and Qianlong (乾隆). They ruled the largest land empire of the time from 1662 to 1796, a period heralded by scholars as one of the most stable in China's history.

Territorial Expansion

Kangxi, the first of these three emperors, came to power in 1662, and under his leadership, the Qing dynasty quickly consolidated territory in southern and southwestern China that had previously been controlled by three warlords. In addition, the Qing also expanded and solidified borders. To suppress resistance by Ming dynasty loyalists who had retreated to Taiwan, they captured the island in 1683 and made it part of the Qing empire (see Item 3.C on the companion website for an overview of Taiwan's history). The Qing then solidified the northeast border of China by signing the Treaty of Nerchinsk with Russia in 1689 (see Chapter 4, Document 4.2). A subsequent treaty outlining the border west of the 1689 treaty was signed in 1727 under the Yongzheng emperor.[1] The Manchus defeated the Eastern Mongols in the 1630s and the nomadic Zunghar tribes (western Mongols) in 1696. They also invaded Tibet (*Xizang* 西藏) (an area almost twice the size of the state of Texas) in 1720, continuing a long legacy of Chinese involvement in and efforts to control the region (see Item 3.D on the companion website for an overview of Tibet's history). In the 1750s, Manchus conquered the vast, primarily Muslim territory of Xinjiang (新疆). Over the course of a century, the Qing had significantly increased land holdings north, south, and west, which included people of many ethnicities. As the empire expanded, however, the Manchus also faced the task of coping with periodic rebellions, which were often led by secret societies such as the White Lotus (see A Closer Look at the end of the chapter).

Manchu and Chinese Cultures Integrate

Throughout their rule, the three emperors (Kangxi, Yongzheng, and Qianlong) balanced ways to maintain military and civil power with practices that integrated Confucian-trained Chinese intellectuals into the Manchu government. On the one hand, the Manchus established dominance by requiring Chinese men to wear a braided queue in the Manchu style. They prohibited Manchu women from binding their feet, which limited intermarriage between Manchu women and Chinese men since Chinese men believed bound feet to be a sign of refinement. The Qianlong emperor also persecuted Chinese writers suspected of harboring anti-Manchu sentiments. On the

---

[1] The Treaty of Kiakhta

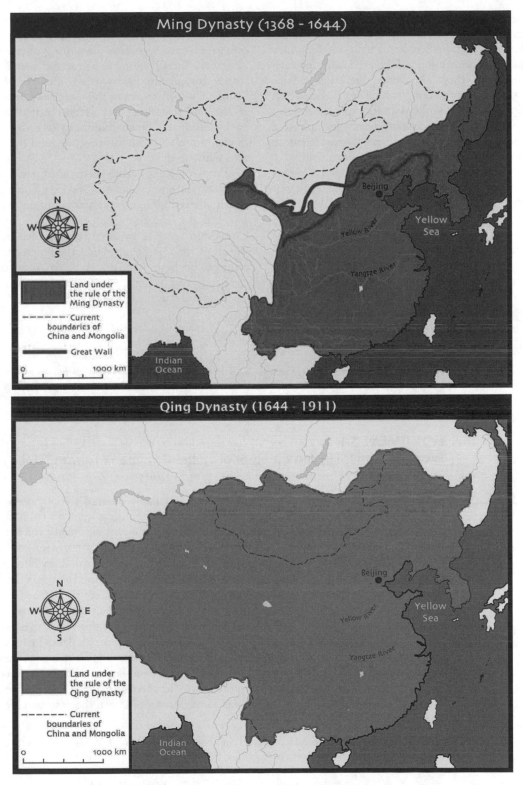

(Minneapolis Institute of Art)

other hand, when the Qing established six ministries of government (Civil Affairs, Finance, Rituals, War, Justice, and Public Service), they had a Manchu and a Chinese leader for each ministry. They also kept the civil service examination system, which was based on knowledge of four key Confucian books and five ancient Chinese classics. They even added a special exam in 1679 for men of great talent, to draw more Chinese into their government.

The three emperors incorporated Chinese culture to make the Chinese more accepting of their rule. The Kangxi emperor not only studied and debated proper moral behavior and values found at the heart of the ancient classics, but wrote his "Sacred Edicts" in 1670, summarizing sixteen maxims that he considered to embody Confucius's most important moral values. In 1724, the Yongzheng emperor added his own comments to these edicts and mandated that they be publicly presented to the common people twice a month. The Qing court sponsored literary endeavors, such as the writing of encyclopedias. The Qianlong emperor sponsored a major compilation of famous literary and historical works known as the *Complete Library of the Four Treasuries*. He is also noted for having studied Tibetan Buddhism in order to model himself as a Buddhist savior kind to his non-Chinese subjects.

Emperors Kangxi, Yongzheng, and Qianlong expanded the empire and solidified key borders, which allowed China to prosper culturally and economically. The few Europeans who visited China were stunned by the sheer opulence and wealth of the Qing court. Until the nineteenth century, the high standard of living, material resources, and inventions of Manchu China were unrivaled in the rest of the world.

Primary Sources

DOCUMENT 3.1:
Excerpts from "Shi Lang's Memorial on the Capture of Taiwan," 1683

Cannon shot and arrows fell like rain; smoke and flame covered the sky. It was impossible to see even a foot beyond the ships.... The fighting went on from the early morning until the late afternoon. Our sailors fought without regard for their own lives and used all of their energy to attack and kill the bandits. Eighteen of the bandits' big gunboats were set aflame and destroyed by our navy's incendiary buckets and grenades. Eight other heavy gunboats were sunk by cannon fire. Thirty-six large "birdboats," sixty-seven silk junks, and five refitted foreign ships were also burned and destroyed. Moreover, our navy used the wind to propel incendiary boats into other bandit ships; one "birdboat" and two silk junks were destroyed in this way. The rebellious bandits fought feverishly and when their forces were exhausted, [they] packed gunpowder in holds of their own ships and blew themselves up. In this way, they burned nine gunboats and thirteen "birdboats." Some bandits panicked and jumped into the sea and, in this way, we captured two "birdboats," eight silk junks, and twenty-five two-masted junks. What was to be burnt was burnt; those to be killed were killed....

SOURCE: Rpt. in Pei-Kai Cheng, Michael Lestz, and Jonathan Spence, eds., *The Search for Modern China: A Documentary Collection* (New York: W.W. Norton, 1999) 50–51.

 Go to **www.chinasince1644.com** for the full text of **Document 3.1.**

DOCUMENT 3.2: Excerpts from the *Analects of Confucius*

Confucius is believed to have been born around 551 B.C.E., during the time of the Warring States and great political disorder in China. He became a scholar and traveled from province to province hoping to spread his ideas about good moral behavior and the proper way for rulers to treat their subjects. While he never had the impact he hoped for during his lifetime, Confucius's thoughts were recorded by his students in the Analects. *Since the Han dynasty (206 B.C.E.–220 C.E.), Confucius's ideas have shaped Chinese society and were used as the foundation for political and social life in dynastic China long after his death.*

1.2 You Zi (a disciple of Confucius) said, "It is rare for a man whose character is such that he is good as a son and obedient as a young man to [go against] his superiors… Being good as a son and obedient as a young man is perhaps the root of a man's character."

1.6 The Master said: "At home, a young man must respect his parents; abroad, he must respect his elders. He should talk little, but with good faith; love all people, but associate with the virtuous. Having done this, if he still has energy to spare, let him study literature."

1.16 The Master said, "Don't worry if people don't recognize your merits; worry that you may not recognize theirs."

2.3 The Master said, "Guide them by edicts, keep them in line with punishments, and the common people will stay out of trouble but will have no sense of shame. Guide them by virtue, keep them in line with the rites, and they will, besides having a sense of shame, reform themselves."

2.7 Nowadays people think they are dutiful sons when they feed their parents. Yet they also feed their dogs and horses. Unless there is respect, where is the difference?

2.15 Confucius said, "To study without thinking is futile. To think without studying is dangerous."

SOURCES: D.C. Lau, trans., *Confucius: The Analects* (Hong Kong: The Chinese University Press, 2000). Simon Leys, trans., *The Analects of Confucius* (New York: W. W. Norton, 1997).

 Go to **www.chinasince1644.com** for the text of **Document 3.2**.

DOCUMENT 3.3: The Kangxi Emperor's "Sacred Edicts," 1670

1. Highly esteem filial piety and the proper relations among brothers in order to give due importance to social relations.
2. Give due weight to kinship in order to promote harmony and peace.
3. Maintain good relations within the neighborhood in order to prevent quarrels and lawsuits.
4. Give due importance to farming and the cultivation of mulberry trees in order to ensure sufficient clothing and food.
5. Be moderate and economical in order to avoid wasting away your livelihood.

6. Make the most of schools and academies in order to honor the ways of scholars.

7. Denounce strange beliefs in order to elevate the true doctrine.

8. Explain laws and regulations in order to warn the ignorant and obstinate.

9. Show propriety and courtesy to improve customs and manners.

10. Work hard in your professions in order to quiet your ambitions.

11. Instruct sons and younger brothers in order to prevent their committing any wrong.

12. Put a stop to false accusations in order to protect the good and honest.

13. Warn against giving shelter to deserters in order to avoid punishment with them.

14. Promptly and fully pay your taxes in order to avoid forced requisition.

15. Get together in groups of ten or a hundred in order to put an end to theft and robbery.

16. Free yourself from resentment and anger in order to show respect for your body and life.

SOURCE: Paul Brians et al., ed., *Reading About the World*, Volume 2 (Fort Worth, TX: Harcourt Brace CustomBooks, 1999). http://www.wsu.edu/~wldciv/world_civ_reader/world_civ_reader_2/kang_hsi.html

Go to **www.chinasince1644.com** for the text of **Document 3.3**.

DOCUMENT 3.4: "Fan Jin Passes the Juren Examination," an excerpt from *The Scholars* by Wu Jingzi, c. 1740

"This is to announce that the master of your honourable mansion, Fan Jin, has passed the provincial examination in Guangdong, coming seventh in the list. May better news follow in rapid succession!"

Fan Jin feasted his eyes on the announcement, and, after reading it through once to himself, read it once more aloud. Clapping his hands, he laughed and exclaimed, "Ha! Good! I have passed." Then, stepping back, he fell down in a dead faint. His mother hastily poured some boiled water between his lips, whereupon he recovered consciousness and struggled to his feet. Clapping his hands again, he let out a peal of laughter and shouted, "Aha! I've passed! I've passed!" Laughing wildly he ran outside, giving the heralds and the neighbours the fright of their lives. Not far from the front door he slipped and fell into a pond. When he clambered out, his hair was dishevelled, his hands muddied and his whole body dripping with slime. But nobody could stop him. Still clapping his hands and laughing, he headed straight for the market.

They all looked at each other in consternation, and said, "The new honour has sent him off his head!"

His mother wailed, "Aren't we out of luck! Why should passing an examination do this to him? Now he's mad, goodness knows when he'll get better."

"He was all right this morning when he went out," said his wife. "What could have brought on this attack? What *shall* we do?"

SOURCE: Wu Jingzi, *Rulin waishi* [*The Scholars*], trans. Yang Xianyi and Gladys Yang (Beijing: Foreign Languages Press, 1999).

Go to **www.chinasince1644.com** for the full text of **Document 3.4**.

DOCUMENT 3.5: Excerpts from "Yuanchun Visits Her Parents on the Feast of Lanterns," *A Dream of Red Mansions* by Cao Xueqin, 1792

For a long time they waited in silence, Jia She and the young men of the family by the entrance of the west street, the Lady Dowager and the women in front of the main gate.

Then two eunuchs wearing scarlet uniforms rode slowly up to the entrance of the west street. Dismounting, they led their horses behind the screens, then stood to attention, their faces turned towards the west. After some time another pair appeared, then another, until there were ten pairs lined up and soft music could be heard in the distance.

And now a long procession approached: several pairs of eunuchs carrying dragon banners, others with phoenix fans, pheasant plumes and ceremonial insignia, as well as gold censers burning Imperial incense. Next came a curved-handled yellow umbrella on which were embroidered seven phoenixes, and under this a head-dress robe, girdle and slippers. After this came attendant eunuchs bearing a [Buddhist] rosary, embroidered handkerchiefs, a rinse-bowl, fly-whisks and the like.

Last of all, borne slowly forward by eight eunuchs, came a gold-topped palanquin[2] embroidered with phoenixes....

SOURCE: Hsueh-chin Tsao and Ngo Kao, *A Dream of Red Mansions*, trans. Yang Hsien-yi and Gladys Yang (Boston: Cheng & Tsui Company, 1996) 116.

Go to **www.chinasince1644.com** for the full text of Document 3.5.

DOCUMENT 3.6: Excerpts from "A Worthless Son Receives a Fearful Flogging," *A Dream of Red Mansions* by Cao Xueqin, 1792

The sight of his father paralyzed Huan with fright. He pulled up short, hanging his head.

"What are you rushing about for?" demanded Jia Zheng.... As he shouted for the servants who accompanied Huan to school, the boy saw a chance to divert his father's anger.

"I wasn't running to begin with," he said. "Not until I passed the well where that maid drowned herself. Her head's swollen up like this, and her body's all bloated from soaking in the water. It was such a horrible sight that I ran away as fast as ever I could."

Jia Zheng was astounded. "What maid here had any reason to throw herself into a well?" he wondered. "Such a thing has never happened before in this house. Since the time of our ancestors we have always treated our subordinates well. Of late, though, I've neglected household affairs and those in charge must have abused their power, resulting in this calamitous suicide. If word of this gets out, it will disgrace our ancestors' good name."

He called for Jia Lian, Lai Da and Lai Xing. Some pages were going to fetch them when Huan stepped forward and caught hold of his father's gown, then fell on his knees.

---

[2] A covered litter, or elaborate arm chair, carried by poles on the shoulders of two or more men.

"Don't be angry, sir!" he begged. "No one knows about this except those in my lady's apartment. I heard my mother say...." He stopped and looked around, and Jia Zheng understood. At a glance from him the servants on both sides withdrew.

"My mother told me," Huan went on in a whisper, "that the other day Brother Baoyu grabbed hold of Jin Zhuan in my lady's room and tried to rape her. When she wouldn't let him, he beat her. That's why she drowned herself in a fit of passion." Before he had finished Jia Zheng was livid with fury.

"Fetch Baoyu! Quick!" he roared....

SOURCE: Hsueh-chin Tsao and Ngo Kao, *A Dream of Red Mansions*, trans. Yang Hsien-yi and Gladys Yang (Boston: Cheng & Tsui Company, 1996) 200–201.

 Go to **www.chinasince1644.com** for the full text of **Document 3.6**.

DOCUMENT 3.7: "Portrait of the Qianlong Emperor (r. 1736–1796) as the Bodhisattva Manjusri," by Jesuit missionary Giuseppe Castiglione

This painting shows Qianlong in the center of a *thangka*—a Tibetan religious painting of a divinity. Bodhisattvas are individuals who have achieved great moral and spiritual wisdom, and Manjusri is the Tibetan Bodhisattva of Wisdom. The inscription on the painting states that Manjusri is the ruler of the Buddhist faith. Qianlong embraced Buddhism, frequently studying it at his court. *(Courtesy of Freer Gallery of Art, Smithsonian Institution, Washington, D.C.)*

 Go to **www.chinasince1644.com** for the color painting in **Document 3.7**.

DOCUMENTS 3.8a–n
Photographs of the Forbidden City, Beijing, 2006–2007

(Photos by Julie Newport)

 Go to **www.chinasince1644.com** Document **3.8a-n**
for additional photographs of the Forbidden City.

Activities

ACTIVITY 1: Responding to Reading about the Qing Dynasty

Read the introductory essay and prepare to discuss:

1. Why were the Manchus able to gain power?
2. How did the status of the Manchus as foreigners affect their rule?
3. What about the three emperors stands out to you?
4. What characteristics would you assume early Qing leaders had (qualities, skills, abilities) that contributed to their success?
5. Compare the Manchu occupation of China to that of another military power occupying a country.

ACTIVITY 2: Examining the Capture of Taiwan

1. Read "Shi Lang's Memorial on the Capture of Taiwan" (3.1)
2. Create a comic strip to go with an assigned passage of the battle. Incorporate language or adjectives that were used to describe enemy forces and Qing Forces.
3. Share your comic strip in a group assigned by your teacher.
4. Be prepared to discuss in your group:

   Which side was superior and why? How were the enemies treated when they were captured? Based on the way the Qing treated the rebels, what message were they sending?

ACTIVITY 3: Mapping the Qing Dynasty

Examine maps of China (Items 3.A, 3.B on the companion website). Locate and compare the size of:

- the Manchu homeland
- China under the Ming dynasty
- China's borders under the Qing after a century of their rule
- China's borders today

When you have become familiar with the maps, you will discuss in class:

1. What does this expansion tell you about the Qing? What would they have needed in order to do this?
2. What challenges does any empire face when adding so much territory? (e.g. consider treatment of minority groups, differences in culture, organization, communication, etc.)

Extended Activity:

Look up maps showing the boundaries of earlier Chinese dynasties (for example, see Chapter 3 Activity Websites on the companion website) and prepare to discuss the implications of the changes in China's borders over the centuries.

ACTIVITY 4: Analyzing and Writing about Cultural Values

Part 1: Categorize

Individually, in pairs or in groups, read assigned excerpts from the *Analects of Confucius* (3.2). Put the analects in your own words, then decide what general category each belongs to (family, government, education, etc).

Part 2: Paraphrase and Categorize

Read and paraphrase the Kangxi emperor's sixteen "Sacred Edicts" (3.3). Again, categorize the edicts, as you did with the *Analects*. Discuss:

1. What are the similarities/differences between Kangxi's edicts and the *Analects*?
2. What did the Qing emperor emphasize?
3. According to the Qing emperor, what qualities make a good subject? What behavior should be avoided?
4. How could these edicts have been used to solidify the emperor's power and create harmony in society?
5. What conclusions can be drawn from the similarities between the Kangxi edicts and Confucius's *Analects*?

Writing Connections:

Choose from the following:

1. Write an essay addressing how leaders can consolidate and solidify their control over their subjects. Consider:
   a. How did the Qing emperors consolidate and solidify their control?
   b. How have other empires achieved these goals?
2. Write an essay addressing how cultural values are imposed or spread. Consider:
   a. What materials in your culture are used to disseminate values and ideals?
   b. What do you believe are the most effective ways to promote civility and harmony among people?

ACTIVITY 5: Using Literature to Learn about Society

Part 1: Respond to Reading

Read the excerpt from *The Scholars*, "Fan Jin Passes the Juren Examination" (3.4). Prepare to discuss:

1. What elements of Chinese society are evident in the story? Cite the evidence in the text.
2. What do you think is the basis of Wu Jingzi's criticism of the examination system? Why does he use satire to make his point?
3. Do you think that he is justified?
4. How would having an examination system such as this for all civil service jobs affect government?
5. Should people pass exams to serve in certain jobs? Which jobs? Is this fair for everyone?

Part 2: Respond in Writing to Another Reading

Read the excerpts from *A Dream of Red Mansions*. (Document 3.5 details a visit to the wealthy Jia family by one of their daughters who was one of the emperor's courtesans. Document 3.6 gives insight into the hierarchy and relationships in the Jia family.)

For Document 3.5, write an essay that addresses the following:

1. What did the family do in preparation for the courtesan's visit?
2. Who were the eunuchs? What was their role?
3. What was the role of the imperial courtesans in society?
4. What does this description show about China at that time?

For Document 3.6, first diagram the family hierarchy. Then prepare to discuss:

1. How do various members of the household react to Jin Zhuan's suicide? What is thought to have pushed the maid to suicide? What conclusions can be drawn from the reactions?
2. What has Baoyu done to enrage his father and how does the father respond?
3. Which behavior is considered the worst? Why?
4. Who ultimately speaks to Jia Zheng about the way he punished his son? What happens next?
5. What does it mean to be "filial" in Chinese culture?
6. What questions do you have and where might you find answers?

Take notes for a class discussion or write an essay to answer: How does literature help us learn about another culture and era? What are the advantages and disadvantages of relying on literature for insights?

Alternatively, write a reaction piece describing your impressions of a wealthy family during the Qing dynasty.

ACTIVITY 6: **Interpreting Visual Art**

In the 1720s, the Qing rulers were drawn into Tibet and added the devoutly Buddhist region to the area under their control. (For more information about Tibet's history, read the essay in Additional Resources on the companion website.) Examine the painting "Portrait of the Qianlong Emperor (r. 1736–1796) as the Bodhisattva Manjusri" (3.7).

1. Describe the painting. What do you notice?
2. What relationship does the painting suggest exists between Manjusri—the Bodhisattva of Wisdom—and the Qianlong emperor?
3. What do you think Qianlong's objective was in commissioning this painting?
4. What can we learn about the Qing dynasty from this painting?
5. What are some other examples of government figures taking on a guise for a similar purpose?

Extended Activity:

■ Find an article about an ethnic minority or national group within China and its relationship with the Chinese government today (for example, the Uyghur or Tibetans).

■ Find information about an ethnic group anywhere in the world that wants independence from what it feels is rule by a foreign power.

Summarize the information you find and prepare to share it with classmates.

ACTIVITY 7: **Exploring the Forbidden City**

Examine the photographs of the Forbidden City (3.8a–n) and research online how the palace functioned for 500 years, until the early 1900s. You will then discuss as a class:

1. What is most striking about how the palace functioned?
2. How did the Forbidden City reflect the relationship among various elements of Chinese society?
3. What additional information does it give us about the Qing dynasty?
4. Compare the way the Forbidden City functioned to the government structure and operations in another country in the same time period (e.g. France, Great Britain, the North American colonies, or Japan during the period 1650–1750).

EXTENDED RESEARCH:
···

To further your understanding of Qing dynasty China, research any one of the following topics and present your findings in a paper, digital presentation, or visual display.

- The role of eunuchs in the imperial court
- Secret societies (such as White Lotus, Triad, etc.)
- The role of concubines
- *A Dream of Red Mansions* theme parks in China today
- Present-day Chinese soap operas set during the Qing dynasty
- Tibetan Buddhism
- Taiwan

Suggested Resources

Books

Barmé, Geremie R. *The Forbidden City*. Cambridge: Harvard University Press, 2008.
A history of the Forbidden City in Beijing, China, with information about the dynasties and rulers who resided in the palace.

Bosse, Malcolm. *The Examination*. New York: Farrar, Straus & Giroux, 1994.
This historical novel gives a sense of the civil service examination system and secret societies.

Cao, Xueqin. *The Story of the Stone*. Trans. David Hawkes. Vol. 1. London: Penguin, 1973.
A translation of the famous novel also known as *A Dream of Red Mansions*.

Websites

The Art of Asia: Ch'ing Dynasty
http://www.artsmia.org/art-of-asia/history/dynasty-ching.cfm
Site from the Minneapolis Institute of Arts with history and maps of the Chinese dynasties. Includes curator videos.

Discovery Atlas China Revealed: Chinese Architecture, The Forbidden City
http://dsc.discovery.com/videos/discovery-atlas-china-revealed-chinese-architecture.html
A video about the architecture and history of the Forbidden City.

History & Maps, Ming Dynasty Map
http://www.artsmia.org/art-of-asia/history/ming-dynasty-map.cfm
Maps from the Minneapolis Institute of Arts showing China's shifting boundaries across the millennia.

■ A CLOSER LOOK

The White Lotus Society Rises in Protest

Though the early Qing years were times of relative peace and stability, small rebellions did occur, many inspired by secret societies. The White Lotus Society first emerged in the late thirteenth century during another period when China was ruled by foreigners. The Society originated in Sichuan Province in central China and its members were millennialists: they believed that the end of the world was close at hand. The Society drew on a sort of folk Buddhism, Daoism, and a belief in the support of the "Eternal Venerable Mother" goddess. Smaller branches believing in the same principles appeared again and again in later centuries. They usually rose in objection to the ruling dynasty of the time, but especially objected to the foreign Manchu rule.

White Lotus rebels, under the leadership of Wang Lun, emerged in the eighteenth century with the goal of reestablishing the Ming dynasty, whom they saw as the legitimate rulers of China. Most White Lotus followers were poor peasants, workers, and demobilized soldiers—those disaffected by society. The White Lotus also appealed to women, as the Society promoted social equality. While it is not clear whether there was a specific trigger to their rebellions, the movement suggests deep discontent in society.

Several factors may have led to the rise of the White Lotus Society: the poor management of emergency granaries (for use in time of famine), cruel and brutal treatment by Manchu soldiers, a growing population, high taxes, and government corruption. During the Qing dynasty, followers of the White Lotus often clashed with local officials and landlords and had to be subdued by the military. While these societies did not overthrow the Qing, they ultimately contributed to the dynasty's demise.

■ *Discuss: What secret and/or illegal organizations do you know of elsewhere in the world that destabilize a government? How do they operate?*

Inside Beijing's Forbidden City
http://today.msnbc.msn.com/id/26054286/ns/today-today_in_beijing/t/exclusive-inside-beijings-forbidden-city
A behind-the-scenes tour of the Forbidden City with "Today Show" host Matt Lauer and historic preservationist Henry Ng.

Recording the Grandeur of the Qing: The Southern Inspection Tour Scrolls of the Kangxi and Qianlong Emperors
http://www.learn.columbia.edu/nanxuntu/start.html
An interactive website about the Qing dynasty. From the Metropolitan Museum of Art and Columbia University.

Films

The Emperor's Eye (58 mins; 1990)
This documentary captures the preeminence of the arts in Chinese culture.

CHAPTER RESOURCES

Primary Sources

DOCUMENT 4.1a & b: Stamps issued commemorating Jesuit missionary Ferdinand Verbiest

DOCUMENT 4.2: Excerpts from Treaty of Nerchinsk Signed by China and Russia in 1689

DOCUMENT 4.3: Excerpts from the letter King George III of England wrote to the Chinese emperor and sent with Lord Macartney, 1792

DOCUMENT 4.4: Two edicts from the emperor Qianlong in reply to Lord Macartney's mission to China, September 1793

DOCUMENT 4.5: Requests by English merchants and responses from a Chinese official, 1793

DOCUMENT 4.6: A description of various European countries and their people by Xie Qinggao, a Chinese sailor, between 1783 and 1797

DOCUMENT 4.7a & b: Excerpts from a letter by William Trotter of Philadelphia, trading in Guangzhou, 1797

DOCUMENT 4.8: Excerpts from a letter Edward King wrote from Guangzhou to his brother, October 31, 1835

DOCUMENT 4.9a & b: Examples of *chinoiserie* (ca. 1800 and ca. 1810)

DOCUMENT 4.10: Excerpts from a letter of instructions from the owners of the vessel *Mentor* to Captain John Suter, 1816

DOCUMENT 4.11: "A Voyage with Opium Smugglers" by William Hunter, between 1825 and 1844

Supplementary Materials

ITEM 4.A: Opium Trade statistics

ITEM 4.B: *Qianlong Meets Macartney: Collision of Two World Views*, a play by John Watt

 Excerpts of these primary source documents appear in this chapter. Go to **www.chinasince1644.com** for the full version of these documents and for the Supplementary Materials.

CHAPTER 4

China's Foreign Relations (1644–1839)

By Shirley Moore Huettig

Chapter Contents

Key Idea

Despite restrictions enforced by the Qing dynasty, an active exchange of goods and ideas continued to exist between China and the Western powers. However, in the mid-eighteenth century, Europeans, especially Great Britain, began pressuring the Qing government for broader access to Chinese markets.

Guiding Questions

What diplomatic and trade relationships did the Qing dynasty establish with foreign nations?

What roles did missionaries play in China in the seventeenth and eighteenth centuries?

Why did the Qing restrict trade with Westerners but allow relative freedom of trade with other Asian nations?

How and why did Western nations try to change diplomatic and trade relations with China? To what extent were they successful in the period 1638–1839?

Terms to Know

astronomy	homage
cartography	kowtow
chinoiserie	Manchuria
decentralized	memorial
"factory"	tributary relationship

Essay

Until the late seventeenth century the Chinese world view was one of concentric circles in which China, known to Chinese then and now as *Zhongguo*, the "Middle Kingdom," was at the center and all people on the borders and beyond were considered subordinate or "barbarians" (*manyi* 蛮夷). International relations and trade were conducted using a tributary system in which foreign trade missions would pay homage to the Chinese emperor, bring him gifts, and conduct trade under tightly controlled conditions. The Qing (清), foreign invaders themselves from Manchuria (*Manzhou* 满洲),[1] recognized the need to interact carefully with people along their borders. They created a series of agencies to communicate with various groups of foreigners, reflecting their view of the nations involved.

Early Management Approaches

The Office of Border Affairs (*Lifan Yuan* 理番院) had been created in 1638 by Nurhaci, who had led the conquest of China, to address the growing challenges from peoples north and west of China, such as the Russians and Mongolians. Qing emperors saw these peoples as a threat because they sought territorial expansion into China, so their movement and trade within China was carefully controlled and monitored.

The Board of Rites (*Li Bu* 礼部) was responsible for non-Chinese people whose cultures were similar to the Chinese and who were not seen as a territorial threat, such as Koreans, Japanese, and Vietnamese. They were allowed much more lenient trade rights, though they were still limited to coastal cities and not permitted to travel inland. Early European traders were also included in this group because they did not at first fit into the other categories.

The Imperial Household (*Neiwu Fu* 内务府) was responsible for overseeing the activities of European missionaries. The missionaries impressed the elites with their scientific and mathematical knowledge. They were welcomed into the imperial court and served as advisors to the emperor in technology, astronomy, and determining the calendar. In fact, several Jesuit missionaries held the important position of director of the Bureau of Astronomy from the beginning of the Qing era to the late eighteenth century.[2] Jesuit missionaries had also spread thinly into northern and western China. Their roles, however, were strictly limited so as to keep them from encroaching too much into Chinese society. Eventually, Kangxi (康熙) (r. 1661–1722) expelled missionaries who refused to accept his position that Confucian rites were civil ceremonies that did not conflict with Catholic faith. The pope's position and the Chinese response (expulsion of the Jesuits) weakened the Jesuit role, leaving room for future Protestant missionaries to gain influence.

In the late 1600s, China's international relations began to change significantly. European and American missionaries participated in trade agreements and Western nations pressured the emperor for new diplomatic relations and broader trading rights. In 1689, the Chinese signed the Treaty of Nerchinsk[3] with Russia (see Document 4.2) and, significantly, retreated from their traditional tributary system for the first time, acknowledging Russia as a sovereign state and giving the Russians trading rights in Kiakhta. China continued to maintain tight control over who traded in China and where they were allowed to ply their trade.

---

[1] Now referred to as Northeast China

[2] Directors included Father Ferdinand Verbiest in the late seventeenth century, best known for his updated map of the world. In the late eighteenth century, Father Michel Benoist introduced Copernicus's heliocentric theory, in addition to many other scientific discoveries from Europe, to the emperor and his government.

[3] Jesuit missionaries helped with the negotiations.

The Canton System

By 1759, the British, who by then dominated the China trade among the European nations, formally petitioned the emperor for more lenient trade rights, access to higher officials in the Chinese government, and fewer taxes levied on their trade. In response, the Qing government created an even more restrictive system to protect itself against European incursion: the Canton System (*Guangdong Tizhi* 广东体制). European traders were only allowed to trade in Canton, a southeastern port city now known as Guangzhou. Furthermore, Chinese authorities restricted Westerners to one section of the city where the foreigners had their living and business quarters, called "factories." The Chinese permitted Westerners to live there only during the tea-trading season (after which time they had to return to Portuguese-controlled Macao) and insisted they conduct their business with Chinese intermediaries, the *Cohong* or *Hong* merchants (*hangshang* 行商). In 1793, frustrated by the limitations, the British sent Lord Macartney on a mission to the emperor, again requesting changes in trade policies. Through a series of misunderstandings and cultural conflicts, the mission failed and left the Chinese increasingly resistant to European pleas for greater freedom in China.

Active Trade

Despite the restrictions, trade flourished between China and the West. Europeans and merchants from the newly founded United States of America bought large quantities of tea, silk, and porcelain.[4] In addition, ideas and artifacts from China and Western cultures become known and appreciated by the other. *Chinoiserie*, a style of art and architecture reflecting a strong Chinese influence (though idealized and fanciful) became popular in Europe. Europeans had begun to imitate China's blue-and-white porcelain during the Ming era and later started to include Chinese-inspired design and images on furniture and small pagoda-styled garden buildings. In China, meanwhile, the Qianlong (乾隆) emperor hired Westerners to work collaboratively with Chinese architects to build his summer palace, the Yuan-mingyuan (圆明园), in a mixed Italianate and Chinese style.

By the late eighteenth century, Great Britain's trade deficit with China had grown to alarming levels.[5] China required payment in silver, but silver was increasingly expensive, and British merchants began to import opium as the medium of exchange. Taking vast quantities of opium grown in their colony in India, the British shipped it to China, where growing numbers of addicts kept demand high. By the early 1800s, China was experiencing a trade deficit with Great Britain; the tables had turned. The emperor and court officials were appalled by the rate of addiction and wrote several edicts; first in 1800 the government banned importation and domestic production of opium, then in 1813 smoking it was banned as well. Tension between China and Great Britain over the smuggling of opium into the country grew until in 1839 it erupted into war.

---

[4] In 1784, the *Empress of China* sailed out of New York City bound for Guangzhou, opening the United States–China trade.

[5] By 1800, the East India Company, which operated all British trade to India and China, was buying more than 23 million pounds of tea a year, at a cost of £3.6 million (Spence, *The Search For Modern China*, 122.) When converted into the purchasing power of the dollar in 2010, this is equivalent to approximately $21.2 billion (www.measuringworth.com).

Primary Sources

DOCUMENT 4.1a & b: Stamps issued commemorating Jesuit missionary Ferdinand Verbiest

 Go to **www.chinasince1644.com** for colored images and the text of **Document 4.1a & b**.

DOCUMENT 4.2: Excerpts from the Treaty of Nerchinsk signed by China and Russia in 1689

II

Likewise, the river called Argun which falls into the river Amur is thus decreed the frontier, so that all lands that make up the left side, going along that river to its very sources, are under the dominion of the Khin khan [Chinese ruler]; likewise, all lands contained on the right side are in the domain of the czarist majesty of the Russian state, and all buildings on the southern bank of that river Argun shall be moved to the other side of that same river.

III

The town of Albazin which was built by the czarist majesty will be destroyed to its foundations and those people living there with all military and other supplies shall be returned to the side of the czarist majesty, and none of their losses, however small the things, shall be left there.

IV

Fugitives, whether they were, up to this peace decree, from either the side of the czarist majesty or from the side of the Bugdykhan highness are [permitted] to be on either side without being exchanged, but those who after this decreed peace shall pass over, such fugitives shall be expelled without delay from either side and [turned over] immediately to the frontier voevodas.[6]

SOURCE: Rpt. in Pei-Kai Cheng, Michael Lestz, and Jonathan Spence, eds., *The Search for Modern China: A Documentary Collection* (New York: W.W. Norton, 1999) 53–54.

Go to **www.chinasince1644.com** for the full text of **Document 4.2**.

DOCUMENT 4.3: Excerpts from the letter King George III of England wrote to the Chinese emperor and sent with Lord Macartney, 1792

We rely on your Imperial Majesty's wisdom and justice and general benevolence to mankind so conspicuous in your long and happy reign, that you will please to allow our Ambassador and Representative at your court to have the opportunity of contemplating the examples of your virtues and to obtain such information of your celebrated institutions, as will enable him to enlighten our people on his return; he, on our part, being directed to give as far as your Majesty shall please to desire it, a full and free communication of any art, science or observation either of use or curiosity which the industry, ingenuity and experience of Europeans may have enabled them to acquire; and also that you will be pleased to allow to any of our subjects frequenting the coasts of your dominions, and conducting themselves with propriety, a secure residence there, and a fair access to your markets, under such laws and regulations as your Majesty shall think right, and that their lives and properties shall be safe under your imperial protection....

SOURCE: *British Illustrations*

Go to **www.chinasince1644.com** for the full text of **Document 4.3**.

DOCUMENT 4.4: Two edicts from the emperor Qianlong in reply to Lord Macartney's mission to China, September 1793

I have perused your memorial: the earnest terms in which it is couched reveal a respectful humility on your part, which is highly praiseworthy. In consideration of the fact that your Ambassador and his deputy have come a long way with your memorial and tribute, I have shown them high favour and have allowed them to be introduced into my presence. To manifest my indulgence, I have entertained them at a banquet and made them numerous gifts. I have also caused presents to be forwarded to the Naval Commander and six hundred of his officers and men, although they did not come to Peking, so that they too may share in my all-embracing kindness.

As to your entreaty to send one of your nationals to be accredited to my Celestial Court and to be in control of your country's trade with China, this request is contrary to all usage of my dynasty and cannot possibly be entertained....

Our dynasty's majestic virtue has penetrated unto every country under Heaven, and Kings of all nations have offered their costly tribute by land and sea. As your

---

[6] Local administrators with political and judicial powers

Ambassador can see for himself, we possess all things. I set no value on objects strange or ingenious, and have no use for your country's manufactures....

SOURCE: *Chinese Cultural Studies: Emperor Qian Long: Letter to George III, 1793*

 Go to **www.chinasince1644.com** for the link to **Document 4.4**.

DOCUMENT 4.5: Requests by English merchants and responses from the Chinese official, 1793

Request II: When we [the English] pass through [the river] between Guangzhou and Macao, both toll tax and goods tax are to be collected. If this is required by the original regulation, we beg your Excellency to give us a list of what we should pay; if these taxes are not required by the original regulation, we beg your Excellency to abolish them.

Endorsement: The toll tax and the goods tax were originally illegal and were abolished in the eleventh month of the fifty-eighth year of [the emperor] Qianlong, by official proclamation. We have punished the soldiers and servants one by one who dared to demand this illegal levy.... Now we shall publish another official proclamation to renew the prohibition. If they still dare to demand money, we shall allow the barbarians[7] to present a petition of accusation in order to try them...."

SOURCE: Lo-shu Fu, *A Documentary Chronicle of Sino-Western Relations (1644–1820)* (Tucson: University of Arizona Press, 1966) 327–328.

 Go to **www.chinasince1644.com** for the text of **Document 4.5**.

DOCUMENT 4.6: A description of various European countries and their people by Xie Qinggao, a Chinese sailor, between 1783 and 1797

England is located southwest [*sic*] of France and could be reached by sailing north from St. Helena for about two months. It is a sparsely settled island, separated from the mainland, with a large number of rich families. The dwelling houses have more than one story. Maritime commerce is one of the chief occupations of the English, and wherever there is a region in which profits could be reaped by trading, these people strive for them, with the result that their commercial vessels are to be seen on the seven seas. Commercial traders are to be found all over the country. Male inhabitants from the ages of fifteen to sixty are conscripted into the service of the king as soldiers. Moreover, a large foreign mercenary army is also maintained. Consequently, although the country is small, it has such a large military force that foreign nations are afraid of it....

SOURCE: Jeannette Mirsky, ed., *The Great Chinese Travelers*, (New York: Pantheon, 1964) 266–71. Rpt. in Mark A. Kishlansky, ed., *Sources of World History*, vol. 2 (New York: HarperCollins College Publishers, 1995) 126–128.

Go to **www.chinasince1644.com** for the full text of **Document 4.6**.

---

[7] Common word for "foreigner," anyone who was not literate in the Chinese language and literature.

DOCUMENT 4.7a & b: Excerpts from a letter by William Trotter of Philadelphia, trading in Guangzhou, 1796

The City of Canton [Guangzhou] is situated on the north side of the River Zhu [Pearl River]...about 80 miles from the Sea; it is surrounded by a thick wall about 20 feet in height, and according to information about 10 miles in circumference. There are several arched passages through the walls, by which the inhabitants of the Suberbs [*sic*] have communication with the City; to these passages are large iron gates, which are guarded during the day and shut every night. Of the interior part of the City, we can only judge from the suberbs, as the jealous laws of Chinese prohibit all Foreigners from entering. I was assured by a respectable Merchant they were much the same. The suberbs of Canton are very extensive and exceeding populous. The streets are irregular and very narrow, and so crowded with People that a stranger frequently finds great difficulty in passing them. The Houses are built of brick and wood and generally more than a story high, with a kind of balcony facing the street. The front part of the Houses and especially those near the European Factories are fitted up as shops, which [are] painted and gilded in a fancified manner. The Warehouses of some of the Silk Merchants are very large and well stocked with the valuable article they trade in.

SOURCE: William Trotter to William Sansom, 13 April 1796, William Trotter letter, Massachusetts Historical Society, Boston.

Go to **www.chinasince1644.com** for the text of Document 4.7a. Document 4.7b, also on the companion website, has longer excerpts from Trotter's letter.

DOCUMENT 4.8: Excerpts from a letter Edward King wrote from Guangzhou to his brother, October 31, 1835

I arrived in this city on Thursday evening the 29th ... [I] intend taking on board a Cargo of Teas for home...

People live here in great style and have everything very comfortable. Servants in abundance one for every person. I have been much pleased with the appearance of the Chinese. They are extremely neat, that is the better class. Our passage up from Linten was quite interesting though. We were confined in a small fishing boat covered up to prevent our being seen. We saw I should think a million or more of people in Boats. All the way up the river from Whampoa there are villages of 50,000 and more. There are hundreds of kinds of boats. That is of different forms and sizes, from the sampan to the junk of 1,000 tons. Opposite the city, the river is completely covered with Boats, which are anchored in which are thousands of inhabitants....

What I have seen of the shops has pleased me. The Chinese are a shrewd set. Silks are high, 20% more than last year.... The Chinese are a very industrious people. They are always busy about something. I today went with Mr. Coolidge to see some of the Hong Merchants. We called on Hougus, the senior Hong Merchant. He is quite old, about 80 years of age. He is the richest man in Canton, and one of the most intelligent. We also saw Toushing and Kingqua who are also Hong merchants. The Hong merchants are the only persons allowed by the Government to sell Teas to foreigners.

SOURCE: Edward King to George King, 31 October 1835, Edward King papers, Massachusetts Historical Society, Boston.

 Go to **www.chinasince1644.com** for the full text of **Document 4.8**.

DOCUMENT 4.9a & b: Examples of *chinoiserie*

Blue and white porcelain platter, ca. 1800

Blue and white porcelain lunch plate, ca. 1810

(Courtesy of Lovers of Blue and White.)

DOCUMENT 4.10: Excerpts from a letter of instructions from the owners of the vessel *Mentor* to Captain John Suter, 1816

Your Ship is equipped and provisioned for a three years' Voyage and you are furnished with a Cargo both for trade with the natives and Russian settlements in that quarter of the Globe. Although they prepared for two Seasons it would be highly beneficial if the Voyage could be accomplished in one, and we think it very possible that this may be the case. If when you arrive on the Coast you think there is a fair probability of your being able to collect, the first Season, both from the Russians and Natives, a quantity of Furs, equal to Three thousand Merchantable Sea Otter Skins, we recommend your finishing your Voyage [from there to Guangzhou, China] by all means the first year,…

The articles which compose your Russian assortment are probably better than have ever been carried there before, the Rum is not lower than third proof and the Brandy is all fourth, the Wine may want to be fined which can easily be done with a little Isinglass, Milk or Eggs. For the Natives you have the best assortment we have known to have been carried. The Muskets are unequalled by any ever shipped from this Country and will sell very readily. As more of the same kind will undoubtedly follow, we recommend your selling them as expeditiously as possibly without undervaluing them.…

We leave you at full liberty to pursue any course which you may deem for our interest either by purchasing Furs, by killing them or employ the Ship in any other way, taking care however never to attempt any illicit trade against which your Ship is not insured, although She is against all the usual and ordinary perils of the Voyage. When you arrive at Canton [Guangzhou] you will find instructions from us for your future government. Should you not you will apply to Messrs Perkins & Company who will assist you in transacting your business then.…

SOURCE: Bryant Sturgis to John Suter, 6 August 1816, John Suter papers, Massachusetts Historical Society, Boston.

Go to **www.chinasince1644.com** for the full text of Document 4.10.

DOCUMENT 4.11: "A Voyage with Opium Smugglers" by William Hunter, between 1825 and 1844

Needless to say, the opium trade was prohibited by Imperial edicts as well by proclamations of the Guangzhou authorities. The Chinese who dealt in "foreign mud" [opium] were threatened even with capital punishment, but so perfect a system of bribery existed (with which foreigners had nothing whatever to do) that the business was carried on with ease and regularity.…

The [official and his secretary] were then invited to the cabin to refresh, which being done, we proceeded to business. The Mandarin [Chinese official] opened by the direct questions, "How many chests have you on board? Are they all for Namao? Do you go further up the coast?"…Then came the question of [the bribe], and that was settled on the good old Chinese principle (that customs in such matters are the same everywhere). Everything being thus comfortably arranged, wine drunk, and [cigars] smoked, His Excellency said: "I announce my departure."…

SOURCE: W. C. Hunter, *The "Fan Kwae"*[8] *at Canton Before Treaty Days, 1825–1844* (London: Kegan Paul, Trench and Company, 1882) 64–70. Rpt. in Hyman Kublin, ed., *China: Selected Readings* (Boston: Houghton Mifflin, 1968) 117–120.

Go to **www.chinasince1644.com** for the full text of Document 4.11.

Activities

ACTIVITY 1: Examining Jesuit Contributions

Examine the two commemorative postage stamps (4.1a and 4.1b) and see Chapter 4 Activity Websites for additional resources related to this activity. Answer the following questions individually or in a class discussion:

1. Why would Chinese emperors have been so interested in astronomy and cartography? Why would they want to know more about Western advances in particular?

2. What roles did Jesuits play in the imperial government of China in the seventeenth and eighteenth centuries?

3. Why were Ferdinand Verbiest and Johann Adam Schall von Bell such important figures at this time?

4. Choose one of the five instruments shown on the stamp from Macao and learn how it was used. Why would each instrument have been important to the emperor?

5. Why would Belgium and Macao create these commemorative stamps of Verbiest?

Extended Activity:

Examine Verbiest's map using the link in Chapter 4 Activity Websites on the companion website.

1. Which parts of the map are most accurate?

2. Which are very different from modern maps?

3. Why do you think some parts of the map are accurate and others are not?

4. Consider again, based on this evidence, why the emperor would have wanted Western cartographic expertise.

---

[8] *Fan Kwae* is another Chinese word for "barbarian," a foreigner, someone not literate in Chinese.

ACTIVITY 2:
Collaborating and Analyzing the Treaty with Russia

Your class will be divided into six groups. Each group will read a part of the Treaty of Nerchinsk (4.2) and will prepare a presentation that paraphrases the agreed-upon point in the treaty.

Be sure to use a map if explaining geographical terms. After presenting prepare to discuss as a class:

1. Identify the boundaries on a map. What did Russia and Qing dynasty China gain and lose?

2. What do you notice about the stipulations of the treaty?

3. Why was the treaty so significant for the Manchus?

4. Why was this treaty an exception to the tributary system?

5. What does the treaty say about the Qing dynasty?

ACTIVITY 3:
Trade between Great Britain and China: A Jigsaw

Part 1: Collaborate

You will be assigned to one of three teams. Each team will become experts on one of the following documents: 4.3, 4.4 or 4.5. Each team member will read the document on his or her own. The team will then gather to discuss:

1. Who is the author? What tone (collegial, condescending, patronizing, sub-servient, etc.) does the author use? Is it consistent throughout the document?

2. Who is the recipient?

3. When was the document written?

4. What is the purpose of the document? What does the author want?

5. Does the author comment on the recipient or his country? What kinds of things does he write? Is he complimentary? Critical?

6. What promises, if any, does the author make to the recipient?

7. If you were the recipient of this document, how would you respond to its tone and content?

8. Individually, write a response as if you were the recipient writing back to the author of the document.

Part 2: Present and Evaluate

Reconvene in groups of three, with each member of the new group an expert on a different document. Share with each other pertinent details related to your document (date, author, tone, content, etc.) Then discuss:

1. To what extent are the authors of the documents in agreement? On which points do they disagree?

2. In your opinion, is one author more reasonable than the others? What evidence do you see of misunderstandings between cultures? How might these misunderstandings have been avoided or cleared up?

3. As a group, draft a letter addressing the authors of all the documents. Imagine you are a "disinterested third party" and make recommendations for resolving the points of conflict found among these documents.

Part 3: Present

Return to a whole class discussion and share the letters of resolution drafted in your groups.

Creative Extension:

To further explore the issues involved in the Macartney mission, perform *Qianlong Meets Macartney: Collision of Two World Views*, a play by John Watt. (See Item 4.B under Supplementary Materials on the companion website.)

ACTIVITY 4: Exploring Foreigners' Perceptions

Read documents 4.6, 4.7a and 4.8. For each document, answer the following questions.

1. What is the nationality of the author? What foreign culture or nation is he describing?

2. What is the author doing in that part of the world?

3. What part of the culture does the author discuss the most? Do you think the answer to question 2 is related to your answer to this question? How?

4. How is the author's description different from what you expected?

5. Is the author's tone complimentary or derogatory? Or is it neutral—merely descriptive? Is there any evidence of cultural bias?

6. Compare the writing of these three authors, commenting on the presence or absence of cultural bias. What does this suggest to you about their cultures at the time of writing?

Writing Extension:

Imagine you are a member of one of the cultures being described. Write a response to the author regarding his description of your culture.

ACTIVITY 5: *Chinoiserie*: Discovering Legends and Images

Reread the section on *chinoiserie* in the introductory essay to this chapter, and read about the Spode Willow Pattern (see Chapter 4 Activity Websites on the companion website). Examine the porcelain in the images and answer the following questions:

1. Who was Josiah Spode, and why did he produce blue and white porcelain dishes?

2. Why would Europeans have adapted, or made up, a legend to go with the Spode dish pattern?

3. Why do you think the Willow Pattern was the most popular one? How do you think the legend played into that popularity?

Creative Extensions:

Choose one:

- Draw your own interpretation of the legend of the Willow Pattern.

- Read the longer excerpts from William Trotter's letter (4.7b on the companion website) and design your own porcelain pattern based on one of Trotter's descriptions. Remember, your pattern should be "idealized and fanciful" and show both Chinese and European influences.

ACTIVITY 6: Mapping and Analyzing Early Nineteenth Century Trade between China and the United States

1. On an outline map of the world, trace the routes of the ships *Mentor* and *Rose* described in 4.10 and 4.11 as best you can from the landmarks provided in the text. Illustrate on each leg of the journeys those items being transferred to the next location.

2. About how far from Guangzhou (Canton) was the Russian trade that the *Mentor* engaged in (4.10)?

3. Which leg of the journey was the longest for the *Mentor*?

4. About how far from Guangzhou (Canton) did Hunter's vessel, the *Rose*, "wander" (4.11)?

5. Based on your knowledge of the China trade, what items do you think Captain Suter would have been instructed to purchase and take back to Boston?

6. What kind of advice and warnings did the ship owners (Bryant and Sturges) give Captain Suter regarding trade and getting the best deal? Cite evidence from the text.

7. Once at sea, how did ship captains communicate with ship owners 200 years ago?

8. Compare how trade was conducted in 1816 to what you know about international trade today.

9. Why might traders have resorted to trading opium instead of the items mentioned in Suter's letter?

10. Based on the statistics from Item 4.A (on the companion website), evaluate the extent to which opium was a large part of trade in China by the time Suter's ship the *Mentor* arrived in 1816.

11. What, if anything, surprises you about the description of the illegal opium trade in William Hunter's account (4.11)?

EXTENDED RESEARCH:

Research any of the topics below and present your findings in a paper, a visual display, or a digital slideshow such as PowerPoint®.

■ Tea use in Great Britain and/or the British North American colonies in the eighteenth century

■ The tributary system (e.g. relations between China and Korea)

■ Trade conducted on the traditional Chinese sailing vessels called "junks" by Westerners

■ Hong merchants

■ Hong merchant Pan Changyao, known as Conseequa to Westerners, an exceptionally wealthy man

■ The Kangxi and Qianlong emperors

■ Using the descriptions in William Trotter's letter (4.7b), compare any one aspect of life in 1797 Guangzhou (Canton) to another country in the same time period (e.g. a city in South America to Guangzhou; vessels in Europe to vessels in China; the lives of women in the United States to the lives of women in China; formal gardens in France to the merchant's garden outside Guangzhou).

Suggested Resources

Books

Brook, Timothy and Bob Tadashi Wakabayashi. *Opium Regimes: China, Britain, and Japan, 1839–1952*. Berkeley: University of California Press, 2000.

Ghosh, Amitav. *Sea of Poppies*. New York: Farrar, Straus and Giroux, 2008.
A novel set in the nineteenth-century during the Opium Wars.

Kerr, Phyllis Forbes. *Letters from China: The Canton-Boston Correspondence of Robert Bennet Forbes, 1838–1840*. Mystic, Conn.: Mystic Seaport Museum, 1996.

Spence, Jonathan D. *The Memory Palace of Matteo Ricci*. New York: Viking, 1984.

Websites

Asian Export Art, Peabody Essex Museum
http://pem.org/collections/9-asian_export_art
The Peabody Essex Museum holds one of North America's premier collections of Asian export art with many images available online.

Chinese Export Art, Victoria and Albert Museum
http://www.vam.ac.uk
Search for "Chinese export art" from the homepage of the museum website. Room 47f of the collection includes objects made in China and brought to the West by merchants.

■ **A CLOSER LOOK**

Opium: From Use to Abuse

Opium is harvested from the unripe seedpods of the opium poppy. The seedpods release a milky latex that turns into a gummy substance when it comes in contact with air. Raw opium can be ground into powder, or sold as lumps, cakes, or bricks, and when treated further, morphine, codeine, and heroin can be made from it. Opium and all the drugs created from it are called opiates. People have known about the medicinal and sedative properties of opium for millennia. It has been widely used as a painkiller, but in addition to alleviating pain, opium gives users a feeling of calm, well-being, and drowsiness.

Turkish and Arab traders first brought opium to China in the late sixth or early seventh century. For some 1,000 years the Chinese swallowed raw bitter-tasting opium, using it in limited quantities to reduce pain and stress.

In the 1720s, smoking a mix of opium and tobacco started to become popular. The Portuguese imported opium into China early in the eighteenth century, and the British became the leading suppliers by the early 1770s. The drug also made its way overland through Tibet and Burma into China's western provinces.

In Britain opium was used as a mild "recreational drug" at social gatherings of friends. It could be used during surgical operations or during dental surgery to mask pain. This is why the British initially felt that importing opium into China was not intrinsically bad. As addiction in China increased, the British saw it was having a negative effect on the Chinese population. However, importing opium was so profitable that the British continued to trade it to realize high profits.

By 1729, addiction had increased so dramatically that the Yongzheng emperor issued an edict prohibiting selling opium for anything but medicinal use. This had little effect. From 200 chests of opium in 1729, British imports increased to more than 4,000 chests in 1796 (see Item 4.A on the companion website). Addiction grew so high that it began to affect both the Qing troops and scholar-officials responsible for local and provincial governing. Despite further imperial edicts that banned importation, domestic production, and later, smoking of opium, the problem only grew worse.

■ *Discuss: What responsibility does a supplier of a drug bear for increasing addiction? What else might the European merchants have used for trade?*

The Chinese Rites Controversy, 1715, Internet Modern History Sourcebook
http://www.fordham.edu/halsall/mod/1715chineserites.asp
Decrees from the Kangxi Emperor and Pope Clement XI.

Great Universal Geographic Map, World Digital Library
http://www.wdl.org/en/item/4136/
A map created by Matteo Ricci in 1602 showing five continents. It is the oldest surviving map in Chinese to the show the Americas.

Rise & Fall of the Canton Trade System: China in the World, 1700–1860s, Massachusetts Institute of Technology Visualizing Cultures
http://ocw.mit.edu/ans7870/21f/21f.027/rise_fall_canton_01/index.html
Essays and images about the Canton Trade System from the Massachusetts Institute of Technology, in partnership with the Peabody Essex Museum.

Salem's International Trade, Salem Maritime National Historic Site
http://www.nps.gov/sama/historyculture/trade.htm
The National Park Service site about Salem, Massachusetts, and trade with China.

CHAPTER RESOURCES

Primary Sources

DOCUMENT 5.1: Painting, "View of Guangzhou," ca. 1800

DOCUMENT 5.2: Painting, "Factory site, Guangzhou," 1865

DOCUMENT 5.3: Excerpts from Lin Zexu's letter to Queen Victoria, 1839

DOCUMENT 5.4: Excerpts from William Gladstone's speech to Britain's House of Commons, 1840

DOCUMENT 5.5: Excerpts from the Treaty of Nanjing, August 1842

DOCUMENT 5.6: Excerpts from the Treaty of Wangxia, July 3, 1844

DOCUMENT 5.7: Excerpts from "The Land System of the Heavenly Kingdom," 1853

Supplementary Materials

ITEM 5.A: "Hong Xiuquan and the Taiping Rebellion," an essay

ITEM 5.Ba–c: Photographs from the Presidential Palace, Nanjing, commemorating the Taiping Rebellion, 2006

ITEM 5.C: Replica of a robe worn by Hong Xiuquan, Nanjing, 2006

 Excerpts of these primary source documents appear in this chapter. Go to **www.chinasince1644.com** for the full version of these documents and for the Supplementary Materials.

CHAPTER 5

Nineteenth-Century Strife

By Liz Nelson

Chapter Contents

The Opium Wars
Unequal Treaties
The Taiping Rebellion

Key Idea

Great Britain and its allies fought two wars in part to protect their lucrative opium trade, but more broadly to coerce China into becoming part of the Western trade and diplomatic system. These wars and the subsequent "unequal treaties" were watershed events in Chinese history. Together with the rebellions that broke out in various provinces, they put immense political and economic pressure on the Qing dynasty.

Guiding Questions

Why did hostilities break out between China and Western nations in the 1840s and again in the late 1850s?

What were the short-term and long-term results of the treaties signed between Western nations and China?

Why do many historians—Chinese and Western—consider the Opium Wars as the beginning of modern Chinese history?

What appear to have been the root causes of the rebellions that broke out across China during this time period?

Terms to Know

barbarian	*tael*
gunboat diplomacy	tariff
Manchu	treaty

Essay

In the increasingly globalized world of the 19th century, China's position as arbiter of civilization was first challenged and then shattered by the newly industrializing Western states. Buffeted by internal challenges as the population of China skyrocketed and resources remained limited, the Qing also had to face external pressures as first the English and then several other Western nations realized the wealth they could reap from China with their new military superiority. The first Opium War, where Britain militarily forced China to accept its imports of opium in order to correct the imbalance of trade caused by the British thirst for tea, set the tone for the next 100 years. Thus began what is known to this day as "The Century of Humiliation."

Westerners Smuggle Opium

British exports of opium to China from its colony India multiplied sevenfold in the second half of the eighteenth century, to 4,570 chests—each holding 130 to 160 pounds of opium.[1] Despite Chinese imperial decrees banning domestic production, importation, and use, British exports to China rose to 40,000 chests of opium in 1838,[2] and they sold the drug to merchants from other nations, such as the United States, to export to China, too. Not only were merchants and corrupt officials reaping huge profits, but so was the British treasury in the form of taxes from the trade. (For further information on the opium trade, see chapter 4.)

Britain's Gunboat Diplomacy

In 1838, the emperor appointed Lin Zexu (林则徐) (see A Closer Look) to cut opium importation off at its source: Guangzhou (广州).[3] Lin imposed increasingly severe penalties on users and traffickers and destroyed 20,183 chests of confiscated opium—cargo he insisted the foreigners surrender. In response, British merchants, who had lost the most in the confrontation, pressured their government for a military response. The debate in Great Britain was extensive and the vote in the House of Commons close, but the advocates for a military response prevailed 271 to 262. Parliament never officially declared war; rather, the nation with the most formidable navy in the world sent a fleet to exact "satisfaction and reparation."

The first Opium War (*Yapian Zhanzheng* 鸦片战争) (1839–1842) was fought in fits and starts and consisted primarily of the British blockading harbors and seizing several key Chinese cities. When British forces threatened Nanjing (南京), the Qing dynasty capitulated and agreed to the terms of the Nanjing Treaty. Britain's steam-powered Royal Navy and state-of-the-art weapons forced China to open five ports to trade, to pay $21 million in reparation, and to cede to Britain the island of Hong Kong (*Xianggang* 香港) "in perpetuity." The emperor refused, however, to legalize opium, writing: "nothing will induce me to derive revenue from the vice and misery of my people." Sadly, the emperor's stand had no effect on the quantities of the drug smuggled into China.

In 1843, the Treaty of the Bogue (*Humen Tiaoyue* 虎门条约) extended further rights to the British, including the critical most-favored-nation clause: whatever additional rights China

[1] Jonathan D. Spence, *The Search for Modern China* (New York: W.W. Norton, 1999) 129-130.

[2] Spence, 151

[3] Formerly known as Canton

gave to other nations would immediately apply to the British, too. The United States signed their first treaty with China, the Treaty of Wangxia (*Wangxia Tiaoyue* 望厦条约), in July 1844; the French signed the Treaty of Whampoa (*Huangpu Tiaoyue* 黄埔条约) with the Qing government the following October.

Social Unrest

While their first direct confrontation with powerful Western nations resulted in a shocking loss of face for the Qing government, internal rebellions in the mid-nineteenth century had a far more devastating effect on the people, as well as on Qing power. Violence, dislocation and famines, which were in part a result of the chaos, left tens of millions dead or homeless by the time order was restored.

The Taiping Rebellion (*Taipingtianguo Yundong* 太平天国运动) (1851–1864) was the most significant of four major rebellions at this time. It began in Guangxi Province (广西) under the leadership of Hong Xiuquan (洪秀全). Hong (1813–1864), himself a Hakka (*kejiaren* 客家人), initially attracted followers primarily from among this group of minority people, known as "guest people" because of their origins in Northern China, far from their present home. The growing economic problems among the lower classes of South China further fueled interest in Hong's group. With the opening of new ports to the tea trade after the crumbling of the Canton System, the industry that had grown up around transporting tea to Guangdong collapsed, displacing many local laborers. Opium addiction in the area soared. Hong's message, gleaned from Christian missionary tracts he had picked up during a failed attempt to pass the civil service exams in Canton, informed Hong's new ideology—a hybrid of Anti-Confucian, communitarian and quasi-Christian teachings. This blend of ideas—part Chinese and part foreign—would become more and more common in China, as foreigners' presence became more widespread and interactive with the general populace.[4] In December 1850, Qing forces tried but failed to quash the movement, which was growing rapidly. Soon thereafter Hong appointed himself Heavenly King of the *Taiping Tianguo* (太平天国) (Heavenly Kingdom of Great Peace). The movement became committed to destroying the Manchu Qing dynasty, an idea that resonated with Hong's disaffected followers.

The Taiping egalitarian, puritanical ideology appealed to China's masses who were feeling the effects of an economy unable to keep up with population growth, the pall of opium addiction, and the waning appeal of a Confucian system that seemed to be failing its main constituency: the peasants. In the fall of 1851, the Taiping began to conquer one city after another, massacring all people of Manchu descent as they marched north. In March 1853, they took Nanjing, established a theocracy, and ruled for eleven years. Their rebellion affected sixteen of China's eighteen provinces but never succeeded in toppling the Qing dynasty. Ultimately the Taiping failed for a variety of reasons including a collapse of their leadership (see Item 5.A on the companion website for a detailed account of the Taiping Rebellion).

But the Qing court would also have to wage costly battles against more rebellions such as the Nian Rebellion (1851–1868) in North China and the Muslim Dungan Revolt (1862–1877) and Miao revolts (1854–1873) in China's western areas before social unrest was quelled. These rebellions coincided with the Taiping Rebellion and emerged for many of the same reasons: the impoverishment of China's peasantry, increased taxation to pay for escalating military costs, and the government's inability to live up to its perceived role as succor of the people. The two western rebellions (Muslims in the northwest and Miao in the southwest) further revealed how tenuous Qing control over newly acquired ethnic and religious minority populations could be.

---

[4] Mao Zedong's appropriation of Communism has frequently been compared to Hong's adaption of Christianity, for example; the adaptation of Indian Buddhism in China is an earlier example of such hybridization.

The Second Opium War (1856–1860)

While Qing dynasty officials were embroiled in suppressing the Taiping and other rebellions, the British, French, and Russians (with Americans in tow) pushed the Qing for further concessions. The British, for example, wanted to live wherever they wished in Guangzhou, rather than be restricted to the area designated for foreigners. They insisted on having an ambassador at the imperial court in Beijing, who could argue on behalf of the merchants. Qing officials absolutely refused to allow foreigners into their capital, seeing it as an admission to equal status.

The second war, like the first, concentrated for the most part on port cities and around access to key waterways. Chinese and Manchu soldiers fought valiantly, but once again, their antiquated weapons were no match for Western technology. After two years of sporadic conflict, and with the British and French navies threatening to sail up to Beijing, the Qing government signed the Tianjin Treaty (*Tianjin Tiaoyue* 天津条约) in 1858. Although the Western powers did not get everything they wanted in the treaty, they were mindful of the concurrent Taiping threat. "If you humiliate the Emperor beyond measure [by entering the capital], if you seriously impair his influence over his own subjects...[you] throw the country into confusion and imperil the most lucrative trade you have in the world," warned Lord Elgin, Britain's senior official in China. But as hostilities continued, the British and French eventually took the capital. First, though, they plundered the imperial Summer Palace, just outside Beijing's city walls. Then, to avenge the death of several British prisoners of war, on October 18, 1860 Lord Elgin ordered the palace buildings burnt to the ground. A week later, Chinese officials signed the Convention of Peking (*Beijing Tiaoyue* 北京条约),[5] in which the emperor apologized for the execution of the British captives, agreed to pay 8 million *taels*[6] of silver in reparation, opened Tianjin to trade, and permitted a British ambassador to maintain year-round residency in the capital. The French signed a similar agreement the following day.

While the Europeans and Americans had been coercing the Chinese into granting them more favorable commercial rights, the Russians had been pressing for territorial gains north of the Amur River and east of the Ussuri River. Taking advantage of China's weakness they, too, were part of the agreements reached with the Convention of Peking, which gave Russia more than 300,000 square miles of formerly Chinese territory. As a result of the most-favored-nation clause, they also benefited from anything the British and French had gained. China's "Century of Humiliation" had begun.

---

[5] Former name for Beijing

[6] A *tael* is approximately one ounce

Primary Sources

DOCUMENT 5.1: Painting, "View of Guangzhou," ca. 1800

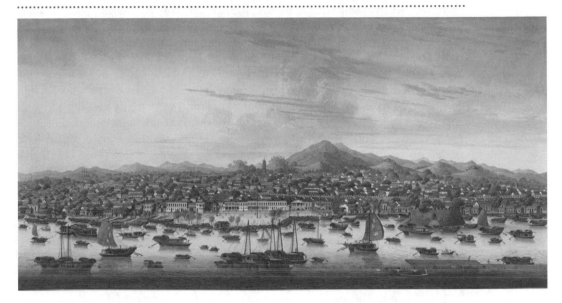

DOCUMENT 5.2: Painting, "Factory site, Guangzhou," 1865

(Images courtesy of the Peabody Essex Museum, Salem, Massachusetts)

Go to **www.chinasince1644.com** for color images of **Documents 5.1** and **5.2**.

DOCUMENT 5.3:
Excerpts from Lin Zexu's letter to Queen Victoria, 1839

We find your country [Great Britain] is sixty or seventy thousand *li* from China. Yet there are barbarian ships that strive to come here for trade for the purpose of making a great profit. The wealth of China is used to profit the barbarians. That is to say, the great profit made by barbarians is all taken from the rightful share of China. By what right do they then in return use the poisonous drug to injure the Chinese people? Even though the barbarians may not necessarily intend to do us harm, yet in coveting profit to an extreme, they have no regard for injuring others. Let us ask, where is your conscience? I have heard that the smoking of opium is very strictly forbidden by your country; that is because the harm caused by opium is clearly understood. Since it is not permitted to do harm to your own country, then even less should you let it be passed on to the harm of other countries—how much less to China! Of all that China exports to foreign countries, there is not a single thing that is not beneficial to people: they are of benefit when eaten, or of benefit when used, or of benefit when resold: all are beneficial.

SOURCE: Ssu-yü Teng and John Fairbank, *China's Response to the West: A Documentary Survey, 1839–1923* (Cambridge, MA: Harvard University Press, 1954). Rpt. in Mark A. Kishlansky, ed., *Sources of World History*, vol. 2 (New York: HarperCollins CollegePublishers, 1995) 266–269. http://cyber.law.harvard.edu/ChinaDragon/lin_xexu.html

 Go to **www.chinasince1644.com** for the full text of **Document 5.3**.

DOCUMENT 5.4: Excerpts from William Gladstone's speech to Britain's House of Commons, 1840

[The Chinese government] gave you notice to abandon your contraband trade. When they found you would not do so, they had the right to drive you from their coasts on account of your obstinacy in persisting with this infamous and atrocious traffic [in opium]… justice, in my opinion, is with them; and whilst they, the Pagans, the semi-civilized barbarians have it on their side, we, the enlightened and civilized Christians, are pursuing objects at variance both with justice and with religion… a war more unjust in its origin, a war calculated in its progress to cover this country with a permanent disgrace, I do not know and have not read of. Now, under the auspices of the noble Lord [Macaulay], that flag is become a pirate flag, to protect an infamous traffic.

SOURCE: qtd. in W. Travis Hanes III and Frank Sanello, *The Opium Wars: The Addiction of One Empire and the Corruption of Another* (Naperville, IL: Sourcebooks, Inc., 2002) 78–79.

 Go to **www.chinasince1644.com** for the full text of **Document 5.4**.

DOCUMENT 5.5: Excerpts from the Treaty of Nanjing, August 1842

II.

His Majesty the Emperor of China agrees, that British subjects, with their families and establishments, shall be allowed to reside, for the purposes of carrying on their mercantile pursuits, without molestation or restraint, at the cities and towns of Guangzhou, Xiamen, Fuzhou, Ningbo, and Shanghai…

III.

It being obviously necessary and desirable that British subjects should have some port whereat they may [maintain] and refit their ships when required, and keep stores for that purpose, His Majesty the Emperor of China cedes to Her Majesty the Queen of Great Britain, &c., the Island of Hong-Kong, to be possessed in perpetuity by Her Britannic Majesty, her heirs and successors, and to be governed by such laws and regulations as Her Majesty the Queen of Great Britain, &c., shall see fit to direct.

IV.

The Emperor of China agrees to pay the sum of 6,000,000 of dollars, as the value of the opium which was delivered up at Guangzhou in the month of March, 1839, as a ransom for the lives of Her Britannic Majesty's Superintendent and subjects, who had been imprisoned and threatened with death by the Chinese High Officers….

Go to **www.chinasince1644.com** for the full text of Document 5.5.

DOCUMENT 5.6: Excerpts from the Treaty of Wangxia, July 3, 1844

ARTICLE XVII.

Citizens of the United States residing or sojourning at any of the ports open to foreign commerce, shall enjoy all proper accommodation in obtaining houses and places of business, or in hiring sites from the inhabitants on which to construct houses and places of business, and also hospitals, churches and cemeteries. The local authorities of the two Governments shall select in concert the sites for the foregoing objects, having due regard to the feelings of the people in the location thereof… any desecration of said cemeteries by subjects of China shall be severely punished according to law….

ARTICLE XXI.

Subjects of China who may be guilty of any criminal act towards citizens of the United States, shall be arrested and punished by the Chinese authorities according to the laws of China: and citizens of the United States, who may commit any crime in China, shall be subject to be tried and punished only by the Consul, or other public functionary of the United States, thereto authorized according to the laws of the United States. And in order to the prevention of all controversy and disaffection, justice shall be equitably and impartially administered on both sides.

Source: Jules Davids, ed., *American Diplomatic and Public Papers: The United States and China* (Wilmington, DE: Scholarly Resources, Inc., 1973) 122–124.

 Go to **www.chinasince1644.com** for the full text of **Document 5.6**.

DOCUMENT 5.7:
Excerpts from "The Land System of the Heavenly Kingdom," 1853

Throughout the [Taiping] empire the mulberry tree is to be planted close to every wall, so that all women may engage in rearing silkworms, spinning the silk, and making garments. Throughout the empire every family should keep five hens and two sows, which must not be allowed to miss their proper season. At the time of harvest, every sergeant shall direct the corporals to see to it that of the twenty-five families under his charge each individual has a sufficient supply of food, and aside from the new grain each may receive, the remainder must be deposited in the public granary. Of wheat, pulse, hemp, flax, cloth, silk, fowls, dogs, etc., and money, the same is true; for the whole empire is the universal family of our Heavenly Father, the Supreme Lord and Great God....

For every twenty-five families there must be established one public granary, and one church where the sergeant must reside. Whenever there are marriages, or births, or funerals, all may go to the public granary; but a limit must be observed, and [money] not be used beyond what is necessary. Thus, every family that celebrates a marriage or a birth will be given one thousand cash and a hundred catties of grain....

SOURCE: Franz H. Michael, *The Taiping Rebellion: History and Documents*, vol. 2, Documents and Comments (Seattle: University of Washington Press, 1971) 313–315, 319–320.

 Go to **www.chinasince1644.com** for the full text of **Document 5.7**.

Activities

ACTIVITY 1: Examining Visual Sources before Reading

Before reading any of the materials for this lesson, examine the two paintings of Guangzhou (5.1 and 5.2).

1. What does each painting show?

2. Which countries had a presence in Guangzhou (Canton) in 1800? Which had a presence in 1865? How can you tell? Had anything changed in the way in which these countries were present?

3. Compare the two paintings, citing all the differences and similarities.

4. What might be the reasons behind the differences? Discuss the significance (or lack thereof) of each change.

5. What surprises you about the paintings?

Now read the unit overview and the introductory essay to the chapter. Re-examine the paintings. What do they reflect? What changed from your original impression of the paintings?

ACTIVITY 2: Evaluating the Controversy Over the Opium Trade

After reading Commissioner Lin's letter intended for Britain's Queen Victoria (5.3), consider:

1. What do you learn about trade between China and Western nations from this document?

2. What is the overall tone of the letter?

3. How does the letter reflect Chinese perceptions of themselves and China's traditional values?

4. On what arguments did Lin Zexu base his appeal?

5. In what other situations have people used similar arguments? What were the results?

6. How do Commissioner Lin's efforts to eradicate opium use in China compare to efforts to eliminate drug abuse around the world today?

Now compare Lin's arguments with those that William Gladstone, a member of the British Parliament, gave in his speech (5.4).

1. From Gladstone's speech what can be concluded about the members of Parliament and their knowledge of the ethical issues involved in the opium trade?

2. What factors likely led Parliament to vote in favor of a military response?

Creative Extension:

Create an anti-opium-importation poster, either from the point of view of members of Britain's Parliament who opposed the trade or from the point of view of someone on Commissioner Lin's staff.

ACTIVITY 3: Comparing Unequal Treaties

You will be defining the word "treaty" as a class. What would you expect to read in a treaty between two countries? You will be assigned to read either the Treaty of Nanjing between China and Great Britain (5.5) or the Treaty of Wangxia between China and the United States (5.6). Complete the following with a partner who will read the other treaty.

1. List the key components of each treaty in your own words.

2. Why did these and several subsequent treaties between Western nations and China earn the term "unequal treaties"?

3. Analyze the similarities and differences between the two treaties. How does the content of each treaty reflect the motives of Britain and the United States?

4. Now compare either treaty with the Treaty of Nerchinsk between Russia and China in 1689 (Chapter 4, Document 4.2). What conclusions can be drawn from the differences among the treaties? How had the position of Qing dynasty China changed?

Role Play You will be assigned to play one of the following six roles: member of a negotiating team who represented China, Great Britain or the United States; the Emperor or a member of Parliament or the U.S. Senate. Each of the negotiating teams will report to their governments on the terms of their respective treaties and convince them that the treaty should be ratified. The Emperor, members of Parliament, or the U.S. Senate should be prepared to ask questions to ensure that the treaty is in their country's interest. Parliament and the Senate representatives will vote; the Emperor will deliver a final opinion.

ACTIVITY 4: **Reflecting in Writing**

Choose one of the following options:

1. W. Travis Hanes, in his book *Opium Wars*, describes this period of Chinese history as "a cultural confrontation—a confrontation between two great world civilizations, one new and one ancient, each believing itself to be the pinnacle of civilization on the planet" (12). Refer to Chapter 4 for additional information, and then write an essay in response to this statement.

2. Write a diary entry from the perspective of a scholar-official in the Qing court, William Gladstone, Commissioner Lin, or an American or British ship owner who has been involved in the opium trade, explaining your view of the war and subsequent treaties.

3. Write an essay suggesting how China should respond to these encounters with the West in order to protect its interests.

ACTIVITY 5: **Concluding Discussion**

Prepare to discuss in class:

1. Why does China consider the wars and signing of the treaties as the beginning of its "Century of Humiliation"?

2. How might you expect these events in the nineteenth century to affect China's foreign policy today?

ACTIVITY 6: **Analyzing the Taiping Rebellion**

Read a summary of the Taiping Rebellion (Item 5.A). Then, working with a partner, examine "The Land System of the Heavenly Kingdom" (5.7).

1. List the principles upon which the government was established.
2. Summarize the organizational structure.
3. Why might this type of government have appealed to so many people?
4. How does the Heavenly Kingdom compare to other forms of government or utopian communities?

ACTIVITY 7: **The Taiping in Nanjing**

You will work in a small group to examine the photographs taken in the wing dedicated to the Taiping Rebellion at the Presidential Palace in Nanjing (Item 5.Ba–c) and of the replica of Hong's robe (Item 5.C). Discuss:

1. What can you conclude from the appearance of the two rooms?
2. What, if anything, surprised you about the rooms? Why?
3. List words to describe the statue of Hong Xiuquan.
4. Does the king's robe contradict or support the principles of the Heavenly Kingdom? How? What is the significance of the color?

EXTENDED RESEARCH:

To explore this period of Chinese history further, research:

- The Nian Rebellion (1851–1868)
- Muslim revolts in Yunnan (1855–1873) and in Shaanxi and Gansu provinces (1862–1873)
- The treaties of Tianjin between China and the United States (June 18, 1858), and China and Great Britain (June 26, 1858) (see Suggested Resources).
- The Taiping Rebellion by reading Katherine Paterson's novel *Rebels of the Heavenly Kingdom* (see Suggested Resources)

Suggested Resources

Books

Hanes, W. Travis III and Frank Sanello. *The Opium Wars: The Addiction of One Empire and the Corruption of Another*. Naperville, Ill.: Sourcebooks, 2002.

Paterson, Katherine. *Rebels of the Heavenly Kingdom*. New York: Puffin Books, 1983.
A young adult historical novel about how two teenagers experienced the Taiping Rebellion.

Platt, Stephen R. *Autumn in the Heavenly Kingdom: China, the West, and the Epic Story of the Taiping Civil War*. New York: Alfred A. Knopf, 2012.

Spence, Jonathan D. *God's Chinese Son: The Taiping Heavenly Kingdom of Hong Xiuquan*. New York: W.W. Norton, 1996.
An analysis of Hong Xiuquan, who led the Taiping.

Waley, Arthur. *The Opium War through Chinese Eyes*. Stanford: Stanford University Press, 1968.
History of the first Opium War, recording the feelings and sufferings of common people affected by the war.

Wang, Dong. *China's Unequal Treaties: Narrating National History*. Lanham, MD: Lexington Books, 2005.
Based on primary sources, this book examines treaties signed by China between 1842 and 1946.

Websites

The Opium War and Foreign Encroachment, Asia for Educators
http://afe.easia.columbia.edu/special/ china_1750_opium.htm
Student readings, primary sources, and discussion questions about the Opium War.

"The Signing of the Treaty of Tien-sin," The Argus
http://trove.nla.gov.au/ndp/del/article/ 7304800
A digital newspaper article from Melbourne, Australia, about the Treaty of Tianjin between China and Great Britain.

Taiping Rebellion (1850–1864), Asia for Educators
http://afe.easia.columbia.edu/special/ china_1750_taiping.htm
An overview of the Taiping Rebellion with teaching activity suggestions.

The Western Encounter with China, 1600–1900
http://digital.library.mcgill.ca/westchina/ trade.htm
An online exhibition from McGill University with a brief overview of the time period and primary sources about diplomacy, the Boxer Uprising, and *chinoiserie*.

■ **A CLOSER LOOK**

Lin Zexu: The Commissioner Takes Charge

In 1838, the emperor appointed Lin Zexu (1785–1850) to enforce the ban on opium by cutting it off at the source: Guangzhou (Canton). Commissioner Lin was an exemplary official by all accounts. He held a *jinshi* degree, having passed the most difficult of the civil service exams. A literary scholar, reformer, and skilled diplomat, he was incorruptible.

Lin took a multifaceted approach to the opium problem: favoring rehabilitation for addicts, appealing to Britain's Queen Victoria on moral grounds, and destroying drug-relat-ed paraphernalia. By the spring of 1839, he had arrested 1,600 Guangzhou residents and confiscated 42,000 opium pipes. By mid-summer, he had seized 14,000 drug-filled chests. After a battle of wills, he forced Western merchants to surrender the opium on their vessels: 20,000 chests (worth about $12 million), which the commissioner destroyed. In future, he declared, if any vessel were found to have opium on board, he would order the entire crew executed.

In Britain, economics peppered with national pride trumped moral arguments and the British with their allies fought two wars in part to protect the lucrative opium trade. Commissioner Lin's best efforts were no match for Britain's gunboat diplomacy. By 1879, opium imports to China had risen to an astronomical 105,000 chests.

■ *Discuss: How else might Commissioner Lin have approached the task of ridding Guangzhou and hence inland China of opium? Were his efforts doomed to fail? Why or why not?*

CHAPTER RESOURCES

 Excerpts of these primary source documents appear in this chapter. Go to **www.chinasince1644.com** for the full version of these documents and for the Supplementary Materials.

CHAPTER 6

Exploring Solutions (1861–1894)

By Shirley Moore Huettig

Chapter Contents:

The Self-Strengthening Movement

Missionaries in China

The Chinese Diaspora

Key Idea:

The period 1861–1894 witnessed the Chinese turning to ideas that included both accommodation and resistance in order to strengthen themselves in their dealings with foreign powers. In addition to their increased contact with foreign governments and traders, the Chinese witnessed a flood of missionaries into their country, as well as an exodus of Chinese individuals to other parts of the world.

Guiding Questions:

How did the Chinese both accommodate and resist foreigners?

What initiatives did the Chinese launch as part of the Self-Strengthening Movement?

What was the relationship between missionaries and the Chinese?

What factors contributed to the large number of Chinese people choosing to emigrate in the late nineteenth century?

What were some common experiences of Chinese people working and living overseas?

Terms to Know

accommodation

coolies

conservative

diaspora

immigrant

incursion

indentured servitude

missionary

progressive

proselytize

restoration

Essay

In the second half of the nineteenth century, the Qing (清) dynasty was faced with growing incursion from foreign nations and dissatisfaction from within China. Conservative and progressive voices within China argued over the country's relationship with the outside world—some calling for a rejection and exclusion of all foreign knowledge, while others urged learning from the foreigners to be better able to resist them. For some Chinese, one of the most visible examples of Western incursion was the presence of missionaries, especially from Britain and the United States, whose numbers in China grew significantly after 1860. Finally, in response to conditions at home, thousands of Chinese chose to leave in search of a better life in areas as far flung as Australia, the West Indies, and the United States.

Self-Strengthening and the Tongzhi Restoration (1860–1874)

Although the Qing dynasty was greatly weakened after the internal rebellions and the foreign treaty settlements of 1860, it was able to continue in power. Many Chinese intellectuals saw the dynasty's survival as threatened, and knew that drastic measures were required. The world was changing around China, they recognized, and China needed to change too, in order to survive. These Chinese officials urged major shifts in policy, suggesting that the Chinese engage and learn from foreigners so as to resist further incursions. This "self-strengthening" (*ziqiang* 自强), while encouraging what many considered radical change (learning from Westerners), was actually inherently conservative. These reformers proposed adopting Western technologies and techniques, but insisted that the Confucian canon remain the "essence" of Chinese learning and outlook, explicitly rejecting the influence of any other philosophy or

attitudes. Even these superficial changes were opposed by another faction at the Qing court, led by Manchu Grand Secretary Woren. Woren and his adherents believed that China was not in decline, and the best way to proceed was to carry on unchanged. Most of the arguments between those who called for self-strengthening and those who rejected it revolved around education, the traditional foundation of Chinese government. A major supporter of self-strengthening was the provincial leader Zeng Guofan (曾国藩),[1] who recorded in his diary:

> If we wish to find a method of self-strengthening, we should begin by considering the reform of government service and the securing of men of ability as urgent tasks, and then regard learning to make explosive shells and steamships and other instruments as the work of first importance. If only we could possess all their [Westerners'] superior techniques, then we would have the means to return their favors when they are obedient, and we would also have the means to avenge our grievances when they are disloyal.[2]

Unfortunately, despite the efforts of a number of visionary and talented individuals, China made little headway in developing industry and military technology compared to achievements in the West and Japan. The self-strengtheners claimed success and called the period "The Tongzhi Restoration" (*Tongzhi Zhongxing* 同治中兴) implying that the dynasty had been restored to its pre-Opium War glory after the reforms. But this "restoration" was in name only. "They never dreamed of remaking China into a

---

[1] Zeng Guofan was a Confucian statesman/general/scholar, who brought an end to the Taiping Rebellion by defeating the Taiping in Nanjing (see Chapter 5).

[2] Ssu-yü Teng and John King Fairbank. *China's Response to the West: A Documentary Survey 1839–1923*. (Cambridge: Harvard University Press, 1954) 62.

modern state," writes Immanuel Hsü in *The Rise of Modern China*. "In fact, they strove to strengthen the existing order rather than to replace it. They had absolutely no conception of economic development, industrial revolution, and modern transformation."[3] The movement did, however, mark "the beginning of industrialization…in China."[4]

Empress Cixi (慈禧), who had served as regent for her son the Tongzhi emperor, supported self-strengthening. But after the movement proved to be a sham with defeat in the Sino-Vietnamese/French War (1885), she began to retrench. At first, she tried to balance calls for traditional versus Western education and policy. Later, however, she became convinced that it was only through the restoration of the traditional Confucian system of government that she would retain her power over the young emperors and, therefore, the government, and her views became more conservative, even reactionary.[5]

Foreign Relations

In 1861 the Qing government created the *Zongli Yamen* (总理衙门) (Office for the General Management of Affairs Concerning the Various Countries).[6] It was headed by Prince Gong (*Gong Qinwang* 恭亲王), the Tongzhi emperor's uncle, who had gained important experience in dealing with foreigners in his role negotiating the 1860 peace settlement with the British, French, and Russians (see chapter 5). He had come to appreciate that the West had good ideas to offer in the realm of manufacturing as well as international law and treaties. As a result, several schools to train

translators and interpreters were set up on the eastern seaboard. The first, the *Tongwen Guan* (同文馆), had a curriculum that included foreign language, taught mostly by missionaries who were restricted from proselytizing at any time, as well as Western science, technology, and mathematics, also taught by foreigners, and classical Chinese studies.

Despite the best efforts of the *Zongli Yamen*, foreign nations continued their encroachment on what the Chinese had long considered tributary lands. In 1879, Japan occupied the Liuqi Islands and was quickly followed by Russia in the Ili Valley in 1881, France in Vietnam in 1885 and Laos in 1893, and Britain expanding its empire into Burma in 1886.[7] Within China's borders, foreigners continued to extract more favorable trade arrangements and greater access to interior sections of the country.

Missionaries

After 1861, Europeans and Americans also made their presence felt in China with a significant increase in missionary activity, both Protestant and Catholic. These missionaries sent fundraising reports about China back to their home countries, which helped spark interest in Chinese customs, opium use, and orphans, as well as providing fodder for burgeoning ideas about the West's "Civilizing Mission"—ideas which would come to fruition in the New Imperialism of the turn of the century (see chapter 7). In China, missionaries used the funds they raised to begin building clinics, orphanages and schools, where they offered Western curricula including English language, science and technology, medicine and law, as well as religious studies. Catholic missions emphasized religious conversion, while some Protestants maintained a more secular curriculum, especially as formulations of the Social Gospel became more prevalent among missionary communities. In dramatic contrast to Chinese tradition, missionaries opened schools for girls.

---

[3] Immanuel C.Y. Hsü, *The Rise of Modern China*, 4th ed. (New York: Oxford University Press, 1990) 288.

[4] Hsü, p. 290

[5] Joanna Waley-Cohen, *The Sextants of Beijing: Global Currents in Chinese History* (New York: W.W. Norton, 1999).

[6] Prior to this, China's foreign relations were divided among three bureaus (see Chapter 4).

[7] In Japan the Liuqi Islands are called the Ryukyu Islands

Despite these seemingly useful contributions, the presence of Western missionaries was fraught with tension, which periodically erupted in violence. In 1870, The Tianjin Massacre (*Tianjin Jiaoan* 天津教案) was sparked when rumors began spreading through China that missionaries were buying Chinese babies to use their body parts in the preparation of exotic medicines. These rumors seemed to be confirmed by the actual practices of missionaries, who would often actively seek out orphans to bring into their missions. These infants, many already weakened by abandonment, would frequently die in their care, often after having been baptized, leading to even more frantic speculation on the connection between baptism and death. When Chinese kidnappers, arrested outside of Tianjin, admitted to having sold babies to the nuns in that city, relations—already strained by the erection of a Catholic cathedral on the grounds of an imperial temple—went from bad to worse. An angry mob gathered and burned down the cathedral, the orphanage, and other local churches. They also murdered nuns, the French consul, priests, and other foreigners and Chinese Christians.

The Tianjin Massacre led to an international outcry and a necessitated a formal apology from the Qing government to France. Official relations between the Qing government and the Christian missions deteriorated, as did popular relations between local Chinese and foreign missionaries. This tension would culminate in yet another bloody incident, the Boxer Uprisings (*Gengzi Guobian* 庚子国变) in 1899–1900. Meanwhile, Christianity remained unpopular with mainstream Chinese, and converts were few and far between. For many Chinese, the rigid definition of religion insisted on by Christian missionaries could not accommodate important Chinese cultural traditions and beliefs such as ancestor worship. In addition, the behavior of missionaries themselves, who encouraged women to leave the inner quarters and frequently engaged in activities incomprehensible to the Chinese, was offensive and unacceptable.

Nonetheless, the presence of these new faces, ideas and mentalities deep in China's heartlands would have a long-lasting impact on diversifying the opportunities available to China's thinkers and activists.

Emigration

As countries abolished slavery and the Atlantic slave trade slowed, a huge international demand for labor arose.[8] Despite Confucian ethics, which emphasized that an adult son should remain at home in order to take care of aging parents, and a Qing edict (1672) that prohibited Chinese individuals from emigrating, an estimated 3 million impoverished Chinese, especially from rural areas, left in the late nineteenth century in search of a better life overseas.[9] They boarded ships in southern China only to find crowded, unhealthy passage to work on plantations, in mines, and on railroads in the Caribbean, Southeast Asia, Latin America, South America, Australia, and the United States. Once there, the immigrants found the work to be little better than slave labor. Belying its image as a land of equal opportunity, the United States greeted Chinese immigrants with discrimination, derision, and physical harm. Immigrants in many other lands fared similarly. Forced to watch out for themselves, Chinese immigrants settled together in neighborhoods, creating "Chinatowns" in large cities such as Havana, Cuba; Georgetown, Guyana; Liverpool, England; and San Francisco, United States.

---

[8] Peru abolished slavery in 1854, for example, the United States in 1865, and Cuba in 1886.

[9] Wei Djao, *Being Chinese: Voices from the Diaspora*. (Tucson: University of Arizona Press, 2003) 26. This figure covers the period between 1840 and 1911.

Primary Sources

DOCUMENT 6.1: Excerpts from letter from Zeng Guofan and Li Hongzhang to *Zongli Yamen* (the Foreign Relations Bureau) on sending young men abroad to study, March 1871

[After a delegation sent by the empress dowager Cixi] had traveled in various countries... they saw the essential aspects of conditions overseas, and they found that cartography, mathematics, astronomy, navigation, shipbuilding, and manufacturing are all closely related to military defense. It is the practice of foreign nations that those who have studied abroad and have learned some superior techniques are immediately invited upon their return by academic institutions to teach the various subjects and to develop their fields. Military administration and shipping are considered as important as the learning that deals with the mind and body, and nature and destiny of man. Now that the eyes of the people have been opened, if China wishes to adopt Western ideas and excel in Western methods, we should immediately select intelligent young men and send them to study in foreign countries....

Source: Rpt. in William Theodore de Bary and Richard Lufrano, *Sources of Chinese Tradition*, vol. 2 (New York: Columbia University Press, 2000) 241.

 Go to **www.chinasince1644.com** for the full text of Document 6.1.

DOCUMENT 6.2: Excerpts from the autobiography of Yung Wing, *My Life in China and America*, describing his efforts to modernize China, 1909

The proposition was for the government to send picked Chinese youths abroad to be thoroughly educated for the public service.... As to the character and selection of the students: the whole number to be sent abroad for education was one hundred and twenty; they were to be divided into four installments of thirty members each, one installment to be sent each year for four successive years at about the same time. The candidates to be selected were not to be younger than twelve or older than fifteen years of age. They were to show respectable parentage or responsible and respectable guardians. They were required to pass a medical examination, and an examination in their Chinese studies according to regulation—reading and writing in Chinese—also to pass an English examination if a candidate had been in an English school....

Source: Wing Yung, *My Life in China and America* (New York: Henry Holt and Company, 1909) 173, 183–184.

 Go to **www.chinasince1644.com** for the full text of Document 6.2.

DOCUMENT 6.3: Excerpt from letter by Zhu Yixin in response to the Self-Strengthening Movement, late 1800s

The barbarians do not recognize the moral obligations between ruler and minister, parent and child, elder brother and younger brother, husband and wife. There is your change in principles. Do you mean that the classics of our sages and the teachings of our philosophers are too dull and banal to follow, and that we must change them so as to have something new? Only if we first have principles can we then have institutions. Barbarian institutions are based on barbarian principles. Different principles make for different customs, and different customs give rise to different institutions. Now, instead of getting at the root of it all, you talk blithely of changing institutions. If the institutions are to be changed, are not the principles going to be changed along with them?

SOURCE: William Theodore de Bary and Richard Lufrano, *Sources of Chinese Tradition*, vol. 2 (New York: Columbia University Press, 2000) 277.

Go to **www.chinasince1644.com** for the full text of **Document 6.3**.

DOCUMENT 6.4: Excerpts from the writings of British evangelical Protestant missionary J. Hudson Taylor regarding the foundation and functioning of the China Inland Mission in 1865

A journey taken in the spring of 1855 with the Rev. J. S. Burdon of the Church Missionary Society (later the Bishop of Victoria, Hong Kong) was attended with some serious dangers…. We went to Tongzhou [in Jiangsu Province], and of our painful experiences there the following journal will tell….

A respectable man came up, and earnestly warned us against proceeding, saying that if we did we should find to our sorrow what the Tongzhou militia were like…. After this my wheelbarrow man would proceed no farther, and I had to seek another, who was fortunately not difficult to find…. Long before we reached the gate, a tall powerful man, made tenfold fiercer by partial intoxication, let us know that all the militia were not so peaceably inclined, by seizing Mr. Burdon by the shoulders…. At once we were surrounded by a dozen or more brutal men, who hurried us on to the city at a fearful pace…. We demanded to be taken before the chief magistrate, but were told that they knew where to take us, and what to do with such persons as we were, with the most insulting epithets…. He all but knocked me down again and again, seized me by the hair, took hold of my collar so as to almost choke me, and grasped my arms and shoulders, making them black and blue….

As we were walking along Mr. Burdon tried to give away a few books that he was carrying, not knowing whether we might have another opportunity of doing so; but the fearful rage of the soldier, and the way he insisted on manacles being brought, which fortunately were not at hand, convinced us that in our present position we could do no good in attempting book distribution….

SOURCE: J. Hudson Taylor, *The Autobiography of a Man Who Brought the Gospel to China* (Minneapolis: Bethany House, 1986) 64, 66, 68–69.

Go to **www.chinasince1644.com** for the full text of **Document 6.4**.

DOCUMENT 6.5: Letters from Southern Baptist missionary Lottie Moon, published in the *Foreign Mission Journal*, October 1888 and June 1898

June 30, 1898

Tongzhou, China

Dear Dr. Willingham,

I have visited during this Quarter [three months] twenty different towns & villages. At many of them, I remained several days. At others, I have made but brief visits, going out after dinner & returning about sun-set. I have had much to encourage me in the work. The people are very friendly & more ready to listen to the gospel than I have ever known them to be. In two places, there are, apparently, some genuine inquirers. I have been pressingly invited to go to a new village to visit a family said to be very favorably disposed to Christianity & I have promised to go. It is a source of sorrow that I cannot meet the numerous calls. I have simply to decide what cases & places most urgently demand attention & to neglect many others to which I would gladly go, were I free to do so. We need at least three more single women here. Miss Hartwell is doing noble work in the school, but, thus far, this year has been unable to leave the city. There are about thirty towns & villages connected with the Tongzhou station, that ought to have visits of several days duration, at least twice a year. With our present force, this is simply impossible.

We are rejoiced at the good news from the Convention. To have that awful debt rolled off, what a blessing.

With best wishes & earnest prayers for a blessing upon your labors,

Yrs. sincerely,

L. Moon.

SOURCE: Lottie Moon to Robert J. Willingham, 30 June 1898. *Lottie Moon Letters*, ed. International Mission Board (Southern Baptist Convention), accession no. 192. https://solomon.imb.org/public/ws/lmcorr/www/lmcorr/SimpleSearch

 Go to **www.chinasince1644.com** for additional letters from Lottie Moore.

DOCUMENT 6.6: Excerpts from a report by the commissioner of three northern ports describing the Tianjin Massacre, June 1870

I find that in the Tianjin region, since summer began the weather has been hotter and drier than usual, and the popular mood is unsettled. Among the populace, rumors have been rife. There are those who say that [the foreigners] use medicine to kidnap youths and children. There are those who say that there are cases of the corpses and bones of youths and children being exposed in the public cemetery. There are those who say that the exposed corpses are all those abandoned by the church. Also, there are those who say that the Catholics gouge out eyes and cut out hearts. Rumors spread in great confusion, but without any firm basis....

People from everywhere were summoned by gong. The church was burnt down, and also the Renci Hall outside the Eastern Gate was destroyed by fire. In other places "preaching halls" were pulled down. Missionaries and those practicing the faith, both Chinese and foreign, were injured and killed. Your servant rushed to supervise with the local civil and military officials and also sent troops to put down [the disturbance]. Alas, the masses were [too] numerous, with the force of a mob, and in a short while the killing, wounding, burning, and destroying were already *faits accomplis.*…

SOURCE: Gengyin Chonghou, untitled memorial, 23 June 1870, trans. Howard R. Spendelow. http://www9.georgetown.edu/faculty/spendelh/china/TJ700623.htm

Go to **www.chinasince1644.com** for the full text of **Document 6.6**.

DOCUMENT 6.7: Excerpts from the "Autobiography of Mr. Kwan Hong Kee," describing his early years in Australia, January 1938

In 1885, Kwan Hong Kee borrowed $100 from his brother to pay for his passage from Hong Kong to Australia. He worked as a cook on board the vessel. After arriving in Sydney, he borrowed more money to send a letter home, letting his family know he had arrived safely, and to buy European clothes. His first job was in Newcastle as a cook in a Chinese store. He was provided with room and board but received no pay.

Each day after cooking breakfast, I worked as a hawker selling goods until 4 o'clock in the afternoon, when it was time to cook the evening meal. I did this for a period of three months, after which through another friend I got work in Sydney at "Sarm Choy" store. This store imported and sold Chinese goods. My wages were fifteen shillings a week. After two years I was promoted to salesman and received one pound a week. [Four years later] my work included selling, back store work, receiving and delivering goods, in fact all general work. I tried my best, my boss was pleased with my work over the six years. I then returned to China again and married.…

SOURCE: Kwan Hong Kee, "Autobiography of Mr. Kwan Hong Kee," Hong Kong, January 1938. *Golden Threads,* Australian Museums & Galleries Online, Nov. 2003. http://amol.org.au/goldenthreads/stories

Go to **www.chinasince1644.com** for the full text of **Document 6.7**.

DOCUMENT 6.8: Excerpts from a contract of indenture for Chinese emigrants sailing to Guyana, 1873

1. I agree to work in British Guyana as I may be directed by the Government Immigration Agent or for any person to whom he may transfer this Contract.…

3. I agree to do any kind of work that I may be lawfully directed to do, whether in town or country, in fields, in factories, in private houses &c.…

8. Wherever I may work or in whatever family I may be employed, I must obey the lawful regulations there in force; on the other hand should I at any time feel aggrieved at the conduct of my master towards me, all reasonable facility shall be afforded me, for laying my complaint before the proper officers of the Colony....

12. Every day, food will be issued as follows; 8 oz. salt meat and 2½ lbs. of other articles, all of which shall be good and wholesome....

14. Each year there will be given me one suit of clothes and one blanket....

19. I the said coolie now agree that my wages shall be four dollars a month and I declare my willingness, before my departure, to go to British Guyana, it is therefore understood that hereafter if I hear or ascertain that the labourers in British Guyana receive more wages than myself, I must still be satisfied with the wages and other compensating advantages secured to me by this Contract....

SOURCE: Trev Sue-A-Quan, *Cane Reapers: Chinese Indentured Immigrants in Guyana* (Vancouver, BC: Riftswood Publishing, 1999) 323–327.

 Go to **www.chinasince1644.com** for the full text of Document 6.8.

DOCUMENT 6.9a & b: Excerpt from "Our Misery and Despair" by Denis Kearney of the California Workingmen's Party and a letter in response by Kwang Chang Ling, published in the *San Francisco Argonaut*, 1878

From Kwang Chang Ling's response:

▪ You are continually objecting to [the] morality [of the Chinese]. Your travelers say he is depraved; your missioners call him ungodly; your commissioners call him unclean... Yet your housewives permit him to wait upon them at table; they admit him to their bedchambers; they confide to him their garments and jewels; and even trust their lives to him by awarding him supreme control over their kitchens and the preparation of their food. There is a glaring contradiction here....

▪ The slender fare of rice and the other economical habits of the peasant class [of China], which are so objectionable to your lower orders and the demagogues who trumpet their clamors, are not the result of choice to Chinamen; they follow poverty. The hard-working, patient servants that you have about you today love good fare as well as other men, but they are engaged in a work far higher than the gratification of self-indulgence; they are working to liberate their parents in China [from poverty].... When this emancipation is complete, you will find the Chinamen [sic] as prone as any human creature to fill his belly and cover his back with good things.

SOURCE: Kwang Chang Ling, letter in *San Francisco Argonaut*, 1878. *Becoming American: The Chinese Experience*, PBS. http://www.pbs.org/becomingamerican/ce_witness2.html

 Go to **www.chinasince1644.com** for the full text of Document 6.9.

DOCUMENT 6.10:
Cartoon in Australia's *Queensland Figaro*, April 1888

 Go to **www.chinasince1644.com** for the cartoon in **Document 6.10**.

DOCUMENT 6.11:
Statistics of Chinese Immigrant Ships to Guyana, 1853–1879

 Go to **www.chinasince1644.com** for the text of **Document 6.11**.

DOCUMENT 6.12a–d:
Photographs of Chinatowns around the world today

Chinatown in Sydney, Australia *(Photo by Liz Nelson)*

Go to **www.chinasince1644.com** for additional photographs in **Document 6.12**.

Activities

ACTIVITY 1: Exploring Solutions: Reading and Discussing

Part 1: "Text on Text" Discussion

In groups of three, read and respond to each document (6.1, 6.2 or 6.3; see Item 6.A on companion website for directions on "Text on Text" discussions).

1. How does this person feel about China's relationship with foreign countries?

2. What does he think should be done in response? What specific solutions does he recommend? Does he advocate "self-strengthening" or maintaining the status quo?

3. Are you convinced by his argument? Why or why not?

Part 2: Inside/Outside Class Discussion

You will be assigned to a group with a mix of "experts" on each of the three documents 6.1, 6.2, and 6.3.

One group sits in a tight circle in the middle of the room with its members facing each other. The other group sits in a larger circle around the first group. The inner group begins a discussion of the questions addressed in part 1. When the discussion concludes, the groups switch. The new inside group can add to the first group's discussion as well as address the original questions. When this new discussion concludes, the groups switch again. The first group returns to the middle to finish the discussion of the questions.

ACTIVITY 2:
The Missionary Presence: Reading, Discussing, and Writing

Part 1: "Text on Text" Discussion

After reading documents 6.4–6.6, and "A Closer Look, Dr. Peter Parker: Beyond Evangelical Work," work in small groups to answer the following questions (see Item 6.A on the companion website for directions):

1. What was the role of missionaries in China?
2. How well did the missionaries integrate with the Chinese population?
3. How did the missionaries treat the Chinese? How did the Chinese treat the missionaries?
4. How were the authors of these documents similar to and different from each other?

As a class you will discuss opinions about missionaries in China.

Writing Extension:

Write a letter either as a church elder or a Chinese official to one of the denominations sending the missionaries, with recommendations regarding their presence in China. Would you advocate "self-strengthening" or maintaining the status quo? Would you allow missionaries to stay? What restrictions, if any, would you place on their activities (traveling, proselytizing, or conducting business)? Be sure to support your argument with evidence from the documents.

ACTIVITY 3: The Chinese Diaspora: Reading and Discussing

Part 1: Collaborate

Working in small groups, examine documents 6.7–6.10 and discuss:

1. Why did Chinese people leave China? Where did they go?
2. What factors contributed to the discrimination Chinese immigrants experienced?

Creative Extension:

Role Play with a partner. One person is a Chinese immigrant; the other is an American. Create a dialogue showing either a challenge or an opportunity for a Chinese immigrant in America.

Part 2: Respond to Reading

Conduct an Inside/Outside group discussion (see Activity 1, Part 2 for directions) on the issue of Chinese immigration.

ACTIVITY 4: Analyzing Data from Shipping Records

Refer to the instructions in Item 6.B on the companion website to prepare for working with the shipping records (6.11 on the companion website). Answer the following questions:

1. Which ship made the most voyages to Guyana? How was the name of the ship ironic?

2. What was the height of the immigration from China to Guyana? How did you define the "height" of the trade? Based on your knowledge of Chinese history (see Chapter 5), how can you explain the increase in emigration?

3. From which Chinese port did most ships sail? What was the second most common port of departure?

4. Which was the longest voyage? Which was the shortest? What was the average length of a voyage from China to Guyana?

5. At what time of year did most voyages take place? In which months did these voyages generally not sail? Why do you suppose this was?

6. What was the greatest number of people transported on one ship? The least number? Notice the difference between the numbers in column L and those in column R. How might you account for the differences? What was the greatest number of people "lost" on one voyage? How might you account for the change in the number who embarked and those who disembarked on the *Montmorency* in 1861?

7. Who accounted for the most emigrants: men, women or children? Why do you suppose this was true?

Propose other questions and experiment with other sorting methods to further examine the data for information about emigration from China to Guyana.

ACTIVITY 5: Emigration

For documents 6.7–6.11, create a corresponding written or visual response. For example:

1. Write an editorial to a newspaper in a country to which Chinese people immigrated. Address the topic of assimilation or treatment of the Chinese immigrants. Be sure to support your argument with evidence from the documents.

2. Design a political cartoon from the Chinese perspective that summarizes the experience of the Chinese immigrant: conditions, reception, family life, etc.

3. Create a sculpture or write a poem in response to any one of the documents.

4. Write a report to the *Zongli Yamen* (the Foreign Relations Bureau) from a Chinese official sent out to investigate the conditions in Guyana, Peru, or San Francisco.

ACTIVITY 6: Chinatown Brainstorming

In brainstorming, members of a group all respond by calling out words that they associate with the image. A recorder writes down all of the ideas; there is no censoring in brainstorming. Don't criticize or question anyone's idea.

As a class, brainstorm about Chinatown:

1. What is a Chinatown?
2. What do you expect to see? What don't you expect to see?
3. Where do you think Chinatowns are located?

Working in small groups, examine one of the photographs 6.12a–d. One member of each group should record the group's ideas. On a single sheet of paper, record at the top the names of the students in the group and the location of the Chinatown.

1. Brainstorm for five minutes together, with the recorder writing down all the responses. Consider: What do you see? What don't you see that you might have expected? What surprises you about the image?

2. When the time is up, put the paper on which the group's ideas were recorded in the middle so all can see. Write several summary statements about the image, using the responses from the whole group.

3. Reconvene as a class and share one summary statement from your own work. (Statements can be read out loud or written on the board for others to record.)

4. Discuss the many ideas elicited by the pictures. To what extent did the images of Chinatowns match the ideas from the initial brainstorming?

NOTE: This activity can also be done using the topic of the reactions of native populations to Chinese immigration, referring to Document 6.10.

EXTENDED RESEARCH:

Choose one of the topics below and create a final product (a paper, a digital presentation using a program such as PowerPoint, or a creative response) to share the information with classmates.

1. Choose another country that has faced or currently faces the need to modernize, and show how the country did it (e.g. Japan, Russia, or a developing country today).

2. Where else besides China did missionaries go in the nineteenth century? How were their experiences similar and different from those of missionaries in China?

3. Where do missionaries go today? How do they work?

4. Search online for Chinatowns all over the world. Using a world map or Google Earth, mark all the cities where Chinese immigrants created communities in the past that are still present today.

Suggested Resources

Books

Lee, Erika and Judy Yung. *Angel Island: Immigrant Gateway to America*. New York: Oxford University Press, 2010.
A history of the Angel Island Immigration Station.

McCunn, Ruthanne Lum. *God of Luck*. New York: Soho Press, 2007.
A novel about a young Chinese man kidnapped in southern China, shipped to Peru, and coerced to work there.

McCunn, Ruthanne Lum. *Thousand Pieces of Gold*. Boston: Beacon Press, 1981.
The true story of Lalu, a rural Chinese girl sold into slavery to a saloon owner in a gold-mining town in the American West.

Min, Anchee. *Empress Orchid*. Boston: Houghton Mifflin, 2004.
A fictional account of the last empress of China who begins her journey to power as a teenage concubine in the Chinese Emperor's court.

Min, Anchee. *The Last Empress*. Boston: Houghton Mifflin, 2007.
The sequel to *Empress Orchid*. This novel tells the story of Empress Dowager Cixi and her control of the Qing Dynasty from 1861–1908.

Sue-A-Quan, Trev. *Cane Reapers: Chinese Indentured Immigrants in Guyana*. Vancouver, BC: Riftswood, 1999.
This book tells the experiences of the author's own ancestors as many of the Chinese who were "hired" to work in the Caribbean and South America. *Cane Ripples* is the sequel to *Cane Reapers*. Both books contain accounts of the Chinese Diaspora beyond the United States.

Woo, X.L. *Empress Dowager Cixi: China's Last Dynasty and the Long Reign of a Formidable Concubine, Legends and Lives during the Declining Days of the Qing Dynasty*. New York: Algora, 2002.

Yep, Laurence. *Dragonwings*. New York: Harper & Row, 1975.
A Newbery Honor Book, *Dragonwings* tells the story of a child who leaves his mother and grandmother in China to join his father in San Francisco. The book captures the experiences of Chinese immigrants and the traditions they brought with them to an often hostile new setting.

Websites

Ancestors in the Americas, Center for Educational Telecommunications
http://cetel.org/
The companion website to the PBS series *Ancestors in the Americas*. The site includes documents, video clips, and viewer's guides.

Angel Island: Poetic Waves, Chinese Immigration History
http://www.poeticwaves.net/
This site examines Chinese detention at Angel Island and includes poetry carved into the walls of detention cells.

Asia for Educators, Columbia University
http://afe.easia.columbia.edu/
Select the 1750–1919 section for essays and primary sources about the Self-Strengthening Movement.

The Chinese in California, 1850–1925, American Memory, The Library of Congress
http://memory.loc.gov/ammem/award99/cubhtml/cichome.html
Primary sources about Chinese immigrants in California. Materials are from the University of California, Berkeley and California Historical Society.

Chinese in Guyana: Their Roots
http://www.rootsweb.ancestry.com/~guycigtr/
Trev Sue-A-Quan's website about the history of Chinese immigrants in Guyana.

Chinese Immigration and the Chinese in the United States, National Archives
http://www.archives.gov/research/chinese-americans/guide.html
Overview and primary sources about Chinese immigration to the United States.

Cixi: The Woman Behind the Throne
http://www.smithsonianmag.com/history-archaeology/da-cixi.html
An article from Smithsonian Magazine by Amanda Bensen.

Immigration Explorer, The New York Times
http://www.nytimes.com/interactive/2009/03/10/us/20090310-immigration-explorer.html
An interactive map exploring immigration to the United States from 1880 to 2000.

International Mission Board Archives and Records Services
http://archives.imb.org/solomon.asp
This site provides a collection of Lottie Moon's correspondence.

Li Hung Chang's Scrapbook, University of California
http://archive.org/stream/lihungchangsscr00ligoog
A digitized version of Li Hung Chang's (Hongzhang) writings on Christianity and missionaries in China.

Origins: History of Immigration from China, Immigration Museum Australia
http://museumvictoria.com.au/origins/history.aspx?pid=9
This site about immigrant communities in Victoria, Australia, includes background information and a photo gallery.

Ruthanne Lum McCunn Author Website
http://mccunn.com/
Ruthanne Lum McCunn's official website. Includes reader's guides to her books and video interviews.

The Yung Wing Project
http://www.ywproject.com
A website dedicated to Yung Wing, the first Chinese graduate of an American university.

Films

Ancestors in the Americas (108 mins; 1998)
Part I: Coolies, Sailors, Settlers; Part II: Chinese in the Frontier West; Part III: Crossing a Continent, Crossing the Pacific.

■ **A CLOSER LOOK**

Dr. Peter Parker: Beyond Evangelical Work

Peter Parker (1804–1888) was the first Protestant medical missionary to China. He was born in Framingham, Massachusetts, the son of devout farmers. After graduating from Yale College in 1831, he studied medicine and theology. In 1834, he earned his M.D., was ordained as a Presbyterian minister, and sailed for Guangzhou. There he opened an opthalmic hospital.

Throughout his years in China, he specialized in diseases of the eye, but also performed other surgeries, especially ones involving removal of tumors. Dr. Parker introduced Western anesthesia (sulphuric ether) to China. Medicine and preaching were of equal importance to him. He offered free treatment at the hospital to rich and poor alike and held regular religious services there. His goal, he said was to "open China for the gospel with the lancet."

During the first Opium War, Dr. Parker left China, did extensive fundraising back in the States, then returned to China in 1842. Two years later, he took on a diplomatic role: he was of invaluable assistance to U.S. envoy Caleb Cushing in his efforts to negotiate the first treaty between the U.S. and China. From 1855 to 1857, Dr. Parker served as the American Commissioner and Minister to China.

■ *Discuss Peter Parker's work in China. Compare it to the work of earlier missionaries (see Chapter 4). How was Dr. Parker's presence similar to and different from that of other Westerners in Guangzhou? Do present-day missionaries combine their evangelical work with social services, too? Where? How?*

■ A CLOSER LOOK

Li Hongzhang: Reformer and Diplomat

Li Hongzhang (1823–1901) was a central figure in China's Self-Strengthening Movement and foreign policy in the late nineteenth century. He was born in Anhui Province near the capital city of Hefei, and at the young age of twenty-four, passed the highest level civil service examination, the *jinshi*.

Li gained notice and promotions for his military and administrative abilities leading forces against the Taiping, Nian, and Tianjin rebellions (see Chapter 5). He worked tirelessly to quell aggression against the Qing dynasty, as well as against foreigners. His military successes were due to a well-paid and loyal army, but also to foreign-made arms and patrol boats, which he used after witnessing their effectiveness. By the early 1870s, Li had been promoted to the grand council of the empire and was appointed the superintendent of trade, a position that put him in regular contact with the international community. In this role, Li effectively led Chinese foreign policy.

With his experience using Western technology in battle and negotiating treaties with foreign countries, Li Hongzhang became an early and staunch supporter of strengthening the empire. He ardently supported the use, and later the construction, of Western artillery, as well as efforts to bring Western education to China, including the China Education Mission begun by Yung Wing.

Li Hongzhang continued to play an important role in Chinese foreign relations, traveling to the United States to advocate for more lenient immigration laws following the Chinese Exclusion Act in 1882. Li died only months after signing the treaty ending the Boxer Uprising and negotiating the withdrawal of foreign troops from Beijing in 1901 (see Chapter 7, Document 7.2).

■ *Discuss why the Qing government depended on Li's military and diplomatic skills so often. What appear to have been his strengths?*

■ **A CLOSER LOOK**

Empress Cixi: The Power Behind the Throne

Cixi was born in 1835 to a low-ranking Manchu government official. She moved to Beijing during her childhood and was offered to the Xianfeng emperor as a concubine when she was fifteen years old. Chosen from a group of sixty young girls, Cixi entered the Forbidden City as a low-ranking concubine with little power, but when she gave birth to the only male offspring of the Xianfeng emperor in 1856, Cixi quickly moved up the ranks among the most favored women, second only to the emperor's mother.

When the Xianfeng emperor died, his heir apparent was only five years old, which left the leadership of the country in turmoil. Cixi, an intelligent, realistic, and energetic woman, knew well how the court operated. Through a series of plots, alliances, and executions Cixi positioned herself as the de facto ruler of China as empress dowager for her son, the Tongzhi emperor, and later her nephew, the Guangxu emperor. She was the power behind the throne for forty-seven years, from 1861 to her death in 1908.

During most of her reign, the empress made conservative decisions, fighting to maintain the traditional Confucian system of government that she had manipulated to put her in power and keep her there, and resisting the incursion of foreign manufacturers and ideas into China. But at times Cixi made non-traditional choices, such as the handing over of military leadership against the Taiping to Han Chinese generals rather than to Manchu generals traditionally favored by the Manchu Qing dynasty.

Among Empress Cixi's most questionable decisions was her use of the budget intended for the Imperial Navy to renovate the Summer Palace, including having a marble boat built, which never floated. Harshly criticized, Cixi continued to make decisions that would maintain both her power in the government and the splendor she associated with her station.

In the end, the Empress Cixi is generally blamed for contributing to the fall of the Qing dynasty and the imperial system in China because of her self-serving motives and poor decisions. She died three years before the Republican Revolution of 1911.

■ *Read more about Empress Cixi and then discuss: In what ways did she benefit China? What decisions did she make that give credence to historians' generally negative portrayal of her?*

CHAPTER RESOURCES

Primary Sources

DOCUMENT 7.1: Woodblock print of Treaty of Shimonoseki negotiations

DOCUMENT 7.2: Excerpts from "Li Hongzhang Negotiates with Japan, 1895"

DOCUMENT 7.3: Excerpts describing Emperor Guangxu and his 1898 reforms

DOCUMENT 7.4: Excerpts describing the activities of the "Boxers" during the uprising, by Fei Qihao, 1900

DOCUMENT 7.5: Excerpts from a letter written by missionary Nellie N. Russel to relatives in Chicago, describing the Boxer Uprising, 1900

DOCUMENT 7.6: Interviews with individuals recalling the Shining Red Lanterns movement

DOCUMENT 7.7a: Excerpts from the preface to *China the Yellow Peril: At War With the World* by J. Martin Miller, 1900

DOCUMENT 7.7b–d: Photographs included in *China the Yellow Peril: At War With the World*, by J. Martin Miller, 1900 (only on the companion website)

DOCUMENT 7.8: Excerpts from "The Yellow Peril," an essay by Jack London, 1904

DOCUMENT 7.9: Excerpts from Sun Yat-sen's Reform Proposal, 1893 (not available on the companion website)

DOCUMENT 7.10: Excerpts from a revolutionary proclamation published by the *Zhonghua Tongmeng Hui* (Chinese Alliance Association), 1907 (not available on the companion website)

DOCUMENT 7.11: Excerpts from "The Revolutionary Army," by Zou Rong, 1903

DOCUMENT 7.12: Photograph of Sun Yat-sen's mausoleum, Nanjing, 2006

DOCUMENT 7.13: Sign describing Sun Yat-sen, 2006

DOCUMENT 7:14: Excerpts from Emperor Puyi's abdication

Supplementary Materials

Item 7.A: Map showing the encroachment of foreign powers on Chinese territory in the late nineteenth century

Item 7.B: Chart Comparing Three Revolutionary Documents

Item 7.C: Guide to Clips from *The Last Emperor*

 Excerpts of these primary source documents appear in this chapter. Go to **www.chinasince1644.com** for the full version of these documents and for the Supplementary Materials.

CHAPTER 7

The End of Imperial Rule

By Jamie Moore

Chapter Contents

Key Idea

China's humiliating defeat by Japan in 1895 precipitated reforms and violence. Ultimately, a combination of internal and external pressures such as land shortages, famine, and high population; foreign encroachment on Chinese territory; and an increasing sense of nationalism brought an end to two thousand years of dynastic rule, paving the way for a new period in Chinese history.

Guiding Questions

What factors led to the Boxer Uprising? What effects did the uprising have?

How were the revolutionary goals for a "new China" that were held by various factions similar and different? How did they become more radical over time?

What role did foreign pressure (Western and Japanese) play in the demise of the Qing dynasty?

What immediate and long-term factors led to the fall of dynastic China?

How did Sun Yat-sen symbolize a new direction for China? How is he portrayed in China today?

Terms to Know

abdication	mausoleum
Boxer Uprising	Meiji Restoration
feudal Japan	reparation
imperial power	*tael*
industrialized	tributary relationship
Manchu	

Essay

By the end of the nineteenth century, the Qing (清) dynasty was crumbling. In addition to growing territorial pressures from European powers, China had to contend with an increasingly strong Japan, which had imperialistic dreams of its own.

The Rise of Japan

While both Japan and China had come under political and economic pressure from the West in the middle of the nineteenth century, the two countries responded differently. In 1868 Japan began a tremendous transformation known as the Meiji ("Enlightened Rule") Restoration. Beginning in 1868, Japan consciously reached out to the West to incorporate Western institutions and technologies into their polity. In this way Japan built a powerful militarized and industrialized nation that not only was able to resist Western pressure but competed with the West in empire-building. This strategy was particularly important as Western nations entered into a period known as "the New Imperialism," where a nation's strength and stature were determined by how many colonies the nation could subdue and command.

In the latter part of the nineteenth century, Japan began to encroach on countries that had a long-standing tributary relationship with China. First, in 1879, Japan annexed the Liuqi Islands.[1] Fifteen years later a rebellion broke out in Korea, and China intervened, sending reinforcements in support of Korea's Joseon dynasty. The Japanese sunk one of the ships carrying Chinese soldiers to Korea, and war broke out between China and Japan. The Sino-Japanese War was a disaster for China, quickly demonstrating Japan's new military strength. Now Japan concluded its own "unequal treaty" with China (see Chapter 5 for the initial series of unequal treaties). In the 1895 Treaty of Shimonoseki (*Maguan Tiaoyue* 马关条约), China was forced to give up Taiwan to the Japanese and to open four more cities to Japanese trade including Chongqing (重庆) far up the Yangzi River (*Chang Jiang* 长江). China also agreed to recognize "the independence of Korea." (In reality, however, Korea became a Japanese colony.) The Chinese had to allow the Japanese to build factories in their Chinese ports and to pay the Japanese reparations of 200 million *taels* (*liang* 两) of silver.[2] China's defeat at the hands of the country that had once looked up to them as the source of civilization was profoundly humiliating to China's educated populace. The Treaty of Shimonoseki brought the age of New Imperialism to China, and the conclusion of the treaty with territorial concessions to Japan was followed by a "Scramble for Concessions" among Western powers, all of whom wanted similar strongholds in China. It was during this time that Hong Kong was "leased" to England and the Germans took control of the Shandong peninsula in a "semi-colonial" arrangement.

In 1905, Japan further demonstrated its strength to the rest of the world by winning a war against Russia. For the first time, the "yellow man" had beaten the white man, and fear of the "yellow peril" began to spread in the West. Distrust and racism targeting the Chinese in the United States had begun in the mid-nineteenth century and led to the Chinese Exclusion Act of 1882, which limited the number of Chinese eligible to immigrate. In Australia the Immigration Restriction Act of 1901 was written to achieve similar ends. Japan's climb to power only increased the West's anxiety over the rise of Asian power and further exacerbated discrimination against individuals of Chinese heritage. Yet at the same time, the strength of an Asian nation was inspiring to progressive Chinese.

---

[1] In Japan the Liuqi Islands are known as the Ryukyu Islands.

[2] A *tael* is approximately one ounce.

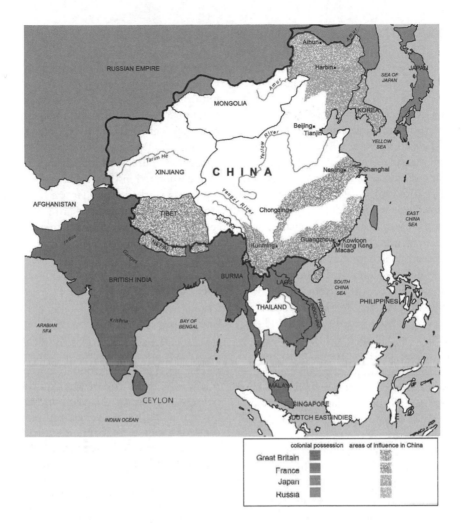

	colonial possession	areas of influence in China
Great Britain		
France		
Japan		
Russia		

"Hundred Days Reforms"

By the end of the nineteenth century, China was a country of sharp contrasts. Evidence of modernization and industry could be found along the coast, where contact with the outside world was the strongest, but not inland. The Qing bureaucracy and the vast majority of Chinese were still firmly rooted in tradition and age-old practices. When Western powers increased their claims in China, this only heightened fears among the Chinese. Some, though, recognized that change needed to occur in China if the country were to survive and keep its independence. Among them was the relatively young emperor Guangxu (光绪). In late 1898, he issued a number of edicts, which became known as the Hundred Days Reforms (*Bairi Weixin* 百日维新). He insisted on changes in education and economic development. He ordered the rebuilding of the navy and training of militias, and he mandated that the bureaucracy be made more efficient. His aunt, the empress dowager Cixi (慈禧) promptly quashed his efforts. She placed the emperor under "house arrest" (in the Forbidden City) and executed many of his key advisors.

The Boxer Uprising

Meanwhile, outside of Beijing (北京), calls for change took a different form. In the late 1800s and early 1900s many secret societies had formed in China, continuing a long historical tradition of rural anti-government protest (see A Closer Look in chapter 3). During this period, however, the secret societies also opposed the increasing presence of Western missionaries. The Boxers United in Righteousness (*Yihequan* 义和拳) emerged in Shandong Province in 1898. As in the case of past secret societies, they practiced martial arts (giving them their name "Boxers"), used magic to ward off evil, and took oaths. Some believed they had special powers that could even protect them from bullets. The group appealed mostly to landless, young peasants, as well as boatmen, disbanded soldiers, and vagrants whose lives had been devastated by famine and/or poverty. Young women also joined the Boxers, including a group called the Shining Red Lanterns (*Hongdengzhao* 红灯照). The Boxers blamed the problems of society on foreigners and Chinese Christian converts. Initially, they destroyed their property. Then in June of 1900, violence escalated when Boxers killed foreigners and Chinese Christians in Tianjin (天津), Beijing, and other cities. The empress dowager Cixi at first wavered in her support of the Boxers, then publicly backed them. Alarmed, foreign nations (including Japan, Russia, Great Britain and the United States) raised a force of 20,000 soldiers and began in August of 1900 to subdue the uprising that was holding many of their citizens under siege. The foreign powers insisted China execute Boxer supporters and pay staggering reparations: 450 million *taels* of silver.[3] Among other concessions, China was to cancel civil service exams for five years in cities where foreigners had died.

Qing Reforms

Finally, following humiliation after humiliation, Qing rulers of the early 1900s seemed ready for reform. In 1905, they sent delegates to five Western countries to study their governments, and they ended the centuries-old examination system. In 1908, the empress dowager Cixi stated that a full constitutional government would be incorporated in China within nine years. The Qing also worked to modernize schools and restructure and centralize the army. Unfortunately for the Qing, many forward-thinking Chinese considered this too little, too late.

Revolution of 1911

The Boxer Uprising, foreign encroachment throughout China, and other problems such as high taxes (issued to pay for new reforms and reparations) and catastrophic flooding led people to call for the end of Manchu rule.[4] Fear of being carved up by the West and anger at the government's ineffectiveness spurred a growing sense of nationalism. Chinese students who had studied abroad and experienced Western and Japanese industrialized, modern societies led the drive to overthrow the Qing dynasty.

The most famous of the revolutionaries was Dr. Sun Yat-sen (*Sun Zhongshan* 孙中山) (1866–1925), who came to be the leader of the Revolutionary Alliance (*Tongmenghui* 同盟会) in the early 1900s. The goal of Sun Yat-sen and his followers was to expel the Manchus, restore China to the Chinese, and establish a republic. They met in secret, raised funds from expatriates, and, most importantly, gained support in the army and among provincial leaders (see A Closer Look for further information on Sun Yat-sen).

In November 1908, the empress dowager Cixi died. A day earlier, in a suspicious coincidence, so had the (imprisoned) emperor

---

[3] This represented more than twice the government's total annual revenue.

[4] The Manchus, a foreign people from what are now Liaoning, Heilongjiang, and Jilin provinces, had invaded Ming dynasty China in the early 1600s and in 1644 established the Qing dynasty (see Chapter 3).

Guangxu. Puyi (溥仪)—a toddler—was named emperor and Manchu regents as his "advisors." In October, an accidental bomb explosion sparked the revolution. Within weeks, many of the provinces joined the uprising. The Qing called on Yuan Shikai (袁世凱)—leader of a powerful North China army and a general in the Qing military—to put down the rebellion.

He, however, worked both sides, negotiating the best position for himself. On December 25, 1911, Sun Yat-sen who had been gathering support for the revolution overseas, returned to China to be named provisional president of the Republic. In February 1912 the Qing court abdicated, and two thousand years of dynastic rule ended. A new age for China began.

Primary Sources

DOCUMENT 7.1:
Woodblock print of Treaty of Shimonoseki negotiations

Japanese and Chinese officials negotiate the treaty at Shimonoseki in 1895 to end the Sino-Japanese War.

Courtesy of Freer Gallery of Art, Smithsonian Institution, Washington, D.C.

 Go to **www.chinasince1644.com** for the color version of the woodblock print in **Document 7.1**.

DOCUMENT 7.2:
Excerpts from "Li Hongzhang Negotiates with Japan, 1895"

H.E[5]. LI. And if I sign this gruesome Treaty I am certain to bring down another avalanche of curses on my head. Think of it!... The Chinese in [Taiwan] are

---

[5] H.E. stands for His Excellency.

unwilling to remove and are equally unwilling to sell their property. If hereafter Proclamations are issued requiring them to do so and they revolt, the Chinese Government cannot be held responsible.

H.E. ITO. My Government will assume all future responsibility.

H.E. LI. I have received a telegram from the Governor of [Taiwan] stating that the [Taiwanese] have revolted and swear that they will not be subject to Japan.

H.E. ITO. Let them revolt. We can manage that.

H.E. LI. This is not said to alarm you. I am telling you the truth out of good-will.

H.E. ITO. I have heard of it.

H.E. LI. If the [Taiwanese] kill the officials and band together to resist, you must not blame me.

H.E. ITO. Let China transfer the sovereignty to us and the whole responsibility will be assumed by the Japanese Government... Our intention is to send troops and officials to take [Taiwan] over within a few weeks after the Treaty has been ratified.

H.E. LI. Someone can be appointed to consult with the Governor of [Taiwan] about all matters pertaining to the transfer.

H.E. ITO. As soon as ratifications have been exchanged the Chinese officials should proclaim the transfer to the [Taiwanese] and we will send troops and officers to take charge...

H.E. LI. One month is rushing the matter. The Zongli Yamen[6] and myself are too far removed from [Taiwan] to know the actual situation there. It would be much better for China to delegate the Governor of [Taiwan] to arrange with the Japanese Governor on the spot what the conditions of transfer shall be. Then, the Treaty having been exchanged we shall be on friendly terms and arrangements can readily be made.

H.E. ITO. One month is sufficient.

SOURCE: Rpt. in Pei-kai Cheng, Michael Lestz, and Jonathan Spence, eds., *The Search for Modern China: A Documentary Collection* (New York: W.W. Norton , 1999) 173–174.

Go to **www.chinasince1644.com** for the full text of **Document 7.2**.

DOCUMENT 7.3:
Excerpts describing Emperor Guangxu and his 1898 reforms

The *Peking[7] Gazette* continued to come daily, bringing with it the following twenty-seven decrees in a little more than twice that many days. I will give an epitome of the decrees so that the reader at a glance may see what the emperor undertook to do. Summarized, they are as follows:

1. The establishment of a university at Beijing.
2. The sending of imperial clansmen to foreign countries to study the forms and conditions of European and American government.
3. The encouragement of the arts, sciences and modern agriculture.

[6] Chinese bureau that managed foreign affairs; see Chapter 6.

[7] Today the city is officially called Beijing.

4. The emperor expressed himself as willing to hear the objections of the conservatives to progress and reform.

5. Abolished the literary essay as a prominent part of the governmental [civil service] examinations…

12. Special rewards were offered to inventors and authors.

13. The officials were ordered to encourage trade and assist merchants.

14. School boards were ordered established in every city in the empire.

15. Bureaus of Mines and Railroads were established.

16. Journalists were encouraged to write on all political subjects.

17. Naval academies and training-ships were ordered.

SOURCE: Isaac Taylor Headland, *Court Life in China: The Capital, its Officials and People* (New York: Fleming H. Revell, 1909) 137–139.

Go to **www.chinasince1644.com** for the full text of Document 7.3.

DOCUMENT 7.4: Excerpts describing the activities of the "Boxers" during the uprising, by Fei Qihao, 1900

As we traveled, the young soldier who had taken my horse away walked close behind my cart, never taking his eyes off me. I thought that he was angry because I had objected to giving him the horse, so I gave little attention to it. Then I noticed something strange in his way of looking at me, as if there was something he wished to say to me. After we had gone on a little farther with the soldier walking behind the cart, still keeping his eyes on me, he heaved a great sigh, and said: "Alas for you—so very young!"

The soldier walking at the side looked sternly at the speaker and said something to him, which I could not hear, but I heard the reply: "This is our own countryman, and not a foreigner." When I saw the expression on their faces and heard these words, suddenly it flashed across me that they had some deep meaning, and I asked the young soldier what was up.

"I don't know," he replied.

"If anything is going to happen," I said, "please tell me."

He hung his head and said nothing, but followed still close to the cart, and after a while said to me plainly: "You ought to escape at once, for only a short distance ahead we are to kill the foreigners."

SOURCE: Fei Ch'i-hao, *Two Heroes of Cathay*, ed. Luella Miner (New York: Fleming H. Revell, 1903) 63–128.

Go to **www.chinasince1644.com** for the full text of Document 7.4.

DOCUMENT 7.5: Excerpts from a letter written by missionary Nellie N. Russel to relatives in Chicago, describing the Boxer Uprising, 1900

That afternoon about 4 o'clock the first attack on us here was made, and the bullets fell like rain for a few moments. Just before we came here, very early one morning,

Mr. Ament went in around the back way to our place and the sight made him sick. The houses, two churches, printing office, school buildings, all were in ruins. Most of the brick walls had been carried away, and not enough wood was left in the place to make a toothpick he said…. We heard from the Chinese officials of the taking of the forts at Tianjin, but we did not believe it, for it did not seem possible such a thing would be done with the ministers shut in the enemy's country—and that a heathen one—with no possible way out. The day after we came in here the custom-houses were fired and the Austrian legation was abandoned. The Boxers, flourishing knives, approached the legation, and the machine guns were turned on them, killing and wounding sixty. This only drove them away for the time. They started fires all about us. The next few days we had to fight fire. We ladies formed in line and passed back the pails and other receptacles for water. Such an olio of articles for fighting fire and for one's life—pitchers, large and small, wash bowls of all sizes, pails, tin cans, flower pots, etc. The Chinese seemed determined to burn us out, and it was not till all about us was either burnt by them, or by us as a protection, that they gave up that time.

SOURCE: Qtd. in J. Martin Miller, *China, the Yellow Peril: At War With the World* (Chicago: Monarch Book Co., 1900) 423–424.

Go to **www.chinasince1644.com** for the full text of **Document 7.5**.

DOCUMENT 7.6: Interviews with individuals recalling the Shining Red Lanterns movement

3. [The town of] Fenglou had the Shining Red Lantern. All the Shining Red Lanterns were women who dressed up completely in red. They waved red fans and carried red lanterns and they could get wind or rain or ride the clouds and call in the mist. Two women facing each other would wave their fans and while waving them would ascend into the sky. That was the kind of thing they did…I used to go to watch the hustle and bustle…

—*Interview with Zhang Yuqi, age 82, Ma Village, Sanlitun Commune, Renping County, January 1966.*

5. Girls who joined the Boxers were called "Shining Red Lanterns." They dressed all in red. In one hand they had a little red lantern and in the other a little red fan. They carried a basket in the crook of their arm. When bullets were shot at them they waved their fans and the bullets were caught in the basket. You couldn't hit them! Some were also possessed by spirits and would say that they were Ma Guiying or Hu Jinchan [famous women warriors who were often portrayed in popular dramas in North China].

—*Interview with Zhu Yunze, age 82, Zhu village, Yeguantun Commune, Renping County, December 1965.*

SOURCE: Pei-kai Cheng, Michael Lestz, and Jonathan Spence, eds., *The Search for Modern China: A Documentary Collection* (New York: W.W. Norton, 1999) 185–186.

Go to **www.chinasince1644.com** for the full text of **Document 7.6**.

DOCUMENT 7.7a: Excerpts from the preface to *China the Yellow Peril: At War With the World* by J. Martin Miller, 1900

Never before has one nation of the world stood against allied civilization as China has stood against Europe and America in the unique contest [the Boxer Uprising]—military, diplomatic and commercial—which is here related…

In a prolonged journey through the Chinese Empire in 1899, the author gathered the historical and descriptive matter which comprise the chapters devoted to those phases of the subject, as well as many of the photographs, which appear as illustrations…. Careful study has been made of the works of the best authors, English, German, French, and American, with assurance that the best book is the one that seeks the best sources for its complete information. The resulting work is here presented with the hope and belief that it will prove of service to its readers.

Source: J. Martin Miller, *China, the Yellow Peril: At War With the World* (Monarch Book Co., 1900) 9–10.

 Go to **www.chinasince1644.com** for the full text of **Document 7.7** and for **Documents 7.7b–d** of the photographs included in *China the Yellow Peril: At War With the World* by J. Martin Miller, 1900.

DOCUMENT 7.8:
Excerpts from "The Yellow Peril," an essay by Jack London, 1904

The menace to the Western world lies, not in the little brown man, but in the four hundred millions of yellow men should the little brown man undertake their management. The Chinese is not dead to new ideas; he is an efficient worker; makes a good soldier, and is wealthy in the essential materials of a machine change. Under a capable management he will go far. The Japanese is prepared and fit to undertake this management. Not only has he proved himself an apt imitator of Western material progress, a sturdy worker, and a capable organizer, but he is far more fit to manage the Chinese than we are. The baffling enigma of the Chinese character is no baffling enigma to him. He understands as we could never school ourselves nor hope to understand. Their mental processes are largely the same. He thinks with the same thought-symbols as does the Chinese, and he thinks in the same peculiar grooves. He goes on where we are balked by the obstacles of incomprehension. He takes the turning, which we cannot perceive, twists around the obstacle, and, presto! is out of sight in the ramifications of the Chinese mind where we cannot follow.

Source: Jack London, "The Yellow Peril" (1904). Rpt. in *Major Problems in Asian American History*, Lon Kurashige and Alice Yang Murray, eds. (Boston: Houghton Mifflin, 2003) 182.

 Go to **www.chinasince1644.com** for the full text of **Document 7.8**.

DOCUMENT 7.9: Excerpts from Sun Yat-sen's Reform Proposal, 1893

I have always felt that the real reason for Europe's wealth and power lies less in the superiority of its military might than in the fact that in Europe every man can fully develop his talent, land resources are totally utilized, each object functions to its maximum capacity, and every item of merchandize [*sic*] circulates freely…these four items are the most basic if our nation is to become wealthy, strong, and well governed. For our nation to ignore these four items while concerning itself exclusively with ships and guns is to seek the insignificant at the expense of the basic…

It has been thirty years since we began to imitate the West. We have language schools, as well as military and naval academies, to train specialists in Western affairs. We have mining and textile enterprises to open up financial resources. We have steamship and railroad companies to facilitate transportation. Yet we still lag behind Europe in overall achievement. Why? The reason is that we have not, really, embarked upon the completion of the four tasks, as described above, on a nationwide basis. When we do, given China's human and natural resources, we should be able to overtake Europe in twenty years.

SOURCE: Pei-kai Cheng, Michael Lestz, and Jonathan Spence, eds., *The Search for Modern China: A Documentary Collection* (New York: W.W. Norton, 1999) 169–171.

DOCUMENT 7.10: Excerpts from a revolutionary proclamation published by the *Zhonghua Tongmeng Hui* (Chinese Alliance Association), 1907

A PUBLIC DECLARATION

Since the beginning of China as a nation, we Chinese have governed our own country despite occasional interruptions. When China was occasionally occupied by a foreign race, our ancestors could always in the end drive these foreigners out, restore the fatherland, and preserve China for future generations of Chinese. Today when we raise the righteous standard of revolt in order to expel an alien race that has been occupying China, we are doing no more than our ancestors have done or expected us to do. Justice is so much on our side that all Chinese, once familiarizing themselves with our stand, will have no doubt about the righteousness of our cause….

We…strive not only to expel the ruling aliens and thus restore China to the Chinese but also to change basically the political and economic structure of our country. While we cannot describe in detail this new political and economic structure since so much is involved, the basic principal behind it is liberty, equality, and fraternity. The revolutions of yesterday were revolutions by and for the heroes; our revolution, on the other hand, is a revolution by and for the people….

At this juncture we wish to express candidly and fully how to make our revolution today and how to govern our country tomorrow.

1. *Expulsion of the Manchus from China.* The Manchus of today were known as the Eastern Barbarians *Dong Hu* during bygone years. Toward the end of the Ming dynasty they repeatedly invaded our border areas and caused great difficulties. Then, taking advantage of the chaotic situation in China, they marched southward and

forcibly occupied our country. They compelled all Chinese to become their slaves, and those who did not wish to subjugate themselves were slaughtered, numbering millions. In fact, we Chinese have not had a country for the past two hundred and sixty years. Now that the day has finally arrived when the brutal and evil rule by the Manchus must come to an end, we do not expect much resistance when our righteous army begins to move. We shall quickly overthrow the Manchu government so as to restore the sovereignty of China to the Chinese....

2. *Restoration of China to the Chinese.* China belongs to the Chinese who have the right to govern themselves. After the Manchus are expelled from China, we will have a national government of our own....

3. *Establishment of a Republic.* Since one of the principles of our revolution is equality, we intend to establish a republic when we succeed in overthrowing the Manchu regime. In a republic all citizens will have the right to participate in the government, the president of the republic will be elected by the people, and the parliament will have deputies elected by and responsible to their respective constituents. A constitution of the Chinese Republic will then be formulated, to be observed by all Chinese. Anyone who entertains the thought of becoming an emperor will be crushed without mercy.

4. *Equalization of landownership.* The social and economic structure of China must be so reconstructed that the fruits of labor will be shared by all Chinese on an equal basis....

To attain the four goals as outlined above, we propose a procedure of three stages. The first stage is that of a military rule.... [D]uring the first stage, the Military Government, in cooperation with the people, will eradicate all the abuses of the past; with the arrival of the second stage the Military Government will hand over local administration to the people while reserving for itself the right of jurisdiction over all matters that concern the nation as a whole; during the third or final stage the Military Government will cease to exist and all governmental power will be invested in organs as prescribed in a national constitution. This orderly procedure is necessary because our people need time to acquaint themselves with the idea of liberty and equality. Liberty and equality are the basis on which the Republic of China rests....

The brilliant achievements of China have been known throughout the world, and only recently has she suffered numerous difficulties. We shall overcome these difficulties and march forward....

SOURCE: Pei-kai Cheng, Michael Lestz, and Jonathan Spence, eds., *The Search for Modern China: A Documentary Collection* (New York: W.W. Norton, 1999) 202–205.

DOCUMENT 7.11:
Excerpts from "The Revolutionary Army" by Zou Rong, 1903

I offer to my most revered and beloved 400 million countrymen of the great Han people to prepare them for the path they are to follow:

- China is the China of the Chinese. Countrymen, you must all recognize the China of the Chinese of the Han race.
- Not to allow any alien race to lay their hands on the least rights of our China....

- To set up a central government, which will act as a general body to run affairs.
- In each area and province a deputy to a general assembly is to be elected by vote in public elections. From these deputies, one is to be elected by vote to serve as provisional president to represent the whole country A vice-president is also to be elected, and all *zhou* [prefectures] and *xian* [counties] are to elect a number of deputies.
- The whole population, whether male or female, are citizens.
- All men have the duty to serve as citizen-soldiers.
- Everybody has the duty of bearing the burden of taxation.

SOURCE: John Lust, trans., *The Revolutionary Army: A Chinese Nationalist Tract of 1903* (Paris: Mouton, 1968).

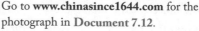 Go to **www.chinasince1644.com** for the full text of **Document 7.11**.

DOCUMENT 7.12:
Photograph of Sun Yat-sen's mausoleum, Nanjing, 2006

The mausoleum was built just outside Nanjing by the Guomindang government in 1926 to honor Sun Yat-sen. Nanjing, at that time, was the capital of China. The stairway is 323 meters long and 70 meters wide. One of the signs in English reads: "The map of the whole mausoleum looks like an alarm bell, which symbolizes the never-ending struggling spirit of Dr. Sun Yat-sen and his devotion of himself to the cause of waking up the masses and saving the Chinese nation and state." The site continues to be visited by tens of thousands of people every year. This photograph was taken on a weekday in May. *(Photo by Liz Nelson)*

Go to **www.chinasince1644.com** for the photograph in **Document 7.12**.

DOCUMENT 7.13: Sign describing Sun Yat-sen, 2006

(Photo by Liz Nelson)

Go to **www.chinasince1644.com** for the photograph in Document 7.13.

DOCUMENT 7.14: Excerpts from Emperor Puyi's abdication, 1912

The Whole Country is tending towards a republican form of government. It is the Will of Heaven, and it is certain that we could not reject the people's desire for the sake of one family's honor and glory.

We and His Majesty the Emperor hand over the sovereignty to the people. We decide the form of government to be a constitutional republic.

In this time of transition, in order to unite the South and the North, We appoint Yuan Shikai to organize a provisional government, consulting the people's army regarding the union of the five peoples, Manchus, Chinese, Mongolians, Mohammedans [Muslims], and Tibetans with their territories. These peoples jointly constitute the one great Republic of China.

We and His Majesty the Emperor will retire to a peaceful life and will enjoy the respectful treatment of the nation.

This was signed by the emperor, by Yuan Shikai as prime minister, and also by the other ministers.

SOURCE: Eva March Tappan, ed., *China, Japan, and the Islands of the Pacific*, The World's Story: A History of the World in Story, Song, and Art, vol. 1 (Boston: Houghton Mifflin, 1914) 261.

Go to **www.chinasince1644.com** for the full text of **Document 7.14**.

Activities:

ACTIVITY 1: Overview of the Manchu Decline

Review events from earlier in the nineteenth century (see Chapters 4–6), and read the introductory essay. Write an overview of the reasons for the Manchu decline incorporating your thinking on the following:

1. What was going wrong for the Manchus?
2. How was the population changing, and what effect might this have had?
3. What role did modernity play in the demise of the dynasty?
4. What were the effects of foreign encroachment? How did the Manchu government respond? What might they have done differently?

ACTIVITY 2:
Examining the Results of the Sino-Japanese War, 1895

Look at the painting of the negotiations (7.1) and write down everything you notice.

1. Who is depicted in the painting?
2. What differences in posture and dress can you see?
3. From looking at this painting, what can you infer about each side and the negotiations?

Read the transcript of negotiations between the Chinese delegate Li Hongzhang and the Japanese delegate Ito Hirobumi at Shimonoseki (7.2).

1. What tone does each delegate take with the other?
2. What is each side trying to convey?
3. Who has the upper hand, and why?

As a class you will discuss the final treaty and its cost to China.

1. How do you think the Chinese intelligentsia felt?
2. How were the Chinese perceived by the rest of the world?
3. How does the tone of the negotiations compare to the painting?

Creative Extension:

Westerners including missionaries wrote copiously about the situation in "the Orient." In the voice of a missionary, write a letter home explaining how the treaty affected or didn't affect different people such as a Westener, a Chinese traditionalist, and a Chinese reformer.

ACTIVITY 3: Analyzing the Effects of Imperialism in China

View the map "Imperialism in the Nineteenth Century" (Item 7.A) and see Chapter 7 Activity Websites on the companion website for additional resources. Remember that in the eighteenth century, China had strongly resisted foreign influence. Examine all the places where Western powers had influence in and around China.

Prepare to discuss as a class or in a small group.

1. How did Western powers gain influence in China?
2. What areas did they control and why?
3. What does this tell us about the Qing dynasty in the nineteenth century?
4. How does this compare to the Qing dynasty of the eighteenth century? (See Chapter 4.)
5. Compare the Qing territorial expansion of the seventeenth century with the growing foreign influence of the nineteenth century (see Chapter 3 and Item 3.B). What conclusions can you draw?
6. If this map of the late nineteenth century were shown to a Chinese citizen of the time, how might he or she feel? (Remember that many educated Chinese people were aware of what had happened to India and countries in Africa at the hands of imperialists.)
7. How did the situation faced by the Chinese reflect the wider trend of European encroachment around the world?

ACTIVITY 4: Analyzing and Promoting Emperor Guangxu's Reforms

Examine the emperor's proposals for change (7.3). In small groups, discuss:

1. What subjects did the emperor's reforms include?
2. What problems did these proposed reforms appear to address?
3. Based on the proposed reforms, what did Emperor Guangxu see as the role of government?
4. Would it be possible to do all that he proposed? What would it have taken to accomplish his goals? What countries have undertaken and succeeded at such wide-ranging reforms?
5. Which, if any, government departments or ministries in your country address these subjects?

Creative Extension:

Draw a cartoon for a Western newspaper of the period about emperor Guangxu's reforms. Express support or dislike and include a title or caption.

ACTIVITY 5: Exploring the Boxer Uprising

You will work in a group of three on one of the documents related to the Boxer Uprising/Shining Red Lantern Movement (7.4–7.6). After reading it closely, discuss in your group:

1. Who created or wrote the text, and for what purpose?
2. How does this affect the content of the document?
3. List at least six key pieces of information from the document.
4. How does this document further inform you about the Boxer Uprising?
5. Was religion the issue? If so, in what way? If not, what was at the heart of the violence?

Jigsaw to form new groups of three in which each member has read a different document. Share with each other the information you extracted from your primary source. In a class discussion you will compare the Boxer Uprising to other episodes of significant social unrest such as the White Lotus, and the Taiping, Nian and Muslim Rebellions.

1. How was the Boxer Uprising similar to and different from other social unrest?
2. What conclusions can you draw from the comparisons?
3. How might the Boxer Uprising have been used by the government to promote nationalism?
4. How does the Boxer Uprising compare to anti-religious violence that erupted in China later in the twentieth century?

ACTIVITY 6: The Rise of the "Yellow Peril"

Read the preface to J. Martin Miller's book *China the Yellow Peril: At War With the World* and examine several photographs he included in his book (7.7a–d on the companion website). Take notes on the following questions:

1. What ideas are included in the choice of words in the title? What does the title lead you to expect?
2. What does Miller say was his purpose in writing this book?
3. How did he go about writing it? Was it a reasonable way to approach the writing of a country's history? Why or why not?
4. What responses do the photos evoke now? What responses do you think they were likely to evoke in 1900? Why do you think Miller chose to include them?
5. How might a book such as this affect people's opinions and views of China, Asia, and/or Chinese Americans?

Read and prepare to discuss the excerpts from Jack London's essay "The Yellow Peril" (7.8).

1. What is the significance of the title?
2. What is most striking about this essay?
3. How does London describe the Chinese? The Japanese? The West? Make a three-column table and list examples of each.
4. What does London see as the connection between the Chinese and Japanese?
5. Why does London not fear the "Brown Peril"?
6. When did the "Yellow Peril" become a concern for Westerners? Why?
7. Writing in 1904, what did London see as the future? Were his predictions accurate? In what way?

After reading both excerpts, write what you think was the source of Western fears.

Creative Extension:

Role play a conversation between Miller and London where they discuss the position they think their government should take toward supporting a revolutionary government or sustaining imperial rule in China.

ACTIVITY 7: Comparing Three Revolutionary Documents

You will be assigned to a small group.

1. As a group, study one of three revolutionary documents (7.9-7.11) and complete the section about that document using the chart on Item 7.B in Supplementary Materials on the companion website.
2. The groups will then jigsaw so that the new groups represent and share the thinking of each of the revolutionary documents.
3. Discuss similarities and differences as a group and complete the chart 7.B. Be prepared to share your ideas with the class.

ACTIVITY 8: Examining the Legacy of Sun Yat-sen

Read about Sun Yat-sen in the introductory essay and A Closer Look at the end of the chapter. Examine the photographs of his mausoleum (7.12) and the sign describing Sun Yat-sen (7.13). Prepare to discuss:

1. Why would the Guomindang government have decided to build this for Sun Yat-sen? Compare the layout to other important historic sites in China, such as the Temple of Heaven in Beijing and the Monument to Martyrs in Nanjing.
2. Why do you think he was so widely admired over other revolutionaries?
3. When you read the sign, pay attention to the language used. What did the Chinese government want people to think about Sun Yat-sen?

4. What can you conclude from the fact that both the Guomindang government and the Chinese Communist Party claim Sun Yat-sen as the father of the nation? (See Chapter 9 for more information.)

Creative Extension:

Write an obituary about Sun Yat-sen for a foreign newspaper extolling his early efforts and ideas for the development of a "new China."

ACTIVITY 9: Manchu Abdication

The Qing dynasty ended in 1911. You will read the Manchu abdication edict as a class (7.14) and discuss:

1. What do you notice about the edict?
2. What language is used? What is the tone?
3. What was the role of Yuan Shikai in the revolution?
4. What role is the emperor hoping for in the future? Do you think that this will happen? Why or why not?

Watch part of the film *The Last Emperor* up to the Japanese invasion. See "Guide to Clips from *The Last Emperor*," item 7.C in Supplementary Materials on the companion website. What do you learn about life within the confines of the Forbidden City? How does the life of the Qing leaders compare with that of leaders in other countries around the world in the same time period?

ACTIVITY 10: Reflecting on the End of the Imperial Era

As a class, you will brainstorm based on classwork and readings: What were the immediate and long-term reasons for the fall of the Qing dynasty? When finished, pick one or two reasons that the majority agree were the most significant. Explain in writing why the top reasons the majority of the class agreed upon were so significant.

EXTENDED RESEARCH:

In groups or individually, research revolutions in other countries in the world (e.g. the United States, France, or countries in Africa, South America, or Central America). Each group will have a different country. Address:

1. What happened in the country you selected?
2. What factors caused the people to revolt? Was there a final straw, or was it a culmination of events?
3. How does this revolution compare to the 1911 revolution in China?

Each group will present its findings and then join in a class discussion about revolution in general and the forces that guide it.

Suggested Resources

Books

Aisin-Gioro Pu Yi. *From Emperor to Citizen: The Autobiography of Aisin-Gioro Pu Yi.* Trans. W.J.F. Jenner. New York: Oxford University Press, 1987.
The autobiography of the last Qing emperor who came to the throne as a toddler.

Bergère, Marie-Claire. *Sun Yat-sen.* Stanford: Stanford University Press, 2000.

Rowe, William T. *China's Last Empire: The Great Qing.* Cambridge, Mass.: Belknap Press of Harvard University Press, 2009.

Silbey, David. *The Boxer Rebellion and the Great Game in China.* New York: Hill and Wang, 2012.

Websites

"En Chine: Le gâteau des Rois et…des Empereurs," Bibliothèque Nationale de France
http://gallica.bnf.fr/ark:/12148/bpt-6k716261c/f8
A French political cartoon from 1898 depicting China as a cake or pie being divided by Great Britain, Russia, France, and Japan.

Fei Ch'i-hao: The Boxer Rebellion, 1900, Internet Modern History Sourcebook
http://www.fordham.edu/Halsall/mod/1900Fei-boxers.asp
A Chinese account of the Boxer Uprising.

Yellow Promise / Yellow Peril: Foreign Postcards of the Russo-Japanese War (1905–1905), Massachusetts Institute of Technology Visualizing Cultures
http://ocw.mit.edu/ans7870/21f/21f.027/yellow_promise_yellow_peril/
Essays by John W. Dower and visual narratives and lessons about the relationship between China, Japan, and Russia in the early twentieth century.

Films

The Last Emperor (162 mins; 1987)
The film poignantly captures the anachronism of a child-emperor coming to power in China in the early twentieth century and the subsequent political turmoil.

■ **A CLOSER LOOK**

Dr. Sun Yat-sen: Father of the Nation

Sun Yat-sen was born in 1866 to a poor rural family near Guangzhou (formerly Canton). He received his early education in a local village school, but the rest of his schooling took place at assorted educational institutions associated with missionary efforts in Hawaii (where his elder brother had a business), Hong Kong, and Guangzhou. He completed medical school in Hong Kong in 1892.

As he experienced more of the industrialized West, he became increasingly involved with revolutionaries, including members of secret societies. Influenced by Western ideas and a nationalistic desire to improve China, he formed an organization called the Revive China Society (*Xingzhonghui*), which eventually had branches in a number of countries. In 1894, he wrote to a high-ranking Qing official explaining his ideas for how China needed to reform and modernize (see 7.9). His ideas were ignored and in 1895, he helped plan an uprising in Guangzhou. The plot was exposed, and Sun Yat-sen fled to Hong Kong and then Japan. Living in exile, he cut his queue and began to wear Western clothes. In 1896, he was briefly arrested in London by Qing authorities but was able to effect a dramatic rescue, which made him internationally famous. For years Sun Yat-sen traveled in Europe, the United States, and Japan, speaking, writing, and raising funds.

By 1905, he had refined his ideas and developed the Three Principles of the People (Sanmin Zhuyi): nationalism, democracy, and social welfare. He also organized the Revolutionary Alliance (Tongmenghui), whose goal was to overthrow the Qing dynasty and establish a Chinese republic. Sun Yat-sen's message and desire for revolution appealed to many who had studied abroad, as well as women and the poor, who felt marginalized.

Between 1906 and 1911, the Alliance planned several uprisings, all of which failed.

Sun Yat-sen was not in China at the time of the revolution of October 1911, but returned in December to accept the title of Provisional President of the Chinese Republic. Though his tenure as leader was brief, Sun Yat-sen worked until his death trying to promote a unified Republican nation in the face of constant opposition from warlords (see Chapter 9). He died of cancer in early 1925 while he was in Beijing to negotiate with warlord leaders. Despite his many setbacks, the vast majority of Chinese regard Sun Yat-sen as the father of the nation (*Sun Guofu*).

■ *To read more about Dr. Sun's ideas in his essay "Fundamentals of National Reconstruction," see the companion website.*
Discuss: How was Sun Yat-sen similar to and different from revolutionary leaders in other countries?

■ A CLOSER LOOK

Qiu Jin: Revolutionary Heroine

Today Qiu Jin is considered a heroine for her fight as a revolutionary against Manchu rule in China. She was born in 1875 to a relatively well-to-do family and was one of the few girls in China to receive an education. In 1904, unhappy in the marriage her parents had arranged, Qiu Jin left her husband and two children to study in Japan.

Like others who studied abroad, she was struck by Western ideas and modernization. She attended a vocational school, but her passion lay with revolutionary politics and feminist issues. Qiu Jin wrote on both topics, pushing for an overthrow of the Qing as well as for greater equality between men and women, and an end to practices such as foot-binding, female infanticide, and arranged marriages.

In 1906, she returned to China, where she taught at a school in Zhejiang Province and founded the *Chinese Women's Journal*. Contemporaries considered Qiu Jin's occasional preference for men's clothing and participation in military drills shocking. She continued her efforts to bring political change to China by working to unite different revolutionary groups to better ensure success. But in 1907, Qing officials captured and executed her for participating in revolutionary activities.

After the fall of the dynasty, Qiu Jin became an inspiration for girls all over China. A nationalist and revolutionary, she had the courage to take a stand against the government and a society that oppressed women.

■ *Compare Qiu Jin to female role models in other countries.*

UNIT THREE

Struggles to Create a Unified China

(1911–1949)

UNIT OVERVIEW

By Ryan Bradeen and Liz Nelson

The words highlighted in this overview are key people, concepts, or movements that appear in the chapters that follow.

The fledgling Republic of China built from the ashes of the Qing dynasty was soon itself in tatters, with the country split between bickering **warlords** constantly battling for power. While the armies fought, young men and women from all walks of life tried to find solutions to the deep-seated problems that threatened to destroy the country. From this dangerous and unsettled period, the leaders of New China would emerge. The carving of China into independent territories during the Republican period echoed the fragmentation

that had followed the end of many previous dynasties[1]. One of the most notable aspects of Chinese history is that during these chaotic periods, peasants and intellectuals alike believed that a politically unified China should be the goal.

In China's earlier periods of disunity, vicious warfare and turmoil created desperate times for the general populace. The rural population suffered from the destruction of crops, the marching of armies back and forth across their lands, the loss of young men pressed into military service, endless taxes, and the disruption of economic activity. Cities were the targets of conquests, and as a result urban residents were often caught in the middle of pitched battles, their homes and business confiscated or destroyed, their families separated. The turmoil of the Republican era (1911-1949) was no different; modern weaponry made the conflicts only more deadly and devastating.

Throughout China's history, the downfall of powerful empires and fragmentation of the country into contending regions also had surprising and positive side effects: great outpourings of intellectual activity. In the confusion of periods of disunity, no single philosophy, religion, or ideology was held up by the central

---

[1] At the end of the Han Dynasty (220 C.E.) China was divided for more than 300 years as many kingdoms fought one another. Again at the end of the Tang dynasty (907 C.E.) China experienced fifty-three years of regional warfare. There have been many such periods of disunity and regional warfare in China's long history.

TIMELINE (1911–1949)

1910–1945: Japanese colonial rule in Korea

1911–1912: Republican Revolution and the founding of the Republic of China

1912: Guomindang (the National People's Party) formed

1913: United States extends full diplomatic recognition to the Republic of China

1913: 13th Dalai Lama returns to Tibet and assumes temporal and spiritual leadership

1914: World War I breaks out after the assassination of Archduke Franz Ferdinand

1915: Japan issues the Twenty-One Demands

1916–1928: Warlord Period

1917: Russian Revolution

1918–early 1920s: Red Scare in the United States

1918: Armistice between Allies and Germany signed on November 11

1919: Paris Peace Conference concludes with the signing of the Treaty of Versailles

1919: May Fourth Movement begins

1920: League of Nations founded in Paris

1920: Nazi Party formed in Germany

1921: Chinese Communist Party formally organized at First Congress in Shanghai

1922: Soviet Union established

1926: Communists and Guomindang work together in First United Front: Northern Expedition against warlords

1927: Guomindang turn on Communists in Shanghai

1929: World economic crisis follows "Black Friday"; stock exchange collapse in New York

1929: Joseph Stalin, general secretary of the Communist Party of the Soviet Union since 1922, becomes de facto dictator

1930: Indochina Communist Party founded

1931: Mukden (Shenyang) Incident

1932: Franklin Delano Roosevelt sworn in as 32nd president of the United States

1933: Japan withdraws from the League of Nations

1933: Adolf Hitler appointed chancellor of Germany

1934: Puyi becomes emperor of Manchukuo under Japanese auspices

---

government as the official belief system to which the populace should adhere. Therefore, philosophers, scientists, and writers were much freer to explore new intellectual territory.[2]

[2] During the Warring States period (475–221 B.C.E.), for example, intellectual activity is described with the moniker "One Hundred Schools of Thought," referring to the many philosophers of religion, government, war, and diplomacy who established schools, traveled broadly, and freely debated during this period of chaos. Confucius and several of his most important disciples, the early Daoists, Sun Zi (author of *The Art of War*), and the founders of Legalist thinking all grew out of this vibrant intellectual environment.

During the first half of the twentieth century, a similar **intellectual vitality** characterized China.

China was not stagnant economically during this period. New railways were built, telegraph lines were put up, new banks and factories were formed. But all of these efforts had only limited success because of the destructive warfare that kept breaking out in various provinces as the warlords and their armies fought each other.

Out of the political and military upheaval created by the warlords and the intellectual turmoil resulting from the **May Fourth Movement**, two leaders emerged who would lead

1934: Soviet Union joins the League of Nations

1934–1935: Long March

1936: Zhang Xueliang and his supporters kidnap Chiang Kai-shek in Xi'an, Second United Front formed

1937: Japan occupies eastern China; Nanjing Massacre

1939: World War II begins: Nazi Germany invades Poland, and France and Britain declare war on Germany

1941: Japan attacks Pearl Harbor; the United States declares war on Japan, Germany, and Italy

1941–1945: Japan occupies Vietnam

1943: Cairo Conference; Chiang Kai-shek and Madame Chiang Kai-shek meet with President Roosevelt and British Prime Minister Winston Churchill

1945: "V-E Day" ends war in Europe

1945: United States drops two atomic bombs on Japan; Japan surrenders August 14

1945–1952: Japan occupied by Allied Powers, chiefly the United States

1945: World Bank founded

1945: Korea liberated from Japanese control but soon divided into zones of occupation by the United States and Soviet Union

1945: Taiwan, under Japanese control since 1895, is returned to China

1945: Ho Chi Minh declares the founding of the Democratic Republic of Vietnam

1946–1954: First Indochina War between France and the Viet Minh

1946: Marshall Mission to China

1946–1949: Civil war in China

1947: New constitution in Japan creates a parliamentary state

1947: India and Pakistan gain independence from Great Britain

1947: Taiwan becomes a separate province of China

1948: Mahatma Gandhi assassinated

1949: India adopts a constitution

1949: On October 1 Mao Zedong declares the founding of the People's Republic of China

1949: Chiang Kai-shek and Guomindang forces flee to Taiwan

China on a path to resurgence: **Mao Zedong** and **Chiang Kai-shek**. Each man would come to the fore of opposing political factions, the **Chinese Communist Party** (CCP) and the **Guomindang**, with competing beliefs about how to unify the nation and heal the deep political and social wounds. Mao was primarily concerned with conditions in rural China, where the vast majority of the population lived. His proposals called for sweeping change—revolution—to overturn the long-standing rural social structures and empower the peasants. Chiang, on the other hand, proposed to lead citizens into a reinvigorated Chinese lifestyle rooted in ancient traditions. At times, these two leaders would collaborate, forming "united fronts" against the common enemies. But more often they saw each other as deadly archrivals to be destroyed for the sake of the nation.

By the early 1930s, the power of the warlords had diminished as the Guomindang and the CCP grew into increasingly potent military and political organizations controlling more and more of China's land mass. But the two parties had to contend with a menacing **Japanese Army** that threatened the entire nation with colonialization. One could picture the situation as a boxing match with three contenders in the ring at the same time, each trying to knock out the other two. In 1934, Chiang and his Guomindang forces, determined to eliminate the Communists, drove the CCP out of southeastern China on the legendary **Long March**; the Communists regrouped at Yan'an in Shaanxi Province.[3]

As the Japanese continued to encroach, two of Chiang's generals kidnapped him to try to force him into creating a **United Front** against Japan. The **Xi'an Incident**, as it became known, ended with a fragile alliance among the Chinese warring factions. China's armed forces, however, were no match for Japan's imperial army. By the end of 1937, the Japanese occupied key cities and the most fertile regions in eastern China. Chiang's Guomindang government retreated into the country's interior, to Chongqing. The Communists continued to rebuild their strength in Yan'an. The horrors of the **Nanjing Massacre** were followed by years of brutal occupation by the Japanese, which included **biological warfare**.

After World War II ended, any semblance of cooperation between the CCP and the Guomindang disappeared. Representatives of the United States tried to broker a collaborative new government, and when that failed to materialize, they supported Chiang Kai-shek's efforts to take control of China. The CCP, on the other hand, had help from the Soviet Union. The **civil war** that had plagued the country in the 1930s broke out again in 1946. The Guomindang government was unable to stem spiraling inflation, nor could it effectively counter the compelling communist ideology that spread throughout China. As the CCP's People's Liberation Army (PLA) mounted one successful military campaign after another, the Guomindang government retreated to the island of Taiwan. On October 1, 1949, Mao Zedong proclaimed the founding of the **People's Republic of China**.

---

[3] North central China, in a region north of the city of Xi'an.

CHAPTER RESOURCES

Primary Sources

DOCUMENT 8.1: "Medicine," a short story by Lu Xun, first published in *Xin Qingnian* (*New Youth* magazine), May 1919

DOCUMENT 8.2: Excerpts from Act 2 of *Teahouse,* a play by Lao She, 1957

DOCUMENT 8.3: Table of Contents from *Xin Qingnian* (*New Youth* magazine), Vol. 6 No. 5, May 1919

DOCUMENT 8.4: Excerpts from "Why I Write Poems in the Vernacular" by Hu Shi, in *Xin Qingnian* (*New Youth* magazine), May 1919

DOCUMENT 8.5: Excerpts from "My View on Marxism" by Li Dazhao, in *Xin Qingnian* (*New Youth* magazine), May 1919

DOCUMENT 8.6: Slide show "Duolun Road" on the New Culture Movement in the 1920s and 30s in Shanghai

DOCUMENT 8.7: Excerpts from a memoir by Li Xiuwen (1890–1992), describing the political turmoil of the 1920s

DOCUMENT 8.8: Clips from Northeast Historic Film (Archives), 1934 (on companion website)

CLIP 1: "Americans Living in Shanghai"

CLIP 2: "The Paper Chase"

CLIP 3: "An American Family Tours the Countryside"

Supplementary Materials

ITEM 8.A: Map of areas controlled by warlords, 1925

 Excerpts of these primary source documents appear in this chapter. Go to **www.chinasince1644.com** for the full version of these documents and for the Supplementary Materials.

CHAPTER 8

The Early Republican (1912–1916) and Warlord (1916–1928) Periods

By Ryan Bradeen and Nan Ye

Chapter Contents

The Rise and Fall of the Republic
The Reign of the Warlords
Intellectual Vitality
The May Fourth Movement

Key Idea

Like the end of many previous dynasties, the fall of the Qing was followed by a period of division when competing warlords battled for power. But the disunity also heralded intellectual exploration that led to the development of ideas and the emergence of leaders who would found a New China.

Guiding Questions

What were the characteristics of the Early Republican Period?

Why did warlords come to power and how did they preserve their power?

Why did the political disunity of the Early Republican Period lead to intellectual vitality?

What were the characteristics and legacy of the May Fourth Movement?

Terms to Know

Guomindang
ideology
Nationalist
propaganda
Republic of China (ROC)
Treaty of Versailles
vernacular
warlords

Essay

The overthrow of the Qing (清) dynasty ushered in a shockingly brief period of hope for rejuvenating China and tackling the dire issues that confronted the nation. After working for years to bring about the downfall of the Manchu government, Sun Yat-sen (*Sun Zhongshan* 孙中山) was elected president of the Republic of China (*Zhonghua Minguo* 中华民国) on January 1, 1912. He held the post for six weeks.

The troops who had mutinied against the Manchus were no match for the imperial armies stationed around the capital. Without the support of the Qing military—especially its most senior general, Yuan Shikai (袁世凯)—the Republic would be short-lived. On the very day of his election, Sun Yat-sen sent a telegram to Yuan Shikai, stating "[The presidency] is actually waiting for you, and my offer will eventually be made clear to the world."[1] Yuan accepted the offer, forced the abdication of the last Manchu emperor, and on February 13, 1912 became president of the Republic of China.

The new government immediately planned national elections for December 1912. Sun Yat-sen's Guomindang Party (*The National People's Party* 国民党) won a majority of seats.[2] It soon became apparent, however, that Yuan Shikai had no intention of following the new Republican laws. The newly elected Guomindang party leader, Song Jiaoren, was assassinated by figures associated with Yuan Shikai. By October 1913, Yuan had outlawed the Guomindang and forced its members out of the legislature. Hunted by Yuan's troopers, Sun Yat-sen slipped out of the country, leaving Yuan as virtual dictator of the Republic of China.

While Yuan Shikai had eliminated the Guomindang—his most pressing threat—he had also undermined his own support among the military, many of whom genuinely believed that the Republic was China's best chance to modernize the nation. The final straw was Yuan's December 1915 attempt to install himself as the new emperor of China. Massive protests sprang up all over the country. Even Yuan's old officers rebelled, declaring themselves and their provinces independent. Coincidentally, within six months, Yuan was dead of kidney failure. The Republic of China survived, but only in name. For the next decade, the Republican government carried on at the whim of whichever military leader was strong enough to control the capital, but the central government did not have complete control over the country. The basic functions of law, order, and public works were left to the provinces.

The Reign of the Warlords

The men who assumed control of the provinces in the period between 1916 and 1928 most often were provincial army commanders. These generals-turned-warlords were a varied group. The most prominent were professional soldiers who had been trained in China's New Army, established in 1895 under the command of Yuan Shikai. Many were committed to the ideal of a unified China, especially one in which they themselves would play a starring role. Some warlords, like Yan Xishan in Shanxi Province, were quite progressive, establishing schools and promoting social reforms. Others were little more common criminals who had consolidated a base through corruption, crime, and intimidation.[3]

The handful of major warlords who dominated the 1910s and 1920s commanded sizeable regions, populations, and deposits of resources. For example, the smallest of the major warlord regions, Yan Xishan's Shanxi Province, was approximately the same geographic size as modern Greece or Louisiana and had huge quantities of coal, aluminum, and other strategic minerals. With such resources at his

---

[1] Qtd. in Jonathan D. Spence, *The Search for Modern China* (New York: W. W. Norton, 1999) 263.

[2] Formerly spelled Kuomintang and abbreviated as KMT, the Guomindang are also known as the Nationalists.

[3] Spence, 284.

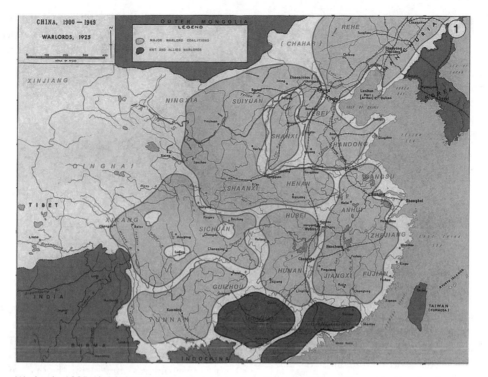

Warlords, 1925: Light-shaded areas represent major warlord coalitions; darker-shaded areas were controlled by the Guomindang and allied warlords.
(Courtesy of the United States Military Academy.)

disposal, a warlord could create a mini-state generally independent from the rest of China. Within their mini-states some warlords established a government, set up schools along modern lines, paved roads and encouraged commerce. They issued proclamations using patriotic language, and they acted as head-of-state within the territories they controlled.

Since the cornerstone of warlord authority hinged upon control of military force, a warlord's first priority was to secure funds to pay and equip his soldiers. The size of these armies was not small. By the mid-1920s, nearly two million Chinese soldiers were under arms in warlord armies spread across the country.[4] Scholars estimate that in the years between 1917 and 1927, more than 600,000 people were

killed in battles between warlords.[5] The cost of these armies outstripped the normal tax revenue of the provinces. Warlords, therefore, created new taxes on basic necessities like salt, established toll roads, or forced farmers to pay as many as twenty years' taxes in advance. Others turned to more criminal activities like reviving opium production or subdividing their territories to local criminals in return for payment and military service. Many warlords took out large loans from foreign banks to shore up their positions in the rapidly shifting domestic alliances and intrigues that characterized the period. As a result, most political leaders and the general populace continued to believe that a politically unified China was the natural state to which honorable rulers should strive to return.

---

[4] By comparison, during the 1920s the U.S. Army had only 175,000 soldiers in its ranks.

[5] R.J. Rummel, *China's Bloody Century* (New Brunswick, NJ: Transaction Publishers, 1991). www.hawaii.edu/powerkills/NOTE2.HTM

Intellectual Vitality

Yet, as in earlier periods of disunity in China, the turmoil of the Republican period sparked a great outburst of intellectual activity. The established elite and younger generations sought to find solutions to the country's dizzying array of problems in government and politics, culture and education, social organization and economics, and foreign relations and the military. The elimination of the imperial exam system left Chinese writers and students open to explore much more freely than under the Qing.[6] They drew upon the deep well of Chinese philosophy and political thought as well as the many currents of European, American, and Japanese ideas that were circulating in translated articles and books, in university and school classrooms, and through interaction with European and American businessmen, missionaries, and teachers stationed in the treaty ports.

Chinese men and women also traveled and studied abroad in large numbers. Many studied in Japan, which was held up as a model of an Asian nation that had avoided domination by foreign powers and modernized its institutions and society. Others studied in the United States or Europe, where they were exposed to the heated intellectual debates among socialists, communists, fascists, feminists, labor union activists, progressives, anarchists, liberal democrats, and capitalists that characterized the early twentieth century outside of China as well. Among those who traveled to Europe were 100,000 Chinese men who served as laborers supporting Allied forces in France against Germany in World War I. Upon their return to China, some of these students, laborers, and travelers became schoolteachers, translators, newspaper editors, writers, and political and social activists who tried to apply the ideas they had absorbed in their travels to the challenges that China confronted.

New Publications

Those who did not travel abroad benefited through the development of new schools and small local newspapers that published articles on political and social issues. Often these journals were short-lived, as their radical views eventually brought the unwelcome attention of the local warlords. But as quickly as they could be shut down, new papers would spring up to replace them. The new journalism created a constant flow of information that stirred people's minds and hearts with new ideas, stimulated discussions of deep-seated cultural and political problems, and inspired hope for rejuvenating the nation before it collapsed under the many internal and external pressures pushing and pulling against it.

Even the warlords themselves, as they constructed their regimes to govern their territories, were drawn into the intellectual currents of the day. Yan Xishan of Shanxi Province believed he had created a flawless ideology for governing his region by combining the best features of "militarism, nationalism, anarchism, democracy, capitalism, communism, individualism, imperialism, universalism, paternalism, and utopianism."[7] In many ways, the chaotic and bloody Republican period echoed the era of the "One Hundred Schools of Thought" (*Baijia Zhengming* 百家争鸣) from which the philosophies of Confucianism (*Rujia* 儒家) and Daoism (*Daojia* 道家) emerged in the sixth century B.C.E. (Refer to Primary Source's *The Enduring Legacy of Ancient China* for more information on Confucianism and Daoism.)

---

[6] A series of increasingly difficult exams open only to men had served as the system whereby government officials would ideally be appointed on merit rather than family status and connections (see Chapter 2). As a man passed each exam, he would become eligible for a position of greater authority. From the Song dynasty (960 C.E.) on, the exams were based on mastery of four key Confucian books, including the *Analects*, and five ancient classics. These exams were abolished under the Qing in 1905.

[7] Qtd. in Spence, 284.

The May Fourth Movement

The events of May 4, 1919, galvanized intellectuals and the general populace throughout China as people recognized the desperate need for radical change to Chinese society. Three days earlier, news had reached Beijing that at the Paris Peace Conference to end World War I, the Allied Powers had awarded Japan all of Germany's colonial possessions in China's Shandong Province (山东省).[8] This was in exchange for the naval assistance the Japanese had provided against the Germans. Students in Beijing's major universities marched to the homes of several prominent politicians to protest the treaty. Soon thereafter, outraged students, teachers, workers, and businessmen in nearly one hundred cities around China protested against the settlement. In Paris, Chinese students and workers surrounded the Chinese delegation's quarters, preventing the representatives from signing the Treaty of Versailles.

These initial protests evolved into a wide range of actions and organizations all over the country, including the formation of student and labor unions, boycotts of foreign (particularly Japanese) goods, and the printing of radical newspapers, magazines, and books. The May Fourth Movement (*Wusi Yundong* 五四运动) is considered to be the most important intellectual period in twentieth-century China.

Out of the protests, study groups, and unions formed in the May Fourth Movement, the leaders of China's resurgence would eventually emerge. Its future political leaders, such as Mao Zedong (毛泽东), Chiang Kai-shek (*Jiang Jieshi* 蒋介石), Zhou Enlai (周恩来), and Deng Xiaoping (邓小平), were all deeply influenced by the May Fourth Movement and its reaction against warlords and foreign imperialism. China's most creative writers and thinkers of the century forged their craft in the pages of the newspapers and journals that circulated through the nation during this era. Lu Xun (鲁迅), considered to be the founder of modern Chinese literature, wrote many of his most famous works in the years immediately surrounding the May Fourth Movement. Ba Jin (巴金), Lao She (老舍), Mao Dun (茅盾), and Hu Shi (胡适) were among the famous writers of novels, short stories, poems, and plays who found their voice in this turbulent period.

All sought to make sense out of their lives and foresee a hopeful future for their country, even as the crows and vultures of warlordism and imperialism descended upon the corpse of the imperial tradition. While terribly chaotic and dangerous to live through, the Republican period produced writers and leaders who, through their accomplishments, laid the foundation for a new China that today is a resurgent world power.

---

[8] The Treaty of Versailles was signed at the conclusion of the conference.

Primary Sources

DOCUMENT 8.1: "Medicine," a short story by Lu Xun, first published in *Xin Qingnian* (*New Youth* magazine), May 1919

"You know, that little bastard was really too much—even tried to get the jailer to rebel against the emperor!"

"Aiya! Have you ever heard the likes of that?" A man in his twenties is filled with overweening righteous indignation.

"Well, it was like this. Redeye Ah-yi went to question him and find out whatever he could, but the Xia kid acts as though it's just a regular conversation and starts tellin' Redeye how the Great Manchu Empire belongs to all of us. Now stop and think for a second, does that sound like talk you'd expect out of a human being? Redeye knew right from the start there was no one in the kid's family except his old mother, but he never imagined he could be *that* poor – couldn't squeeze a single copper out of him. Now that means Ah-yi is pissed off to begin with, right? Then the Xia kid's gotta go rub salt in the wound by talkin' *that* kinda stuff. Well Ah-yi gave him a couple good ones right across the mouth!... Gettin' hit didn't faze that punk one little bit. His only comeback was to say, 'Pitiful, pitiful.'"…

SOURCE: Lu Xun, *Diary of a Madman and Other Stories*, trans. William A. Lyell (Honolulu: University of Hawaii Press, 1990) 55.

 Go to **www.chinasince1644.com** for the full text of **Document 8.1**.

DOCUMENT 8.2:
Excerpts from Act 2 of *Teahouse*, a play by Lao She, 1957

FOURTH ELDER CHANG: I was arrested by you gentlemen here in 1898, and spent more than a year in prison for saying that "the Great Qing Empire is about done for."

SONG ENZI: You have a remarkable memory. Life treating you well these days?

FOURTH ELDER CHANG: Thanks to you, yes. I got out of prison just before the year 1900, and joined the Boxers to help the dynasty oust the foreigners.[9] We did battle with the foreigners a few times; but despite all our efforts the Great Qing Empire collapsed in the end. Well, it deserved to collapse. I'm a Bannerman myself, but I must speak the truth.[10] Now, every day I'm up at dawn and get together two baskets of vegetables, and by mid-morning I have them all sold. Because I earn my own keep I'm healthier than ever. If the foreigners ever venture to attack again, I'll be ready for them. I'm a Bannerman. Bannermen are Chinese too! And how've you two been keeping?

WU XIANGZI: We muddle along. When there was an emperor, we served the emperor; when Yuan Shikai became president, we served President Yuan Shikai. And now… Song Enzi, how would you put it?

SONG ENZI: Now we serve whoever puts food in our bellies….

SOURCE: Lao She, *Teahouse*, trans. John Howard-Gibbon (Hong Kong: Chinese University Press, 2004) 78.

 Go to **www.chinasince1644.com** for the full text of **Document 8.2**.

---

[9] The Boxer Uprising took place in 1900; see Chapter 7.

[10] As the Manchus invaded China in the early 1600s, they organized their forces into eight military units known as "banners" that consisted of soldiers and their family members. The system remained in place until the Qing dynasty ended in 1912.

DOCUMENT 8.3: Table of Contents from *Xin Qingnian* (*New Youth* magazine), Vol. 6 No. 5, May 1919

···

New Youth Magazine
Vol. 6 No. 5
(Eighth Year of the Republic; Published in May 1919)

SOURCE: *Xin Qingnian* (*New Youth* magazine), Vol. 6 No. 5 (1919). Trans. Diana Lin.

Go to **www.chinasince1644.com** for the text of Document 8.3.

DOCUMENT 8.4: Excerpts from "Why I Write Poems in the Vernacular" by Hu Shi, in *Xin Qingnian* (*New Youth* magazine), May 1919 (See definition of *vernacular* in glossary)

···

I clearly stated that "Classical Chinese is a half dead language and should not be taught using a methodology used to teach a live language." I also stated that "so-called live language is a language that is used in daily life, such as English, French and vernacular Chinese. The so-called dead languages, such as [ancient] Greek and Latin, are not used daily, in other words, they're dead....

[T]he literary revolution that I propose is based on the current situation of Chinese literature and has little to do with the new literature movements in Europe and America. The reason that I sometimes quote Western literary history, (specifically the part when European authors began to write in their native languages three or four hundred years ago), is only because the need for vernacular literature in China today is very similar to the need in Europe then. If we study what those countries accomplished, we will reduce our conservatism and increase our courage....

SOURCE: Hu Shi, "Why I Write Poems in the Vernacular," *Xin Qingnian*, May 1919: 488–499. Trans. Nan Ye.

Go to **www.chinasince1644.com** for the full text of Document 8.4.

DOCUMENT 8.5: Excerpts from "My View on Marxism" by Li Dazhao, in *Xin Qingnian* (*New Youth* magazine), 1919

I have not done much research on Marxism; therefore it is bold of me to attempt to talk about Marxism here. However, ever since the Russian Revolution, Marxism is about to sweep through the world. Countries such as Germany, Austria, and Hungary started their revolutions one after another following Marxist ideology. While Marxism caught people's attention around the world and stirred up great changes, it also generated many misunderstandings and misinterpretations.

Although our study of Marxism is slight, there has been a great deal of interest in, and criticism of, his works in various countries as a result of the 100th anniversary [of Marx's birth] in 1918. We have collected and edited these writings to introduce them to our readers in this Marxism edition of *New Youth* magazine. I believe it is not without benefit for readers to gain some insight into this world-altering theory through our discussions. If there are any errors due to the authors' limited knowledge of Marxism, we hope our dear readers will offer their corrections.

SOURCE: Li Dazhao, "My View on Marxism," *Xin Qingnian*, May 1919: 521–537. Trans. Nan Ye.

Go to **www.chinasince1644.com** for the full text of Document 8.5.

DOCUMENT 8.6: Slide show "Duolun Road" on the New Culture Movement in the 1920s and 30s in Shanghai

Go to **www.chinasince1644.com** for the slide show of Document 8.6.

DOCUMENT 8.7: Excerpts from a memoir by Li Xiuwen (1890–1992), wife of an army officer, describing the political turmoil of the 1920s

In the war years,[11] we moved often from city to city. We couldn't eat and sleep peacefully. Suddenly an order would be given by army headquarters to move. The families would hurry to pack and follow the army by boat or by sedan chair.

---

[11] Between 1912 and 1927

Sometimes we heard the noise of cannons. Sometimes the enemy advanced behind us. It was hard for a woman to take these adverse conditions.

Whenever we arrived in a new city, we rented a place to live, or we stayed in the barracks. There wasn't much discipline in the army. The people were terrorized by the soldiers. When the army came into a city, people locked their doors. The shops stopped doing business. Some stores had their doors half open. If the merchants got paid for their merchandise, they would open their doors wide and continue to do business….

SOURCE: Li Xiuwen, unpublished memoir.

Go to **www.chinasince1644.com** for the full text of Document 8.7.

DOCUMENT 8.8: Clips from *Northeast Historic Film* (Archives), 1934

Go to **www.chinasince1644.com** for the clips of Document 8.8.

Activities

ACTIVITY 1: Examining the Common People

After reading the introductory essay, read the story "Medicine" (8.1) and prepare to discuss the following questions either as a class or in small groups.

1. The blood-soaked bun is the symbolic key to understanding the story. For what reasons did revolutionaries like the Xia boy shed their blood? For what reasons did the Hua family purchase the blood? How would Lu Xun, the author, account for the differences in the purposes between revolutionaries and more ordinary people like the Hua family?

2. Why did the Xia boy feel sorry for Redeye? Why did the people at the teahouse feel sorry for the Xia boy?

3. Do you think Mother Xia understands her son's cause? Give two reasons to support your opinion.

4. Reread the section at the end of the story about the red-and-white wreath placed on the revolutionary's grave. Here you can almost hear the author's voice. Who do you think placed the wreath at the revolutionary's grave? Why?

5. What do you learn about life in China in 1919 from this short story? Cite evidence from the text.

6. What do you think might be the author's purpose for writing the story? How do you think the story might have influenced the May Fourth Movement?

7. What other literature do you know that has political overtones?

ACTIVITY 2: Examining the Revolutionary

Part 1: Write

Working in pairs or individually, develop a first-person narrative from the perspective of one of the characters in "Medicine": Little Bolt (the sick boy), Big Bolt (the boy's father), Uncle Kang (the executioner), Redeye (the prison warden), Mother Xia (the revolutionary's mother), or a teahouse customer. In your narrative, make sure you address the following issues in a fictionalized style.

- Your relationship to the Xia boy
- Your place in society
- Why the boy was executed and whether it was justified
- What the Xia boy would or should do differently if he were given a second chance to carry out his cause

Part 2: Present

Jigsaw: Reconvene in new groups of five or six students in which each student represents a different character. Present your first-person narratives to the group.

Part 3: Synthesize

Compile the narratives and create a third-person narrative introducing the Xia boy, the revolutionary.

ACTIVITY 3: The Republic and Its People

Read Act 2 of Lao She's *Teahouse* (8.2) before class. In class, you will choose roles and perform the play. To prepare, consider the following questions:

1. Analyze the different characters' philosophies and the strategies that they rely on to survive and adapt to the social changes during this period.
2. Categorize the characters according to their philosophies and survival strategies. Create a description of the general philosophy and strategy of each category.
3. What do you learn about life in and around Beijing in 1922? How had things changed (or not) since 1919?
4. What do you think might have been Lao She's purpose in writing this play?

Creative Extension:

- Voices in the Head: Choose a moment from the play, and be prepared to either 1) freeze in place as a character in the play while classmates share what you could be thinking or 2) to say what your character might be thinking.

- Create a cartoon, a poster, or a woodblock print that reflects a sense of the times as Lao She depicts them.

ACTIVITY 4: Analyzing the May Fourth Movement

After reading the table of contents of *New Youth*'s May 1919 issue (8.3) and two excerpts from that issue (8.4 and 8.5), prepare to discuss as a class:

1. How did publications like *New Youth* mobilize intellectuals to think, discuss, and debate about social, political, and literary issues in Chinese society?

2. What kind of new cultural ideas and thoughts did magazines like *New Youth* stimulate in young intellectuals who carried out the May Fourth Movement?

ACTIVITY 5: Evaluating the Writing System

After reading excerpts from "Why I Write Poems in the Vernacular" (8.4) (See definition of *vernacular* in glossary), answer the following questions.

1. What might have been some of the reasons that motivated young intellectuals like Hu Shi to promote writing in vernacular Chinese?

2. What kind of challenges do you think they might have encountered in promoting writing (including poetry writing) in the vernacular?

3. From the proposed rules for writing in the vernacular, what can you conclude about writing in the traditional style using classical Chinese?

4. Who would benefit from such a literary revolution? Why?

5. List some immediate effects that writing in the vernacular could have on early twentieth-century Chinese society. What might be the long-term significance of the change?

6. How is this movement tied to the goals and ideology of the May Fourth Movement?

ACTIVITY 6: Examining the Intellectuals

Look at the slide show "Duolun Road" (8.6), and use books and online sources to learn about the lives of Hu Shi, Li Dazhao, Lu Xun, and others. Discuss, then write an essay about one of the questions.

1. What did Hu Shi, Li Dazhao, and Lu Xun have in common? How were they different? What did all the individuals commemorated on Duolun Road have in common?

2. What ideologies did they embrace and what paths did they embark on as their lifelong careers?

3. What influence did they have on Chinese people and society in the long term?

ACTIVITY 7: Political Turmoil of the 1920s

While reading excerpts from Li Xiuwen's memoir (8.7), consider:

1. What do you learn about the life of soldiers and their families during the early warlord era from this document?

2. How did the political turmoil affect people's lives both in the countryside and in cities? Cite evidence from the text.

3. The excerpt describes how people, the army and their families celebrated the 1925 unification in Guangxi, thinking there would be no war again. When did the "normal and safe life" they dreamed of eventually come?

4. What is the relationship between the Chinese perception of war and peace depicted in the memoir and the strong emphasis on political stability and economic prosperity by the current Chinese government?

Creative Extension:

As a class, create a photo montage or a mural to show the problems of life in the warlord era. Contribute one event illustrating a problem and place it in the proper chronological order.

ACTIVITY 8: Examining Westerners' Perspective

After viewing the film clips from the Northeast Historic Film archives (Document 8.8 on the companion website), you will discuss as a class, in a group, or with a partner:

1. What surprised you in the film clips?

2. What do you see in Clip 1 that is similar to what you would expect to see in a wealthy family in the United States during the early 1930s? What is different?

3. In Clip 2, Westerners are shown riding their horses over farm fields. Based on what you know about Chinese traditional views on farming, what does this suggest about the relationship between the average foreigner in 1930s China and the average Chinese person? The mounds in the background of the shot are possibly ancestral gravesites, though it is hard to be 100 percent positive without excavating the site. Suppose the mounds are indeed grave mounds. Considering Chinese reverence for their ancestors, how might this affect the Chinese farmers' reaction to foreigners riding across their fields? What might be concluded about foreigners' attitude toward Chinese people in general, and rural Chinese in particular?

4. In Clip 3, how would you describe the interactions the American family had with the local villagers? What do you think was the villagers' attitude toward the touring Westerners? What was the Westerners' attitude towards these villagers?

5. What conclusions can you draw from the three film clips?

6. These were homemade family films (like a modern-day home video). How does that affect the content? How might a homemade film be different from a documentary, for example?

Suggested Resources

Books

Buck, Pearl S. *The Good Earth*. New York: Washington Square Press, 1931.
A novel about a farmer and his family confronted by new practices that threaten to wash away old traditions. It includes themes of women's rights, family, class conflict, spiritual and moral trials, and hardships of the modern world. Buck won the Pulitzer Prize for this work, and in 1938, won the Nobel Prize for Literature.

Dong, Stella. *Shanghai: The Rise and Fall of a Decadent City*. New York: William Morrow, 2000.
A history of the city at the center of China's turbulent revolutionary years.

Hahn, Emily. *The Soong Sisters*. New York: Doubleday, 1941.
Written by an American expatriate living in China, this biography offers insight into the inner workings of the Republican era.

Lan, Hua R. and Vanessa L. Fong. *Women in Republican China: A Sourcebook*. Armonk, NY: M.E. Sharpe, 1999.
Essays by activists of the May Fourth Movement.

Lao She. *Blades of Grass: The Stories of Lao She*. Trans. William Lyell. Honolulu: University of Hawaii Press, 1999.
A collection of short stories set in the era of the early Republic.

Lao She. *Rickshaw*. Honolulu: University of Hawaii Press, 1979.
A novel about a rickshaw puller hoping to make a successful life for himself against the backdrop of revolution, warlords, and social chaos.

Lu Xun. *Diary of a Madman and Other Stories*. Trans. William Lyell. Honolulu: University of Hawaii Press, 1990.

Ng, Janet and Janice Wickeri. *May Fourth Women Writers: Memoirs*. Hong Kong: Research Centre for Translation, the Chinese University of Hong Kong, 1996.

Spence, Jonathan and Annping Chin. *The Chinese Century: A Photographic History of the Last Hundred Years*. New York: Random House, 1996.

Zarrow, Peter Gue. *China in War and Revolution, 1895-1949*. New York: Routledge, 2005.

Websites

Asia for Educators, Columbia University
http://afe.easia.columbia.edu
Select the 1900–1950 section for primary sources and essays on Republican China and the May Fourth Movement.

Before and After the May Fourth Movement, Asia for Educators, Columbia University
http://afe.easia.columbia.edu/special/china_1750_mayfourth.htm
An overview, primary sources, and discussion questions about the May Fourth Movement.

Chinese Warlords
http://commons.wikimedia.org/wiki/Chinese_Warlords
Images of Chinese Warlords.

Lu Xun
http://chineseposters.net/themes/luxun.php
Biographical information and posters of Lu Xun.

May Fourth Movement, 1919
http://chineseposters.net/themes/may-fourth-movement.php
Background information and posters of the May Fourth Movement.

Virtual Shanghai
http://www.virtualshanghai.net/Photos/Images
A website about the history of Shanghai from the mid-nineteenth century to the present. It includes documents, maps, images, and essays.

Films

China in Revolution, vol. 1 of *China: A Century of Revolution* (120 minutes, 2007)
This documentary provides footage of the Republican Period and interviews with Chinese people who lived through this era.

The Last Emperor (162 mins; 1987)
This film poignantly captures the anachronism of a child-emperor coming to power in China in the early twentieth century and the subsequent political turmoil.

Rickshaw Boy (120 mins; 1982)
An adaptation of Lao She's novel *Rickshaw*. The film captures the grim realities of life for the urban working poor in 1920s China.

Writers and Revolutionaries (60 mins; 1992)
Volume IV of the ten-part *Pacific Century* series focuses on the role of intellectuals in the rise of twentieth-century nationalism and progressivism in the East.

■ **A CLOSER LOOK**

Chen Duxiu: In the Thick of Things

Chen Duxiu (1879–1942), the first party secretary of the Chinese Communist Party, had always been a nonconformist. Born in Anhui Province and tutored by his grandfather, Chen received a classical Chinese education, but in an informal setting. This, combined with his exposure to Western political and philosophical theories while studying in Japan, led Chen to critically examine conventional Chinese beliefs and practices.

When only twenty-five years old and still studying in Japan, Chen founded his first newspaper. This paper and all of his later publications would promote revolutionary ideas using Chinese vernacular language instead of the classical Chinese language used in most other publications. Upon his return to Shanghai in 1915, Chen established *New Youth*, the single most important journal of the Republican era. It was read eagerly by students, thinkers, and revolutionaries around the nation. People gathered in groups to read the precious articles and passed them around until the paper was in tatters.

During his early career, Chen was a strong supporter of the Republican government. But by 1919, Chen wrote, "A false signboard 'Chinese Republic' has been hanging for eight years now but it is still the old medicine which is being sold."[12]

Following the 1919 student protests in Beijing, Chen was at the center of the May Fourth Movement, which spread across the country in waves largely tuned to the circulation of issues of his *New Youth*.

Disillusioned with the workings of the supposedly democratic Republic, Chen searched for other means to address China's many fundamental political and social problems. As early as 1919,

communism appeared to offer Chen an attractive alternative, one he saw as having demonstrated clear success in transforming Russian society. By early 1920, Chen was at the center of efforts by Chinese revolutionaries and Soviet agents to organize a Chinese Communist Party. In 1921, he was elected party secretary of the CCP at its founding meeting in Shanghai. Chen held this post until 1927, when he was forced to resign due to disputes with Soviet advisors and other CCP leaders. After his resignation Chen was imprisoned by the Guomindang for five years, after which he gradually faded from prominence among China's revolutionary leaders.

■ *Discuss publications that you believe have had an impact on people's views and on political activism. What role can and should the media play in politics?*

---

[12] Chen Duxiu, "Basis for the Realization of Democracy," *Xin Qingnian* (*New Youth* magazine), Vol. 1, 14. Qtd. in Benjamin Schwartz, *Chinese Communism and the Rise of Mao* (Cambridge, MA: Harvard University Press, 1961) 13.

CHAPTER RESOURCES

Primary Sources

DOCUMENT 9.1: "Hometown," a short story by Lu Xun, first published in *Xin Qingnian* (*New Youth* magazine), May 1921

DOCUMENT 9.2: Excerpts from "The Guidelines of New Life Movement" by Chiang Kai-shek, *Central Daily News*, May 15, 1934

DOCUMENT 9.3: Excerpts from "Report on an Investigation of the Peasant Movement in Hunan" by Mao Zedong, March 1927

DOCUMENT 9.4: "The Long March," a poem by Mao Zedong, 1935

DOCUMENT 9.5: "Jinsha Jiang" ("The River of Golden Sand"), an anonymous account describing this segment of the Long March, 1934–1935

DOCUMENT 9.6: "The Bridge of Iron Chains," an account describing crossing the Luding Bridge on the Long March, 1934–1935

DOCUMENT 9.7: "Jiajin Shan" ("The Great Snow Mountain"), an anonymous account describing a segment of the Long March, 1934–1935

DOCUMENT 9.8: Excerpts from "Political Mobilization for the War of Resistance," a lecture by Mao Zedong, May 1938

DOCUMENT 9.9: "Manifesto on the Seizure of Chiang Kai-shek," a telegram sent to the nation by General Zhang Xueliang, December 12, 1936

DOCUMENT 9.10: "The Rebellion in Xi'an," a report in the *Manchester Guardian Weekly*, July 16, 1937 (only on companion website)

DOCUMENT 9.11a & b: Photographs at site of the seizure of Chiang Kai-shek outside Xi'an, 2006

DOCUMENTS 9.12a–c: Cartoons by Sapajou in *The North China Daily News*, 1936–1937

DOCUMENT 9.13: Photograph of Zhou Enlai, Mao Zedong, and Bo Gu, 1937

Supplementary Materials

ITEM 9.A: Guidelines for "Hometown" character interviews, Activity 1, part 3, Creative Extension

ITEM 9.B: Map of the Long March

ITEM 9.C: Map of China under Chiang Kai-shek, 1928–1937

 Excerpts of these primary source documents appear in this chapter. Go to **www.chinasince1644.com** for the full version of these documents and for the Supplementary Materials.

CHAPTER 9

United Fronts: The Guomindang vs. the Communists (1921–1937)

By Ryan Bradeen and Nan Ye

Chapter Contents

Key Idea

As the Republic of China frayed into competing warlord territories, two major forces emerged: the Guomindang led by Chiang Kai-shek and the Communist Party of China. Throughout the 1920s and 1930s, these two forces would twice form united fronts against common enemies; and twice these alliances would break apart in bitter feuds. The rivalry between the Guomindang and the Communists would define the era and determine the path of modern China.

Guiding Questions

How did the political situation that led to the First United Front compare to the one that led to the Second United Front?

How does the gap between urban China and rural China during this era reflect the political contest between the Guomindang and the Communists?

How did the Long March and the Xi'an Incident shape the future of the Chinese Communist Party?

How was the Chinese Communist Party able to survive this era against the economically, politically, and militarily superior Guomindang?

Terms to Know

feudal
gentry

soviet (as in Jiangxi Soviet, for example)
Chinese Communist Party (CCP)

Essay

In July 1921, thirteen men filtered secretly into a Shanghai girls' school shuttered for summer vacation. Over the next ten days, they would launch a national Chinese Communist Party (*Zhongguo Gongchandang* 中国共产党) that unified the numerous small cells spread across the country. Chen Duxiu (陈独秀), editor of the revolutionary journal *New Youth* (*Xin Qingnian* 新青年), was elected leader of the party.

Among those attending the meeting was a young Communist from Hunan Province, Mao Zedong (毛泽东). Born in 1893, Mao was the eldest son of prosperous farmers. He received a progressive education in a modern high school, and in 1918 was given a position as a clerk in Peking University's library.[1] There he began to study communism under the direction of Li Dazhao (李大钊), the university's head librarian and China's leading authority on communism. In December 1919, Mao returned to Hunan, where he became a teacher and a contributor to local political publications.

Delegates at the founding of the Chinese Communist Party (CCP) discussed the structure of the party, its goals, and how to achieve them. Their main priorities included: unifying the nation, addressing the exploitation of rural Chinese by landlords, eradicating foreign imperialism in China, and preparing the way for a socialist revolution. One of the most disputed topics was what attitude the CCP should take towards the Guomindang (国民党).[2] Some argued that Sun Yat-sen (*Sun Zhongshan* 孙中山) was just another warlord and should be resisted as such. Others believed that, although they did not agree with all of Sun's ideas, they should support his attempts to unify the nation. It would take another year for CCP leaders to agree to seek an alliance with the Guomindang in order to defeat the warlords.

---

[1] Peking is Beijing written in the Wades-Giles romanization system.

[2] Formerly spelled Kuomintang and abbreviated as KMT, the Guomindang are also known as the Nationalists.

Sun Yat-sen, the Guomindang, and the First United Front

After fleeing into exile in 1913, Sun Yat-sen had gradually rebuilt the Guomindang in Guangzhou, but his position remained fragile. The CCP, with its backing from the Soviet Union, was an attractive partner. In 1919, the newly founded Soviet Union had renounced its colonial privileges in China. The Russians offered advisors to help the Guomindang improve its governing ability, as well as military equipment and financial support. The Russians hoped that Sun would become a critical ally to them in Japan's ambitions in Manchuria and Siberia. In early 1924, the Guomindang began to accept CCP members into its own ranks, forming the First United Front (*Diyici Tongyi Zhanxian* 第一次统一战线). Chen Duxiu, Li Dazhao, Mao Zedong, Zhou Enlai, and many other CCP members were given important posts within the Guomindang.

One of the immediate outcomes of the First United Front was the establishment of the Whampoa Military Academy in Guangzhou. The academy trained young recruits in modern military techniques based on Russian models and with Russian equipment. The commandant of the Whampoa Academy was a young officer named Chiang Kai-shek (*Jiang Jieshi* 蒋介石) who had just returned from training in Moscow.

Chiang Kai-shek was born in 1887 in the Yangzi Delta region to a family of upper-class salt merchants. After training in Japanese military academies, Chiang returned to Shanghai after the 1911 Republican Revolution and joined the Guomindang. In addition to his political work, Chiang learned to navigate Shanghai's seamy underside, where opium-running, dirty politics, revolution-making, and crime intersected with China's wealthiest business circles and foreign dignitaries. Chiang rose through the ranks of the military, becoming a trusted protégé of Sun Yat-sen. Following Sun's unexpected death in early 1925, Chiang Kai-shek, possessing the loyalty of the officers he had trained at Whampoa, became one of the highest-ranking members of the Guomindang.

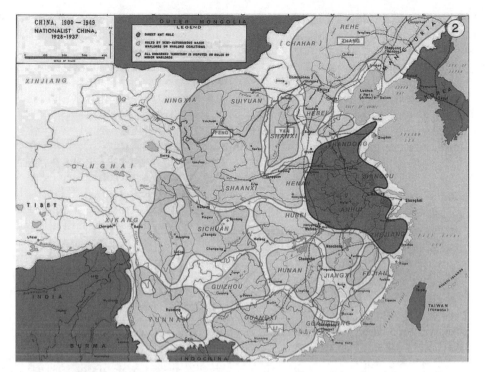

Nationalist China 1928–37: Dark-shaded areas were regions under direct Guomindang rule; light-shaded areas were ruled by semi-autonomous major warlords or warlord coalitions; unmarked territories were in dispute or ruled by minor warlords. *(Courtesy of the United States Military Academy.)*

The Northern Expedition Against the Warlords

On July 1, 1926, the Guomindang army marched out of Guangzhou. As Chiang Kai-shek would later say, the moment had come for the Guomindang to prove "whether or not the Chinese nation and race [could] restore their freedom and independence."[3] This campaign, called the Northern Expedition (*Beifa Zhanzheng* 北阀战争), involved three thrusts against the warlords of southeastern China. Experienced CCP labor and peasant organizers—Mao Zedong among them—were sent ahead to arrange strikes and sabotage to weaken the warlords before the Guomindang army even arrived.[4] In many cases, warlord soldiers

defected to the Guomindang side or fled when faced with their more disciplined and better-equipped forces. By early 1927, the Northern Expedition had overrun warlord opposition in seven provinces south of the Yangzi River, including the major cities of Shanghai, Nanjing, and Wuhan.

The Shanghai Purge

Momentum, public support, and international opinion all pointed towards a rapid reunification of China under Guomindang leadership. But the success of the initial stage of the Northern Expedition revealed rifts in the alliance between the Guomindang and the CCP. Chiang Kai-shek, emboldened by his recent successes, decided to break with the Communists, whom he saw as a threat to China's tradition and economy.

---

[3] Qtd. in Spence, *The Search for Modern China* (New York: W. W. Norton, 1999) 329.

[4] Mao Zedong was the head of the Peasant Training Institute.

On April 12, 1927, soldiers loyal to Chiang attacked Communist party members and labor unions in Shanghai. During this purge, known as the Shanghai Purge (*Shanghai Datusha* 上海大屠杀), hundreds of CCP activists and sympathizers were killed and protests brutally put down. In the following months, Guomindang forces hunted down Communists all over China. Leaders fled for their lives, and the party itself was dispersed into small, disconnected cells. Mao Zedong, for example, escaped with a ragtag band of CCP soldiers and bandits to the mountainous border between Hunan and Jiangxi provinces. The First United Front was over. It had gone a long way towards achieving its goal of national reunification, but at great cost for the Chinese Communist Party.

The Nanjing Government (1928–1937) and Japan

The stunning success of the Northern Expedition, combined with his elimination of the CCP leaders and their allies, left Chiang Kai-shek as the undisputed head of the Guomindang. By January 1928, he had been named commander in chief of the Guomindang, as well as chairman of the Central Executive Committee.

Chiang, however, did not have long to enjoy his triumph. Despite the new government's wide popularity, the Guomindang was desperately short of money. From his new capital in Nanjing, Chiang reactivated many of his contacts in the Shanghai underworld, who helped the Guomindang strong-arm the Shanghai business community into giving the government massive "loans," ostensibly to fund the next stage of the reunification campaign.

By early 1928, the Guomindang had raised enough money to send its armies into the field again. Guomindang forces, allied with several warlords including Yan Xishan of Shanxi Province (see Chapter 8), crossed the Yangzi River headed towards Beijing. Beijing was controlled by Zhang Zuolin, another powerful warlord who also ruled Manchuria in China's northeast.

As Guomindang troops moved into North China, however, they entered an arena in which Japanese business interests and the Japanese army were major power brokers.[5] Zhang Zuolin, for example, had built his powerful army with Japanese advisors, equipment, and funds.

In May 1928, Japanese soldiers stationed in Shandong Province clashed with Guomindang troops, forcing Chiang Kai-shek to reroute his army. Weeks later, with Chiang poised to defeat Zhang Zuolin and capture Beijing, Japan pressured Zhang to retreat to Manchuria, while Japanese troops committed to guarding the passes into Manchuria against a Guomindang advance. As Zhang's train approached Manchuria's capital, however, Japanese agents assassinated the warlord, hoping to provoke a wider war in North China that would give them an excuse to invade Manchuria. But Zhang's son, Zhang Xueliang (张学良), assumed his father's leadership of Manchuria and quickly pledged allegiance to the Guomindang. The Japanese would have to wait until 1931 to conquer Manchuria.

The Jiangxi Soviet

Chiang Kai-shek was reluctant to enter into a full-scale war with Japan. He was already facing a series of rebellions by warlords, and, more ominously from his point of view, the remnants of the Chinese Communist Party had regrouped and seized control of several large rural regions. Chiang established a policy of "internal pacification first, then external resistance." He intended to face Japan only when he had the full weight of a completely unified Chinese nation behind him. While perhaps tactically sound, this policy was hugely unpopular with the general populace.

In January 1931, Guomindang armies attempted to overpower the largest of the new CCP refuges, the Jiangxi Soviet (*Jiangxi*

---

[5] In 1919, the Treaty of Versailles transferred China's Shandong Province from the Germans to the Japanese. Japan had also colonized Korea in 1910.

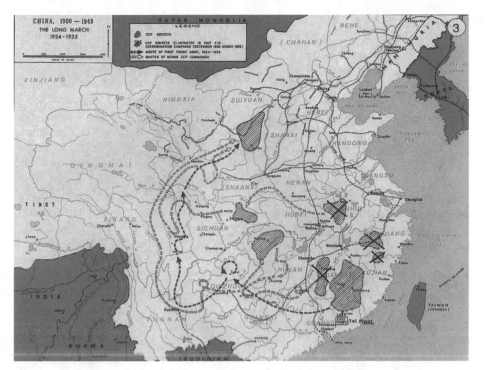

Long March: Shaded areas were controlled by the Chinese Communist Party; darker line is the route of the First Front Army 1934–35; the lighter line represents the routes of minor CCP commands. *(Courtesy of the United States Military Academy.)*

Suwei'ai 江西苏维埃). What had started in 1928 as a hideout for Mao and his small group of CCP followers had grown into a sizeable Communist enclave. Eventually covering an area larger than the state of Massachusetts with a population of more than three million people, the Jiangxi Soviet declared itself an independent country and established its own government, currency, postal service, and army. Chiang's first four attempts to encircle and destroy this new Communist base were soundly defeated by Mao's skillful use of guerrilla tactics. But in 1933, employing ideas from his Nazi German advisors, Chiang's methodical Fifth Encirclement Campaign gradually whittled down CCP territory by blockading the entire region with tightening rings of roads, barbed wire fences, and block houses armed with machine guns, as well as air cover provided by Italian airplanes and pilots.

The military campaign was accompanied by a political program called the New Life Movement (*Xin Shenghuo Yundong* 新生活运动), which was designed to counter Communist social reforms by reinvigorating the populace's Confucian values and nationalistic sentiment. Chiang founded an organization called the Blueshirts,[6] strident anti-Communist partisans, who acted as enforcers of the public morals emphasized in the New Life Movement. In skirmish after skirmish, Chiang's troops defeated the Red Army (*Hong Jun* 红军) in 1934. Other CCP officials took over command from Mao, but they, too, were unable to break Chiang's noose. The days of the Jiangxi Soviet were numbered.

---

[6] So named for the simple blue shirts worn by members and modeled on similar paramilitary organizations in Nazi Germany and in Mussolini's Italy: the Brownshirts and the Blackshirts.

The Long March

In October 1934, 80,000 CCP personnel broke out of the Guomindang stranglehold. Over the next fourteen months, the Communists doggedly marched west and north, sometimes in circles, to avoid the pursuing Guomindang armies in what became known as the Long March (*Chang Zheng* 长征). CCP leaders fiercely debated the causes of their defeat in Jiangxi and how to carry on their fight after the Soviet Union's withdrawal of support. Those who had pushed Mao Zedong out of power were demoted, and Mao assumed command of the Long March. He successfully kept the tattered Communist forces together, despite relentless Guomindang pressure and the rugged terrain and climate of western China. The losses were staggering: only one in ten of those who had set out from Jiangxi made it to Yan'an (延安), a town in China's northwestern Shaanxi Province where a small Communist base had survived. In the end, they had marched farther than the distance from the northern tip of the state of Maine to Key West, Florida, and back again.

The Xi'an Incident and the Second United Front

While the weary Long March survivors recuperated in northwestern China, Chiang Kai-shek maneuvered to wipe out this last Communist base and also to contain Japan's most recent advances into Chinese territory. To confront the Communists, Chiang assigned General Zhang Xueliang, the Manchurian warlord, to move his troops to Xi'an and destroy the Yan'an Soviet. With the CCP finally destroyed, Chiang believed, a fully unified nation could concentrate its forces against the Japanese, who in late 1935 had moved south of the Great Wall to annex eastern Hebei Province around Beijing. Protests against Guomindang inaction had spread across all of China's major cities, calling for an end to the civil war and for united action against the Japanese.

Zhang Xueliang, from his post in Xi'an, was caught in conflicting currents. He was loyal to Chiang Kai-shek, but Zhang and his soldiers, all Manchurian, were reluctant to fight other Chinese given that the Japanese had killed Zhang's father and occupied their homeland. When Communist leader Zhou Enlai approached Zhang about forming a second united front against the Japanese, Zhang took action.

In December 1936, Chiang Kai-shek flew to Xi'an to inspect Zhang's preparations for what he believed would be the last campaign against the Communists. After several days of tense debates, electrified by student protests calling for a united front, Zhang Xueliang seized the Guomindang leader and placed him under house arrest. Zhang and his generals issued a nationwide call for a united front to ally the Guomindang, the CCP, and all warlords against the Japanese.

The Xi'an Incident (*Xi'an Shibian* 西安事变), as it was called, paralyzed the nation and was monitored with consternation by governments around the world. Among the Communists, some, including Mao Zedong, believed that Chiang should be publicly tried and executed, eliminating their archenemy once and for all. But others in Yan'an and Moscow, including Joseph Stalin himself, worried that there was no one else of Chiang Kai-shek's stature who could hold together a unified front against the Japanese. After two weeks of intense negotiations, General Zhang released Chiang Kai-shek. Immediate deliberations to establish a Second United Front (*Di'erci Tongyi Zhanxian* 第二次统一战线) with the Communists began, and open war with Japan loomed on China's horizon.

Primary Sources

DOCUMENT 9.1: "Hometown," a short story by Lu Xun, first published in *Xin Qingnian* (*New Youth* magazine), May 1921

It was Runtu. Although I recognized him right off, he was not at all the Runtu who lived in my memory. He seemed twice as tall now. The round and ruddy face of yesteryear had already turned pale and grey, and it was etched with deep wrinkles. The rims of his eyes were swollen and red just like his father's. I knew that most farmers who worked close to the sea got that way because of the wind. He was wearing a battered old felt hat, and his cotton clothes were so thin that he was shivering. His hands held a paper package along with his pipe. They were not the smooth and nimble hands that I remembered. Now they were rough, clumsy, and as cracked as pine bark.

I was beside myself with enthusiasm, but didn't know how to begin and simply said, "Brother Runtu, you've come…"

There was so much I wanted to say. There were so many words waiting to gush out one after the other like pearls on a string: hornchicks, jumperfish, Guanyin hands, *zha*—but at the same time I was aware of something damming them up inside me, so that they simply swirled around in my brain without a single one coming out.

As he stood there his expression was a mixture of happiness and melancholy. His lips began to move, but not a single word came out. Finally he assumed a very respectful attitude and addressed me in a loud clear voice: "Master!"

I shuddered as I realized what a wretched thick wall now stood between us. I too was at a loss for words….

SOURCE: Lu Xun, *Diary of a Madman and Other Stories,* trans. William Lyell (Honolulu: University of Hawaii Press, 1990) 96.

Go to **www.chinasince1644.com** for the full text of Document 9.1.

DOCUMENT 9.2: Excerpts from the "Guidelines of the New Life Movement," by Chiang Kai-shek, *Central Daily News*, May 15, 1934

There are two kinds of people who are skeptical of the New Life Movement. One [kind] considers *li, yi, lian, chi* [propriety, righteousness, modesty, and a sense of shame] no more than some polished behaviors. They argue that if our knowledge and technology are below other nations, no matter how beautiful and benevolent our behavior may be, our country still would not be saved. This kind of argument is a result of reversing the importance of moral conduct with that of knowledge and technology, because knowledge and technology are by-products of the pursuit of perfect moral conduct. Otherwise, knowledge and technology will be used for ill purposes, harming others and not necessarily benefiting oneself. Therefore, *li, yi, lian, chi* can not only save the country, but also strengthen our country….

SOURCE: Chiang Kai-shek, "The Guidelines of New Life Movement," *Central Daily News*, 15 May, 1934. Trans. Nan Ye.

Go to **www.chinasince1644.com** for the full text of Document 9.2.

DOCUMENT 9.3: Excerpts from "Report on an Investigation of the Peasant Movement in Hunan," by Mao Zedong, March 1927

[T]he rise of the peasant movement is a colossal event. In a very short time, in China's central, southern and northern provinces, several hundred million peasants will rise like a mighty storm, like a hurricane, a force so swift and violent that no power, however great, will be able to hold it back. They will smash all the trammels that now bind them and rush forward along the road to liberation. They will sweep all the imperialists, warlords, corrupt officials, local tyrants and evil gentry into their graves. Every revolutionary party and every revolutionary comrade will be put to the test, to be accepted or rejected as they decide. There are three alternatives. To march at their head and lead them? To trail behind them, gesticulating and criticizing? Or to stand in their way and oppose them? Every Chinese is free to choose, but events will force you to make the choice quickly....

SOURCE: *Selected Works of Mao Zedong* (Beijing: Foreign Languages Press, 1967).

Go to **www.chinasince1644.com** for the full text of Document 9.3.

DOCUMENT 9.4: "The Long March," a poem by Mao Zedong, 1935

The Red Army fears not the trials of the Long March,
Holding light ten thousand crags and torrents.
The Five Ridges wind like gentle ripples
And the majestic Wumeng roll by, globules of clay.
Warm the steep cliffs lapped by the waters of Golden Sand [River],
Cold the iron chains spanning the Dadu River.
Minshan's thousand *li* of snow joyously crossed,
The three Armies march on, each face glowing.

SOURCE: Mao Zedong, *Mao Zedong Poems* (Beijing: Foreign Language Press, 2003) 37.

Go to **www.chinasince1644.com** for the full text of Document 9.4.

DOCUMENT 9.5: "Jinsha Jiang" ("The River of Golden Sand"), an anonymous account describing a segment of the Long March, 1934–35

Nearer and nearer we drew to the shore. The outline of the town was now visible and the lights became brighter. Shadows could be seen moving about and shouts were audible. A fierce battle was impending. My heart tightened. Grabbing my Mauser I looked intently at the approaching town. As the boat drew up along the bank, I pushed lightly the two sitting next to me who quickly jumped ashore and mounted the stone steps holding their rifles.

"Hey! You, why have you come back so late?" said a cracked voice in a Yunnan accent.

The two made no immediate response. Then we heard one say quietly: "Don't move!"

As soon as I heard that, I led the others up the steps, and before they knew a thing, the two enemy sentries were captives. The depositions of the captives were more or less like the boatmen's. I ordered the 1st Platoon to go up the street and attack the Guomindang regular troops and the 2nd Platoon to attack the police. I stayed on the jetty. They were to report back to me. The boats were sent for reinforcements. According to plan, I made the messenger gather some rushes and burn them by the riverside as a signal that our company had succeeded in crossing.

Source: *Stories of the Long March* (Beijing: Foreign Languages Press, 1958) 35–50.

 Go to **www.chinasince1644.com** for the full text of **Document 9.5**.

DOCUMENT 9.6: "The Bridge of Iron Chains," an account describing crossing the Luding Bridge on the Long March, 1934–35

The next day we received an order reading as follows: "Our Left Route Army has been given until the 25th to take the Luding Bridge. You must march at the utmost speed and act in the shortest possible time to accomplish the glorious mission. We are confident you can do it. Are preparing to congratulate you on your victory." Below was the forceful signature of General Lin Biao....

We couldn't stop. Time was too precious. As we marched we held a meeting of military and political officers to discuss what we should do. First we issued a number of rallying cries: "The 4th Red Regiment has a glorious battle record. We must complete our mission and preserve our glory!" "Emulate the 1st Red Regiment, which captured Anshunchang. Compete with them and take the Luding Bridge!" "Our mission is glorious but very difficult. We can pass the test!" We set six the following morning as the deadline for reaching our objective....

To cross the Wild Tiger Mountain you have to go up some forty *li*, then come down the same distance. It is a dangerous climb, with the Dadu River on the right, high cliffs on the left, and the path just a narrow twisting trail. People say it's the neck of the road between Anshunchang and the Luding Bridge, and that's no exaggeration in the least....

Source: Yang Zhengwu, "The Fight at Luding Bridge," *Stories of the Long March* (Beijing: Foreign Languages Press, 1958) 61–76.

 Go to **www.chinasince1644.com** for the full text of **Document 9.6**.

DOCUMENT 9.7: "Jiajin Shan" ("The Great Snow Mountain"), an anonymous account describing a segment of the Long March, 1934–35

By nightfall we had crossed, at an altitude of 16,000 feet, and that night we bivouacked in a valley where there was no sign of human life. While most of us were stretched out exhausted, General Zhu De came around to make his usual inspection. He was very weary, for he had walked with the troops. Yet nothing ever prevented him from making his rounds. He gave me half of a little dried beef, which he had in his pocket. He encouraged everyone and said we had crossed the worst peak, and it was only a few more days to Mougong.

To avoid enemy bombers, we arose at midnight and began climbing the next peak. It rained, then snowed, and the fierce wind whipped our bodies, and more men died of cold and exhaustion.

The last peak in the range, which we estimated to be eighty *li* [twenty-seven miles] from base to summit, was terrible. Hundreds of our men died there. They would sit down to rest or relieve themselves and never get up. All along the route we kept reaching down to pull men to their feet only to find that they were already dead....

Source: "Across the Snow Mountain," *Stories of the Long March* (Beijing: Foreign Languages Press, 1958) 79–84.

Go to **www.chinasince1644.com** for the full text of **Document 9.7**.

DOCUMENT 9.8: Excerpts from "Political Mobilization for the War of Resistance," a lecture by Mao Zedong, May 1938

The mobilization of the common people throughout the country will create a vast sea in which to drown the enemy, create the conditions that will make up for our inferiority in arms and other things, and create the prerequisites for overcoming every difficulty in the war. To win victory, we must persevere in the War of Resistance, in the united front and in the protracted war. But all these are inseparable from the mobilization of the common people. To wish for victory and yet neglect political mobilization is like wishing to "go south by driving the chariot north," and the result would inevitably be to forfeit victory.

What does political mobilization mean? First, it means telling the army and the people about the political aim of the war. It is necessary for every soldier and civilian to see why the war must be fought and how it concerns him. The political aim of the war is "to drive out Japanese imperialism and build a new China of freedom and equality;" we must proclaim this aim to everybody, to all soldiers and civilians, before we can create an anti-Japanese upsurge and unite hundreds of millions as one man to contribute their all to the war....

The richest source of power to wage war lies in the masses of the people. It is mainly because of the unorganized state of the Chinese masses that Japan dares to bully us. When this defect is remedied, then the Japanese aggressor, like a mad bull crashing into a ring of flames, will be surrounded by hundreds of millions of our people standing upright, the mere sound of their voices will strike terror into him, and he will be burned to death….

Source: *Selected Works of Mao Zedong, Volume II* (Beijing: Foreign Languages Press, 1967).

 Go to **www.chinasince1644.com** for the full text of **Document 9.8**.

DOCUMENT 9.9: "Manifesto on the Seizure of Chiang Kai-shek," a telegram sent to the nation by General Zhang Xueliang, December 12, 1936

Generalissimo Chiang Kai-shek, surrounded by a group of unworthy advisers, has forfeited the support of the masses of our people. He is deeply guilty for the harm his policies have done the country. We, Zhang Xueliang and the others, undersigned, advised him with tears to take another way; but we were repeatedly rejected and rebuked….

The Military and Civilians in the Northwest unanimously make the following demands:

1. Reorganize the Nanjing Government, and admit all parties to share the joint responsibility of saving the nation.
2. Stop all kinds of civil wars.
3. Immediately release the patriotic leaders arrested in Shanghai.
4. Release all political prisoners throughout the country.
5. Emancipate the patriotic movement of the people.
6. Safeguard the political freedom of the people to organize and call meetings.
7. Actually carry out the Will of Dr. Sun Yat-sen.
8. Immediately call a National Salvation Conference….

Source: Rpt. in James Bertram, *First Act in China: The Story of the Sian Mutiny* (New York: Viking Press, 1938) 126–127.

 Go to **www.chinasince1644.com** for the full text of **Document 9.9**.

DOCUMENT 9.10: "The Rebellion in Xi'an," a report in the *Manchester Guardian Weekly*, July 16, 1937

The Guardian's *reporter wrote the article based on Mme. Chiang's (Soong Meiling's) account, which she published under the title* Xi'an: A Coup D'Etat.

 Go to **www.chinasince1644.com** for the full text of **Document 9.10**.

DOCUMENT 9.11a & b: Photographs at site of the seizure of Chiang Kai-shek outside Xi'an, 2006

The poster reads: "National Historical Red Tourist Site: Xi'an Incident Site in commemoration of the 70th anniversary of the Xi'an Incident." From left to right, the photographs are of Chiang Kai-shek, Zhang Xueliang, and Yang Hucheng.

This meeting room was in the suite of rooms Chiang used before he was placed under house arrest.
(Photos by Liz Nelson)

Go to **www. chinasince1644.com** for the photographs in **Document 9.11a & b.**

DOCUMENTS 9.12a–c:
Cartoons by Sapajou in *The North China Daily News*, 1936–1937

THE NORTH-CHINA DAILY NEWS, MONDAY, DECEMBER 14, 1936

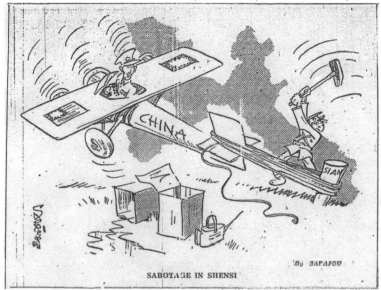

SABOTAGE IN SHENSI

 Go to **www.chinasince1644.com** for the other two cartoons in Document 9.12.

DOCUMENT 9.13:
Photograph of Zhou Enlai, Mao Zedong, and Bo Gu, 1937

The three men were key figures in the Chinese Communist Party. *(Peabody Museum of Archaeology and Ethnology, Harvard University/Lattimore Foundation.)*

 Go to **www. chinasince1644.com** for the photograph in Document 9.13.

Activities

ACTIVITY 1: Evaluating the New Life Movement

Part 1: Analyze

After reading the introductory essay, read Lu Xun's short story "Hometown" (9.1) and consider the following:

1. What tone is set at the outset of the story?
2. What words does the narrator use to describe "life" (see page 9 of the story)?
3. What feelings does the narrator express?
4. What kind of "new life" do you think the narrator is proposing toward the end of the story?

Part 2: Discuss

After reading Chiang Kai-shek's "Guidelines of the New Life Movement" (9.2), you will discuss with a partner:

1. What were the central concepts in Chiang's New Life Movement?
2. In what spheres of life did he suggest they should be applied?
3. Do Chiang's guidelines echo any other philosophical or religious approach to living? If so, which ones and how are they alike?
4. Which guidelines to New Life do you agree with? Why? With which do you disagree? Why?
5. What role can or should government play in people's personal behavior?

Writing Extension:

Consider this statement from "Guidelines of the New Life Movement," (9.2): "Strong morals must be the foundation of all learning. Basic needs, such as food and clothing, and accumulation of knowledge and technology, are secondary." Write a response piece agreeing or disagreeing. Give specific examples from the text to support your position.

Part 3: Respond to Reading

Read Mao Zedong's report on the peasant associations (9.3) and consider the questions:

1. What were the peasant associations doing?
2. How had power shifted in the rural areas Mao describes?
3. What was Mao's attitude toward violence?
4. Compare Mao's approach to "new life" to Chiang Kai-shek's.

Creative Extension:

Consider the impact of Chiang's New Life Movement and Mao's peasant actions on Chinese people by imagining how three major characters (the narrator, Runtu, and Second Sister Yang) in Lu Xun's story "Hometown" (9.1) might have responded to each. Pairs will assume the roles of an interviewer and one of Lu Xun's characters, then conduct live interviews with the characters or videotape interviews outside of class (see Item 9.A on the companion website for guidelines).

Part 4: Synthesize

In reality, Mao's peasant revolution eventually overthrew Chiang's government and led to the establishment of People's Republic of China in 1949. Chiang's New Life Movement failed to gain momentum at the time, but lived on in Taiwan after 1949.

1. List three reasons to explain the success of Mao's call for peasant revolution. Use specifics from Lu Xun's story and the documents to illustrate your point.

2. List three reasons to explain the failure of the New Life Movement at the time. Use specifics from the story and the documents to illustrate your point.

ACTIVITY 2: Analyzing Accounts of the Long March

Part 1: Respond to Mao's Poem

After reading Mao Zedong's poem "The Long March" (9.4) you will participate in a "Quaker Read." Read the poem a second time and highlight words, phrases, or lines that are particularly powerful or that create a vivid image in your mind. As a class, you will share your selected images by reading them aloud at random. Listen while others read a selection they highlighted, and share your selections when moved to do so. (Periods of silence are also allowed.) Then be prepared to discuss the following questions:

1. What is the tone of the poem?

2. For what purpose might Mao have written this poem and other poems during the Long March?

3. Mao's poems are written in a traditional Chinese style that echoes that of much-loved poets of the Tang dynasty, particularly Li Bai (701–762 c.e.). Why might Mao have chosen this style as opposed to a more modern poetic form influenced by European or American writers?

Part 2: Write

Read the three accounts describing the Red Army's experience at three famous landmarks: "The River of Golden Sand," "The Bridge of Iron Chains," and "The Great Snow Mountain" (9.5. 9.6, and 9.7). Think about the following questions and share your most significant insights in a written conversation with a partner. See directions for written conversation below.

1. What is the tone of each account? Are they similar? How is it similar or different across accounts?

2. What impression do you get of the Red Army soldiers? How are Guomindang soldiers portrayed?

3. What are the highlights in each account?

4. How do they differ in perspective from Mao's "Long March" poem?

5. Whose account of events appears to be more authentic, Mao's or the soldiers'?

6. Whose account would have been more useful to the Communists' efforts to build support among the populace? Why?

Written Conversation: Write a letter! Use formal greetings ("Dear _____ ") and closings.

■ Write for 3 minutes. No stopping. No talking.

■ Pass letter to your left.

■ Read and respond in writing for 2 minutes. No stopping. No talking!

■ Pass back to original writer (to your right).

■ Read and respond in writing for 2 minutes. No stopping. No talking!

■ After 3/4 turns, talking is allowed.

ACTIVITY 3: Transforming Narratives

Part 1: Present Monologues

Form three groups. Each group is responsible for one of the three landmarks (Golden Sand River, the Bridge of Iron Chains, or the Great Snow Mountain). Identify the location of the site on the map (Item 9.B). To get a sense of the terrain over which the Red Army marched, look at a topographic map in Additional Resources on the companion website or use Google Earth to look up the locations. Based on information given in the accounts as well as supplemental research from text and online sources, each member of a group should develop a monologue from the perspective of a Long Marcher that describes the Red Army's experiences at the landmark. The monologues when presented to the class should do the following:

1. Describe the topographical characteristics of the area in which the landmark is located and the challenges the topography posed to Red Army troops.

2. Describe the other challenges that the Red Army encountered in this area, such as Guomindang troops, climate, disease, scarcity of food, or other obstacles.

3. List the advantages and strengths the Red Army possessed when they faced these obstacles.

4. Describe the strategies the Red Army used to overcome the obstacles.

Part 2: Summarize

Read or take notes on the monologues at key junctures along the Long March. Write a paragraph summarizing the key elements that eventually contributed to the Red Army's success in completing the Long March.

Part 3: Discuss

These three accounts (9.5, 9.6, 9.7) were among many published in 1958. Prepare to discuss in class:

1. How might the time span between when the Long March took place (1934–1935) and the date of publication affect the narratives?

2. What other factors, such as the political conditions in 1958 (see Chapter 13), might have affected the narratives?

3. Even though the Long March was essentially a retreat from superior Guomindang forces, it has taken on mythic proportions since the PRC was founded in 1949. Why might this event be viewed as so important?

4. Are there similar achievements or events in other countries that compare to the Long March? How do other countries remember or commemorate events they consider pivotal in their histories?

ACTIVITY 4: Examining Political Mobilization for the Anti-Japanese National United Front

Part 1: Synthesize in Writing

Read Mao Zedong's "Political Mobilization for the War of Resistance" (9.8) and create a Chinese Communist Party propaganda leaflet to convince Guomindang officers and soldiers to support a United Front with the CCP to resist the Japanese invasion. The leaflet should include key wording from Mao's lecture and achieve the following aims:

■ Instill patriotism and confidence in the officers and soldiers for resisting Japanese invasion.

■ Encourage Guomindang officers and soldiers to mobilize civilians such as workers, peasants, merchants, and students to support the United Front.

Part 2: Write

Read Zhang Xueliang's telegram to the nation explaining the kidnapping of Chiang Kai-shek (9.9) and review the information in the introductory essay. Write an editorial on General Zhang's seizure of Chiang for either a CCP newspaper or a Guomindang newspaper. The editorial should:

■ Outline the political circumstances under which the incident happened.

■ Explain Zhang's motive in taking the action.

- Predict possible outcomes of the kidnapping incident and suggest a solution to the situation.
- Call on the readers to take steps to help achieve the best solution.

ACTIVITY 5: Analyzing the Xi'an Incident

Read General Zhang's telegram (9.9) and "The Rebellion in Xi'an" (9.10) and complete the following assignment.

Part 1: Compare

Prepare to discuss in class:

1. How do the perspectives of these two accounts of the same incident differ from each other?
2. Of the eight demands presented to Chiang Kai-shek by force, which ones did he refuse and which ones did he comply with? Why?
3. In 1946, Chiang ordered Yang Hucheng, the other general involved in the kidnapping, to be executed along with his whole family, but he put Zhang under house-arrest instead. Why do you think he spared Zhang's life? Why did he wait until after the end of World War II to have General Yang's death sentence carried out?
4. After the Long March, the Xi'an Incident is considered "a historical turning point for China."[7] What might be the significance of the Xi'an Incident in the ultimate success of the CCP?
5. Examine the photos of the site where Chiang was captured and where the negotiations took place (9.11a & b). How has the Chinese government chosen to memorialize the Xi'an Incident?
6. General Zhang Xueliang lived under house arrest in Taiwan and later, after Chiang's death, lived in Hawaii, where he died at the age of 101. Why do you think that despite repeated invitations, he never returned to mainland China?

Part 2: Debate

Divide into two groups (one takes the perspective of Zhang Xueliang, the other of Chiang Kai-shek) and debate the pros and cons of cooperation with the Communists against Japanese invasion.

---

[7] Wording used at the museum created at General Zhang's headquarters in Xi'an.

ACTIVITY 6: Analyzing Perspectives on the Xi'an Incident

Examine the three cartoons from the *North China Daily News* (9.12a–c) and answer the following questions:

"Sabotage in Shensi [Shaanxi Province]," December 14, 1936

1. The two figures depicted in the cartoon are actual people involved in the Xi'an Incident. Who are they?
2. What is the artist's attitude toward the figure in the plane?
3. The *North China Daily News*, the paper in which these cartoons ran, was owned by British businessmen in Shanghai. Explain why this paper would have had this perspective.

"Who Did It?" December 17, 1936

1. The two figures depicted here represent two countries with a keen interest in the events at Xi'an. They are placed in geographically accurate positions to China's northwest and northeast. What countries do the figures represent?
2. Why might they be interested in the development of the Xi'an Incident? What stake do they have in the outcome?
3. How does this cartoon reflect the international perspective on the political situation in China at this time? Would European and American governments be as likely to watch the events of the Xi'an Incident as the countries depicted in the cartoon? Why or why not?

"Don't Do It, Sister!" January 24, 1937

1. The two figures depicted here represent generalized images of China and Spain. What events in "Madrid" would make that city a sister to "Sian"?[8]
2. What is the message that "Madrid" tries to convey to "Xi'an"? In other words, don't do what?
3. What is the tone of this cartoon? How does it differ from the first two?

Overall:

1. How did the cartoons change over the course of about six weeks? Why might that have been?
2. Among all the key players in the Xi'an Incident, whose voice is not depicted in the cartoons? Why?
3. Based on your understanding of the artist's perspectives reflected in these cartoons, describe the artist's likely response to the outcome of the Xi'an Incident and the resulting change in the political situation in China.

---

[8] "Sian" is an older spelling of "Xi'an."

ACTIVITY 7: Citing Evidence: What Can a Photograph Tell Us?

Examine the photograph of Zhou Enlai, Mao Zedong, and Bo Gu (9.13) and consider the following questions:

1. What are your impressions of the three Chinese Communist Party leaders depicted in the photo? Describe each person's attitude, expression, and appearance, using two or three adjectives for each category.

2. How do your impressions of these individuals differ from your expectations of CCP leaders prior to seeing this photo?

3. This photo was taken in June 1937, nearly two years after the successful but devastating Long March. In what ways do you think the experience affected the men's appearance as well as their attitude?

4. Pay close attention to their clothing and point out two differences between Mao's attire and that of the others. How do these differences suggest Mao's leadership within the Party? What else could they suggest?

5. Do these men, especially Mao and Zhou, look approachable? How would that have affected their ability to work with and recruit peasants?

6. The fourth person in the photo was not identified. Assuming he is a junior assistant to Mao, how would you interpret the way he gazes at Mao? In other words, what could be going through his mind at such a moment in history?

Search online or in a library to find a photograph of Chiang Kai-shek from the 1930s. Describe his attitude, expression, and appearance. Compare it to that of the CCP leaders in the 1937 photograph.

Suggested Resources

Books

Dong, Stella. *Shanghai: The Rise and Fall of a Decadent City*. New York: William Morrow, 2000.
A history of the city at the center of China's turbulent revolutionary years.

Gray, Jack. *Rebellions and Revolutions: China from the 1800s to 2000*. New York: Oxford University Press, 2002.
A concise and accessible introduction to China's recent history.

Hahn, Emily. *The Soong Sisters*. New York: Doubleday, 1941.
Written by an American expatriate living in China, this biography offers insight into the inner workings of the Republican era.

Li, Laura Tyson. *Madame Chiang Kai-Shek: China's Eternal First Lady*. New York: Atlantic Monthly Press, 2006.

Lu Xun. *Diary of a Madman and Other Stories*. Trans. William Lyell. Honolulu: University of Hawaii Press, 1990.

Snow, Edgar. *Red Star Over China*. New York: Grove Press, 1993.
A U.S. journalist's account of the Chinese Communist movement and its leadership until the late 1930s. Originally published in 1937.

Spence, Jonathan and Annping Chin. *The Chinese Century: A Photographic History of the Last Hundred Years*. New York: Random House, 1996.

Sun Shuyun. *The Long March: The True History of Communist China's Founding Myth*. New York: Doubleday, 2006.

Sun retraces the route of the Long March, interviewing survivors and uncovering truth to the myth of how China's Communist Party escaped the Guomindang.

Taylor, Jay. *The Generalissimo: Chiang Kai-shek and the Struggle for Modern China*. Cambridge: Belknap Press of Harvard University Press, 2009.

Yu Hua. *To Live: A Novel*. Trans. Michael Berry. New York: Anchor Books, 2003.

This contemporary novel chronicles the life of the son of a wealthy family who gambles away his fortune, survives war and famine, and manages to endure the myriad twists and turns of the Guomindang and Communist periods.

Websites

Chinese Civil War Map
http://commons.wikimedia.org/wiki/ File.Chinese_civil_war_map_03.jpg
A map of the Long March, 1934–1935. From the History Department of the U.S. Military Academy, West Point.

"Fundamentals of National Reconstruction," Sun Yat-sen
http://academic.brooklyn.cuny.edu/core9/ phalsall/texts/sunyat.html
An important political statement by Sun Yat-sen, founder of the Nationalist Party, in 1923.

An Illustrated History of the Communist Party of China
http://china.org.cn/english/features/ 45954.htm
This site contains background information and photographs from important moments in the early history of the Chinese Communist Party.

Mao Zedong Library
http://marx2mao.com/Mao/Index.html
Translations of Selected Works of Mao Zedong volumes 1–5.

"A Statement on Chiang Kai-Shek's Statement," Mao Zedong
http://marx2mao.com/Mao/SCKS36.html
From December 28, 1936, in response to Chiang's "Admonition to Zhang Xueliang and Yang Hucheng."

Films

China in Revolution, vol. 1 of *China: A Century of Revolution* (120 minutes; 2007)
This documentary provides footage of the Republican Period and interviews with Chinese people who lived through this era.

The Last Emperor (162 mins; 1987)
This film poignantly captures the anachronism of a child-emperor coming to power in China in the early twentieth century and the subsequent political turmoil.

To Live (133 minutes; 1994)
This film spans four decades of the twentieth century in China. It tells the story of a couple and their two children as they struggle to survive the constantly changing political climate. In Mandarin with subtitles.

Writers and Revolutionaries (60 mins; 1992)
Volume IV of the ten-part *Pacific Century* series focuses on the role of intellectuals in the rise of twentieth-century nationalism and progressivism in the East.

■ A CLOSER LOOK

The Soong Sisters:
"One Loved Money; One Loved Power; One Loved China"

In 1878, twelve-year-old "Charlie Soong" (Sung Yaoju) moved to Boston, Massachusetts to begin his apprenticeship with a Chinese merchant family. He didn't last long and soon signed up as a crew man on a U.S. Revenue Service cutter. The vessel's captain and his wealthy friends in North Carolina helped arrange for Charlie to be educated as a Methodist missionary at Trinity College (later Duke University).

In 1886, he returned to China to preach. He shifted from missionary work to the printing of Bibles and then opened a noodle factory, equipped with the latest Western machinery. A firm supporter of Sun Yat-sen's Revolutionary Alliance (see Chapter 7) and the need to modernize China, Charlie Soong wanted his three daughters as well as his three sons to be proficient in English and college-educated. The girls initially attended a private

American school in Shanghai before traveling to the United States to pursue college degrees.

Soong Ailing, the eldest, left home when she was fourteen to study at Wesleyan College for Women in Georgia—the first Chinese woman to do so. After graduating, she would return to China, work briefly for Sun Yat-sen, and then marry H. H. Kung, a prominent banker and direct descendant of Confucius.

■ A CLOSER LOOK

Madame Sun Yat-sen

Soong Qingling, born in 1893, joined her older sister in Georgia in 1908, where she, too, earned a degree from Wesleyan. In 1913, she returned to China and took over from Ailing as Sun Yat-sen's personal secretary. Two years later, as her family was arranging a marriage for her, Qingling and Sun Yat-sen (her senior by twenty-eight years) eloped. Her parents were appalled; Charlie Soong considered himself betrayed by his close friend.

Sun Yat-sen continued his efforts to unify China as a republic but died prematurely in 1925. After Chiang Kai-shek routed the Communists

and their supporters in Shanghai in the spring of 1927, Soong Qingling broke with the Guomindang and gave her support to the Chinese Communist Party. As a result of her dramatically different political views, Qingling became estranged from her sisters.

In the 1930s, with the Japanese threatening to occupy more and more of China, she supported a united front. In 1939, Soong Qingling founded the China Defense League, an organization that gathered donations and medical supplies from abroad. In later years, the organization became the China Welfare Institute, dedicated to providing maternal and infant

medical care and promoting education.

After the founding of the People's Republic of China in 1949, she held a number of government posts, including vice-chairperson of the PRC and vice-chairperson of the National People's Congress. She represented China on many occasions, traveling to several countries, among them the USSR, India, and Indonesia. She also wrote *The Struggle for New China* and founded and contributed to the magazine *China Reconstructs* (now known as *China Today*). Soong Qingling died in Beijing in 1981. Her home has been declared a historical landmark.

■ A CLOSER LOOK

Madame Chiang Kai-shek

Soong Meiling had insisted on going to Georgia with Qingling in 1908, even though she was just ten years old. For several years she was privately tutored before she began at Wesleyan. In 1913, since both her sisters had returned to Shanghai, Meiling transferred to Wellesley College in Massachusetts to be close to a brother who was at Harvard. She graduated with a degree in English literature in 1917.

Meiling first met Chiang Kai-shek in 1922. Several years would pass before they married, since Chiang already had two wives,[9] and the Soong family insisted he divorce them and convert to Christianity.

Madame Chiang Kai-shek played an active role in the Guomindang government and in promoting the New Life Movement, which she helped develop. Described as a "dazzling and imperious politician,"[10] she helped negotiate a peaceful resolution to the Xi'an Incident.

She is probably best remembered as China's eloquent and elegant "ambassador" to the United States during China's War of Resistance against Japan (see Chapter 11). She traveled across the Pacific several times to raise awareness of China's plight, and in February 1943, seeking financial aid, she was the first Chinese individual and only the second woman to address a joint session of Congress. That November, she served as Chiang's interpreter at the Cairo Conference with President Roosevelt and Winston Churchill, the British prime minister. Twice she appeared on the cover of *Time* magazine.

After the Allies defeated Japan and China's civil war resumed (see Chapter 12), Madame Chiang again sought financial assistance from the U.S. President Truman refused. "They're thieves, every damn one of them," he would insist later, referring to Guomindang leaders and the rampant corruption. It appears likely that the extended Soong family had siphoned hundreds of millions of dollars of U.S. aid intended for the war.[11]

Soong Meiling was in the United States when the PRC was founded; she joined her husband in Taiwan in 1950. After Chiang Kai-shek's death in 1975, when Chiang's eldest son by his first wife took over as president, she left Taiwan.[12] She continued to play a role in organizations such as the International Red Cross Committee and the British United Aid to China Fund, but spent most of her remaining years in New York. Madame Chiang died in October 2003 at age 105.

■ *What factors might explain how these three women were all so central to the story of China's development in the 20th century?*

[9] Polygamy, marrying more than one woman, was legal in China at the time and common among wealthy or prominent men.
[10] "Madame Chiang Kai-shek, a Power in Husband's China and Abroad, Dies at 105," *New York Times*, October 24, 2003.
[11] "Madame Chiang Kai-shek…Dies at 105," *New York Times*, October 24, 2003.
[12] Neither Soong Qingling nor Soong Meiling had children.

CHAPTER RESOURCES

Primary Sources

DOCUMENT 10.1 Excerpts from *Tell the People: Talks with James Yen about the Mass Education Movement*, by Pearl S. Buck, 1945

DOCUMENT 10.2 Photograph of Five Character Plaque in Lijiang, April 2006

DOCUMENT 10.3 Excerpts describing the founding of schools from *Tell the People: Talks with James Yen About the Mass Education Movement* by Pearl S. Buck, 1945

DOCUMENT 10.4: Excerpts describing the Fellow Scholar Association from *Tell the People: Talks with James Yen About the Mass Education Movement* by Pearl S. Buck, 1945

DOCUMENT 10.5 Photograph "Shanghai Street," 1937

DOCUMENT 10.6a–e: Photographs taken on an American's "grand tour" of China, 1913

DOCUMENT 10.7: Excerpts from *Family* by Ba Jin, 1931

DOCUMENT 10.8: Excerpts describing view of family from *A Daughter of Han: The Autobiography of a Chinese Working Woman* by Ida Pruitt, 1945

DOCUMENT 10.9: Excerpts from a memoir by Li Xiuwen (1890–1992), describing growing up female

DOCUMENT 10.10 Excerpts from the Peking United International Famine Relief Committee's Report on the North China Famine, 1922

DOCUMENT 10.11: Excerpts from a memoir by Li Xiuwen (1890–1992) describing life in the village where she grew up, early 20th century

DOCUMENT 10.12: Excerpts from "Agrarian Problems in China," in *Peasant Life in China* by Fei Xiaotong, 1946

DOCUMENT 10.13: Excerpts from the novel *Rickshaw* by Lao She, 1936

DOCUMENT 10.14: Excerpts describing working life, from *A Daughter of Han: The Autobiography of a Chinese Working Woman* by Ida Pruitt, 1945

DOCUMENT 10.15: Clips from Northeast Historic Film (Archives) from 1934 (on companion website)

> **CLIP 1:** "Images from the Countryside"
>
> **CLIP 2:** "Hong Kong, Shanghai and Beijing"

Supplementary Materials

ITEM 10.A: Photograph analysis worksheet

ITEM 10.B: Questions pertaining to Document 10.7

ITEM 10.C: Questions pertaining to Documents 10.8 and 10.9

ITEM 10.D: Questions pertaining to Documents 10.10–10.12

ITEM 10.E: Questions pertaining to Documents 10.13 and 10.14

 Excerpts of these primary source documents appear in this chapter. Go to **www.chinasince1644.com** for the full version of these documents and for the Supplementary Materials.

CHAPTER 10

Challenges to Tradition in the Early Republic

By Cara Abraham

Chapter Contents

Challenges to Confucian Tradition
Reform Efforts
The Lives of Women
Rural China
The Urban Working Poor

Key Idea

The early years of the Republic were marked by both firm attachment to tradition and revitalized efforts by individuals to bring about social change in China.

Guiding Questions

What traditional customs were Chinese men and women practicing in the first thirty years of the twentieth century?

What were some of the ways in which reformers sought to bring about change?

What factors impeded social change?

To what extent did reformers work within the existing social structure to bring about change?

How much change took place for women, peasants, and the urban working poor?

How far did the changes go in creating a basis for a "modern" society?

Terms to Know

concubine	mission schools
Confucian hierarchy	modernization
foot binding	reform
indentured servitude	rickshaw
indigenous	

Essay

In the first decades of the twentieth century, at a time of significant political instability, China underwent important social change. In addition to reformers who published literature and essays in new political journals (see Chapter 8 for examples), there were individuals "in the field" studying social issues and implementing reforms. They sought to reduce the gap between the rich and poor. Many also worked to advance health care and to improve the lives of women. There were important efforts to encourage the vernacular as the medium of written language, rather than Classical Chinese, and to extend educational opportunities to the greater populace.

Following the Boxer Uprising (*Gengzi Guobian* 庚子国变) of 1900, the Qing (清) government had to pay indemnities to Western nations (see Chapter 7). The United States used these payments to provide scholarships for Chinese students to study in the United States. More than a thousand young Chinese also took advantage of a work-study program in France, Zhou Enlai (周恩来) and Deng Xiaoping (邓小平) among them. Peasant workers returning from labor in Europe during World War I brought tales of their extraordinary experiences back to the Chinese countryside when they returned. Japan also became an increasingly popular destination for study abroad and became arguably the most important portal for new ideas into China.

The students and others who returned to China brought a new cosmopolitanism to their homeland. They saw China at the cusp of an as yet undefined beginning. Anarchism, democracy, constitutional monarchy, and communism were some of the political ideas that became current among China's educated elite. China was also a focus for visionaries from all walks of life and nations who brought their causes with them as they visited China: birth control activist Margaret Sanger lectured in China in this period, as did philosopher, psychologist, and educational reformer John Dewey and Indian Nobel laureate in literature Rabindranath Tagore.

Protestant and Catholic congregations from the United Kingdom, the United States and other Western nations funded Christian mission schools in China, which were instrumental in extending education to girls. Chinese students returned from overseas studies and themselves started up many new schools. These schools grew in size and scope, particularly in major port cities around China. Other missionary endeavors already present in China expanded their reach, often without demanding conversion from their constituents. The Social Gospel movement gathered steam during this period among Methodists, Presbyterians, and Baptists, all prominent in China, calling for improved living conditions for the poor all over the world. This progressivist strain gave birth to the YMCA organization, which became an important gathering point and educational force in Chinese cities, spearheading social projects across the country and encouraging a new emphasis on physical fitness and public health.

The Qing dynasty had abolished the civil service examination system in 1905; subsequently many of the younger generation of the scholar-official and literati class led reform movements.[1] Increased literacy led to an explosion in print media in which authors challenged old ways of thinking about marriage, family, and success. Increasing numbers of poor women from rural areas worked in newly urban areas where factories and workshops for the global markets were springing up. They were followed later by educated women leaving the inner quarters. This period saw important efforts to end foot binding and indentured servitude. Reformers challenged the Confucian hierarchy. They also questioned the practice of arranged marriages, and romantic love became a new and important theme, particularly in China's cities.

---

[1] See Chapter 2 to learn about the traditional role of the educated elite in Chinese society.

Rural China

The hope and promise of the 1911 Nationalist Revolution (*Xinhai Geming* 辛亥革命) quickly came face to face with the political realities of early twentieth-century China. First warlords ruled China, often more interested in their own political standing than in the welfare of their constituents. Then in the late 1920s and early 1930s, Chiang Kai-shek's Guomindang government took power. The Guomindang, challenged by warlords, the Chinese Communist Party, and encroaching Japanese (see Chapter 9), as well as their own ineptitude, were unable to create an effective administration in rural areas. Meanwhile, a well tuned indigenous philanthropic sector managed to take care of large-scale refugee problems and widespread hunger in remarkably effective ways. Reform came incrementally, given the challenges of the decades.

Many impoverished peasants moved to the cities, hoping to find steady work. Violence became endemic as warlords battled each other, Guomindang battled Communists, and the Japanese began their violent incursion into China's heartland. Families trying to escape the violence and growing poverty were often separated. Young men with no other prospects joined militias or armies or were conscripted into them. The instability worsened the lives of villagers and made their livelihood, agriculture, increasingly precarious as they no longer could depend upon a steady source of labor or stable social units to cultivate their land.

Urban Life

People living in coastal cities generally fared better during the Republican era. The wealthier Chinese, in particular, increasingly had access to a sophisticated blend of foreign and Chinese culture. Travel on newly paved roads, fast trains, and later even airplanes opened new avenues for national and international exchange. Cinemas, radios, and mass advertising competed for residents' attention and surplus income. Chinese reformers often found a more welcoming atmosphere in these urban centers. Shanghai (上海), in particular, was an international city in the 1920s and 1930s, home to foreign concession areas where French, English, Japanese, American, and Italian businessmen and their families—among others—resided. Their interests were protected by 22,000 of their own troops and police and 43 warships, ready for use should foreigners feel their interests were under threat.[2] Many expatriates lived a comfortable life largely separated from the impoverished Chinese masses.

The years 1912 to 1937 were filled with chaos and dislocation; nevertheless, Chinese people in all walks of life continued to provide for their families and make plans for the future. Many of the reformers' efforts may be credited with paving the way for China's dramatic modernization.

---

[2] Jonathan D. Spence, *The Search for Modern China.* (New York: W.W. Norton, 1999) 334.

Primary Sources

DOCUMENT 10.1 Excerpts from *Tell the People: Talks with James Yen about the Mass Education Movement*, by Pearl S. Buck, 1945

You remember those symbols, five of them, which are enshrined in practically every Chinese home? They are, you remember, these five characters: heaven, earth, emperor, parent, teacher. Teacher, as you see, is ranked side by side with heaven and earth. The teacher shares the homage and worship of the people with heaven and earth as well as parent and emperor. That tradition, as you know, accounts for the great reverence that the Chinese people, a farmer or laborer, have for the scholar, the teacher. So with an educational atmosphere prevailing in the community, everybody wants to learn, and also to teach....

SOURCE: Pearl S. Buck, *Tell the People: Talks with James Yen About the Mass Education Movement* (New York: The John Day Company, 1945) 44.

Go to **www.chinasince1644.com** for the full text of Document 10.1.

DOCUMENT 10.2 Photograph of Five Character Plaque in Lijiang, April 2006

From top to bottom, the characters read "heaven, earth, emperor, parent, teacher." *(Photo by Cara Abraham)*

Go to **www.chinasince1644.com** for the color photograph in Document 10.2.

DOCUMENT 10.3: Excerpts describing the founding of schools from *Tell the People: Talks with James Yen About the Mass Education Movement* by Pearl S. Buck, 1945

"It required weeks of 'social calls' and group meetings to set the atmosphere. Then the campaign went on almost of itself. A big meeting of the townspeople elected a council to take charge of it. Schools were drawn in, and students volunteered to serve on recruiting teams. Events led up to a mass meeting and parade all around the town to the gaping astonishment of the villagers who had come in to town for market day. There was hardly anyone left unaware of the literacy campaign, what it meant, what it stood for. The recruiting teams went from house to house, and there was no peace for a family until every illiterate between twelve and twenty-five had signed up...."

SOURCE: Pearl S. Buck, *Tell the People: Talks with James Yen About the Mass Education Movement* (New York: The John Day Company, 1945) 17–18.

Go to **www.chinasince1644.com** for the full text of **Document 10.3**.

DOCUMENT 10.4: Excerpts describing the Fellow Scholar Association from *Tell the People: Talks with James Yen About the Mass Education Movement* by Pearl S. Buck, 1945

The creation of a People's Literature was approached scientifically; the writers were trained in the use of language and they studied at first hand the people for whom they were to write. The subjects were stories from Chinese history, general information about modern China, lives of great men and women of China and other nations, simple accounts of scientific discoveries, descriptions of methods of improving agricultural production, information about common ailments and other health knowledge, plays, poems and songs.... We made a special research study of folk songs and folk literature. These are the real living literature of the people. Never written down, but passed on from generation to generation. We had to get those who were familiar with them to recite or sing them while our writers took them down, word for word. Studies of this sort helped to bring our writers to a better understanding of the culture of our race. In folk literature they found a great deal that was fine and true and representative of the best qualities of the Chinese....

SOURCE: Buck, Pearl S. *Tell the People: Talks with James Yen About the Mass Education Movement* (New York: The John Day Company, 1945) 55–56.

 Go to **www.chinasince1644.com** for the full text of **Document 10.4**.

DOCUMENT 10.5 Photograph, "Shanghai Street," 1937

(Getty Images/Hulton Archive/Getty Images)

 Go to **www.chinasince1644.com** for the photograph in **Document 10.5**.

DOCUMENT 10.6d:
Photographs taken on an Ohio man's summer tour of China, 1913

A busy street

Go to **www.chinasince1644.com** for the remaining photographs in **Document 10.6**.

DOCUMENT 10.7: Excerpts from *Family* by Ba Jin, 1931

In contrast to the older generation, Juemin took active measures concerning his marriage. Without the least shyness, he made inquiries about the proposed match. Juehui became his scout. Together with Qin the two brothers formed a committee of three. They discussed tactics—how to block the match with old man Feng's niece, how to publicize the relationship between Juemin and Qin.

As the opening stage of the battle, Juemin made his attitude plain to his Big Brother. Juexin replied that it was not up to him. Juemin requested his stepmother to cancel the match. But Juemin couldn't approach the old man directly and he could find no one with influence to help him. In this family, the Venerable Master Gao [Juemin's grandfather] passed final judgment....

After the preliminary skirmish ended in total failure, Juemin began the second phase of his tactics. He spread the story that unless the family respected his wishes, he would take drastic measures. Since this threat was never permitted to reach the old man's ears, it did not produce any results either.

Then Juemin learned that his horoscope and that of his proposed bride were about to be exchanged, after which a date would be set for the engagement. He heard this news only two weeks after the Venerable Master Gao's birthday. It was then that Juexin had given the old man some indication of Juemin's feelings, but to no avail.

"How dare he disagree?" the patriarch had retorted angrily. "What I say is final!"

SOURCE: Pa Chin, *Family*, trans. Sidney Shapiro (Boston: Cheng & Tsui, 1999 edition).

Go to **www.chinasince1644.com** for the full text of **Document 10.7**.

DOCUMENT 10.8: Excerpts describing view of family from *A Daughter of Han: The Autobiography of a Chinese Working Woman* by Ida Pruitt, 1945

My daughter was a good girl until she was twenty-eight. When she said a word it was a true word, and she did what I told her to do. I was out all day, but while her father lived she was good and safe....But after he died and her husband went away and never returned she learned bad ways from the neighbors in the court....

My daughter had always been a good girl and listened to my words. But now she reproached me for her life. She said that I had spoiled it. The new neighbors in our court became very friendly with my daughter. The woman painted her face. She cut her hair above her temples. It hung over her face in long, parted bangs. She talked all day with my daughter about pleasure. She talked and laughed pleasantly but she was not good. The things she talked about to my daughter were not good.

One day when I came home I found that my daughter had cut her front hair in the same long uneven bangs. I was very angry. I seized the bangs and said that I would tear them out, that only a lewd woman wore such. Good women combed their hair straight back and sensibly. My daughter answered me back and said that she was a married woman now and that she no longer needed to obey me. It was the first time she had ever answered me....

SOURCE: Ida Pruitt, *A Daughter of Han: The Autobiography of a Chinese Working Woman, from the Story Told Her by Ning Lao T'ai-t'ai* (New Haven: Yale University Press, 1945) Chapters 17, 20.

Go to **www.chinasince1644.com** for the full text of **Document 10.8**.

DOCUMENT 10.9: Excerpts from a memoir by Li Xiuwen (1890–1992), describing growing up female

In those days, there were many interesting old formalities and customs in the farming community when a young girl was getting married. The most impressive custom in my memory was the songs-blessing-the-new-bride party. This party given by the bride's female relatives was held the night before the bride left her home. At the party, the ladies took the opportunity to show off their talents and skill making up songs on the spur of the moment. They also took the occasion to amuse and enjoy themselves.

The purpose of the party was a gathering where the female relatives gave praise, congratulations, advice, and good wishes to the bride in songs made up by the participants. First, they brought the bride—a good and obedient girl—to her parents, then to her brothers and sisters. Then they congratulated her for having found a good husband, and they advised her to be an obedient wife and a good daughter-in-law. Finally the songs expressed wishes that she would bear many sons and that she would have a happy and prosperous family.

After the lady relatives finished singing, the bride would sing the songs expressing her sorrow at leaving home and her worries about going to the new family. She hoped her husband would love her and her in-laws would like her....

Source: Li Xiuwen, unpublished memoir.

 Go to **www.chinasince1644.com** for the full text of **Document 10.9**.

DOCUMENT 10.10 Excerpts from the Peking United International Famine Relief Committee's Report on the North China Famine, 1922

The famine of 1920–21 has been a real one. Workers in Shandong [Province] report intense privation. In Zhanhua County, 50 percent of the people in 250 villages were absolutely destitute. In Yucheng, the young crops died close to the earth in the fields which were as dry as the roads, and the starving poor were known to go out and dig up the wheat sprouts, still in the ground, in the fields of the more prosperous neighbors. In Linyi County, where throughout the last six years there had been but one year of good crops, there were in the entire county, but a few pecks of grain and those had been imported. Even chaff had been brought in from other regions. From the province of Hebei, similar reports are made. In the district about Chengde one third of a population of 1,093,000 were in direct need and there were 31,286 deaths from hunger and cold....

Source: Peking United International Famine Relief Committee, *Report on the North China Famine*, 1922, rpt. in Pei-kai Cheng, Michael Lestz, and Jonathan D. Spence, *The Search for Modern China: A Documentary Collection* (New York: W. W. Norton, 1999) 247.

 Go to **www.chinasince1644.com** for the full text of **Document 10.10**.

DOCUMENT 10.11: Excerpts from a memoir by Li Xiuwen (1890–1992), describing life in the village where she grew up, early 20th century

Usually farmers ate rice cooked with sweet potatoes or white potatoes with one dish of home-grown vegetables three times a day. Meat, mixed with vegetables, appeared at the table only on the New Year. People thought of eating melon or vegetables as producing cold in the body, so they ate hot peppers to counteract it. Therefore each family had a hot pepper stone grinding bowl in the house. Some nights, the farmers, after their hard day's work, went out to the river to catch fish, shrimp, and frogs. They would eat the frogs, and dry the fish to save for meals in later days. In the busy farming season, farmers usually ate a little better. At dinner, they added a dish of fried soybeans, cooked dried fish, vegetables, and they might even drink some rice wine. Only the male workers drank rice wine, not female workers. Usually the men and women ate separately. The men's table had better food than the women's table....

SOURCE: Li Xiuwen, unpublished memoir.

 Go to **www.chinasince1644.com** for the full text of **Document 10.11**.

DOCUMENT 10.12: Excerpts from "Agrarian Problems in China," in *Peasant Life in China* by Fei Xiaotong, 1946

There was another dilemma in the Chinese land problem. The national [Guomindang] government with all its promises and policies on paper was not able to carry out any practical measures owing to the fact that most of the revenue was spent on its anti-communist campaign, while, as I have pointed out, the real nature of the communist movement was a peasant revolt due to their dissatisfaction with the land system. Despite all kinds of justification on either side, one thing is clear: that the conditions of the peasants are getting worse and worse. So far no permanent land reform has been accomplished in any part of China since the recovery of the Red Area [Jiangxi Soviet] by the government.

It must be realized that a mere land reform in the form of reduction of rent and equalization of ownership does not promise a final solution of agrarian problems in China. Such a reform, however, is necessary and urgent because it is an indispensable step in relieving the peasants. It will give a breathing space for the peasants and, by removing the cause leading to "revolt," will unite all forces in finding the way to industrial recovery.

SOURCE: Fei Xiaotong, *Peasant Life in China: A Field Study of Country Life in the Yangtze Valley* (New York: Oxford University Press, 1946) 284–285.

 Go to **www.chinasince1644.com** for the full text of **Document 10.12**.

DOCUMENT 10.13:
Excerpts from the novel *Rickshaw* by Lao She, 1936

[Xiangzi] had to save all he could; otherwise he couldn't get his own rickshaw soon. Even if he bought one today and lost it tomorrow, he still had to buy one. This was his ambition, his hope, even his religion. It would simply be a waste of his life if he didn't buy a rickshaw. Thoughts of becoming an official, getting rich, buying property, these were all beyond him. Pulling a rickshaw was all he was good for. To be able to buy a rickshaw was the only reliable hope he could have. He could not face himself if he didn't buy a rickshaw. This hope filled his mind all day long as he counted and recounted his money. Should a day come when he forgot it then he would have forgotten himself and would know he was only a beast of burden, running along the streets without any promise and without any manhood....

SOURCE: Lao She, *Rickshaw: The Novel Lo-t'o Hsiang Tzu*, trans. Jean M. James (Honolulu: University of Hawaii Press, 1979) 39.

 Go to **www.chinasince1644.com** for the full text of **Document 10.13**.

DOCUMENT 10.14: Excerpts describing working life, from *A Daughter of Han: The Autobiography of a Chinese Working Woman* by Ida Pruitt, 1945

But the worst trouble I had with her was the trouble of the eyeglasses. I asked for time off to go down town to have mine mended. She said that that was not necessary. The cook could take them to town the next time he went, and I could wear hers. She took them out of her pocket and gave them to me. They were a very fine pair of bifocals. It was a pleasure to wear them.

The next day I was not feeling well. I had a headache, and so I went to a neighbor's to have my temples cupped for my headache. While there, lying on the bed, I felt the glasses in my pocket, so I took them out, fearing that I would lie on them and break them. The cupping took a long time and we talked about many matters. I forgot the glasses.

After I left, the little boy of the house, a boy of about nine, saw them and said to his mother, "Mother, let me take these to auntie." The children of the family called me auntie. As he was running along the street after me, calling me and the holding the glasses up in his hand, he met a man who stopped him and said, "Let me see them. What is it?" He took them in his hands, put them in his pocket, and ran away. As he had long legs he was soon out of sight. I heard the wails of the child calling me and turned.

"He took the glasses, he took the glasses." Then I was frightened. What should I do? The man was gone. He could not be caught. It was Sunday afternoon. I knew that Miss Mason had gone to church. I went to her house and waited at the gate for her return. When she saw me she said, "Oh, amah. It is Sunday. What are you doing here?" And she was all smiles and pleasant. But when I told her, her face changed. "They were a very valuable pair of glasses. You are a naughty amah. You do not need to come anymore."

So I went home and was very miserable indeed. She did not believe that the glasses had been stolen. She thought that I had sold them or kept them for myself. I felt pressed down till I could not breathe. I had offered to pay for them, but where could I find the money?...

SOURCE: Ida Pruitt, *A Daughter of Han: The Autobiography of a Chinese Working Woman* (New Haven: Yale University Press, 1945) 215.

 Go to **www.chinasince1644.com** for the full text of **Document 10.14**.

DOCUMENT 10.15: **Clips from** *Northeast Historic Film* **(Archives), 1934**

 Go to **www.chinasince1644.com** for the clips of **Document 10.15.**

Activities

ACTIVITY 1: Researching the Mass Education Movement

Part 1: Read and Discuss

Read the statements by James Yen (10.1) and examine the Five-Character Plaque (10.2). Prepare to discuss:

1. How does the use of the word "laboratory" reflect a modern approach to education?

2. How might this attitude affect the success or failure of an educational movement like James Yen's?

3. How would you answer the questions Yen poses?

4. What is the significance of the Five-Character Plaque? Yen writes that such plaques used to be present in "every Chinese home." What does this suggest about traditional values in China?

Part 2: Evaluate

Read about James Yen's efforts to start schools in rural areas (10.3) and examine Pearl Buck's conversation with him (10.1). Evaluate his attempts by answering the following:

1. What inspired James Yen to start educating illiterate Chinese workers?

2. What challenges did James Yen face when starting a modern school in a rural village?

3. What did he need to do to successfully meet these challenges?

4. If the rural villagers understood the value of literacy, why would they still be hesitant about learning to read?

5. Who were the key people who truly made a difference in the campaign to establish schools?

6. How and when were schools set up in your community? How does that compare to Yen's work?

Part 3: Discuss and Create

Read about James Yen's Fellow Scholars Association (10.4).

1. How did the Fellow Scholars Association work? What was expected from Fellow Scholars?

2. How did education influence other aspects of a rural Chinese person's life? Cite evidence from the text.

3. What was the significance of having text be written in the vernacular?

4. What challenges did Yen take on beyond improving literacy? Why?

Creative Extensions:

Choose from among the following and be sure to incorporate your thinking from Parts 1–3:

- Write an article for a community newspaper describing James Yen's work in rural China.

- Create a poster that compares Yen's work to another reform or development effort elsewhere in the world.

ACTIVITY 2: Life in Shanghai, the "Paris of the East"

Examine the photograph "Shanghai Street" (10.5) and complete the analysis worksheet (Item 10.A). Discuss the Western influences that you notice. Then see Chapter 10 Activity Websites for more photographs of Shanghai. Compare and contrast Shanghai and Paris in the 1920s and 1930s. Use a Venn diagram or other graphic organizer to note your observations. Write an editorial for a newspaper explaining why it was or was not justified to call Shanghai the "Paris of the East."

ACTIVITY 3: Examining an American's Perspective

Your teacher will divide the photographs taken by an American tourist in 1913 among the class (10.6a–e). Use the photograph analysis sheet (Item 10.A) to help you note all the details in the images. As the class views each photo on a screen, report on the ten details you consider most important. Discuss as a class:

1. The photographs were taken by an American tourist. How does that affect what is shown? Would a Chinese traveler have taken these same photographs? Why or why not?

2. What have you learned about China in 1913 from these photographs?

3. What issues arise when you generalize about a country roughly the size of the United States based on five photographs?

4. What do you find most striking about the images?

5. What conclusions can you draw about relationships between people in the photos?

Extended Research:

Search online or in a library to find photographs taken in other countries around the same time. Compare those images to the ones from China.

ACTIVITY 4: Comparing Rural with Urban China

View the film clips from Northeast Historic Film (10.15). Prepare to discuss as a class:

1. How is the rural landscape different from the urban ones you have seen?
2. What kind of work did people do in the rural areas? What jobs did people do in the cities? How do the differences reflect the economy?
3. What are the primary means of transportation in the cities depicted in the films?
4. How do rural people and urban people respond differently to foreigners filming them?

ACTIVITY 5: Contrasting Perspectives

Part 1: Write

Write your answers to the following questions. (You will refer to them after you complete the reading for this activity.)

1. What traditional values are upheld by the older generation in your family?
2. What modern values are you, the younger generation, pursuing that may differ from your traditional family values? What traditional family values are you upholding?
3. Have you ever gone against the wishes of your family? What happened? If not, would you ever go against the wishes of your family? Why or why not?

Part 2: Written Response to Reading

Literature of this period reflects many historical truths about the lives of the people. Read the selections from Ba Jin's *Family* (10.7) and answer the questions for each part (Item 10.B).

Writing Extension:

Working in small groups, each member will examine in writing a dilemma faced by one of the characters. (Juexin and his arranged marriage; Juexin and his new job; Juexin taking over his family's affairs; Juemin facing an arranged marriage; Juehui handling his feelings for Mingfeng; Mingfeng facing an arranged marriage as a concubine; Juehui writing for the journal *Dawn*; Qin writing for the journal *Dawn*; Qin entering a coed school; Qin cutting her hair).

Include the following in your writing:

1. What options did the character have to resolve the dilemma?
2. What advice could you give from a 21st century perspective?
3. What advice could you give from the perspective of the era of the novel?

Share your writing with the group.

Part 3: Discuss

Revisit your answers to the questions in Part 1 and discuss your answers to these questions with your classmates.

1. What were the traditional values being upheld by the older generation in the Gao family?

2. What were the modern values being pursued by the younger generation in the Gao family?

3. To what extent were the members of the family in control of their destinies? Were they overwhelmed by the established order of life? Were they swept up by the events of the time? Be prepared to explain your answers.

4. What skills and knowledge would you need to set out on a "new road" like some of the characters in the story?

5. Why do you think the author, Ba Jin, wrote this novel?

6. To what extent could this novel be used by reformers to bring about change? What current novels or movies can you think of that seem to be created with the goal of bringing about change?

Extension Activity:

Contrast the Gao family with the rural family in Pearl Buck's *The Good Earth*. Though told from the perspective of the father, *The Good Earth* also explores the upheaval of this time period and the changes the younger generation tries to make.

ACTIVITY 6: Social Action: Researching and Synthesizing

The changes in Republican-era China affected different people in different ways. Women, peasants, and the urban working poor all faced challenges in surviving and prospering in a changing China. Our information about these people comes from varied sources, as well. Consider the source when reading each selection assigned below. Does the type of source make the information more or less reliable?

You may want to read all the documents, or the class can be divided into "expert groups." If the class splits into groups, your expert group will read the documents about either women, peasants, or the urban working poor. Then you will complete a mobilization campaign to change ancient traditions in order to modernize China. Be sure to refer to the information in the documents when presenting your group's work to the class.

Group One: Women's Lives

Read about women's lives in the excerpts from Ida Pruitt's *Daughter of Han* (10.8), and Li Xiuwen's memoir (10.9) and take notes in response to the questions about each document (Item 10.C). See also Chapter 10 Activity Websites on the companion website for additional resources related to this activity. Then, in small groups, discuss:

1. What was the traditional status of women in society?

2. What physical restraints and social barriers kept women there?

3. What reforms were being proposed to liberate women?

4. What conditions and resources would need to be in place for reform efforts to succeed?

Within your group, organize a public event to advocate for one of the following changes in women's lives:

- Ending foot binding
- Ending arranged marriages
- Ending indentured servitude/slavery

You may want to create a series of slogans to appear on placards and posters. Will you have supporters march in a parade or meet at a rally, or both? Will you have public speakers? Draft a short speech or two that argues persuasively for the changes that your group wants.

Group Two: Peasants' Lives

Read about peasants' lives in the "Report on the North China Famine, 1922" (10.10), Li Xiuwen's memoir (10.11), and Fei Xiaotong's report (10.12) and answer questions about each document (Item 10.D). Then, in small groups, discuss:

1. What were the benefits and hardships in a Chinese peasant's life at this time?

2. What recourse did peasants have when natural disasters, corrupt tax collectors, or harsh landlords reduced their ability to provide enough food for the family?

3. What reforms would you propose to help peasants?

4. What conditions and resources would need to be in place for reform efforts to succeed?

Within your group, plan a new peasants' association to address the ecological, economic, and political problems faced by farmers in the early twentieth century. What will you call your new association? How will you encourage people to join? Will you have public speakers? Draft a short speech or two that argues persuasively for the changes your group wants. (Note: Refer back to Document 9.3 to find out about the Peasant Associations that Mao Zedong observed in 1927.)

Group Three: Lives of Urban Working Poor

The urban poor was the group that the Communist Party targeted to help after its 1921 founding led by the Comintern. Read about the lives of the urban working poor in Lao She's *Rickshaw* (10.13) and Ida Pruitt's *Daughter of Han* (10.14). Answer questions about each document (Item 10.E). Then, in small groups, discuss:

1. What did Xiangzi and Ning Lao do to survive?

2. How were Xiangzi and Ning Lao treated by their respective employers?

3. Do you think each would have been better off with or without an extended family?

4. What could each have done to improve his or her life?

Within your group, organize a public event to advocate for one of the following changes in the lives of the Chinese urban working poor in the 1920s and 1930s by:

- Establishing a minimum wage
- Organizing a labor union

See Chapter 10 Activity Websites on the companion website for additional resources related to this activity. You may want to create a series of slogans to appear on placards and posters. Will you have supporters march in a parade or meet at a rally, or both? Will you have public speakers? Draft a short speech or two that argues persuasively for the changes your group wants.

ACTIVITY 7: **Constructing a newspaper**

In the 1920s and 1930s, newspapers and journals were distributed and read in China's cities and towns by officials, politicians, educators, students, businessmen, and professionals. They contained important information about the affairs of the day and issues of concern. As a class, you will produce one or more newspapers that will serve the same purpose—informing others about the important issues in China, 1912–1937. Each newspaper should contain the following sections:

1. "On the street" interviews with people (students, women, peasants, individuals from the urban working poor) with a picture and a one-to-two sentence caption commenting on the state of China from their particular perspective

2. Reports on activities by the women's movement, labor movement, peasant movement, and student movement

3. Articles that review earlier material (from Chapters 8 and 9) and summarize national political news and international news

4. International updates about what is happening in Japan, Russia, France, Great Britain, and the United States with regard to movements to improve the condition of women, labor, peasants, and/or students (will require additional research)

5. Lyrics (actual or student-invented) to new patriotic songs

6. Op-ed page with letters supporting and opposing current government policies and China's position in the international community

7. Images; for example, the national flag, important people, city street scenes, rural village scenes

8. Want ads seeking the ideal teacher to work in Yen's education efforts

9. Advertisements for consumer products and services appropriate to the period

Suggested Resources

Books

Buck, Pearl S. *The Good Earth*. New York: Washington Square Press, 1931.
A novel about a farmer and his family confronted by new practices that threaten to wash away old traditions. It includes themes of women's rights, family, class conflict, spiritual and moral trials, and hardships of the modern world. Buck won the Pulitzer Prize for this work, and in 1938, won the Nobel Prize for Literature.

Buck, Pearl S. *East Wind, West Wind*. Wakefield, RI: Moyer Bell, 1930.
The story of a Chinese sister and brother who give up old traditions such as foot binding and arranged marriages.

Chang, Jung. *Wild Swans: Three Daughters of China*. New York: Simon & Schuster, 1991.
A tale of three generations of women in China that spans the twentieth century.

Gilmartin, Christina. *Engendering the Chinese Revolution: Radical Women, Communist Politics, and Mass Movements in the 1920s*. Berkeley: University of California Press, 1995.

Hsing, Chun. *Baptized in the Fire of Revolution: The American Social Gospel and the YMCA in China, 1919–1937*. Bethlehem, Pa.: Lehigh University Press, 1996.

Li, Leslie. *Bittersweet*. Boston: C.E. Tuttle, 1992.
This novel recounts the life of the author's grandmother and provides insights into Chinese traditions and values.

See, Lisa. *Shanghai Girls: A Novel*. New York: Random House, 2009.
Two sisters living in Shanghai in the 1930s are sent by their parents to California to be married to Gold Mountain men. Detained at Angel Island for months, they face the harsh reality of their new life outside of Shanghai.

Shen Congwen. "Xiaoxiao." Trans. Eugene Chen Eoyang. *The Columbia Anthology of Modern Chinese Literature*. Ed. Joseph S.M. Lau and Howard Goldblatt. New York: Columbia University Press, 1995. 97–110.
The short story which the film *Girl from Hunan* is based upon.

Spence, Jonathan D. and Annping Chin. *The Chinese Century: A Photographic History of the Last Hundred Years*. New York: Random House, 1996.

Tsukiyama, Gail. *Women of the Silk*. New York: St. Martin's Press, 1991.
Set in rural China in the 1920s and 1930s, this is a story of girls whose families "give them to silk work" in factories.

Wang Ping. *Aching for Beauty: Footbinding in China*. Minneapolis: University of Minnesota Press, 2000.

Zarrow, Peter Gue. *China in War and Revolution, 1895-1949*. New York: Routledge, 2005.
Zarrow addresses social conditions in rural and urban environments as well as social reform movements of the early twentieth century.

Websites

Heavenly Feet Society (Anti-Footbinding League), British Museum
http://www.britishmuseum.org/explore/high-lights/highlight_objects/asia/h/heavenly_feet_society_badge.aspx
A badge from the Heavenly Feet Society, a group in opposition to the Chinese custom of foot binding.

Reaching for Gold: The YMCA and the Olympic Movement in China from 1895–1920, University of Minnesota Libraries
https://www.lib.umn.edu/apps/ymca/reachgold/
An online exhibition about the history of the YMCA in China.

Sidney D. Gamble Photographs, Duke University
http://library.duke.edu/digitalcollections/gamble/
Approximately 5,000 photographs, primarily of China, taken between 1917 and 1932. Search by place to view photographs from different Chinese cities.

Virtual Shanghai
http://www.virtualshanghai.net/Photos/Images
A website about the history of Shanghai from the mid-nineteenth century to the present. It includes documents, maps, images, and essays.

■ **A CLOSER LOOK**

Fei Xiaotong, Sociologist and Anthropologist

Fei Xiaotong (1910–2005) was recognized in China and the United States as a leading expert on China's agricultural society. Educated at Christian mission schools and a graduate of Yenching and Tsinghua universities, he earned his doctorate from the London School of Economics in 1936. Fei originally wanted to become a physician, but like Lu Xun he decided that "China's problem was not sickness, not a medical problem. It was a social problem and a political problem. So I went into the social sciences."

He conducted research in rural areas, studying everything from kinship to religion to marriage customs, but mostly focusing on economics. He discovered that farmers relied upon local industries such as growing silkworms to make a living. His proposal to revive the economic viability of rural areas as the key to reviving China itself was first developed in the 1930s, but was not adopted in China until the 1980s. In the 1950s, Fei also studied ethnic minorities in Guizhou and Guangxi provinces. He taught hundreds of college students in China and lectured at many universities in the United States during World War II. In China, he joined the Democratic League in 1944, an alternative to the Guomindang and the CCP.

A few years after the Communists came to power in 1949, Fei was denounced during the Anti-Rightist Campaign (1957) and again during the Cultural Revolution (1966–1976). He was forbidden to teach, stripped of his official posts, and after he was sent to the countryside to be a farm laborer, many of his papers were destroyed. He returned to Beijing in 1972 and was politically rehabilitated. In 1994, he was awarded the prestigious Ramon Magsaysay Award for Community Leadership established by the Rockefeller Brothers Fund.

■ *For more about Fei and his work, refer to Chapter 1. Document 1.2 has additional excerpts from his book* Peasant Life in China. *Discuss: What was the significance of Fei Xiaotong's research in China's villages? What lessons did he learn?*

Films

Girl from Hunan (110 mins; 1986)
An adaptation of the short story "Xiaoxiao" by Shen Congwen. A teenage girl is sent to marry a toddler in a remote Chinese village. As she matures, she enters into an illicit love affair and has to face the consequences.

Rickshaw Boy (120 mins; 1982)
An adaptation of Lao She's novel *Rickshaw*. The film captures the grim realities of life for the urban working poor in 1920s China.

CHAPTER RESOURCES

 Excerpts of these primary source documents appear in this chapter. Go to **www.chinasince1644.com** for the full version of these documents and for the Supplementary Materials.

CHAPTER 11

China Occupied and Splintered, 1937–1945

By Rachel Zucker Gould

Chapter Contents

Escalating War

The Nanjing Massacre

International Involvement

The Impact of War

Biological Warfare

Key Idea

Between 1937 and 1945, the Chinese fought what they refer to as the "War of Resistance Against Japan," a war that caused extraordinary hardship for the vast majority of Chinese citizens. At the same time, both the Communists and the Guomindang laid the groundwork for a future confrontation.

Guiding Questions

How can a nation divided the way China was in the 1930s defend itself against an aggressive invading force?

Are there rules in warfare? Why? What are they, and how can they be enforced?

What is the impact of warfare and occupation on the lives of ordinary citizens?

What was China's role in World War II?

Terms to Know

biological warfare

collaborator

communism

Generalissimo

nationalism

occupation

Essay

After the Japanese took over Manchuria (*Manzhou* 满洲) and Inner Mongolia (*Neimenggu* 内蒙古) in 1931 and 1936, Japan and China engaged in minor conflicts until July 1937, when the Marco Polo Bridge Incident (near Beijing) finally ignited full-scale war between the two countries. Both countries used this small skirmish between Japanese soldiers, who claimed they were being attacked, and Chinese soldiers, who fiercely resented Japanese presence, as a reason to escalate violence.

Escalating War

As the Japanese advanced farther south, Chinese troops fled Beijing (北京) on July 28, 1937. The Japanese subsequently captured Tianjin (100 km southeast of Beijing) and then attacked Shanghai, the financial center, on August 13. There began a three-month siege, which cost the Chinese approximately 270,000 of their best-trained men. Generalissimo Chiang Kai-shek (*Jiang Jieshi* 蒋介石) appealed to the League of Nations, and on October 6, 1937, the League condemned Japanese incursions into China, but the countries that made up the League were cautious about offending the Japanese; they provided no assistance. The confrontation ended with the Guomindang[1] (国民党) troops withdrawing to Nanjing (南京).[2] China's capital was to be defended "to the last man," insisted Chiang. But in the face of the approaching Japanese bombers and troops, the disorganized Chinese forces held the city for four days and then fled. On December 13, 1937, Nanjing fell to the Japanese.

[1] Spelled Kuomintang (KMT) in Taiwan. The Guomindang were also known as the Nationalists.

[2] China's capital after Chiang Kai-shek came to power in 1927.

The Nanjing Massacre

The battle-wearied Japanese troops initially killed approximately 90,000 Chinese soldiers who had surrendered. They then continued to slaughter men who they suspected were soldiers disguised as civilians. The violence escalated further as Japanese soldiers raped an estimated 20,000 women and girls. Over a seven-week period, the Japanese soldiers massacred between 150,000 and 300,000 men, women, and children. Historians have attempted to explain the appalling violence of the Nanjing Massacre (*Nanjing Datusha* 南京大屠杀) as the culmination of dehumanizing hand-to-hand combat experienced by Japanese soldiers in the earlier Battle of Shanghai, or as the result of the soldiers' frustration and hunger caused by Chinese scorched-earth tactics and rumors of Chinese torture of Japanese prisoners of war. Additionally, Japanese Emperor Hirohito's failure to direct his soldiers to adhere to existing international laws concerning the treatment of prisoners of war implied that human rights did not apply to the Chinese.[3] It is frequently claimed by Chinese journalists, but difficult to verify, that Emperor Hirohito's uncle, Prince Yasuhiko Asaka, Commander of the Central China Area Army, issued a secret directive to "kill all captives." While the exact number of people killed is now a nationalistic point of debate between the two countries, no historian questions the magnitude of the horror.

A Fractured China

Initially, no foreign power came to China's defense. In June 1937, a desperate Chiang Kai-shek ordered the Yellow River (*Huang He* 黄河) dikes blown up. This slowed the Japanese offensive by three months, but the resulting floods killed an unknown but large number of Chinese peasants. The Japanese soon occupied the wealthier, more developed coastal areas

[3] Herbert Bix, *Hirohito and the Making of Modern Japan* (New York: HarperCollins, 2000) 360.

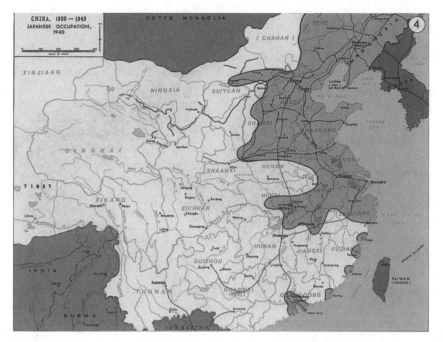

Shaded area in eastern China was under Japanese occupation.
(Courtesy of the United States Military Academy.)

and the most fertile land. After the fall of Nanjing, the Guomindang had retreated to Wuhan (武汉). In October 1938, they moved their capital deep into China—to Chongqing (重庆) in Sichuan Province (四川). In an extraordinary human feat, they dismantled and transported factories, universities, and the entire imperial art collection. Hundreds of thousands of men, women, and children walked hundreds of miles to escape occupied regions. The Japanese established several puppet or collaborationist governments in areas they held or which were under the control of local warlords. External and internal forces had splintered China.

The Communists Grow Stronger

In 1941, the United Front (*Tongyi Zhanxian* 统一战线), which had been loosely cobbled together with help from the Russians, fell apart, and the Guomindang and Communists (*Gongchandang* 共产党) fought the Japanese separately. In several instances, Guomindang troops attacked Communist soldiers rather than focusing on their mutual enemy. Those favoring greater resistance to the Japanese joined the Communists in their stronghold closer to the front at Yan'an (延安) in Shaanxi Province (陕西) (see Chapter 9). This Yan'an Period, from 1937–1945, was a time of regrouping for the Communists. Mao Zedong (毛泽东) had the opportunity to read Marx and adapt aspects of Communist thought to his perception of what China would need to recover from decades of conflict. The two pillars of Maoism—land reform and revolutionary nationalism—were designed to recruit peasants who sought power after generations of disenfranchisement. The lure of land ownership and resistance against the Japanese fueled the growing Communist forces. Membership in the Party rose from 40,000 in 1937 to 800,000 in 1940 and to 1.2 million by 1945.[4]

---

[4] Jonathan D. Spence, *The Search for Modern China* (New York: W.W. Norton, 1999) 436, 456.

International Involvement

While the conflict between Chinese and Japanese forces was reported in the Western press, European countries were coping with the German invasion, occupation, and bombing. An ambivalent United States maintained its official isolationist position.[5] When Japan bombed Pearl Harbor in December 1941, however, everything changed. Great Britain, the Soviet Union, and the United States recognized that by refusing to surrender, the Chinese were tying up two-fifths of Japan's armed forces, preventing them from waging war elsewhere. Western allies began to extend massive loans to the Guomindang government, and to send equipment and fuel via India. At the Cairo Conference of 1943, the Allied powers vowed to eventually defeat Japan and to restore to China all occupied land. They also pledged not to (re)establish their own imperial control in China.

President Franklin Delano Roosevelt sent General Joseph Stilwell to serve as a liaison with Chiang Kai-shek and commander in chief of the American forces in the China-Burma-India region (see A Closer Look at the end of the chapter). Despite many setbacks, gradually the course of the war began to shift. In August 1945, after the United States dropped the second nuclear bomb on Nagasaki, Japan finally surrendered.

Biological Warfare

The Chinese citizenry had endured enormous hardships under Japanese occupation. The Communists' guerrilla tactics and attempts to organize local opposition often met with brutal reprisals: Japanese soldiers eradicated entire villages. In addition, Japanese researchers conducted extensive experiments on prisoners of war and civilians.[6] The most notorious center for these experiments was Unit 731, which had been built outside Harbin (*Ha'erbin* 哈尔滨) in Heilongjiang Province[7] (黑龙江) in 1932. Japanese doctors and their medical staff deliberately infected people with bubonic plague, cholera, anthrax, and dozens of other pathogens. They experimented with ways to manage burns, frostbite, and bullet wounds after first causing the physical trauma. They also conducted "field tests" by dropping plague bombs on several Chinese cities. It is extremely difficult to determine how many people died as a result of this biological warfare. Estimates range from at least 3,000 at Unit 731 alone to more than 200,000 when the germ warfare field experiments are included.

The guerilla fighting by the Communist Red Army (*Hong Jun* 红军) and the tactical attacks by the Guomindang mired two-fifths of the Japanese Army in a costly and unproductive conflict, contributing to Japan's defeat in 1945. However, when the almost decade-long War of Resistance Against Japan (*Kang Ri Zhanzheng* 抗日战争) ended, fighting continued in China, over who would ultimately govern the nation.

---

[5] Nevertheless, the Roosevelt administration authorized the United States Army Air Force to recruit "volunteer" pilots. The "Flying Tigers" fought against the Japanese in China.

[6] In addition to Chinese people, Koreans, Russians, and Mongolians were also victims of this experimentation.

[7] At that time known as Manchuria

Primary Sources

DOCUMENT 11.1:
"Military Door Gods," a print by Huang Yao, late 1930s

Huang Yao, a famous cartoonist of the 1930s from Shanghai, fled to Chongqing to escape the Japanese. His images adorned doors in Guomindang areas throughout the war. The banners say "Defeat Japan, revive China" and the children hold discs that proclaim, "Those who have money should donate money, those who have strength should give strength." The sun emblem was on the Guomindang flag. *(Private collection.)*

 Go to **www.chinasince1644.com** for the color image in **Document 11.1**.

DOCUMENT 11.2:
"Study," a woodblock print by Jing Yun, 1937–1945

Jing Yun was among those who escaped from eastern China to Yan'an, the head-quarters of the Communist forces and the setting for this print. While woodblock is a traditional form of printing, this composition reflects both European influence and Chinese elements, such as use of line and uncluttered or white space. (*Courtesy of the Picker Art Gallery, Colgate University [1968.93].)*

 Go to **www.chinasince1644.com** for the image in **Document 11.2**.

DOCUMENT 11.3: Excerpts from a memoir by Li Xiuwen (1890–1992), describing life under Japanese invasion and occupation

At the beginning of the war, people left their homes in the war zones and came to Guilin for their safety. Those who were wealthy immediately bought houses and properties in the city for them to live in. Some could only afford to rent a house or a few little rooms and some just built the simplest living space with wooden boards and bamboo outside the city....

The city population increased from under 100,000 to 300,000. Government and business offices and civilian organizations moved in and spread all over the city. More new business offices, stores, hotels, restaurants and teahouses were opened. There was a teahouse every block, a restaurant on every other block....

[T]here was an interesting open market where people bought and sold second-hand clothes, personal belongings, furniture and everything that one could think of. The majority of the customers were refugees from other parts of the country. When they arrived in Guilin, they couldn't find work right away. When their savings were exhausted, they had to sell their clothes and belongings for food. Some sold the things that they had no use for anymore, and some reduced their belongings for convenience in traveling. However, when they needed something cheap, they went there to buy. This marketplace was very busy and crowded. When the enemy came close to Guilin, the people sold their belongings and turned them into money to escape from the city....

SOURCE: Li Xiuwen, unpublished memoir.

 Go to **www.chinasince1644.com** for the full text of **Document 11.3**.

DOCUMENT 11.4: Interview with Hsu King-Ming, May 2007

Despite the war, those were our happiest times. We were children. We played despite the Japanese bombing every night. A lot of things didn't seem unbearable. [To escape the Japanese occupation,] we walked from Shanghai to Xi'an, the four of us, (uncles and dad) and hired a person to pull a two-wheeler to pull bedding, no clothes. China still had floods then. Some places we would walk on high ground; sometimes we would take boats. We would eat where we could. Once at an inn after the meal, my father inquired about the meat, and they told us we had eaten human flesh. That is what they told me; I really do not know. Mostly it was steamed buns made of sorghum flour, not white. We stayed in inns. Not many others were traveling because we were supposed to stay in a small group to not gather attention. My family was eight children. We left the youngest three behind in Shanghai to be sent for later....

SOURCE: Hsu King-Ming, interview with Rachel Zucker, May 2007.

 Go to **www.chinasince1644.com** for the full text of **Document 11.4**.

DOCUMENT 11.5: Excerpts from the diary of John Rabe, a witness to the Nanjing Massacre, 1937

Our Chinese servants and employees, about 30 people in all including immediate families, have eyes only for their "master." If I stay, they will loyally remain at their posts to the end....

The rest of the poor servants, most of whom are actually from northern China, simply don't know where to go. I wanted to send off the women and children at least, offered their husbands money for the trip, but they don't know what to do. They want to go back home to the north, but there's war there, too; and so they would rather just huddle here around me. Under such circumstances, can I, may I, cut and run? I don't think so. Anyone who has ever sat in a dugout and held a trembling Chinese child in each hand through the long hours of an air raid can understand what I feel....

Times are bitterly hard here in the country of my hosts, who have treated me well for three decades now. The rich are fleeing; the poor must remain behind. They don't know where to go. They don't have the means to flee. Aren't they in danger of being slaughtered in great numbers? Shouldn't one make an attempt to help them? Save a few at least? And even if it's only our own people, our employees?...

SOURCE: Erwin Wickert, ed., *The Good Man of Nanking: The Diaries of John Rabe* (New York: Vintage, 2000) 5–6.

 Go to **www.chinasince1644.com** for the full text of Document 11.5.

DOCUMENT 11.6: The Empire of Japan's 66th Regiment 1st Battalion Report, December 13 1937

Battalion report: At 2:00 (P.M.) received orders from the Regiment commander: to comply with orders from Brigade commanding headquarters, all prisoners of war are to be executed. Method of execution: to divide the prisoners into groups of a dozen. Shoot to kill separately. It is decided that the prisoners are to be divided evenly among each company…and to be brought out from their imprisonment in groups of 50 to be executed. The vicinity of the imprisonment must be heavily guarded. Our intentions are absolutely not to be detected by the prisoners. Every company is to complete preparation before 5:00 P.M. Executions are to start by 5:00 and action is to be finished by 7:30.

SOURCE: Iris Chang. *The Rape of Nanking: The Forgotten Holocaust of World War II* (New York: Penguin, 1998) 41.

 Go to **www.chinasince1644.com** for the text of Document 11.6.

DOCUMENT 11.7: Photo at Nanjing Massacre Museum, 2006

(Photo by Liz Nelson)

 Go to **www.chinasince1644.com** for the color photograph in Document 11.7.

DOCUMENT 11.8:
"Snow Falls on China's Land," a poem by Ai Qing, 1937

Snow falls on China's land;
Cold blockades China....

On the river of this snowy night,
One small oil lamp drifts slowly
In a rickety boat with a black canopy.
Who sits in there
In the lamplight, head bowed?

—Ah, it's you,
Tousle-haired and grubby-faced young woman.
Wasn't it
Your home
—Warm and happy nest!
That was burnt to the ground
By the brutal enemy?
Wasn't it
A night like this
Bereft of the protection of a man
That, in the terror of death,
You were teased and poked by enemy bayonets?

On such cold nights as tonight,
Our countless
Aged mothers
Huddle together in homes not theirs—
Like strangers
Not knowing
Where tomorrow's wheel
Will take them.
And China's roads
Are so rugged
And so muddy.

Snow falls on China's land;
Cold blockades China....

SOURCE: Ai Qing, "Snow Falls on China's Land," trans. Marilyn Chin, *The Columbia Anthology of Modern Chinese Literature*, ed. Joseph S. M. Lau and Howard Goldblatt (New York: Columbia University Press, 1995) 519–520.

 Go to **www.chinasince1644.com** for the full text of **Document 11.8**.

DOCUMENT 11.9:
Excerpts from "New Faith," a short story by Ding Ling, 1939

He'd left it five days before. Around dawn he'd heard a burst of gunfire coming from just outside the village. He'd leaped out of bed. His wife was already up, and his fifteen-year-old daughter, Jingu, ashen faced, came bursting into the room. Everybody knew what was happening. "Run!" he said. "Get to Granny's house by the back route on the other side of the hill."

"Daddy, oh, Daddy! If we have to die, let's die together."

"Where's my sheepskin vest?"

"Don't worry about your things now! The Japs are nearly here…"

He'd dragged out his bound-foot wife with one hand, his pretty young daughter with the other. Jingu ran crazed with panic. Her face looked hideous, disguised with smears of soot and dirt. They ran ahead of the crowd and soon reached the top of the hill. But then his wife started sobbing. Had their second daughter and their son gotten away? And what about Chen Xinhan's fifty-seven-year-old mother? So leaving the women to flee with the crowd, he slipped off and went back toward the village. People grabbed him, saying, "Don't turn back! Run for your life!" but he didn't know the meaning of fear because his only concern was to rescue his mother. He searched the sweeping tide of people shouting her name…

The village was in total chaos. Bullets flew around his head, people screamed for help. The outlying houses were in flames, and white smoke rolled into the village. There wasn't a soul at his house, just a few chickens darting around the courtyard screeching. He nearly walked right into a hail of bullets. With a shout, he dodged back. He could hear hoofbeats bearing down on him but couldn't risk the time to glance at his rear. The skies were falling, the earth splitting behind him. Crushed, people hadn't the time to draw their next breath; only the sounds of a sharp cry, gasps….

SOURCE: Ding Ling, "New Faith," trans. Jean James and Tani E. Barlow, *I Myself Am a Woman: Selected Writings of Ding Ling*, ed. Tani E. Barlow and Gary J. Bjorge (Boston: Beacon Press, 1989) 283.

Go to **www.chinasince1644.com** for the full text of Document 11.9.

DOCUMENT 11.10: Excerpt from *Shanghai Diary: A Young Girl's Journey from Hitler's Hate to War-Torn China* by Ursula Bacon, 2002

Barely avoiding a collision with a wildly weaving, rattly old automobile, our driver suddenly turned away from the harbor side and entered the web of crowded, narrow, intersecting streets of inner Hongkou. Finally, we came to a stop at a large, run-down building that squatted in an equally run-down courtyard, where a handful of refugees had gathered to greet the new arrivals.

A dark-haired lady in a simple cotton dress stepped forward when the truck squealed to a stop, and with a friendly smile welcomed us in a heavy, unmistakable Viennese dialect. We climbed down from the truck, grabbed our suitcases, and on unsteady sea legs, followed her into the building. A blending of fried onions, stewed cabbage, and a hint of 4711 Cologne greeted us when we entered a large hall-like room. Several rows of rough wooden tables and benches for eating and meeting occupied the center of the hall. The rest of the area was divided into cubicles equipped with two to four cots, which were separated from each other by flimsy sheets or thin blankets hung on clotheslines in an attempt to provide a semblance of privacy....

SOURCE: Ursula Bacon, *Shanghai Diary: A Young Girl's Journey from Hitler's Hate to War-Torn China* (Milwaukie, OR: Milestone Books, 2002) 36.

Go to **www.chinasince1644.com** for the full text of Document 11.10.

DOCUMENT 11.11:
General Joseph Stilwell bust outside the Stilwell Museum, Chongqing

(Photo by Liz Nelson)

Go to **www.chinasince1644.com** for the color photograph in Document 11.11.

DOCUMENT 11.12:
Excerpts from *Red Star Over China* by Edgar Snow, 1968

Bao'an, July 19, 1936

On Land Distribution

SNOW: What is the foremost internal task of the revolution, after the struggle against Japanese imperialism?

MAO: The Chinese revolution, being of bourgeois-democratic character, has as its primary task the readjustment of the land problem—the realization of agrarian reform. Some idea of the urgency of rural reform may be secured by referring to figures on the distribution of land in China today. During the Nationalist Revolution, I was secretary of the Peasant Committee [department] of the Guomindang and had charge of collecting statistics for areas throughout twenty-one provinces.

Our investigation showed astonishing inequalities. About 70 percent of the whole rural population was made up of poor peasants, tenants or part-tenants, and of agricultural workers. About 20 per cent was made up of middle peasants tilling their own land. Usurers and landlords were about 10 per cent of the population. Included in the 10 per cent also were rich peasants, exploiters like the militarists, tax collectors, and so forth. The 10 per cent of the rich, peasants, landlords, and usurers together owned about 70 per cent of the cultivated land.

SOURCE: Edgar Snow, *Red Star Over China: The Classic Account of the Birth of Chinese Communism* (New York: Grove Press, 1968) 445.

Go to **www.chinasince1644.com** for the full text of Document 11.12.

DOCUMENT 11.13: "Chinese Germ Warfare Victims Call for Just Ruling by Japanese Supreme Court," in *China Daily*, June 26, 2006

A group of 180 Chinese who were victims or whose family members were killed by Imperial Japanese Army's germ warfare program, filed a lawsuit with the Tokyo District Court in 1997, demanding 10 million yen each and an apology from the government.

Ichinose Keiichiro, a Japanese lawyer for the plaintiffs, said germ warfare victims had appealed for compensation according to law, and the Japanese court should require the Japanese government to apologize and compensate the victims. Acknowledging the plaintiff's request was the way to realize the rule of justice, said the Japanese lawyer.

"We are not just demanding an apology and compensation from the Japanese government, we are also defending the dignity of the Chinese people," said Lou Xian, another Chinese lawyer for the victims....

SOURCE: Xinhua, "Chinese Germ Warfare Victims Call for Just Ruling by Japanese Supreme Court," *China Daily*, June 26, 2006.

Go to **www.chinasince1644.com** for the full text of Document 11.13.

Activities

ACTIVITY 1: Interpreting Propaganda Art

After reading the introduction on the companion website, examine the two prints (11.1 and 11.2).

Huang Yao's "Military Door Gods" (11.1): The purpose of Door Gods, which remain popular decorations, is to protect homes from evil spirits. List the many details in the image. Then consider:

1. How are these Door Gods like and unlike traditional Door Gods? (Consider color, pose, and symbols.) You can consult page 152 of *The Enduring Legacy of Ancient China* (Cheng & Tsui, 2006) for examples of traditional Door Gods.

2. These Door Gods express one artist's views about his world. What is his perspective? What evidence do you see to illustrate this? How does Huang add to the traditional design of Door Gods as guardians?

3. Why might an artist, especially one who had studied abroad, choose to use traditional folklore figures to express himself?

Jing Yun's "Study" (11.2): You will work in a small group to discuss the setting, the people, and the activities depicted in the woodcut. Then consider the following questions:

1. Looking at how the students and teacher are arranged, what kind of learning is taking place here?

2. What are the workers in front of the cave dwellings doing? What was the artist trying to convey? What is your evidence?

3. Why might a twentieth-century artist choose to use a traditional Chinese form of printing to express himself?

4. What may have been Jing's purpose in creating this piece of art?

5. Both the door gods and the woodcut are political works in support of two different and opposed political groups. How are these two artists' works similar and different?

Creative Extension:

After reading Documents 11.3 and 11.4, design Door Gods from the perspective of Li Xiuwen or Hsu King-Ming. How would their Door Gods be unique? Alternatively, create a pair of Door Gods with symbols and ideas that make your own statement about what you want to guard against and perhaps what you want to "let in" to your life. Explain why you chose the symbols and images that you did.

ACTIVITY 2: Examining War's Impact on Civilians

Part 1: Determining Meaning

Read the excerpts from Li Xiuwen's memoir (11.3) before class. You will work in a small group to examine the map of occupied China (Item 11.A) and identify all the major Chinese cities under Japanese control. Find Chongqing, Yan'an, and Guilin. Compare the map to a topographical map of China (use Google Earth). What areas did Japan target for occupation? Why? Then discuss the memoir:

1. What did you notice about Li Xiuwen's narrative? What new insights did you gain? Cite evidence from the text.

2. Do you think Li gives a trustworthy account of the time period? Why? How do historians verify memoirs and other sources such as diaries, articles, letters, etc.?

3. How would life in your community be different if tens of thousands of people fled from urban centers to your area? What resources would be in short supply? What would be the biggest challenges? What would be the benefits, if any?

4. When Japan's surrender is described, why do you think Li doesn't mention the U.S. bombings of Hiroshima and Nagasaki? How might the end of the war have been viewed in China as compared to the United States or Australia, for example?

As a class you will participate in a "Four Corners" activity.

1. Discuss how the Japanese occupation of coastal China affected civilian life.

2. Create a list of changes and think about which changes would be most important to civilian life. The class will determine the top four changes which will then be posted in the four corners of the room.

3. Go to the corner where you think the change was most significant and discuss your reasons with your peers who are of like mind.

4. With your group, share your reasons (each group will have a turn). You may switch corners if you change your mind at any time during the discussion.

Part 2: Respond to Reading

Read Hsu King-Ming's account of his family's escape (11.4). Then, working in a small group, consider:

1. Hsu was a teenager when he left his home in Shanghai. What can you determine about him and his family from this reading? (For example: class, education level, traditional or non-traditional values, etc.)

2. How can a person be scientifically trained and at the same time believe deeply in the powers of fortune-tellers? Are these beliefs contradictory or can they co-exist?

3. How had the areas that Hsu's family traveled through been affected by the collapse of Chinese control and the influx of westward migrants?

4. Looking at the map (Item 11.A), how do you think Hsu and his family got from Shanghai to Xi'an? What physical barriers did they have to cross?

5. Explain Hsu's father's reaction to finally reaching Xi'an. How far had they traveled, and what did "free China" mean to him?

Be prepared to compare Li's and Hsu's descriptions of leaving their homes in a class discussion.

1. What surprised you in either document? Why?

2. Which events in the accounts are most memorable and what do they illustrate?

3. If you had to leave your home, knowing that it would be occupied by an invading army, what would you take with you? What would you need for the road?

4. How are Li's and Hsu's experiences similar to or different from other materials you have read or seen about war-torn countries?

5. How does the flight of Chinese from occupied regions compare to migrations that are not a result of war? (For example, in the United States consider the Great Western Migration of immigrants in the 1850s, that of African Americans in the South who migrated north to urban areas in the twentieth century, or the Irish migration to the United States during the Great Famine in the 1840s.)

Creative Extension:

Select one scene described by Li Xiuwen or Hsu King-Ming and respond to it by creating a piece of art: for example, a drawing, sculpture, poem, collage, or piece of music.

ACTIVITY 3: Reflecting on the Nanjing Massacre

Part 1: Before Reading

Begin by considering the old saying "All's fair in love and war." Write a response that addresses "All's fair in war." What does this mean? Is it true or should there be rules for warfare? Share your responses. Then come up with and record a possible list of rules that might be effective or necessary in times of war. Some students might believe that no rules are needed or possible. They should explain and defend their position in writing as well.

Part 2: Respond to Reading

Read the excerpts from John Rabe's diary (11.5). Rabe wrote on December 24, 1937 that he "wanted to see these atrocities with [his] own eyes" to be able to speak as an eyewitness later.

1. Why did he think people would need to know about this? What did he expect from the international community?

2. Why did John Rabe stay in Nanjing to protect Chinese people after sending his family away and being told by his employer to flee immediately?

3. What, if anything, surprises you about this diary?

4. How does it challenge your understanding of members of the Nazi Party?

5. How does Rabe's diary deepen your understanding of the war in China?

6. What happened after Rabe returned to Germany?

7. Why do you think Rabe firmly believed that the Nazi Party, which he had joined in 1933, would be interested in and capable of stopping this violence? See Chapter 11 Activity Websites on the companion website for the 25 founding principles of the Nazi Party.

8. Compare the Battalion Report (11.6) to Rabe's diary entries. (Examine style, content, and purpose, for example.)

9. Why are the Japanese officers who wrote the Battalion Report so concerned with concealing the executions from Chinese soldiers? If they truly believed that the executions were permissible, why conceal them?

Part 3: Analyze

Why do humans appear to have such a need to commemorate loss? Together as a class, you will create a list of all the memorials and monuments you can think of. Then star those memorials or monuments that were or are considered controversial because of either the event being memorialized or the design. Some examples might include the Vietnam Veterans Memorial in Washington, D.C.; the Hiroshima Peace Memorial, Hiroshima, Japan; the National Slavery Past Monument in Amsterdam, the Netherlands; and the Monument to the Murdered Jews of Europe in Berlin built on the grounds of the former Nazi headquarters. Hypothesize why these might have been controversial.

Look at the photograph taken at the Nanjing Massacre Museum in Nanjing (11.7). How does this part of the museum convey the loss of hundreds of thousands of lives? Do you think it's effective? Why or why not? See Chapter 11 Activity Websites on the companion website for more photographs of the memorial.

How does a memorial compare to the Battalion Report (11.6) or Rabe's diary (11.5)?

In a group, brainstorm what factual information and emotions you would want to convey in a memorial to the victims of biological warfare or medical experiments. Sketch your design ideas individually.

ACTIVITY 4: Analyzing Literature of the Occupation

Part 1: Quaker Read

After reading excerpts from the poem, the short story, and the memoir (11.8–11.10) you will be assigned to read one of the pieces silently and independently. Then engage in a "Quaker Read": as you read for the second time, select and highlight words, phrases and/or sentences that are particularly powerful or meaningful to you or that create a vivid image in your mind. As a class, share your selected images by reading them aloud at random. Listen while others read a selection they highlighted, and share your selections when moved to do so. (Periods of silence are also allowed.)

Part 2: Literary Analysis

After considering how language is used to engage emotions and develop meaning, analyze these selections by answering the questions under each selection.

"Snow Falls on China's Land," by Ai Qing

1. What do you think Ai Qing is trying to convey in this poem? How does the form or structure of the poem help to convey the meaning?

2. What does the last line mean? How can poetry help people cope with the terrible experiences described here?

3. To whom is the poem directed?

"New Faith," by Ding Ling
Before answering the questions, read about Ding Ling's life in A Closer Look at the end of the chapter.

1. What images dominate parts 1, 2, and 3 of the story? What images dominate the rest of the story? What is the significance of these images?

2. How does the grandmother change from the beginning of the story to the end? (Consider her role, how people view her, and how she views herself.)

3. Why do you think the grandmother had to share her stories? Many people would be silent about a rape, but she forced everyone to listen to what had happened to her. How did her unusual reaction affect her family and the community?

4. What is the author trying to communicate about traditional and newly emerging roles for women? How does this reflect Communist ideology?

5. Based on this story, how did the Communists work to get people to join their movement?

6. Where was Ding Ling when she wrote this short story? Do you think the story was well received by the Communist Party leaders? Why?

Shanghai Diary: A Young Girl's Journey from Hitler's Hate to War-Torn China, by Ursula Bacon

1. How did Ursula feel about leaving home? Why? How would you have felt or reacted in her position? Why?

2. How was China different from Europe in Ursula's experiences? What surprises you about her account?

3. Ursula wrote that her childhood ended. Today, many young people want to stop being a "child" as soon as possible. What could be some advantages to being a child or young adult, specifically in times of great upheaval?

4. What similarities and differences exist between Bacon's account and Hsu's (11.4)? Given that they were of similar ages, is this surprising?

5. What issues may be involved when someone speaks or writes about traumatic events that took place many years earlier?

ACTIVITY 5: Discussing a Western Journalist's Reports

After reading the excerpts from Edgar Snow's book (11.12), A Closer Look on General Joseph Stilwell, and looking at the photograph (11.11), prepare to discuss:

1. Why did the United States choose to support Chiang Kai-shek and the Guomindang but not the Communists, even when both parties were fighting the Japanese?

2. Chiang was storing American resources to fight the Chinese Communists in the future. Why did this frustrate Stilwell?

3. In 1936, Mao told Snow that "the seizure of power is not our (immediate) aim. We want to stop civil war, create a people's democratic government with the Guomindang and other parties, and fight for our independence against Japan" (*Red Star Over China*, 445). List these goals in order of priority for Mao, for Stilwell, and for the Chinese peasants. Why and how might these lists be different?

4. Snow asked Mao to list his goals for China after defeating Japan. What were these goals, and what parts of the population was Mao trying to win over to support his ideas?

5. In this interview with Snow, whom did Mao blame for the problems facing China?

ACTIVITY 6: Debating: Are Reparations the Answer?

Read the news article describing the victims' lawsuit seeking reparations from the Japanese government (11.13). Conduct further research online and in books to learn more about the extent of medical experiments done on people during the Japanese occupation of Manchuria; Unit 731; biological warfare conducted in China; the U.S. response to what Japanese researchers had done in North China; and the most recent developments in the legal case. Half the class will be asked to take the stand that reparations are a necessary next step, and half will be asked to argue that they are not.

EXTENDED RESEARCH:

Conduct further research using books and online sources and present your findings in a paper or a digital presentation.

Suggested topics:

- The Burma Road
- The Flying Tigers
- Unit 731
- U.S. treatment of Japanese individuals involved in biological warfare
- The Nanjing Massacre
- Japanese and Chinese textbook coverage of the war and/or the Nanjing Massacre and other war crimes
- The effects of Japanese war crimes on Chinese-Japanese relations today
- Chiang Kai-shek
- Madame Chiang's role and her speech to the United States Congress
- Compare and contrast the situation of survivors of Japanese biological warfare with that of other groups seeking reparations, such as the descendents of slaves in the United States, Holocaust survivors, and slave wage laborers in Latin America.

Suggested Resources

Books

Bix, Herbert. *Hirohito and the Making of Modern Japan*. New York: Harper Perennial, 2000.

Chang, Iris. *The Rape of Nanking: The Forgotten Holocaust of World War II*. New York: Penguin, 1998.
An account of the 1937 events in Nanking, often considered controversial. For a historian's review of Chang's account, see http://ess.uwe.ac.uk/genocide/reviewswc3.htm by Robert Entenmann.

Ding Ling. *I Myself Am a Woman: Selected Writings of Ding Ling*. Boston: Beacon Press, 1989.

Fenby, Jonathan. *Chiang Kai-Shek: China's Generalissimo and the Nation He Lost*. New York: Carroll & Graf, 2004.

Ha Jin. *Nanjing Requiem: A Novel*. New York: Pantheon Books, 2011.
A novel about an American missionary and college dean who decides to stay in Nanjing during the 1937 Japanese attack.

Honda Katsuichi and Frank Gibney. *The Nanjing Massacre: A Japanese Journalist Confronts Japan's National Shame*. Armonk, NY: M.E. Sharpe, 1999.

Ishikawa Tatsuzō. *Soldiers Alive*. Honolulu: University of Hawaii Press, 2003.
Originally written in 1938, this novella written by a Japanese author describes the march on Nanjing in 1937.

Ropp, Paul. "Civil Wars, Invasion, and the Rise of Communism (1920-1949)." *China in World History*. New York: Oxford University Press, 2010.

Snow, Edgar. *Red Star Over China*. New York: Grove Press, 1993.
U.S. journalist's account of the Chinese Communist movement and its leadership until the late 1930s. Originally published in 1937.

Tobias, Sigmund. *Strange Haven: A Jewish Childhood in Wartime Shanghai*. Chicago: University of Illinois Press, 1999.

Webster, Donovan. *The Burma Road: The Epic Story of the China-Burma-India Theater in World War II*. New York: Farrar, Straus, and Giroux, 2003.

Zarrow, Peter Gue. *China in War and Revolution, 1895-1949*. New York: Routledge, 2005.

Zhao, Yali and John D. Hoge. "Countering Textbook Distortion: War Atrocities in Asia, 1937–1945." *Social Education* 70 (2006): 424–432.

Websites

Asia for Educators
http://afe.easia.columbia.edu/
Select 1900–1950 to view primary sources and a video unit about the Second Sino-Japanese War (1937–1945).

Madame Chiang Kai-Shek Addresses Congress
http://www.history.com/audio/madame-chiang-kai-shek-addresses-congress
Madame Chiang addressed Congress on February 18, 1943, and asked for aid for the Guomindang in their Civil War against the Chinese Communists.

The Memorial Hall of the Victims in Nanjing Massacre by Japanese Invaders
http://www.nj1937.org/english/
The Nanjing Massacre Museum in Nanjing. Site includes photographs and witness statements representing Chinese accounts of the events. Note that this website contains graphic footage from the massacre.

Modern History Sourcebook: The Nanking Massacre, 1937
http://www.fordham.edu/halsall/mod/nanking.asp
From F. Tillman, "All Captives Slain," *The New York Times*, December 18, 1937, pp. 1, 10.

The Nanking Massacre Project: A Digital Archive of Documents & Photographs from American Missionaries Who Witnessed the Rape of Nanking
http://www.library.yale.edu/div/Nanking/
From the Special Collections of the Yale Divinity School Library.

Films

City of Life and Death (135 mins; 2009)
A feature film about the Japanese attack of Nanjing on December 9, 1937.

Nanking (90 mins; 2007)
A documentary about the Japanese invasion of Nanking told through interviews with Chinese survivors, archival footage, and testimonies of Japanese soldiers, interwoven with staged readings of the Westerners' letters and diaries.

Shanghai Ghetto (95 mins; 2002)
This documentary includes interviews with survivors and historians, photographs, and footage of the "Jewish ghetto" and synagogue, which remain in Shanghai today. In English, German, and Chinese with subtitles.

■ **A CLOSER LOOK**

General Joseph Stilwell Enters the Fray

Born in 1883, Joseph Stilwell traced his roots to English settlers who arrived in New England in 1638. He was raised in Yonkers, New York and graduated from West Point in 1904. After serving in World War I, Stilwell divided his time between assignments in China, where he learned to speak fluent Chinese, and teaching Spanish, French, and English at West Point. His service in China included a post as military attaché to the United States embassy from 1935–1939.

Independent-minded and blunt, he earned the name "Vinegar Joe." However, those who served under him also considered him a soldier's general. When President Franklin D. Roosevelt needed a liaison to Generalissimo Chiang Kai-shek, Joseph Stilwell was the obvious choice. Among Stilwell's responsi-bilities was that of ensuring that Lend-Lease supplies from the United States reached Chongqing. He also oversaw the construc-tion of the Ledo Road, which linked to the northern end of the Burma Road and was a vital supply route to landlocked Chongqing.

Stilwell and Chiang Kai-shek did not get along. Stilwell correctly believed that Chiang was hoarding the military supplies from the United States to use against the Communists in the future rather than the Japanese in the present. The American general wanted to reform the dys-functional Guomindang army, a move that Chiang blocked because the upper ranks of his army supported his government. Concluding that Chiang and his government were corrupt, incompetent, and timid, the four-star general routinely referred to him as "Peanut" in his official reports to Washington.

In October 1944, pre-sumably under pressure from Chiang, President Roosevelt recalled Joseph Stilwell. Of his years in China, the general said little except to note: "The trouble was largely one of posture. I tried to stand on my feet instead of my knees. I did not think the knee position was a suit-able one for Americans." Joseph Stilwell died of liver cancer in 1946 at the age of 63. The Ledo Road now bears his name, and the Chinese Communist Party considers him a hero, hon-oring him with a museum in Chongqing, where the general's headquarters once stood.

■ *Why do you think the present Chinese govern-ment honors Stilwell?*

■ **A CLOSER LOOK**

Feminist Writer Ding Ling

Ding Ling is one of the most famous twentieth-century Chinese writers. She was born in Hunan Province in 1904 and educated with the help of her widowed mother. In 1920, sixteen-year-old Ding Ling joined other young intellectuals in Shanghai, in part to avoid the marriage her uncle had arranged. She became deeply involved in the May Fourth Movement (see Chapter 8) and in 1924 married poet Hu Yepin.

Ding published her first short story in 1927, and a collection of her stories the following year. Her work, featuring women struggling with modernity, was extremely popular. In 1931, Ding Ling's husband, who had become active in the League of Left-Wing Writers, was arrested and executed by the Guomindang. Devastated, Ding Ling joined the Communist Party and devoted herself to the cause through her revolutionary writing.

In 1933, the Guomindang arrested her and placed her under house arrest, but she managed to escape three years later and made her way to Yan'an. In time, the Communist Party also tried to stifle her work, especially when she wrote about discrimination against women at Yan'an. *The Sun Shines Over the Sanggan River*, the politically correct novel she wrote in 1949, however, was highly praised.

During the Anti-Rightist campaign in 1957, Ding Ling was once again a target. She was sent to be "reformed through labor" on a farm near the Siberian border. During the Cultural Revolution (see Chapter 14) she endured brutal beatings and was imprisoned from 1970 to 1975. Only after Deng Xiaoping took power did Ding Ling reappear in public. She was a changed woman who no longer spoke about feminist issues or freedom of expression. She died in 1986.

■ *Compare Ding Ling's life story with that of poet Ai Qing (11.8). How would you describe this period in history for writers who were politically inclined? What is the relationship between politics and art? (Consider the prints at the beginning of the chapter as well.)*

CHAPTER RESOURCES

Primary Sources

DOCUMENT 12.1: Excerpt from *China's Destiny* by Chiang Kai-shek, 1943

DOCUMENT 12.2: Excerpt from "Manifesto of the Chinese People's Liberation Army" by Mao Zedong, 1947

DOCUMENT 12.3: Excerpt from General George Marshall's "Personal Statement by the Special Representative of the President," 1947

DOCUMENT 12.4: Letter to the Editor by Ding Keshan, March 30, 1948

DOCUMENT 12.5: Excerpts from a survey sponsored by the North American Chinese Students Christian Association, 1948

DOCUMENT 12.6: "Dead Water," a poem by Wen Yiduo, 1928

DOCUMENT 12.7: Excerpt from Wen Yiduo's speech at the memorial service for Li Gongbu, 1946

DOCUMENT 12.8a–c: Woodblock prints by Li Hua, 1946–1948

DOCUMENT 12.9: Excerpts from reports and writings related to land reform leading up to the founding of the People's Republic of China, 1946–1948

DOCUMENT 12.10: "The People's Liberation Army Captures Nanjing," a poem by Mao Zedong, 1949

Supplementary Materials

ITEM 12.A: Further information and questions related to woodblock prints (Activity 7)

 Excerpts of these primary source documents appear in this chapter. Go to **www.chinasince1644.com** for the full version of these documents and for the Supplementary Materials.

CHAPTER 12

War Continues, 1945–1949

By Philip Gambone

Chapter Contents

The Roots of the Civil War

U.S. Attempts at Mediation

Civil War

The Communist Victory

Key Idea

The Chinese Civil War resulted from a fundamental contradiction between the political objectives of the Guomindang and the Chinese Communist Party. While the Guomindang initially enjoyed international support and material advantages, a combination of their failures and the successful strategies of the Communists led to a Communist victory.

Guiding Questions

What were the respective strengths of the Guomindang and the Chinese Communist Party at the end of World War II?

What role did the United States play in trying to help the two factions form a coalition government? Why?

What attitudes on the part of the Guomindang and the Communists led to a failure to form a coalition government?

What was the military and political stratey of the Guomindang? What was the military and political strategy of the CCP?

Why did the Guomindang lose the civil war?

Terms to Know

Chinese Communist Party (CCP)

coalition

Democratic League

extremist

feudal

Generalissimo

Guomindang (GMD)

manifesto

nationalization

propaganda

reactionary

Essay

With the Japanese surrender in August 1945, World War II came to a close. In China, this signaled the intensification of the struggle for power between the Guomindang (国民党) and the Chinese Communist Party (*Zhongguo Gongchandang* 中国共产党) (CCP).[1] During the War of Resistance Against Japan (*Kang Ri Zhanzheng* 抗日战争) (1937–1945), the two rivals had joined together in an uneasy, bitter alliance (see Chapter 11). Deeply antagonistic, their "coalition" was marked more by suspicion, betrayal, and hostility than by cooperation. As soon as the war was over, each side speedily mustered its forces to try to be the first to receive the surrender of the Japanese, and take possession of their weapons.

Each party enjoyed certain advantages. Under the leadership of Chiang Kai-shek (*Jiang Jieshi* 蒋介石), the Guomindang controlled the major urban areas in unoccupied China. Meanwhile, the Communist forces had grown dramatically during the war against Japan and had the advantage of proximity to Manchuria (*Manzhou* 满洲) in Northeast China, where a strong guerrilla resistance already existed. Mao Zedong (毛泽东) dismissed Chiang as "China's fascist ringleader, autocrat and traitor to the people."[2] The Communists controlled much of the countryside in North China, where the peasants, who numbered about 100 million, saw the CCP as far more sympathetic to their plight.

In an effort to prevent a Communist takeover, the United States ordered the Japanese to surrender only to the Guomindang. The United States further helped the Guomindang by moving half a million men into the areas in North China formerly occupied by the Japanese.

The Chinese Communists also received foreign assistance. Though its help was not as substantial as the aid provided to the Guomindang by the United States, the Soviet Union lent its support to the CCP by turning over weapons, artillery, aircraft, and combat vehicles, which it had confiscated from the Japanese in Manchuria. Furthermore, Japanese prisoners of war were used to train the Communist armed forces.

In the first weeks after World War II, the Guomindang looked to be in the better position. Their armed forces outnumbered those of the CCP (2.7 million to 1 million), and they had more weapons. The Guomindang quickly regained control of most of the major cities in East, Central, and South China. Nevertheless, the Communists did not yield their hold of North China. They used their huge stockpiles of Japanese weapons and advanced into Manchuria, a region rich in minerals and forests. Mao's strategy was to maintain Communist bases in the countryside. From these strongholds, he would mount guerrilla-style attacks and eventually take over the cities.

Attempts at Reconciliation

On August 28, 1945, Mao, escorted by U.S. Ambassador Patrick Hurley, flew to Chongqing (重庆), the wartime capital, for talks with Chiang. Many hoped that civil war could be averted, and at first, a positive outcome seemed a real possibility. The two leaders issued a joint communiqué that acknowledged the importance of peaceful postwar reconstruction. Mao agreed to pull his remaining forces from South China, and the two leaders further agreed to form a unified national army and to resume discussions about China's long-range future. But behind the scenes, the two leaders' distrust of each other festered. Chiang Kai-shek was determined to destroy the Communists. In November 1945, he launched a huge military assault. Mao dug in. He hoped that through ideological work and continued land reform,[3] he would prevail.

---

[1] Guomindang (abbreviated GMD) was spelled Kuomintang (KMT) in the older Wade-Giles system of transcription and was also known as the Nationalist party.

[2] Mao Zedong, "Chiang Kai-shek Is Provoking Civil War," *Selected Works of Mao Zedong*, vol. 4 (Beijing: Foreign Languages Press, 1967) 27.

[3] See Chapter 9, Document 9.3.

In December 1945, U.S. President Harry Truman sent the much respected wartime leader General George Marshall to mediate the dispute. Many in China and the United States were eager to bring the two parties together because they feared the excesses of one-party rule from either side. Twice in 1946, Marshall arranged a truce between the Guomindang and CCP. Talks began about forming a coalition government, but within weeks both sides had violated the truce.

By this time, Mao did not trust the United States. He told an American correspondent: "I doubt very much that the policy of the U.S. government is one of 'mediation.' Judging by the large amount of aid that the United States is giving Chiang Kai-shek to enable him to wage a civil war on an unprecedented scale, the policy of the U.S. government is to use the so-called mediation as a smoke-screen for strengthening Chiang Kai-shek in every way and suppressing the democratic [Communist] forces in China...."[4] Guomindang leaders took measures to ensure that neither the Communists nor the other major opposition party, the Democratic League (*Minzhu Tongmeng* 民主同盟), participated in the National Constitutional Assembly, which met toward the end of 1946 to adopt a new Constitution. In effect, they packed the Assembly with Guomindang supporters, locking out other voices in the formation of China's fledgling "democracy." In January 1947, a deeply frustrated Marshall abandoned his efforts at mediation. Blaming both parties, he wrote, "The greatest obstacle to peace has been the complete, almost overwhelming suspicion with which the Chinese Communist Party and the Guomindang regard each other."[5] China dissolved into civil war.

The Civil War

Early on, most of the battles were won by the Guomindang. Yan'an (延安), an important Communist stronghold, fell to the Guomindang. "How long can the Communist Party keep on?" a U.S. correspondent asked Mao in August 1946. "We can fight to the finish," Mao confidently replied. "We have only millet plus rifles to rely on, but history will finally prove that our millet plus rifles is more powerful than Chiang Kai-shek's aeroplanes plus tanks."[6]

In 1947, the Communists took the offensive in Manchuria. To meet the Communist advance, Chiang committed a half a million men to the campaign and airlifted massive aid to Manchuria's cities. This proved to be a disastrous mistake. The Communists controlled the countryside, and the cities in which the Guomindang were based quickly became isolated from each other. The Communists took Manchuria in November 1948. In the process, Chiang lost some 470,000 of his best troops, in addition to weapons and equipment. With the North firmly in his pocket, Mao turned south.

Communist Victory

Despite the fact that Chiang's army was still superior in terms of equipment and air power, morale within the army and among the civilian populace began to erode. The troops were poorly paid and huge numbers defected. Moreover, some of the Communist military leaders were brilliant strategists; they had a keen understanding of local conditions. Chiang stubbornly refused to listen to better advice from his generals. Pushing his men forward, he exposed them to the superior military tactics of the CCP forces.

On the civilian front, too, there was growing discontent with the Guomindang. Inflation was out of control and the government was riddled with corruption. Many educated Chinese opposed the Guomindang. They pointed to farcical elections, poor leadership, and violations of civil liberties, including the imprisonment, torture, and assassination of critics of the government. "The Government

[4] Mao Zedong, "The Truth About U.S. 'Mediation' and the Future of the Civil War in China," *Selected Works of Mao Zedong*, vol. 4 (Beijing: Foreign Languages Press, 1967) 109.

[5] Department of State Bulletin, January 19, 1947.

[6] *Selected Works of Mao Zedong*, vol. 4, 97–101.

cares for nothing but itself," wrote Zhu Anping, the editor of a popular weekly. "The people have nothing to eat, does it care? It does not.... The Government only protects the wealthy and cares nothing for the poor."[7]

Others, especially the older intellectuals, wanted to reform the Guomindang. They argued that their chances for a democratic society were better with a Guomindang government than one headed by the CCP. Many Chinese were alarmed by the extreme methods the Communists used to address the needs of the peasantry. Beatings, mass killings of landlords, total seizures of land and property—such were the methods peasants adopted, often at the instigation of Communist Party agents.

By the middle of January, first Tianjin (天津) and then Beijing (北京) fell to Communist

General Lin Biao (林彪), and on January 21, 1949, Chiang was forced to resign. The new president tried to negotiate with the Communists, but Mao was not interested. His generals continued pushing south and west. Toward the end of April, Communist troops crossed the Yangzi River (*Chang Jiang* 长江) and took Nanjing (南京). Shanghai (上海) fell in May, Changsha (长沙) in August.

By early fall, it was clear beyond a doubt that the Communists had won the Civil War. At a conference, Mao proudly proclaimed that the Chinese people had stood up. On October 1, 1949, addressing an uproarious crowd at the Gate of Heavenly Peace (*Tiananmen* 天安门) in Beijing, Mao announced the creation of the People's Republic of China. Two months later, remnants of the Guomindang forces fled to Taiwan, where Chiang Kai-shek and a substantial Guomindang military force were already established. The Civil War for political supremacy had ended.

---

[7] Qtd. in Suzanne Pepper, *Civil War in China: The Political Struggle, 1945–1949* (Berkeley: University of California Press, 1978) 144–145.

Primary Sources

DOCUMENT 12.1:
Excerpt from *China's Destiny* by Chiang Kai-shek, 1943

Every Chinese citizen has the right as well as the duty to become a member of the Guomindang. As the central organ directing the work of revolution and reconstruction, the Party treats the people, be they members or non-members, on an equal footing, without the slightest discrimination. It assumes the responsibility of guiding and training the people so that everyone may have the opportunity and the ability to work for the success of the National Revolution, the realization of the Three Principles, the rebuilding of the state and the revival of the nation. It entertains no bias in favor of or against any profession or class. Furthermore, the Guomindang seeks to take care of and give training to every citizen, and does not deny any qualified person his opportunity of service. It welcomes each and every patriotic citizen to join it in a common struggle for the completion of its mission....

SOURCE: Chiang Kai-shek, *China's Destiny*, trans. Wang Chung-hui (New York: Macmillan, 1947) 99–100.

Go to **www.chinasince1644.com** for the full text of **Document 12.1**.

DOCUMENT 12.2: Excerpt from "Manifesto of the Chinese People's Liberation Army" by Mao Zedong,1947

We are the army of the Chinese people and in all things we take the will of the Chinese people as our will. The policies of our army represent the urgent demands of the Chinese people and chief among them are the following:

1. Unite workers, peasants, soldiers, intellectuals and businessmen, all oppressed classes, all people's organizations, democratic parties, minority nationalities, overseas Chinese and other patriots; form a national united front; overthrow the dictatorial Chiang Kai-shek government; and establish a democratic coalition government.

2. Arrest, try and punish the civil war criminals headed by Chiang Kai-shek.

3. Abolish the Chiang Kai-shek dictatorship, carry out the system of people's democracy and guarantee freedom of speech, of the press, of assembly and of association for the people.

4. Abolish the rotten institutions of the Chiang Kai-shek regime, clear out all corrupt officials and establish clean government.

5. Confiscate the property of the four big families of Chiang Kai-shek, T.V. Soong, H.H. Kung and the Chen Li-Fu brothers, and the property of the other chief war criminals; confiscate bureaucrat-capital, develop the industry and commerce of the national bourgeoisie, improve the livelihood of workers and employees, and give relief to victims of natural calamities and to poverty-stricken people.

6. Abolish the system of feudal exploitation and put into effect the system of land to the tillers.

7. Recognize the right of equality and autonomy of the minority nationalities within the borders of China.

8. Repudiate the traitorous foreign policy of Chiang Kai-shek's dictatorial government, abrogate all the treasonable treaties and repudiate all the foreign debts contracted by Chiang Kai-shek during the civil war period. Demand that the U.S. government withdraw its troops stationed in China, which are a menace to China's independence, and oppose any foreign country's helping Chiang Kai-shek to carry on civil war or trying to revive the forces of Japanese aggression. Conclude treaties of trade and friendship with foreign countries on the basis of equality and reciprocity. Unite in a common struggle with all nations, which treat us as equals....

SOURCE: *Selected Works of Mao Zedong,* vol. 4 (Beijing: Foreign Languages Press, 1967) 149–150.

Go to **www.chinasince1644.com** for the full text of **Document 12.2.**

DOCUMENT 12.3: Excerpt from General George Marshall's "Personal Statement by the Special Representative of the President," 1947

[T]he greatest obstacle to peace has been the complete, almost overwhelming suspicion with which the Chinese Communist Party and the Guomindang regard each other.

On the one hand, the leaders of the Government are strongly opposed to a communistic form of government. On the other, the Communists frankly state that they are Marxists and intend to work toward establishing a communistic form of government in China, though first advancing through the medium of a democratic form of government of the American or British type.

The leaders of the Government are convinced in their minds that the Communist-expressed desire to participate in a government of the type endorsed by the Political Consultative Conference last January had for its purpose only a destructive intention. The Communists felt, I believe, that the government was insincere in its apparent acceptance of the PCC [Political Consultative Conference] resolutions for the formation of the new government and intended by coercion of military force and the action of secret police to obliterate the Communist Party....

SOURCE: Department of State Bulletin, January 19, 1947: 83–85, rpt. in Immanuel C.Y. Hsü, *Readings in Modern Chinese History* (New York: Oxford University Press, 1971) 543–546.

 Go to **www.chinasince1644.com** for the full text of **Document 12.3**.

DOCUMENT 12.4: Letter to the Editor, by Ding Keshan, March 30, 1948

[T]he Guomindang's candidate for the National Assembly representative was Dong Xiuming; and there were a few others also seeking election. One cold cloudy afternoon, Dong Xiuming gave a public election speech in the open-air theater... In order to learn something about democracy, I braved the cold wind to listen. When I arrived, except for a few shop apprentices, all those seated in the audience were peddlers from off the nearby streets.... [They said] the police had told them to come.... Then three or four officers brought in over two hundred men who were said to be just then undergoing military training. Only then were all the seats filled. Mr. Dong's speech was very simple and contained no election principles at all... After Mr. Dong had concluded his speech, the *xian* [district] magistrate, Wang Yifang, took over and began to talk. To the "voters" in the audience he said: "I order you to elect Mr. Dong Xiuming. This order is the same as the order telling you that you should go to do repair work on the defense installations. It is wrong for anyone to disobey...." After the meeting, [word went out] to every household: "The *xian* magistrate has spoken. Whoever does not vote for Dong Xiuming will have to go out and work on the defense installations when they need repairs in the future." The result of the election was, of course, that Dong Xiuming received the most votes.

Today is the big opening of the National Assembly and I suppose Mr. Dong Xiuming is already sitting securely in a representative's seat.... Really what a joke it is.

SOURCE: Qtd. in Suzanne Pepper, *Civil War in China: The Political Struggle, 1945–1949* (Berkeley: University of California Press, 1978) 139–140.

Go to **www.chinasince1644.com** for the full text of **Document 12.4**.

DOCUMENT 12.5: **Excerpts from a survey sponsored by the North American Chinese Students Christian Association, 1948**

QUESTION 3: *I feel that peace in China must be sought by:*

	(% of those responding)
no answer	1.8
the Nationalist Government should eliminate the Communist Party	18.0
the organization of a coalition government to include the CCP, the Democratic League, other parties and Independent elements	51.1
The adoption of a federal system	17.9
The division of the country into independent areas	3.2
national rule by the CCP	2.7
let the United Nations arbitrate	1.1
other	4.2

SOURCE: *Kuan-ch'a (The Observer)*, July 17, 1948: 8–9, rpt. in Suzanne Pepper, *Civil War in China: The Political Struggle, 1945–1949* (Berkeley: University of California Press, 1978) 90–92.

Go to **www.chinasince1644.com** for the complete survey on **Document 12.5**.

DOCUMENT 12.6: **"Dead Water," a poem by Wen Yiduo, 1928**

Here is a ditch of hopeless water,
The fresh breeze would not even raise half a ripple.
One might as well throw in a few more tins and scraps of metal
And why not pour in your left-over food and gravy.

Perhaps the green of the copper will turn into emerald,
Rust on the tin cans emerge as petals of peach blossom;
Then let grease weave a layer of patterned muslin,
And bacteria brew vapours of coloured clouds.

Let the dead water ferment into a gully of green wine,
Floating pearl-like crowds of white foam;
The laughter of small pearls will change them to large pearls
Broken by mosquitoes to steal the alcohol.

Even a ditch of hopeless dead water
Can boast of some ornaments.
If the green frogs can't bear the silence,
Then we can say that the dead water can sing.

Here is a ditch of hopeless dead water,
This cannot be a place where beauty lives,
Better let ugliness cultivate it,
And see what kind of world comes of it.

SOURCE: Wen I-to, *Red Candle: Selected Poems*, translated by Tao Tao Sanders (London: Jonathan Cape, 1972) 34.

Go to **www.chinasince1644.com** for the full text of **Document 12.6**.

DOCUMENT 12.7: Excerpt from Wen Yiduo's speech at the memorial service for Li Gongbu, 1946

We all know that, only a few days ago, the most despicable, the most shameless incident occurred in Kunming. What crime had Li Gongbu committed to deserve such an ending in unconscionable hands!... Today I want to know if there are more secret agents here, right here. Step up, you, tell us, why you killed Li Gongbu...

You reactionaries, you try so hard to alienate us from our friends. What shame! You think now that Lianda [University] has moved away and the students have dispersed for the summer, you think we are powerless now. But, secret agents, you are wrong! Look at the thousand and more young people gathered here, our arms linked together. We, the young generation of Kunming, shall not tolerate your reckless action.... We are not afraid of death; we are constantly ready to follow in Li Gongbu's footsteps. The moment we step out of this door, we don't think of stepping back!

SOURCE: Rpt. in Kai-yu Hsu, *Wen I-To* (Boston: Twayne Publishers, 1980) 173.

Go to **www.chinasince1644.com** for the full text of **Document 12.7**.

DOCUMENT 12.8a & b: "Soldiers and People Working Together" and "After the Guard in Charge of Grain Has Gone (Victory)," woodblock prints by Li Hua, 1946–1948

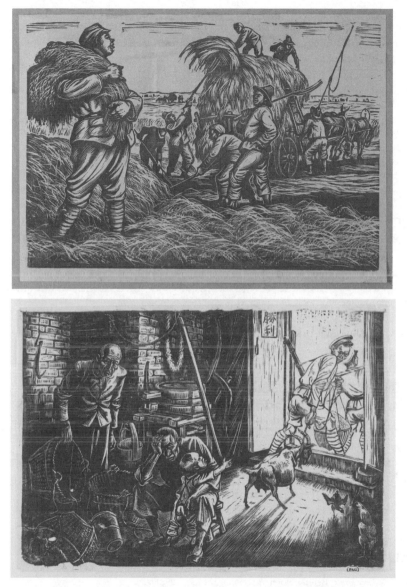

Li Hua (1907–1994) was among the many woodblock print artists who were active during the Chinese Civil War. He drew inspiration from socialist authors like Lu Xun, who was an admirer of woodblock prints as a vehicle for social protest. Li used his art as a way to capture people's lives and to inspire the oppressed to take action.

(Courtesy of the Picker Art Gallery, Colgate University [1968.43, 1968.35])

 Go to **www.chinasince1644.com** for all three woodblock prints in **Document 12.8**.

DOCUMENT 12.9: Excerpts from reports and writing related to land reform leading up to the founding of the People's Republic of China, 1946–1948

The National Land Conference of the Communist Party of China was held in September 1947 in Hubei Province. The law written at the conference was published by the Central Committee of the Communist Party of China on October 10, 1947. It stipulated the following:

Abolish the land system of feudal and semi-feudal exploitation and put into effect the system of land to the tillers.

All the land of the landlords and the public land in the villages is to be taken over by the local peasant associations and, together with all other land there, is to be equally distributed among the entire rural population, regardless of sex or age.

The peasant associations of the villages shall take over the draught animals, farm tools, houses, grain, and other property of the landlords, requisition the surplus of such property of the rich peasants, distribute all this property among the peasants and other poor people who are in need of it and allot the same share to the landlords.

SOURCE: *Selected Works of Mao Zedong* (Beijing: Foreign Languages Press, 1967). Transcribed by the Maoist Documentation Project, revised 2004 by Marxist.org. http://www.marxists.org/reference/archive/mao/selected-works/volume-4/mswv4_24.htm#bm4

 Go to **www.chinasince1644.com** for the full text of Document 12.9.

DOCUMENT 12.10: "The People's Liberation Army Captures Nanjing," a poem by Mao Zedong, 1949

Over Zhongshan swept a storm, headlong,
Our mighty army, a million strong, has crossed the Great River.
The City, a tiger crouching, a dragon curling, outshines its ancient glories;
In heroic triumph heaven and earth have been overturned.
With power and to spare we must pursue the tottering foe
And not ape Xiang Yu the conqueror seeking idle fame.
Were Nature sentient, she too would pass from youth to age,
But Man's world is mutable, seas become mulberry fields.

SOURCE: *Mao Zedong Poems* (Beijing: Foreign Languages Press, 1998) 49.

 Go to **www.chinasince1644.com** for the full text of Document 12.10.

Activities

ACTIVITY 1: Analyzing a Reading from Chiang Kai-shek

After reading the excerpt from *China's Destiny* (12.1), prepare to discuss:

1. What is the overall tone of the first passage? What kinds of appeals does Chiang Kai-shek make to the Chinese population? How effective do you think this passage was in inspiring the Chinese to join the Guomindang cause?

2. In the first passage, Chiang does not specifically mention the Communists. Nevertheless, are there subtle ways in which he expresses criticism of the Communists? Cite evidence of this in the text. Why do you suppose he did not actually name the Communists?

3. In the second passage, Chiang is much more explicitly attacking the Communists. What are some of his criticisms?

4. What does Chiang mean when he refers to the Guomindang cause as the "National Revolution"? What was revolutionary about the Guomindang cause?

5. Taking into account what you have learned about some of the Guomindang tactics, what do you think of Chiang's claim that his party "entertains no bias in favor of or against any profession or class"?

6. Does a political party have a duty to fairly represent itself and competing parties? Why or why not?

ACTIVITY 2: Analyzing a Manifesto by Mao Zedong

After reading Mao Zedong's manifesto (12.2), you will divide into two groups (or smaller groups). One group will be responsible for making a chart of all the phrases Mao uses against Chiang Kai-shek and his government; the other group will make a chart of all the phrases Mao uses to describe the Communist cause. Using the charts as reference points, you will hold a discussion as a class or in small groups comparing the picture that emerges of the two sides in the Civil War.

1. According to Mao, what are the aims of the Communists and their army? In what ways are these aims different from the aims of the Guomindang as expressed by Chiang Kai-shek in Document 12.1? In what ways are the Communists' aims similar to those of the Guomindang? How could the two groups have cooperated?

2. Both Chiang Kai-shek and Mao Zedong claimed to be working for the good of "the people." Did they have the same "people" in mind? Which groups would more likely have been attracted to Chiang's cause? Which groups would have gravitated toward Mao's? Why?

3. How would you describe Mao's style of writing and speaking? What is propaganda? Is this manifesto an example of propaganda? Is Chiang's piece an example of propaganda? Debate these questions.

ACTIVITY 3: Evaluating General Marshall's Assessment

After reading General Marshall's analysis (12.3), consider:

1. How would you assess Marshall's statement? Does he support the Guomindang, the Communists, or is his account even-handed?

2. Marshall wrote that the greatest obstacle to establishing peace between the two factions was "almost overwhelming suspicion." Why do you think this was so? What did each side have to be suspicious about?

3. On the Guomindang (Nationalist) side, Marshall singled out "reactionaries" who were opposed to a coalition. What is a reactionary? What are the political disadvantages of a reactionary stance? Are there times when a reactionary stance is appropriate? Why or why not?

4. What does Marshall see as the faults of the Communist and the Guomindang sides in the breakdown of negotiations? Make a chart comparing and contrasting the faults of the Guomindang and the Communists, as Marshall listed them.

5. Toward the end of his report, Marshall expressed his hope for the end of "one-party rule." Would the Guomindang have been more successful if they had allowed the Communists and other political groups to participate in the government? Why or why not?

Creative Extension:

Write a script or dialogue between three characters—Chiang Kai-shek, Mao Zedong, and George Marshall—in which they try to negotiate a coalition. Use some of the actual words from the first three documents. Give a live or recorded performance acting out your script.

ACTIVITY 4: Writing: Letter to the Editor

After reading Ding Keshan's letter to the editor (12.4), prepare to discuss:

1. What picture of democracy under the Guomindang does this letter give?

2. What is the writer's tone?

3. How do these types of election tactics fit into your definition of "democracy"?

ACTIVITY 5: Analyzing a Survey

Present the answers in the survey (12.5) in a pie graph or bar graph to illustrate in a more visual way the distribution of opinions on each question.

1. Look at the responses to Question 1 in the survey. What is the difference between a cooperative farm and a collective farm? Why do you suppose these students favored cooperatives over collectives?

2. What does "nationalization" mean? Why do you think that over half the students favored nationalization of heavy industry (machinery, manufacturing, etc.) and public utilities? Do you think that other groups in China would have been so supportive of nationalization? What areas of the economy in your country are nationalized?

3. From the students' responses to Question 3, we see that over half of them favored a coalition government, while only 18 percent thought the Guomindang (Nationalist) government should eliminate the Communists. Are students likely to be more liberal than other segments of a society? Why? Do you think a coalition could have worked?

4. What do you make of the students' answers to Questions 4 and 5? How much confidence did they have in the Guomindang government? Why?

Writing Extension:

Imagine you are a Chinese student studying in the United States in 1948. Write a letter home expressing your views of the situation in China. Use ideas that you gather from the survey results and the documents in this chapter.

Address what role intellectuals, and especially students, have in political affairs. Have you ever participated in any political activity? If so, what did you do? Did you feel you made a contribution? What kind of contribution?

ACTIVITY 6: **Listening to the Voice of Dissent**

Part 1: **Make Inferences: Dissent through Poetry**

Choose four adjectives to describe the tone of the poem by Wen Yiduo (12.6). Prepare to discuss:

1. What does "dead water" stand for in this poem?

2. What are some of the other strong images in the poem? What does the poet's attitude seem to be about the possibilities for progress in China?

Characters in Chinese poetry often cannot be precisely translated because the meaning changes subtly depending on the context. This translation is by Tao Tao Sanders. The final stanza of the poem is translated somewhat differently by Kai-yu Hsu in *Wen I-To*:

> Here is a ditch of hopelessly dead water—
> a region where beauty can never reside.
> Might as well let the devil cultivate it—
> see what sort of a world it can provide.

3. How is this different from and similar to Tao Tao Sanders's translation? Who might Wen Yiduo have identified as the "devil" in the next-to-last line?

Creative Extension:

Create two drawings in the woodblock style that illustrate a difference in the two translations.

Part 2: Make Inferences: Dissent Through a Eulogy

Read the excerpt from Wen Yiduo's speech at the memorial service for his friend Li Gongbu (12.7).

1. In the eighteen years between Wen's poem "Dead Water" and this speech, what changes do you detect in his attitude, his writing style, and his subject matter? Cite evidence from the text. What might account for the changes?

2. Do you think Wen was aware of the danger of speaking out so boldly?

3. Kai-yu Hsu writes in his biography of Wen Yiduo, "He regarded patriotism as being as important in literature as 'love, the ephemeralness of beauty, the approach of death, and all universal sentiments suggested by nature'" (Kai-yu Hsu, *Wen I-To*, 100–101). Is "Dead Water" a patriotic poem?

4. Do you think that artists—writers, painters, musicians, actors, etc.—should become involved in politics? Should they create art for political purposes? Why or why not?

5. What artists do you know in other countries who used or use their art to express political beliefs? What effect did the artists' work have on their own lives or on the political process?

Creative Extension:

Present a dramatic reading of Wen Yiduo's speech for the class.

ACTIVITY 7: Analyzing Political Art

Begin by reading a short introduction to the New Woodcut Movement. See Chapter 12 Activity Websites for a link to this introduction. You will work in an expert group to examine one of three woodblock prints (12.8a-c.). In your group discuss the questions below. (Note: Refer to Item 12.A on the companion website for additional information and questions specific to each print.) As an expert on your print, you will join experts on the other two prints, and share information by addressing the questions.

1. Describe the people, things, and place depicted in the print.

2. What is happening? Why?

3. What may have been the artist's purpose in creating this image?

4. What message, if any, is the print communicating?

Then as a class you will discuss:

1. Many of Li Hua's woodcuts were given as traditional New Year pictures (*nianhua*), images that would be pasted on doors during the festival, and often would remain up all year. What effect do you think these images had on the peasants and other people who received and displayed them?

2. Does visual art have the power to change people's thinking? Can you think of examples from today?

Creative Extension:

Create a piece of art (e.g. a sculpture, poem, song, cartoon, or painting) expressing your view on a political or social issue about which you feel strongly. Give it a title, and write a two- to three-sentence caption for your work if it is a visual piece. Explain why you chose the art form that you did. After everyone has had a chance to see everyone else's work, discuss the challenges of this assignment.

ACTIVITY 8: Analyzing Efforts at Land Reform

Land reform was a central tenet of the CCP. Read excerpts describing the efforts (12.9) and prepare to discuss:

1. What was at the heart of the land reform movement? Cite evidence in the text.
2. Why did the Party insist that the rights of "middle peasants" be protected?
3. How did land reform change over this period of time?
4. How was land reform related to the success of the CCP in winning the war?
5. What alternate methods might a government use to address rural poverty?
6. Compare the CCP's land reform programs with Fei Xiaotong's 1946 recommendations for alleviating rural poverty (Chapter 10, Document 10.12).

ACTIVITY 9: Interpreting a Poem by Mao Zedong

1. What is the overall mood of the first four lines of Mao Zedong's poem (12.10)?
2. Who is the "tottering foe" (line 5)?
3. Find out who Xiang Yu was. How did he seek "idle fame"? What comparison is Mao making here?
4. In Mao's view, what has passed from youth to age with this victory? (Keep in mind that the Chinese honor age over youth.)
5. How do you interpret the final line of the poem? Is it a positive image? How so? Find out what the leaves of mulberry trees are used for in China.

Chinese leaders—including emperors, other members of the court, and scholar-officials—were often accomplished poets (see Chapter 2).

6. Do you see Communist leader Mao Zedong's poetry as part of this tradition? Why or why not?
7. Does it seem unusual to you that he would indulge in an activity that was so closely tied to the imperial system of government? What might be his reasons for doing so?
8. Can you think of leaders in other countries who were also creative artists? If so, who? Describe their art and its connection to what was going on in their country at that time.

Creative Extension:

Create a mind map with "Capturing Nanjing" in the middle bubble. Include branches outward for the major concepts and comparisons Mao uses to glorify the achievement. From those, extend branches to the particular words Mao uses to create a sense of heroism and grandiosity.

ACTIVITY 10:
A Debate: How Did the Communists Win the War?

At the beginning of her book *Civil War in China*, historian Suzanne Pepper asks: "Did the Chinese Communists win a genuine mandate to rule, or were they primarily the beneficiaries of Guomindang mistakes and Japanese excesses?" (p. 6) You will either debate the question in class or, alternatively, answer the question in an essay.

Suggested Resources

Books

Birns, Jack. *Assignment, Shanghai: Photographs on the Eve of Revolution*. Ed. Carolyn Wakeman and Ken Light. Berkeley: University of California Press, 2003.

Chiang Kai-shek. *China's Destiny*. Translated by Wang Chung-hui. New York: MacMillan, 1947.
Written in 1943, while China was still fighting the Japanese, this is Chiang's vision for his country.

Mao Zedong. *Selected Works of Mao Zedong*. Beijing: Foreign Language Press, 1967.
Volume 4 covers the period of the Civil War. This series includes many interesting, provocative speeches and essays. Writings of Mao are also available online at http://marx2mao.com/Mao/Index.html.

Pepper, Suzanne. *Civil War in China: The Political Struggle, 1945–1949*. 2nd ed. Lanham, MD: Rowman & Littlefield, 1999.

Snow, Edgar. *Red Star Over China*. New York: Grove Press, 1993.
A U.S. journalist's account of the Chinese Communist movement and its leadership until the late 1930s. Originally published in 1937.

Spence, Jonathan D. *Mao Zedong*. New York: Viking, 1999.

Websites

China's Communist Revolution, BBC News
http://news.bbc.co.uk/hi/english/static/special_report/1999/09/99/china_50/nodhtml.htm
An overview of China's Communist government from 1949–1989.

Nixon's China Game: U.S.-China Relations Timeline, 1945–1949, PBS
http://www.pbs.org/wgbh/amex/china/timeline/index.html
A timeline of Chinese domestic politics and foreign relations between China, the Soviet Union, and the United States from 1945–1949.

Woodcuts
http://depts.washington.edu/chinaciv/graph/9polwood.htm
Information about Lu Xun and Chinese woodcut art of the early twentieth century that was used as a form of protest.

■ **A CLOSER LOOK**

Edgar Snow (1905–1972): Journalist and Activist

In 1937, Edgar Snow ended "Red Horizon," the final chapter in his ground-breaking book *Red Star Over China*, by writing: "The movement for social revolution in China might suffer defeats...but it will not only continue to mature; in one mutation or another it will eventually win, simply because the basic conditions which have given it birth carry within themselves the dynamic necessity for its triumph." It turned out to be a prophetic statement.

By the time he met with Mao Zedong in 1936, Edgar Snow had worked as a foreign correspondent and traveled widely in China for seven years. He spoke some Chinese and was friends with numerous Chinese intellectuals in Beijing and Shanghai. Soong Qingling, the widow of Sun Yat sen (see A Closer Look in Chapter 9), helped arrange for Snow to travel to Yan'an. Once there,

Snow stayed for four months, conducting extensive interviews with leaders of the CCP; he was the first Western journalist to do so.

In 1937, he published *Red Star Over China*, which he described as the "first authentic account of the Chinese Communist Party and the first connected story of their long struggle to carry through the most thorough-going social revolution in China's three millenniums of history."[8] Snow's largely sympathetic account of the Communists introduced the Western world to a movement and individuals about which little was known.

During the McCarthy-era anti-Communist persecutions of the 1950s, Snow was blacklisted in the United States and was only able to sell his articles to foreign journals. He returned to China several times and was the only U.S. journalist given frequent

access to interview CCP leaders. In 1970, on his final visit, Premier Zhou Enlai entrusted Snow with a message for the U.S. government: the "door is open" for improving relations between the two countries. Snow died in February 1972, at almost the same time that President Richard Nixon arrived in China (see Chapter 15).

■ *Discuss: What combination of factors enabled Snow to write his pivotal book? What was the ultimate impact of all of Snow's visits to and writing about China? (For excerpts from Snow's first book, see Chapter 11.)*

■ *Review the chapters in this unit and then consider Snow's prediction quoted in the first paragraph. What conditions was he referring to that gave birth to the social revolution and would ensure its triumph?*

Films

China in Revolution, vol 1 of *China: A Century of Revolution* (120 mins; 2007)
This documentary provides footage of the Republican Period and interviews with Chinese people who lived through this era.

Mao Tse Tung: China's Peasant Emperor (50 mins; 2005)
Archival film and images of Mao's life.

---

[8] Edgar Snow, *Red Star Over China* (New York: Grove Press, 1968) 16.

UNIT FOUR

The People's Republic of China

(1949–2000)

By Kenneth Hammond

The words highlighted in this overview are key people, concepts, or movements that appear in the chapters that follow.

In the autumn of 1949 the leaders of the Chinese Communist Party (CCP) and the Red Army found themselves in command of much of the territory of China. They faced immense challenges in completing the process of military control, and in bringing order and stability to the country. On October 1, 1949, the **People's Republic of China** (PRC) was formally proclaimed by Party Chairman **Mao Zedong**, in Beijing, which became the capital of the new regime.

Over the ensuing months and years, the CCP pursued a wide range of policies that rapidly restored the domestic economy and launched China on a program of development as a socialist state. For the first decade of the PRC's existence, the **Soviet Union** provided significant aid and served as a model for many aspects of China's new system. But the relationship with the Soviets was always a tense one, and by 1960 it broke down as China took a path that the Russians viewed as irrational.

Among the immediate tasks that the CCP undertook were the transformation of the rural economy through **land reform,** the nationalization of major urban businesses and industries, and the restructuring of family life through the **Marriage Law of 1950**, which gave women equal rights in marriage and divorce. These policies yielded immediate results, as the ravages of decades of war and division were healed and China began to grow into a more stable and prosperous society.

In carrying through the early policy reforms, the CCP also faced an internal challenge. When the Party came to power in 1949, there were only about two million members. With a vast and populous country to manage, the Party had to expand its ranks quite rapidly, and this resulted in many new members who were not necessarily devoted to the ideals of socialism, but who saw the Party as a path to security and advancement. This complicated the political landscape and led to an expanding gap between the Party and the people.

Once the initial stage of economic and political transformation was complete, the PRC embarked on a path of socialist modernization, which involved the **collectivization of the agricultural economy** and building up a state-owned industrial sector. Farming was the foundation, and the expansion of grain production in the early and mid-1950s generated

TIMELINE

1949: Mao Zedong announces the founding of the People's Republic of China

1949: Chiang Kai-shek and Guomindang forces retreat to Taiwan

1949: India adopts a constitution

1950: Agrarian Reform Law and Marriage Law are enacted

1950: People's Liberation Army enters Tibet

1950-1953: Korean War begins with North Korea's invasion of South Korea; in late 1950, China enters war on behalf of North Korea

1953–present: Republic of Korea (South Korea) and Democratic People's Republic of Korea (North Korea) are separated by the 38th parallel

1950s: Senator Joseph McCarthy launches the second "Red Scare" in the United States

1953: First Five-Year Plan put into effect

1956: Hundred Flowers Campaign

1957: Anti-Rightist Campaign

1958–1961: Great Leap Forward

1959: PLA represses Tibetan uprising; Fourteenth Dalai Lama leaves Tibet

1960: Soviet Union withdraws all its experts from China

1965–1973: Second Indochina War between the Democratic Republic of Vietnam and the United States; known in the U.S. as the Vietnam War

1966–1976: The Great Proletarian Cultural Revolution

1970: United States begins bombing raids in Cambodia

1971: The People's Republic of China joins the United Nations; Taiwan loses the "China seat" at the UN

1972: President Richard Nixon visits China

1972: Japan and China normalize relations

1972: Park Chung-hee, president of the Republic of Korea (South Korea), declares martial law; he continues as president with control over parliament until his assassination in 1979

1975–1979: Khmer Rouge are in power in Cambodia

---

revenue for the government, which was used to **invest in factories and infrastructure** like railroads and communications networks. But there were divisions among the leaders regarding how best to manage this process. Some, led by Mao Zedong, believed the best way to develop the country rapidly was through voluntarism and popular political mobilization. Others, led by President Liu Shaoqi and top economist Chen Yun, and including the youngest member of the top leadership, Deng Xiaoping (later to become the leader of the CCP), thought it made more sense to develop a corps of technical experts who could use the most advanced and up-to-date technologies

and methods to build the new economic order. These divisions deepened as time went on and ultimately led to violent confrontations between Party factions.

In the mid-to-late 1950s the agricultural sector was the scene of the greatest upheavals. The process of collectivization, in which farming communities were encouraged to share resources and labor to achieve greater production, was pushed into high gear by Mao Zedong in 1957–1958. Wanting to build on early successes, and to unleash the enthusiasm he believed was pent up within the rural villages, he called for a **Great Leap Forward**. But a combination of bureaucratic resistance and

1975: Chiang Kai-shek dies in Taiwan; his son assumes power

1976: Mao Zedong dies September 9

1976: Socialist Republic of Vietnam founded

1978: Deng Xiaoping promotes Four Modernizations

1978: Vietnam invades Cambodia to drive out Khmer Rouge

1979: January 1, the People's Republic of China and the United States formally recognize each other

1979: Deng Xiaoping is the first Chinese leader to visit the United States

1979: One-Child Policy implemented

1980: Special Economic Zones established

1980s: Japan has the world's second largest economy

1988: The first two-party elections held in Taiwan

1989: Tiananmen Square protests

1989: Mikhail Gorbachev, head of state of the Soviet Union, visits China

1989: In November, the Berlin Wall is demolished

1990: October 3, East and West Germany are reunited

1991: Communist Party loses power in the Soviet Union; the country breaks up into a number of independent states

1991: First Gulf War

1992: The first civilian in thirty years is elected president of the Republic of Korea

1997: China regains control of Hong Kong from the United Kingdom

1999: China regains control of Macao from Portugal

2000: Leaders of North and South Korea meet for the first time since the end of the Korean War

2001: China becomes a member of the World Trade Organization

incompetence, along with natural disasters in 1959 and the withdrawal of Soviet aid and advisors in 1960, led to massive drops in grain production, widespread hunger, and even starvation. Deep conflicts within the leadership led to Mao Zedong's being relegated to a secondary role in the day-to-day affairs of the Party, and to a retreat from the policies of mass mobilization that he had championed.

China's economy recovered from the trauma of the Great Leap Forward in the early 1960s, but by 1965 new tensions within the leadership led to renewed conflict. In 1966 the **Great Proletarian Cultural Revolution** broke out, in which Mao and his allies sought to root out what they saw as the bureaucracy and elitism of some leaders within the CCP. But the Cultural Revolution soon became a struggle for power within the Party, and by 1969 a stalemate had set in that paralyzed many aspects of Chinese life for the next decade.

At the same time a shift was underway in China's foreign policy, away from the role as promoter of world revolution and towards a more pragmatic model. The relationship with the Soviet Union had become openly antagonistic, and the CCP, under the guidance of Zhou Enlai, moved toward establishing **relations with the United States.**

The stalemate within the Party over domestic policy was only broken by Mao's death in September 1976. A few weeks later, a coalition of forces within the Party brought down Mao's allies. By 1978 **Deng Xiaoping** emerged as the dominant figure within a new, technocratic elite that now controlled the CCP. This group moved carefully over the next few years to dismantle many aspects of the Maoist economic and social model, and began to move China in the direction of a market economy. Mao's fear that China would "take the capitalist road" was about to be realized.

In the 1980s China went through a period of increasingly **rapid transformation** and development. The agricultural economy was reformed to give private family farms priority, and this led to an immediate jump in production. The reform of the industrial sector and encouragement of private business generated a huge growth in urban incomes and the development of a consumer economy. But the benefits of this growth were not shared in an equal way. While Deng Xiaoping sought to buffer this inequality by arguing that "to get rich is glorious," others saw the accumulation of wealth by individuals with close ties to the Party and government as evidence of widespread corruption. By 1989, frustration and resentment over corruption and the limited opportunities for participation in political affairs resulted in the outbreak of mass protests in Beijing and other cities. The situation grew beyond the control of either the government or the original protest leaders, and eventually resulted in an armed crackdown. Units of the People's Liberation Army (PLA) fought with citizens in the streets around **Tiananmen Square,** killing hundreds of people.

In the wake of 1989, many feared China would turn away from reform and engagement with the outside world. But instead, China renewed its commitment to developing a market economy while retaining features of the socialist state and the leadership of the Chinese Communist Party.

CHAPTER RESOURCES

Primary Sources

Supplementary Materials

 Excerpts of these primary source documents appear in this chapter. Go to **www.chinasince1644.com** for the full version of these documents and for the Supplementary Materials.

CHAPTER 13

The Early Years of the People's Republic of China, 1949–1966

By David Green

Chapter Contents

The Founding of the People's Republic of China (PRC)

Reforms

The Hundred Flowers Campaign

The Great Leap Forward

Foreign Relations

Key Idea

The Chinese Communist Party and Chairman Mao Zedong were driven by revolutionary zeal to transform China into a modern industrialized and proletarian nation. Controversial reforms and campaigns resulted in rapid and widespread change.

Guiding Questions

What steps were taken by the Chinese Communist Party and Mao Zedong to reorganize and reform China after decades of chaos?

What was the purpose and impact of the Hundred Flowers Campaign?

How did the Great Leap Forward affect China's industry, agriculture, and population?

What characterized the relationship between China and the Soviet Union in the 1950s?

Why did Mao begin to lose favor within the Communist Party?

Terms to Know

agrarian	dictatorship	propaganda
bourgeoisie	elites	reform
bureaucracy	imperialism	rural
cadre	inflation	socialist
collective	proletarian	struggle session
commune		

Essay

On October 1, 1949, Mao Zedong (毛泽东) stood atop the Gate of Heavenly Peace (*Tiananmen* 天安门), looking over what is now Tiananmen Square, and proclaimed the founding of the People's Republic of China (PRC) (*Zhonghua Renmin Gongheguo* 中华人民共和国). The challenges facing any government at this point in China's history were staggering. Years of warfare, incessant flooding, extremely low industrial output, and rampant inflation had wreaked havoc on China's people. The Chinese Communist Party (CCP) (*Zhongguo Gongchandang* 中国共产党), often with Chairman Mao Zedong leading the way, enacted radical and often autocratic policies that brought profound change to China's culture, economy, and political organization.

Shortly before proclaiming the PRC, Party leadership had adopted the Common Program for China (*Gongtong Gangling* 共同纲领), which defined and framed the Chinese Communist Party's goals. It outlined a "New Democratic" state that was anti-imperialism, anti-feudalism, and anti-capitalism, one that would empower China's workers and huge peasant population.

The People's Republic of China's communist government was distinct from that of the Soviet Union since it was defined as a "Democratic Dictatorship" (*minzhu zhuanzheng* 民主专政), based on four coexisting social classes: workers, peasants, and two levels of bourgeoisie. At lower levels of government, popular assemblies voted for higher-level representatives. Authority, as the Common Program made clear, lay in the hands of the central government: "All local people's government... shall obey the Central People's Government," giving locally-elected representatives virtually no power. Most governing power was in the hands of the Chinese Communist Party. CCP committees established at the local level sent delegates to committees on the county or provincial level, who, in turn, sent representatives higher still. The top three levels of the Party were the Central Committee (with forty-four members in 1949), the Politburo (with a dozen members) and the Standing Committee (of five[1]). Within the Standing Committee, Mao Zedong was the unchallenged authority, as well as China's leading theorist on Marxism.

Reforms

The early years of the new People's Republic were a heady and transformative time for many in China. The country was poor and had suffered much destruction and dislocation during the previous fifty years of warlord rule, Japanese invasion, and civil war. The soldiers of the People's Liberation Army were a disciplined force whose aim (not always attained) was to treat the common people with respect rather than looting, conscription, or abuse. As soon as they could, the Party set up local "people's governments" to provide aid to the needy and restore basic services and civic order.

The CCP had issued a People's Currency (*renminbi*, RMB 人民币) in May 1949 and immediately upon taking control worked tirelessly to stabilize prices, wages, and lines of communication. As a result, inflation, which had plagued Chiang Kai-shek's government (see Chapter 12), quickly abated.

During the Civil War, the promise of land reform became an important incentive among poor peasants to join the CCP in their fight against Chiang Kai-shek's government. After the Civil War the CCP began to fulfill their promises on a national level. Another priority of the CCP was the passing of the 1950 Agrarian Reform Law (*Tudi Gaige Fa* 土地改革法). Groups of Communist cadres and peasant associations were given the authority to redistribute some 115 million acres of land from landlords to over 300 million peasants. This was a tense and violent process, as the repressed hostilities beneath the surface of village life broke out in struggle sessions where landlords

---

[1] In 1949, the Standing Committee included Mao Zedong (chairman of the CCP), Liu Shaoqi, Zhou Enlai, Zhu De, and Chen Yu.

were denounced. Beatings and deaths were not uncommon during land reform, and it was very easy for struggle sessions to turn into physical confrontations.[2] After completing the campaign, land reform was quickly followed by collectivization in 1953, and many peasants were organized into farming cooperatives. Collectivization was a major aspect of Mao's economic reforms, as he believed that by working cooperatively, China's peasants would be more productive. Collectivization also meant more bureaucratic control in the countryside, and greater influences by the central government; it was the first real introduction of socialism into the countryside. Reform in the early PRC also came with a great deal of coercion and frustration as the peasantry and the Party attempted to understand one another.

The urban economy presented major difficulties to the PRC leaders. Production had almost ground to a halt; drugs and prostitution were widespread. Between 1949 and 1952 the new authorities carried through a series of steps to bring factories, banks, and major retail operations under state management. In 1953, the Chinese government, using the Soviet Union as a model, put into effect its First Five-Year Plan (*Yiwu Jihua* 一五计划). An energized, fiercely patriotic populace threw itself into the work of rebuilding China, and industrial output soared between 1953 and 1957.

Industrial and agricultural reform was followed by social reform. The CCP worked assiduously to correct many of the social ills that had recently befallen China. On a larger scale, the Marriage Law of 1950 gave men and women equal rights to enter into marriage, banned arranged marriages, and allowed either partner to sue for divorce. In the following two years many couples divorced, and the great majority of people quickly remarried, often to people with whom they had secretly been in love for a long time. In the countryside the effects of the Marriage Law were reinforced by the granting of land to women as well as men.

Like Land Reform, the new Marriage Law was the fulfillment of another of the CCP's promises to create a more equitable society. The changes engendered by this law also represented an example of the new power of the CCP. In the 1930s, Chiang Kai-shek's government had also attempted to reform marital relations in China, but failed because it lacked the influence, prestige and control of China that the CCP enjoyed in the 1950s.

Lastly, the new PRC government provided significant new benefits to the people of China. It trained doctors as general practitioners to offer free health services to all people (a policy that lasted into the 1980s). The government organized state-run factories that gave virtually free apartments to their workers, provided childcare and education, and even organized social events such as musical performances and free movies for the people in each "work unit." Chinese living abroad were sufficiently impressed and enthusiastic about the changes taking place in war-torn China that many of them moved back from countries around the world, including the United States, to help rebuild the country. However, those who returned to the PRC after living abroad encountered a difficult environment, and many were accused of being foreign spies and were imprisoned. In spite of the political campaigns that followed, and the ways in which policies and practices sometimes fell short of ideals, most Chinese felt that their lives had been improved by the new People's Government, and appreciated the many services and all-encompassing safety net that it provided.

Continued Revolution and the One Hundred Flowers Campaign

The first decade of life in the People's Republic of China was characterized by one campaign after another. Among them was the 100 Flowers Campaign (*Baihua Qifang* 百花齐放) in 1956. Party leadership was split over whether to include intellectuals, who were not necessar-

---

[2] Jonathan Spence estimates that 1 million people were killed in *The Search for Modern China* (New York: W. W. Norton, 1999) 492.

ily staunch communists, in efforts to transform the nation. But Mao was feeling upbeat about the initial successes of programs like the First Five Year Plan, collectivization, and social reform, and he urged a "campaign of criticism and self-criticism," to keep the revolution alive. Up until Mao's call for more openness, China's intellectuals had hesitated to speak their minds; now they did. Posters, magazine articles, campus demonstrations, rallies, and letters communicated great dissatisfaction. The critics demanded, among other things, an end to corruption among Communist Party cadres and an end to artistic censorship; they also campaigned for a higher standard of living. Within weeks, Mao abruptly changed course. Joining Party leaders who had never backed the campaign, he branded critics as "Rightists" (*youpai* 右派) who opposed the Party. Approximately 300,000 of China's intellectuals—social scientists, economists, writers, scientists—lost their jobs; many were imprisoned or sent to the countryside for re-education. China effectively lost its educated urban professional elite—a loss that would, among other things, seriously affect future economic planning.

The Great Leap Forward

After traveling throughout China in 1956, Mao had come to the conclusion that "the masses can do anything." He also believed that experts, who tended to favor gradual economic development, were actually hindering the potential of the masses. Mao was convinced that China could transform itself into a global economic power if the peasants toiled under a more centralized system that set extremely ambitious industrial and agricultural goals. During the First Five-Year Plan, the nation's industrial output had risen 18.7 percent per year, agricultural production by 3.8 percent. Within fifteen years Mao wanted China to surpass industrial production in the United Kingdom, but much higher agricultural production was essential to pay for this planned industrial growth. In 1958, overruling more cautious long-term planners in

the Party, Mao rallied the populace into another campaign: the Great Leap Forward (*Dayuejin* 大跃进). The idea behind the Great Leap was to put every person in Chinese society to work at massive agricultural and industrial projects. Although China was a relatively poor country, what it lacked in resources it made up for in population. Mao believed that the masses were the key to China's success—the country could accomplish anything if the people sacrificed, worked hard, and acted collectively. A Spartan lifestyle gripped China at the beginning of the Great Leap as cadres were sent into rural China to rally the peasants. A bumper crop in the summer of 1958 inspired the central government to reorganize about 740,000 farm cooperatives—99 percent of the rural population—into 26,000 centralized People's Communes.[3] These communes became massive administration units, containing on average 5,000 households, or 25,000 people,[4] although some grew as large as 20,000 households.[5] Daily life now revolved around these communes. In order to maximize production and ensure efficiency, the communes provided schools, rudimentary healthcare, kitchens, and banks.

The central government also launched a drive to create some 600,000 backyard furnaces throughout the country in order to meet greatly expanded steel production targets. The government encouraged everyone, regardless of his or her job, to melt down all household metals from woks to utensils.

As a result of the euphoria and revolutionary passion, local rural cadres filed exaggerated forecasts for grain production at a time when farmers' incentives and time spent growing crops were diminishing. Simultaneously, the iron produced by overworked peasants in backyard furnaces proved to be unusable. When the Yellow River (*Huang He* 黄河) flooded in 1959

---

[3] Spence, 579.

[4] Immanuel C.Y. Hsü, *The Rise of Modern China*, 4th ed. (New York: Oxford University Press, 1990) 656.

[5] Dikötter, Frank, *Mao's Great Famine: The History of China's Most Devastating Catastrophe, 1958-62* (London: Bloomsbury, 2010) 47-48.

and unrelenting drought afflicted other parts of China, Mao Zedong refused to revise his expectations. He dismissed a famous general who had warned of a growing crisis and cowed Party officials into following his mass revolutionary line. Because of the intensity and scope of the Great Leap, many cadres feared that reporting disappointing crop yields could lead to demotion or even expulsion from the Party. These cadres grossly exaggerated the amount of grain being produced in the countryside in order to impress the central government. In 1958, local cadres reported that 410 million tons of grain had been reaped in the countryside; the actual number was closer to 200 million tons.[6] As a result, too much grain was removed from the countryside in the form of taxes, leaving farming families with little. Rather than respond to concerns over shortfalls, Mao insisted provincial leaders meet the established goals.

By 1961, as a result of government policies, floods, drought, and insect infestations, conditions in the countryside had become catastrophic with extreme famine and deprivation in many regions, and the government began to import far more grain than it exported.[7] The famine, having begun in 1959, would not begin to abate until 1963. The number of those who died prematurely during the Great Leap Forward is difficult to certify; recent estimates vary from 20 million to as many as 45 million deaths.[8] Children were especially hard hit, many suffering from disease and malnutrition. The rate of orphaned children rose tremendously during this period. After the Great Leap, surveys conducted in Hunan found that there were 600,000 more six year olds than three year olds, suggesting that those born in 1961 had a particularly high mortality rate.[9] The period between 1958 and 1961 is still mutely called the "Three Hard Years."

Foreign Relations Through 1960

The CCP and Mao wanted the world to see that China was a nation worthy of respect. They viewed the humiliations of past wars, foreign incursions, and civil conflict as relics of the past, and they were ready to assert new leadership throughout Asia and among the developing countries of the world. The Soviet Union was a significant source of empowerment for Mao, and his first trip abroad to Moscow in 1949 resulted in a multifaceted alliance. Although the relationship was characterized by mutual distrust, Chinese leaders saw the alliance as critical to their economic plans. Utilizing over $300 million in Soviet loans and thousands of Soviet experts on technology, military, and infrastructure, the CCP oversaw construction of new roads, railways, and radio networks that reached all corners of an evolving China.

Party leadership saw China's territorial integrity and the protection of its spheres of influence as high priorities. This commitment to its sphere of influence was soon put to the test when the Korean War began in 1950. At first, China remained neutral; however, when United Nations (UN) troops under General Douglas MacArthur's command pushed north of the 38th parallel, officials in Beijing grew concerned that the army might actually invade China. The People's Republic of China sent 1 million "volunteers" to fight UN forces in North Korea. The addition of Chinese forces into the conflict reversed the trajectory of the war and ultimately cost China between 700,000 and 900,000 casualties.[10]

Although the war resulted in a stalemate, it affected China in two important ways. First, when the war began, President Truman moved the U.S. navy into the Taiwan Strait, assuring that China would not be able to retake the

---

[6] Dikötter, 62.

[7] Denis Crispin Twitchett, & John King Fairbank, eds. *The Cambridge History of China*, vol. 14 (New York: Cambridge University Press, 1978) 381.

[8] Dikötter, 324–325.

[9] Dikötter, 254.

---

[10] Close to 3 million Koreans died in the war, as well as more than 35,000 UN troops, 33,629 of whom were from the United States.

island, which it considered to be part of its territory. Second, it made Mao grow more hostile to Western capitalist countries, and made many Chinese officials paranoid about outside threats. For them, the Korean War proved that many Western countries—particularly the United States—were bent on destroying the People's Republic. The solution to this threat was vigilance, militancy, and the continuation of Mao's revolutionary politics.

The Korean War was not China's only conflict during the early years of the PRC. Beginning in 1950, the CCP reasserted its control over Tibet (*Xizang* 西藏), which had previously been a part of the Chinese empire during the Qing Dynasty. What CCP officials considered to be the reclamation of Chinese territory, many Tibetans saw as an invasion, especially after the Dalai Lama was forced to flee the country after a Tibetan uprising in 1959. Tibetan independence remains an extremely contentious issue even today. The incident demonstrated that the CCP would not brook any challenge to its rule or the cohesion of the PRC.

In the ten years after the founding of the PRC, China saw both progress and disaster, and

faced threats both foreign and domestic. In late 1958, even before the worst of the famine caused by the Great Leap Forward had devastated rural China, members of the CCP began to question some of Mao's most fundamental political and economic philosophies. The most notable, Liu Shaoqi (刘少奇), was among the Party leaders who pushed for Party discipline, economic retrenchment, and a greater emphasis on technology. When Mao accepted some responsibility for the disasters and "retired" from his position, Liu Shaoqi became chairman of the PRC and together with Secretary General Deng Xiaoping (邓小平) took charge of China's economic recovery. However, it was quite clear that Mao, with his remarkable ability to mobilize the country's long-suffering and angry populace, along with his staunch allies in the CCP, continued to wield strong influence. Few dared speak out against him. As the 1960s began, two questions were paramount in China: would the country be able to recover economically from the disaster of the Great Leap Forward; and, how far would Mao allow officials like Liu Shaoqi and Deng Xiaoping to deviate from his radical line in pursuit of this recovery?

Primary Sources

DOCUMENT 13.1: Excerpts from the Common Program of the Chinese People's Political Consultative Conference, September 1949

....

Article 1. The People's Republic of China is a New Democratic or a People's Democratic state. It carries out the people's democratic dictatorship led by the working class, based on the alliance of workers and peasants, and uniting all democratic classes and all nationalities in China. It opposes imperialism, feudalism and bureaucratic capitalism and strives for independence, democracy, peace, unity, prosperity and strength of China....

Article 5. The people of the People's Republic of China shall have freedom of thought, speech, publication, assembly, association, correspondence, person, domicile, change of domicile, religious belief and the freedom of holding processions and demonstrations....

Article 7. The People's Republic of China shall suppress all counter-revolutionary activities, severely punish all Guomindang counter-revolutionary war criminals and other leading incorrigible counter-revolutionary elements who collaborate with imperialism, commit treason against the fatherland and oppose the cause of people's democracy. Feudal landlords, bureaucratic capitalists and reactionary elements in general, after they have been disarmed and have had their special powers abolished, shall, in addition, be deprived of their political rights in accordance with law for a necessary period. But, at the same time, they shall be given some means of livelihood and shall be compelled to reform themselves through labor so as to become new men. If they continue their counter-revolutionary activities, they will be severely punished....

SOURCE: *The Important Documents of the First Plenary Session of the Chinese People's Political Consultative Conference* (Beijing: Foreign Languages Press, 1949).

Go to **www.chinasince1644.com** for the full text of **Document 13.1**.

DOCUMENT 13.2: Excerpt from Lu Dingyi's speech "Let Flowers of Many Kinds Blossom, Diverse Schools of Thought Contend!" May 26, 1956

To artists and writers, we say, "Let flowers of many kinds blossom." To scientists we say, "Let diverse schools of thought contend." This is the policy of the Chinese Communist Party. It was announced by Chairman Mao Zedong at the Supreme State Conference....

If we want our country to be prosperous and strong, we must, besides consolidating the people's state power, developing our economy and education and strengthening our national defence, have a flourishing art, literature and science. That is essential. If we want art, literature and science to flourish, we must apply a policy of letting flowers of many kinds blossom, letting diverse schools of thought contend....

"Letting flowers of many kinds blossom, diverse schools of thought contend" means that we stand for freedom of independent thinking, of debate, of creative work; freedom to criticize and freedom to express, maintain and reserve one's opinions on questions of art, literature or scientific research.

SOURCE: Lu Ting-yi, "Let Flowers of Many Kinds Blossom, Diverse Schools of Thought Contend!" (Beijing: Foreign Languages Press, 1957) 3–35.

Go to **www.chinasince1644.com** for the full text of **Document 13.2**.

DOCUMENT 13.3: Excerpt from "The Masses Can Do Anything," statement by Mao Zedong, September 29, 1958

During this trip, I have witnessed the tremendous energy of the masses. On this foundation it is possible to accomplish any task whatsoever. We must first complete the tasks on the iron and steel fronts. In these sectors, the masses have already been mobilized. Nevertheless, in the country as a whole, there are a few places, a few enterprises, where the work of mobilizing the masses has still not been properly carried out, where mass meetings have not been held and where the tasks, the reasons for them, and the methods have still not been made perfectly clear to the masses or discussed by the masses. There are still a few comrades who are unwilling to undertake a large-scale mass movement in the industrial sphere. They call the mass movement on the industrial front "irregular" and disparage it as "a rural style of work" and "a guerrilla habit." This is obviously incorrect.

However, while devoting ourselves to iron and steel production on a large scale, we must not sacrifice agriculture... The 1959 task in agriculture is to achieve a leap forward even greater than that of 1958. Consequently, we must organize the industrial and agricultural labour force effectively and extend the system of people's communes throughout the whole country....

SOURCE: Mao Zedong, "The Masses Can Do Anything," 29 Sept. 1958. Transcribed by the Maoist Documentation Project.

 Go to **www.chinasince1644.com** for the full text of **Document 13.3**.

DOCUMENT 13.4: Excerpts describing urban living arrangements from *Growing Up in the People's Republic: Conversations Between Two Daughters of China's Revolution*, by Ye Weili and Ma Xiaodong, 2005

YE WEILI: I grew up in Xinhua compound in downtown Beijing.[11] The entire compound occupied more than 70 *mu* of land (about 12 acres). It was divided into work and residential areas.... I don't know how the adults felt about the closeness of the living arrangement. With hindsight I realize they might not have liked it that much, especially when there was a political campaign going on. After a criticism meeting in the office, they would have wanted to avoid their colleagues in the living quarter and privacy would have been desirable. But for us kids who had little sense of the adult world, this living arrangement was great....

Without leaving the compound, one could get almost every type of service. The service was not free but it was cheaper than what would have been charged outside. Besides, you also didn't have to wait in long lines. My parents deposited their money at the compound bank and mailed their letters in the compound post office. When I didn't feel well, I would go to the compound clinic. My parents joined a medical program for children so I didn't need to bring any cash with me. I knew every doctor and nurse there and would try to avoid the ones with a poor reputation.

My favorite places were the library and the auditorium. I spent a lot of time in the library, doing homework in the reading room and browsing the many journals and newspapers on the shelves....

SOURCE: Ye Weili and Ma Xiaodong, *Growing Up in The People's Republic: Conversations Between Two Daughters of China's Revolution* (New York: Palgrave Macmillan, 2005) 33–37.

 Go to **www.chinasince1644.com** for the full text of **Document 13.4**.

---

[11] Xinhua is the Chinese government's official news service; everyone who worked for the news service lived and worked together in the *dayuan* (compound).

DOCUMENT 13.5: Excerpt from Mao Zedong's speech "On the Policies of Our Work in Tibet," April 6, 1952

We must do our best and take proper steps to win over the Dalai [Lama] and the majority of his top echelon and to isolate the handful of bad elements in order to achieve a gradual, bloodless transformation of the Tibetan economic and political system over a number of years; on the other hand, we must be prepared for the eventuality of the bad elements leading the Tibetan troops in rebellion and attacking us, so that in this contingency our army could still carry on and hold out in Tibet. It all depends on strict budgeting and production for the army's own needs. Only with this fundamental policy as the cornerstone of our work can we achieve our aim....

SOURCE: Mao Zedong, "On the Policies of our Work in Tibet," 6 April 1952. Transcribed by the Maoist Documentation Project.

 Go to **www.chinasince1644.com** for the full text of **Document 13.5**.

DOCUMENT 13.6a–d: Propaganda posters, 1957–1959

公社如巨龙，生产显威风

Propaganda posters played a significant role in communicating the goals of the CCP and of Mao himself. They captured the essence of CCP ideology and permeated all levels of Chinese society. The text at the bottom of this 1959 poster reads, "The commune is like a gigantic dragon; production is visibly awe-inspiring." (*Collection Stephan R. Landsberger at the International Institute for Social History, Amsterdam, the Netherlands. http://www.chineseposters.net*)

Go to **www.chinasince1644.com** for additional color posters in Documents 13.6 a–d.

Activities

ACTIVITY 1. Examining the Chinese Communist Party's Founding Principles

Working in a small group, you will read the preamble and articles of the Common Program (13.1). As a class, discuss findings and address the following questions:

1. What is the overall tone of Document 13.1, and what are some examples of that tone?
2. What strikes you about the language used in the preamble?
3. Compare this preamble to the one in the Constitution of the United States of America. Where are the similarities and differences?
4. Compare the complete text of the Common Program to the U.S. Constitution and the Bill of Rights. How are they alike? How do they differ?
5. How does the document hold up as a provisional constitution for the early PRC? Does it feel like a constitution to you? Why or why not?
6. What aspects of this document will clearly serve the people of the PRC? To what extent might it be injurious to them?

ACTIVITY 2: Analyzing the Hundred Flowers Campaign

Read the excerpt from Lu Dingyi's speech (13.2) and consider the following questions:

1. What is the tone of the speech?
2. Who is delivering the speech and what is his position?
3. What are the main themes of the speech?

Assume the identity of a Chinese artist, poet, or scientist who has just heard this speech. With a partner, create a dialogue between any two of these people. The dialogue should reflect the range of thoughts and feelings of people at the time. Be prepared to present your dialogue to the class or to a group.

Review the explanation in the introductory essay of what happened after the campaign.

1. Why do you think the Party and Mao reacted in this way to the criticism?
2. How might removing half of the educated professionals affect society?
3. What does this suggest about Mao's attitude toward highly educated individuals? What other politicians do you know of who have shared Mao's attitude?

Creative Extension:

Prepare to deliver a dramatic reading of Lu Dingyi's speech (13.2).

ACTIVITY 3: Responding to a Statement by Mao Zedong

Read the excerpt of Mao's statement "The Masses Can Do Anything" (13.3).

1. Write passages or words that show Mao's use of patriotism and optimism to motivate the people.

2. Create a graphic organizer such as a chart or mind map (diagram of words/ideas linked around a central word/idea) that shows the range of responses or questions each of the following people might have had about Mao's statement: a former land owner, a rural farmer, an industrialist, an urban resident.

3. Be prepared to discuss your findings in a group. With your group create a "3-2-1": 3 observations about the Chinese peoples' reactions to Mao's statement, 2 questions related to the statement, and 1 conclusion about Mao's leadership.

ACTIVITY 4: Comparing Perspectives on Growing Up in 1950s and 1960s China

Drawing on your prior knowledge and the chapter essay, what do you think it would be like to be a child or student as China profoundly transformed? What might be the experiences of youth in China during the 1950s and early 1960s? Jot down your ideas, then read the description of growing up in Beijing by Ye Weili and Ma Xiaodong (13.4) and consider the following questions:

1. How were the two girls' experiences similar and different?

2. What aspects of China's reforms seemed to affect the girls the most?

3. What was most striking about the girls' experiences? Why?

4. Did the girls' experience match any of your guesses about what children and teens would experience in China during the 1950s and early 60s?

5. Do you relate to any of the experiences described in this reading? Why or why not?

6. What challenges do youth face growing up now? Are there any parallels to the two girls' narratives?

ACTIVITY 5: Analyzing Mao Zedong's Speech on Tibet

The topic of Tibet incites controversy both within and outside of China. Citing historical precedence, Mao advocated strongly for incorporating Tibet into the borders of the PRC, a goal that was eventually realized.

  For more background on Tibet, read "A Brief History of Tibet" on the companion website (Item 13.A in Supplementary Materials), read A Closer Look about the Dalai Lama at the end of the chapter, and study the Map of Provinces in Chapter 1, Item 1.C on the companion website. Then read the excerpt from Mao's speech "On the Policies for Our Work in Tibet" (13.5) and take brief notes on the following issues:

1. What are the main components of the speech?

2. What is Mao's general attitude toward Tibet?

3. What are Mao's concerns about Xinjiang and Tibet?

4. How does the topic of diversity fit into your understanding of this speech?

5. Why might Mao be singling out Tibet as the focus of this speech?

Read the section on Xinjiang in chapter 20 and "A Brief History of Xinjiang" in Supplementary Materials (Item 13.B) on the companion website. Working with a partner, look at the map of China's autonomous regions (Item 1.C on the companion website) and locate both Tibet and Xinjiang. Together, address the following:

1. Go back to the speech and try to identify why Mao might hold such specific attitudes about Tibet.

2. What is geographically interesting and challenging about Tibet's location? Where might this appear in the speech?

3. Answer the same questions for Xinjiang.

4. Given their locations, how would China benefit from exerting influence in Tibet and Xinjiang?

5. What are the disadvantages of exerting such influence?

ACTIVITY 6: Examining Posters as Propaganda Tools

Part 1: Cite Evidence

Before examining the posters, in class you will define the word "propaganda," discuss different avenues of propaganda, and offer examples from your daily life. Then you will consider ways in which a populace could be mobilized in a time when there was no Internet, e-mail, widespread television or radio, and literacy rates were low. In pairs discuss:

1. What would you expect a propaganda poster to look like and why?

2. What would be the key components of an effective propaganda poster?

In pairs, examine "Chairman Mao Provides Us with a Happy Life" (13.6a).

1. What is most striking to you and why?

2. List ten details and explain their significance.

3. What surprised you the most about this poster? Why?

4. Does this poster remind you of any other visual materials you've seen? What are they? How do they compare?

Part 2: Determine Meaning

You will work in a small group with one poster from the 1950s (13.6b, c, or d). Examine it carefully and discuss the following:

1. What do you see?

2. What is the visual message communicated by this poster?

3. Is this an effective propaganda poster? Why might it successfully mobilize people, or not?

4. What aspect of the CCP's and/or Mao's ideology is being communicated? How do you know?

Prepare to present the poster to the rest of the class and share the group's observations.

Creative Extension:

Create your own Chinese propaganda poster about an issue from the early years of the PRC. The poster should demonstrate an understanding of the Chinese style and genre of the 1950s and 1960s. (For additional examples of propaganda posters, see Chapter 13 Activity Websites on the companion website.)

ACTIVITY 7: Analytical Writing

Countries all over the world reacted to the immense changes in China during the 1950s and 1960s. You will be assigned to a team representing the United States, the Soviet Union, England, France, India, or another country.

1. After researching and analyzing how your assigned country reacted to the changes, each member of the team will issue a statement on one of the following events from the perspective of his or her country: the creation of the PRC, the Hundred Flowers Campaign, the Great Leap Forward, or Mao Zedong's leadership.

2. After listening to statements from each "country" team, write an individual essay that captures the different perspectives.

EXTENDED RESEARCH:

Changes for Women

Read the abbreviated version of PRC's Marriage Law of 1950 (see Suggested Resources: Schoppa, R. Keith. *Twentieth Century China: A History in Documents*) and conduct research in books and online to learn about women's traditional roles and rights prior to Liberation. (See also Chapter 1, Document 1.2.) Write an essay that highlights the changes for women brought about by this law. Alternatively, capture the changes in a piece of visual art.

Suggested Resources

Books

Becker, Jasper. *Hungry Ghosts: Mao's Secret Famine*. New York: The Free Press, 1996.

Cheek, Timothy. *Mao Zedong and China's Revolutions: A Brief History with Documents*. Boston: Bedford St. Martin's, 2002.

Chen Jian. *Mao's China and the Cold War*. Chapel Hill: University of North Carolina Press, 2001. Chen examines China's relationship with the Soviet Union in the 1950s and 1960s, the Taiwan Strait crisis, and involvement in Korea and Vietnam.

Dikötter, Frank. *Mao's Great Famine: The History of China's Most Devastating Catastrophe, 1958–1962*. New York: Walker & Co., 2010. Based on documents in Chinese archives that have not previously been available to historians and scholars, Dikötter's work chronicles the policies of the Great Leap Forward and its effect on Chinese society.

Hershatter, Gail. *The Gender of Memory: Rural Women and China's Collective Past*. Berkeley: University of California Press, 2011. Through interviews with 72 men and women in rural Shaanxi province, Hershatter's work provides insights into the impact of the 1950 Marriage Law, land reform, and collectivization.

Hessler, Peter. *Country Driving: A Journey through China from Farm to Factory*. New York: Harper, 2010. A narrative account of how the development and diffusion of cars and roads have changed China. On pages 185–189, Hessler describes changes in land practice from 1949 to the present.

Landsberger, Stefan. *Chinese Propaganda Posters*. Koln: Taschen, 2011.

Schoppa, R. Keith. *Twentieth Century China: A History in Documents*. New York: Oxford University Press, 2004. Includes an abbreviated version of the 1950 New Marriage Law.

Shakya, Tsering. *The Dragon in the Land of Snows: A History of Modern Tibet Since 1947*. New York: Columbia University Press, 1999.

Spence, Jonathan D. *Mao Zedong*. New York: Viking, 1999.

Wemheuer, Felix and Kimberley Ens Manning, eds. *Eating Bitterness: New Perspectives on China's Great Leap Forward and Famine*. Vancouver: UBC Press, 2011. Eleven papers by historians and political scientists examining the events of the early years of the People's Republic of China, including discrepancies in death rates attributed to the famine and the role of women during this time period.

Websites

Chinese Posters: Propaganda, Politics, History, Art **http://chineseposters.net/** Gallery of posters from 1925-2006, including the Mao era, with translations of slogans and social and political context about collections of posters. From the collections of the International Institute of Social History, Amsterdam, and Stefan R. Landsberger.

Commonly Read Speeches and Writings of Mao Zedong (1927–1945), Asia for Educators **http://afe.easia.columbia.edu/special/china_1900_mao_speeches.htm** Speeches highlighting Mao's ideology.

Mao Zedong, 1893–1976, BBC Historic Figures **http://www.bbc.co.uk/history/historic_figures/mao_zedong.shtml** A short biography of Mao Zedong.

Mao Zedong Library **http://marx2mao.com/Mao/Index.html** Translations of Selected Works of Mao Zedong volumes 1–5.

New Marriage Law, 1950 **http://chineseposters.net/themes/marriage-law.php** An overview of the 1950 Marriage Law and propaganda posters from the collections of the International Institute of Social History, Amsterdam, and Stefan R. Landsberger.

The Question of Tibet, Council on Foreign Relations **http://www.cfr.org/china/question-tibet/p15965** An article by Jayshree Bajoria examining the issue of Tibet's political status and conflict with China.

Second Marriage Law of the People's Republic of China
http://newyork.china-consulate.org/eng/lsqz/laws/t42222.htm
The law adopted at the Third Session of the Fifth National People's Congress on September 10, 1980. Amended April 28, 2001.

The Tibet Issue, BBC News
http://www.bbc.co.uk/news/world-asia-pacific-16759913
Perspectives on Tibet from Tibetan and Chinese viewpoints.

Films

All Under Heaven (58 mins; 1986)
Part of the *One Village in China* series, this documentary, directed and produced by Carma Hinton and Richard Gordon, captures the various ways in which the Communist Party of China has tackled the challenge of land reform and gives insight into rural traditions.

The Blue Kite (138 mins; 1993)
The film captures how the turbulent political times affected the lives of citizens. In Mandarin with subtitles.

Mao Tse-Tung: China's Peasant Emperor (50 mins; 2005)
A documentary of Mao's life based on archival film footage and interviews with acquaintances and scholars.

To Live (133 mins; 1994)
This film spans four decades of the twentieth century in China. It tells the story of a couple and their two children as they struggle to survive the constantly changing political climate. In Mandarin with subtitles.

■ **A CLOSER LOOK**

Liu Shaoqi: Mao's Second in Command

Referred to by some as "the other chairman," Liu Shaoqi (1898–1969) left an indelible mark on China's development in the mid-twentieth century. On October 1, 1959, the tenth anniversary of the People's Republic, the newly appointed chairman reflected on the progress of his country: "The first decade has been dedicated to reform. The second should be devoted to reconstruction." Tragically, the opposite occurred.

Liu Shaoqi was born and raised in Yinshan, Hunan Province, not far from Shaoshan, the childhood home of Mao Zedong. Though such beginnings were coincidental, Liu Shaoqi's life paralleled Mao's in many respects. As the theoretician for the CCP, Liu was considered Mao's heir apparent, and he served as chairman of the People's Republic from 1959 to 1966. After briefly attending college in Moscow in the early 1920s, Liu Shaoqi organized several success-ful labor movements back in his homeland, particularly among coal miners. After being elected to the Central Committee of the CCP in 1927 and the Politburo in 1934, Liu became head of the North and Central China bureaus of the Central Committee between 1936 and 1942. In this capacity, Liu Shaoqi faced the daunting challenge of promoting communist ideology in the face of Guomindang efforts to eliminate the Communist Party. His successes as an organizational leader and theorist during this time consolidated his position as a top leader of the CCP.

Liu's seminal work *How to Be a Good Communist* became a central text for the Party. Its unique combination of Confucian and Marxist ideals were appealing to readers of many socio-economic classes, and in 1949, Liu became second vice-chairman of the government and general secretary of the CCP.

The split between Mao and Liu came into the open during the Great Leap Forward and grew increasingly wide as news of the appalling famine began to trickle in from the countryside. Liu and Deng Xiaoping took over government and Party management, but Mao continued to insist that any perceived Party weakness should be open to the "masses" for discussion and debate. As Mao's Cultural Revolution took form and evolved (see Chapter 14), re-establishing Mao as the central figure in Chinese politics and daily life, Liu Shaoqi became the target of an immense campaign to vilify him. In 1967, he and his wife were put under house arrest. Liu died two years later after succumbing to repeated interrogations, physical abuse, and medical neglect.

■ *Find out more about Liu Shaoqi and/or read excerpts from his book* How to Be a Good Communist *(See Suggested Resources on the companion website). Discuss: How did Liu's and Mao's visions for China differ?*

■ **A CLOSER LOOK**

The Dalai Lama Living in Exile

The Dalai Lama is the central figure in both Tibetan Buddhism and Tibetan government. Tibetan Buddhism views the position of the Dalai Lama as a lineage of reborn leaders extending back centuries. The current Dalai Lama, Tenzin Gyatso (born in 1935), is the fourteenth individual to hold the position. He was installed as Tibet's head of state in 1950, one year after Mao Zedong announced the creation of the PRC and sent Chinese armed forces into Tibet.

The Dalai Lama met with Mao Zedong in 1954 when he attended a meeting of the National People's Congress in Beijing. However, tensions between the Chinese government, which considered Tibet a part of China, and Tibetans, who wanted independence, kept increasing, until in 1959 the Tibetans staged a major uprising. The Chinese military responded forcefully. Fearing for his safety and the future of the Tibetan government,

the fourteenth Dalai Lama left his summer residence secretly and was escorted by loyal guards across the Himalayas to safety in India, where he has lived ever since.

As the leader of the Tibetan government in exile, for 61 years he made several appeals for autonomy, acknowledging the highly unlikely chances for independence from China. In April 2001 Lobsang Sangay was elected Prime Minister of the Tibetan government in exile after the Dalai Lama announced he would step down from his political (though not his spiritual) leadership. For the first time these two roles were separated.

The Dalai Lama's emphasis on ethics, non-violent conflict resolution, spirituality, and simple living has won him widespread support throughout the world and beyond the Tibetan cause. He has traveled to forty-six countries, speaking in front of large audiences to discuss topics as diverse as Tibetan Buddhism, environmental responsibility, and morality.

In 1989, as a result of his unfaltering global efforts, the Dalai Lama was awarded the Nobel Peace Prize.

Difficult questions simmer below the surface: what will happen when the fourteenth Dalai Lama passes away? Some Chinese politicians insist that China's government will select the next Dalai Lama. However, most Tibetans, including the present Dalai Lama himself, have suggested that the next reincarnation will be identified outside of Tibet. In the meantime, the Dalai Lama remains a notable figure for many groups of people for many different reasons.

■ *Search the Internet for an account of a recent appearance by the Dalai Lama. What was at the heart of his speech? Why does he continue to draw such large audiences?*

For further information about Tibet's history, see Item 13.A on the companion website. Tibet is also discussed in Chapter 20.

CHAPTER RESOURCES

Excerpts of these primary source documents appear in this chapter. Go to **www.chinasince1644.com** for the full version of these documents and for the Supplementary Materials.

CHAPTER 14

The Cultural Revolution, 1966–1976

By David Green

Chapter Contents

Tensions in the Early 1960s

The Great Proletarian Cultural Revolution

Sent-Down Youth

The Death of Mao Zedong

Key Idea:

The Cultural Revolution grew out of disagreements among the Chinese Communist Party's leaders over how to energize the populace and to continue to develop the nation's economy. The destruction unleashed by this movement affected every element of life in China.

Guiding Questions

What were some of the factors that led to the "Great Proletarian Cultural Revolution"?

How did the role of the Red Guards change over the course of the Cultural Revolution?

What are some different ways in which Chinese youth were affected by the Cultural Revolution?

Other than Mao Zedong, who were the significant political figures during the Cultural Revolution and why were they important?

What are some views of the Cultural Revolution in retrospect?

Terms to Know

class struggle	Mandate of Heaven	"red"
counter-revolution	nationalism	Red Guards
cult of personality	party-state	re-education camp
factionalism	purge	revisionist
Gang of Four	radical	sent-down youth
Little Red Book	reactionary	"victim literature"

Essay

At the height of the Mao cult in the late 1960s, prior to their communal meals, villagers would recite, "We respectfully wish a long life to the reddest sun in our hearts, the great leader Chairman Mao…Having been liberated by the land reform we will never forget the Communist Party, and in revolution we will forever follow Chairman Mao!"[1] Such absolute loyalty to Mao Zedong (毛泽东) was a hallmark of the Cultural Revolution, and epitomized Mao's singular place in Chinese society. While the Communist Party faced a barrage of attacks during the Cultural Revolution, the Mao cult only grew in prominence, producing a generation of students whose loyalty to the Chairman was unyielding.

Tensions in the Early 1960s

Many leading Party members felt that the Great Leap Forward (*Dayuejin* 大跃进) in 1958 was a complete disaster, and Mao himself even admitted to some general errors (see Chapter 13). Following the Great Leap, Communist veterans such as Liu Shaoqi (刘少奇)[2] tried to diminish the personality cult increasingly surrounding Mao, but Mao still had powerful allies in the Party. One of Mao's most important supporters was Lin Biao (林彪), whom Mao had appointed minister of defense and head of the People's Liberation Army (PLA) (*Renmin Jiefangjun* 人民解放军). Lin had worked throughout the 1960s to make Mao's writings required reading, especially in the army. In 1963, Lin Biao ordered everyone in the armed forces to read the newly printed Little Red Book (*Hongbao Shu* 红宝书), filled with "Mao Zedong thought" (*Mao Zedong sixiang* 毛泽东思想). The booklet that could fit into the palm of one's hand would influence a generation of young people.

The Great Proletarian Cultural Revolution Begins

There are many differing explanations as to why the Cultural Revolution occurred and how to judge its impact. One thing appears clear: a serious breakdown had occurred among the top leaders over the future of Chinese society and the recovery of the economy. Liu Shaoqi and Deng Xiaoping (邓小平), who had taken charge of economic recovery after the Great Leap Forward, favored a pragmatic conventional approach. To spur production, they suggested higher salaries and bonuses on a limited scale. Still, to the radical left this sounded like capitalist incentives. Liu and Deng also wanted educated experts to lead the way. Mao Zedong, on the other hand, believed economic planning should stay in the hands of those with strong communist convictions. Frustrated by what he saw as slow economic gains, he believed the Party needed to revitalize communist ideology. In *The Rise of Modern China*, Immanuel Hsü writes, "Mao wanted to re-establish the supremacy of his authority, his line of revolution, his work-style, to revitalize the youth, politicize the masses, and combat old customs, old habits, old culture, and old thinking—and to do so with a single, immediate expurgation."[3]

While the economy recovered, relations with the Soviet Union, one of China's oldest international allies (see Chapter 13), continued to deteriorate. The impetus for these changes lay with the death of Joseph Stalin in 1953, who had enjoyed a good personal relationship with Mao and whose Soviet model was an important basis for Mao's rule. In 1956, Nikita Khrushchev, who succeeded Stalin, criticized Stalin and his cult of personality. The Chinese were taken aback by this "secret speech," and Mao considered Khrushchev's remarks to be a per-

---

[1] Qtd. in Anita Chan, Richard Madsen and Jonathan Unger, *Chen Village: The Recent History of a Peasant Community in Mao's China* (Berkeley: University of California Press, 1984) 170

[2] Liu Shaoqi had temporarily taken Mao's place as chairman of the CCP.

[3] Immanuel Hsü, *The Rise of Modern China*, 4th ed. (New York: Oxford University Press, 1990) 697.

sonal insult. In *The Search for Modern China*, Jonathan Spence explains: "Behind the Soviet-Chinese disagreements that emerged in the late 1950s lay a tangled history of friendship and distrust." The CCP was distressed by Khrushchev's policies in Eastern Europe, his friendlier attitude toward capitalism and the United States in particular, and his unwillingness to share nuclear technology with China. Tensions escalated until in September 1960, the Soviet Union removed all of its 1,390 experts on technology, military, and infrastructure from China. From Mao's perspective, Khrushchev was a revisionist and a traitor who had abnegated the Soviet Union's revolutionary heritage. For all intents and purposes, communism was dead in the Soviet Union.

This had a deep impact on Mao and his supporters; they learned that internal sabotage by revisionist Party elites was just as much a threat to communism as was capitalism. Mao was determined to prevent developments in the Soviet Union from replicating themselves in China. He therefore encouraged the Chinese people to "never forget class struggle," and to redouble their efforts in creating a strong and ideologically pure country. From Mao's perspective, the need for revolutionary vigilance was never more important than in the 1960s. The Sino-Soviet split, as well as Liu Shaoqi and Deng Xiaoping's more moderate approach to the economy, put Mao and his allies on high alert. This new vigilance would provide the fuel for the coming Cultural Revolution (*Wenhua Dageming* 文化大革命).

Although developments at home and abroad had created a well of tension in Chinese society, the trigger for the Cultural Revolution appears to have been an allegorical play that was a thinly veiled critique of the government. Accusing the play of having "traditionalist" content, Mao's wife, Jiang Qing (江青), attacked it as an "anti-socialist poisonous weed." Jiang Qing and other extreme leftists wanted to purify art by having it serve political purposes only. They were also concerned that certain artists, even those who were official party members, were subtly attempting to undermine Mao.

During the early part of 1966, Mao and his allies prepared for a new campaign that would target supposed traitors in the Communist Party. The target of this new campaign quickly expanded from cultural targets to the education system in China. On May 25th, Nie Yuanzi, the Party branch secretary in the Philosophy Department at Beijing University (*Beijing Daxue* 北京大学), created a "Big Character Poster" (*Dazi Bao* 大字报) accusing other professors and university administrators of being anti-Party. Nie was well connected in the Party and was secretly encouraged by leftists close to Mao to criticize Beijing University's president for his supposedly moderate views on education. Mao backed the poster and broadcast its message throughout China. Liu Shaoqi attempted to quell the resulting unrest at the university, but his actions were perceived as another strike against already embittered students and faculty. Revolutionary spirit spread from universities to secondary schools, where groups of students, calling themselves "Red Guards" (*Hong Weibing* 红卫兵), donned arm bands and pledged allegiance to Mao and this new revolution. Schools' normal functions were abandoned, and Mao further encouraged this youthful revolutionary zeal by temporarily making train travel anywhere in China free for students.

For China's youth, this was an exciting time. Like students around the world in the 1960s, many young Chinese had grown disillusioned by an education system which they saw as stagnant, overly formal, and ineffective. Their anger toward authorities and educators for the restraints, the sacrifices, and the limited prospects that characterized their lives fueled their desire to rebel. The Cultural Revolution provided an opportunity to air these grievances. There was also a sense among many students that the Cultural Revolution was their generation's very own revolutionary opportunity. Many young people had grown up hearing tales about the heroic struggle of their forefathers, and some began to fear that they would not have the same chance as their parents to change the course of Chinese history. The outbreak of the Cultural

Revolution seemed to be the opportunity for which they had long waited. In 1966, China's youth presented itself as a new generation of "revolutionary successors."

The Revolution Spreads

In August 1966, the Central Committee of the Chinese Communist Party put forth the "Decision Concerning the Great Proletarian Cultural Revolution" or "The Sixteen Points." It called for "all forces to strike at the handful of ultra-reactionary bourgeois Rightists and counter-revolutionary revisionists, and expose and criticize to the full these crimes against the Party, against socialism, and against Mao Zedong's thought."[4] This spawned a massive outbreak of violence and destruction. "Revolutionaries," bent on isolating and eliminating those who were not in step with Mao's extreme policies, attacked thousands of individuals.

The Cult of Personality and the Role of the Red Guards

During this entire period, the Mao cult continued to grow. Jiang Qing and Minster of Defense Lin Biao promoted Mao Zedong as "our great teacher, great leader, great supreme commander, and great helmsman."[5] All of this was done with Mao's blessing. As August wore on, Mao and Lin Biao made ten appearances at the Gate of Heavenly Peace in Tiananmen Square (天安门广场) to address vast throngs of Red Guards, who made the pilgrimage to Tiananmen Square waving Mao's Little Red Book of quotations in adulation of their leader.

On a more planned level, for Mao, Jiang Qing, and Lin Biao, the revolution centered on consolidating and reclaiming power in the Party for Mao and his supporters. They initiated purges, which escalated to the highest level with the removal and humiliation of Liu Shaoqi and Deng Xiaoping. Countless cadres were disgraced publicly, imprisoned, beaten, and often exiled to the countryside.

Mao called on Red Guards to undo China's "Four Olds" (old ideas, old culture, old customs, and old habits). Teens and young adults interpreted this as a blank check to attack anything deemed Western, feudal, or anti-revolutionary. Uncontrolled violence erupted as students attacked their teachers, school administrators, parents, and known intellectuals. A stunning destruction of Chinese heritage erupted. In the name of Revolution, Red Guards destroyed temples, art, innumerable historical manuscripts, archaeological sites, libraries, sculptures, and artifacts.

Soon after the Cultural Revolution began, students split into different factions, often competing with one another to demonstrate loyalty to Mao, using radical behavior as the measure of that loyalty. The reasons for this factionalism varied. Some Red Guard organizations split over the issue of class origin. Certain factions believed that only students from "red" family backgrounds—parents who were either Party members, farmers, factory workers, revolutionary heroes, or members of the army—could actually participate in the revolution. However, factionalism was also due to genuine differences of opinion about the nature and direction of the Cultural Revolution. Furthermore, students who were persecuted early on for their insistence that students, rather than the Party, should take the lead in the Cultural Revolution tended to join radical factions and advocate for a more aggressive course.

Youthful Red Guards brought their purges to all corners of the country, and extremism reached its apogee in 1967 when radical groups attempted to attack the People's Liberation Army (PLA) in Wuhan (武汉). The confrontation between the PLA and these radical students during the summer of 1967 resulted in numerous casualties. Meanwhile, in Beijing, a group of radical Red Guards attached to the Foreign Ministry also managed to temporarily

---

[4] Qtd. in Michael Schoenhals, ed., *China's Cultural Revolution, 1966–1969: Not a Dinner Party* (Armonk, NY: M. E. Sharpe, 1996) 37.

[5] Qtd. in Jonathan D. Spence, *The Search for Modern China* (New York: W. W. Norton, 1999) 575.

gain the upper hand over their rivals. These students, with the backing of radical patrons in the Party, were extremely critical of those working in the Ministry, and advocated for a much more aggressive foreign policy. This radicalism culminated in August 1967 when a group of students attempted to burn down the British mission in Beijing as a way of retaliating against British colonialism in Hong Kong.

New Purges

The radicalism of 1967, both in places like Wuhan and in China's Foreign Ministry, convinced some—including Mao—that things had gone too far. In response, Mao launched the "Campaign to Purify Class Ranks" to isolate the "bad elements" in China's population. He created investigative teams to locate and re-educate these "bad elements," which included those perceived to be intellectuals, capitalists, and Western-sympathizers. Ironically, Mao's list now included and affected many members of the radical Red Guard, as well as their patrons in the CCP. Purging the class ranks was less about ideology and more about centralization and unity in the Party.

Many officials used this opportunity to attack their enemies, and the movement quickly devolved into chaos. As Mao isolated and purged top cadres, some of their children were labeled as having a "bad background" or coming from "bad elements" as well. Those who were criticized were often denied access to basic services and education. "Re-education camps," where authorities combined hard labor with intense study of Mao's writings and thoughts, sprang up across rural China. Living conditions in these camps were deplorable. Mao also moved to end the student movement, sending "propaganda teams" to many of China's campuses in order to seize control from the students. Many students, called "sent-down youth" (*zhiqing* 知青), were sent into the countryside to either labor or to establish new rural schools dedicated to studying Mao Zedong Thought.

From 1967 to 1969, up to 2 million people, including prominent members of the Party—dedicated Communists—were investigated, sent to be re-educated, and subjected to all manner of physical and mental torture. Unknown numbers of people were killed. Others, humiliated beyond endurance, committed suicide. Many of those who survived grew exhausted and embittered by their ordeals. Although the purges and the persecution of the Cultural Revolution did not abate after 1969, its nature differed. Individuals were still made to suffer, but punishments were more predictable and not subject to the random chaos of the students. The Cultural Revolution would continue, but more on the terms of Mao and his allies.

Lin Biao's Demise

Out of this chaos emerged two competing factions in the central government: Jiang Qing and her radical allies, and Lin Biao and a handful of army generals. In 1969, Mao designated Lin Biao as his successor, but Lin soon began to fall out of favor. By 1970, Mao began to reconsider who should succeed him as Party chairman, and started to doubt whether Lin Biao could carry on his radical policies. As a result, Mao began to lend his support to Jiang Qing's more radical faction. Lin and his family briefly considered using the army to force Mao's hand, but they were outmaneuvered by Jiang's allies. So in September 1971, Lin Biao fled China with his family, apparently headed for the Soviet Union. His plane crashed in Mongolia killing all aboard. The government claimed that Lin had hatched a plot against Mao that failed. While most Chinese figured out that Lin was gone, the government waited a year to announce that Lin had crashed. Lin Biao's death had a profound impact on the Cultural Revolution. As Jonathan Spence describes it, "The credulity of the Chinese people had been stretched beyond all possible boundaries as leader after leader had first been praised to the skies and then vilified."[6]

---

[6] Spence, 586.

The Revolution Ends

Mao, deeply shaken by what he believed were Lin Biao's plots against him, reenlisted separately the help of Deng Xiaoping and Premier Zhou Enlai (周恩来). However, Mao's wife and her closest supporters viewed Deng Xiaoping and especially Zhou Enlai as threats, and they attempted to turn the people against Zhou. The move failed. By the mid-1970s, the populace was exhausted, utterly unable to support another set of purges and protests.

After four years of struggling with cancer, Zhou Enlai died on January 8, 1976. People across China mourned the leader who was seen by many as one of the most selfless and talented members of the CCP (see A Closer Look at the end of Chapter 15). On July 28, a massive earthquake, among the worst in China's historical record, shook Hebei Province (河北). This devastating event is officially reported to have killed almost a quarter of a million people and seriously injured another 160,000. It destroyed the city of Tangshan (唐山) and caused serious damage in Tianjin and Beijing. Many saw the disaster as a signal that Mao had lost the Mandate of Heaven (*Tianming* 天命).[7]

Finally Mao Zedong himself died on September 9, 1976, and with his passing, what little remained of the Cultural Revolution ground to a halt. Many people, even those whose lives were ravaged by Mao's policies, could hardly believe that their leader could die. His cult of personality, his thoughts, and even his image had permeated every facet of Chinese society. But all this adulation no longer protected his associates. Within a month, his wife Jiang Qing and her three closest colleagues—the "Gang of Four" (*Siren Bang* 四人帮)—were arrested by military forces and accused of plotting their own coup against the new leadership, as well as various crimes committed during the Cultural Revolution. It was now their turn to languish in jail while their victims, some of whom had been confined for ten years or more, were at long last released and rehabilitated.

Reflections on the Cultural Revolution

Different people experienced the Great Proletarian Cultural Revolution in different ways. Ye Weili, who experienced the revolution as a teenager, writes that "the texture of everyday life and the multiple shades of grey" are utterly lost in the sea of "victim literature" that permeates our understanding of the Cultural Revolution. She further cautions: "Traumatic as the Cultural Revolution was for us, our history did not begin or end with it. Nor did our life experiences always revolve around politics."[8] While the disastrous elements of this period are undeniable, also important are the family dynamics, conversations, traditions, and resilience that saw the majority of China's population through its crises.

Today, the Cultural Revolution remains a taboo subject in China, although a thaw is beginning. Slowly, more and more people are opening up about their experiences, and even challenging the dominant narrative that settled around the Cultural Revolution after Mao's death. China is truly a country transformed since the days of the Cultural Revolution, embracing capitalist development and trade with Western countries. And yet, China's rapid development has sparked nostalgia for the Maoist period, and even for the Cultural Revolution. Rural people who during the Cultural Revolution experienced improvements in health care through the coming of "barefoot doctors" and in education through village schools, have seen some basic services ended or made overly costly since then. Revolutionary songs are still sung in China, and some admit to missing the sense of

---

[7] For millennia, Chinese tradition dictated that a leader/emperor had to have legitimate authority from the gods—the Mandate of Heaven—in order to rule the country. Huge natural disasters or civil disorder were seen as signs that a ruler had lost this mandate.

[8] Ye Weili and Ma Xiaodong, *Growing Up in The People's Republic of China: Conversations Between Two Daughters of China's Revolution* (New York: Palgrave Macmillan, 2005) 5.

community and egalitarianism that pervaded the Maoist period. Whether this is a longing for times gone by or a reaction to China's breakneck development is difficult to determine.

Nevertheless, the Cultural Revolution continues to have a major impact on Chinese politics and society. While some express a sense of nostalgia for Mao, the party-state apparatus has set its course firmly in the direction of economic growth, ideological dampening, and re-engagement with the outside world. Today, Chinese officials promote "harmony" and stability, virtues that stand directly opposed to the "chaos" that Mao promoted during the Cultural Revolution. While the Party continues to distance itself from the events of the Cultural

Revolution, there has been a push, especially among everyday Chinese people, to preserve the memory of this period. On October 1, 1979,[9] the thirtieth anniversary of the founding of the PRC, Marshal Ye Jianying stated, "Leaders are not gods. It is impossible for them to be free from mistakes or shortcomings. They should definitely not be deified." A year later, he said "We can occasionally slap our own faces, but we cannot, nor do we have time to, start from scratch....If we want to trace the responsibility to the end, we will find that it lies not with Mao alone. It lies in all of us."[10]

---

[9] Three years after Mao Zedong's death
[10] Quoted in Hsü, 782.

Primary Sources

DOCUMENT 14.1: Excerpts from "One Hundred Items for Destroying the Old and Establishing the New," created by Red Guards at the #26 Middle School, Beijing, August 1966

Students at Beijing No. 26 Middle School created a list of 100 instructions for how the Great Proletarian Cultural Revolution should be carried out. They also renamed their school the Maoism School.

1. Under the charge of residential committees, every street must set up a quotation plaque; every household must have on its walls a picture of the Chairman plus quotations by Chairman Mao....

5. With a copy of the *Quotations from Chairman Mao* in the hands of everyone, each must carry it with him, constantly study it, and do everything in accord with it....

11. Every school and every unit must set up highest directive propaganda teams so that everyone can hear at any time the repeated instructions of the Chairman....

24. You landowners who still rode on the people's heads and drank the people's blood after the Liberation, we order you bastards to hurry up and turn over all your private holdings to the state. In a socialist state we absolutely cannot allow you vampires to exist.

25. In a proletarian society, private enterprise cannot be allowed to exist. We propose to take all firms using joint state and private management and change them to state management and change joint state and private management enterprises into state-owned enterprises....

41. Heads of families are not allowed to educate their children with bourgeois ideology. The feudal family-head system will be abolished. No more beating or scolding of children will be tolerated. If the child is not of one's own begetting, no mistreatment is allowed. Children will be consistently educated in Mao Zedong Thought....

SOURCE: Michael Schoenhals, ed., *China's Cultural Revolution, 1966–1976: Not A Dinner Party* (Armonk, NY: M.E. Sharpe, 1996) 212–217.

Go to **www.chinasince1644.com** for the full text of Document 14.1.

DOCUMENT 14.2: "The Red Guards Cut Your Mother's Hair," an excerpt from *Growing Up in the People's Republic: Conversations Between Two Daughters of China's Revolution* by Ye Weili and Ma Xiaodong, 2005

Ma Xiaodong's father spoke of his wife's experiences.

Hewen was forty-two in 1966. She was in the prime of her life, well educated, experienced at work and in good health. But then came the Cultural Revolution. Schools, especially secondary schools, were the first to be turned upside down. Hewen became a black gangster at her school.[11] She was confronted at numerous meetings, where she was spat at, hit by stones, had her body bent in the "jet airplane" position and was forced to don a heavy board over her neck and a dunce hat on her head. She tried her very best to endure all these abuses.

The worst finally came on August 24th when, at a meeting in the school, Hewen was severely beaten along with five other former leaders of the school. Two died on the spot. Hewen's life was spared, but her hair was shaved and wounds covered all her body. When she came back from school, all I could do was to clean the blood from her body. While dressing her wounds, I cried and asked myself why she had to suffer like this. I was afraid that after this horrendous experience Hewen would not want to live anymore. We stayed up the whole night and I tried my best to comfort her and to discourage any thought of suicide....

SOURCE: Ye Weili and Ma Xiaodong, *Growing Up in the People's Republic: Conversations Between Two Daughters of China's Revolution* (New York: Palgrave Macmillan, 2005) 89.

 Go to **www.chinasince1644.com** for the full text of Document 14.2.

---

[11] During the Cultural Revolution, the term "black gangster" was used to brand anyone accused of being anti-Party or anti-socialist. Top administrators in schools, industry, and government were the most likely targets. The label was a reference to criminals who worked in the underworld before the founding of the PRC.

DOCUMENT 14.3: Excerpt from interview with Charles Wang about effects of the Cultural Revolution on his life and on his village, 2012

Charles Wang grew up in a rural village where he experienced the effects of the Cultural Revolution. Charles is now a successful businessman living in a large city an hour's bus ride away from his village.

However, fortune came to me in 1972. After six years the universities reopened to recruit students. And this time no universal national entrance exams were required. The students were recommended by their working units and were called "worker," "peasant," or "soldier" university students. At that time I had already been chosen to teach at the village primary school as a peasant teacher thanks to my time at the high school (less than a year). In addition to the work points I received like the other young peasants in the village, I was given an allowance of half a U.S. dollar a month. I worked hard and the school and the village recommended me to become a university student. I was told to learn English as my major in the Foreign Language University in Xi'an. So, I should say I benefited from the Cultural Revolution as well. But many of my schoolmates were not as lucky as I was. The Cultural Revolution interrupted their education, and they never had a chance to go back to school.

SOURCE: From an unpublished interview with Charles Wang by Carolyn Platt, 2012

 Go to **www.chinasince1644.com** for the full text of Document 14.3.

DOCUMENT 14.4: Excerpt from *Wild Swans: Three Daughters of China* by Jung Chang, 1991

The Rebels' denunciation meetings became more brutal, even though my father was still allowed to live at home. One day he came back with one of his eyes badly damaged. Another day I saw him standing on a slow-moving truck, being paraded through the streets. A huge placard hung from a thin wire that was eating into his neck, and his arms were twisted ferociously behind his back. He was struggling to keep his head up under the forceful pushing of some Rebels. What made me saddest of all was that he appeared indifferent to his physical pain. In his insanity, his mind seemed to be detached from his body....

We watched my father deteriorate mentally and physically with each passing day. My mother went to ask [an acquaintance] for help again. He promised to see what he could do. We waited, but nothing happened: his silence meant he must have failed to get [those in power] to allow my father to have treatment....

SOURCE: Jung Chang, *Wild Swans: Three Daughters of China* (New York: HarperCollins, 1993) 464, 468.

 Go to **www.chinasince1644.com** for the full text of Document 14.4.

DOCUMENT 14.5: Excerpts describing the personal experiences of Nathan Hu during the early stages of the Cultural Revolution, written in 2006–2007

Mao encouraged Red Guards to bring revolutionary zeal to different schools, factories, and governments at all ranks. We could go to any city through free transportation. Our boarding and food were all free. Mao's purpose was to paralyze all the party and government administrations and put power into those people who would follow his political ideology.

I left the middle school when classes were no longer being held, and I returned to my home at my father's university. Children like I, we followed the college students whom we called Big Red Guards. We helped them to print brochures, to write Big-character Posters. Students from the school were divided into two parts. One we called the revolutionary part. The other was called the conservative part. The revolutionaries followed Mao's teachings exactly. They wanted to act against the school leaders. The other side—the conservatives—they tried to protect school leaders. In almost any institution, universities and schools, people divided into these two factions. Sometimes even into three, four, five factions, but generally speaking the two. "Rebellion" was considered a very good word. We called the other group, "protect the emperor group." I was on the side of the revolutionaries, the radicals. I followed the older students....

SOURCE: Nathan Hu, unpublished memoir; interview with Liz Nelson, June 2007.

 Go to **www.chinasince1644.com** for the full text of **Document 14.5**.

DOCUMENT 14.6a & b: Posters from the Cultural Revolution

The slogan on the right side of the poster reads: "Go to the Countryside; Go to the Borderland; Go to the Places Where the Motherland Needs You." On the red cloth, the text says "Become educated by the once poor and low middle class peasants; take roots in the countryside for the Revolution." The poster was created in February 1970 (*Collection Stephan R. Landsberger at the International Institute for Social History, Amsterdam, the Netherlands.*)

This poster shows Dazhai, a village that from 1964 until the late 1970s was held up as a model of success to be copied, regardless of widely varying growing conditions (*Collection Stephan R. Landsberger at the International Institute for Social History, Amsterdam, the Netherlands. http://www.chineseposters.net*)

Go to **www.chinasince1644.com** for the color posters in Document 14.6a & b.

DOCUMENT 14.7: "I Now Knew the Face of Poverty," an excerpt from *Growing Up in the People's Republic: Conversations Between Two Daughters of China's Revolution* by Ye Weili and Ma Xiaodong, 2005

Ye Weili describes her experience as a zhiqing, *one of 12 million "sent-down youth" sent to the countryside between 1968 and 1975 to be re-educated by the peasants.*

It was unsettling to see the poverty surrounding us. There were three scenes I will never forget. One occurred in late fall. By then I had lived in the village for a number of years. Our team harvested potatoes earlier that day. In the evening we were going to divide up the potatoes so that each household would get its share—we received all our grains and vegetables this way. After supper I took a wicker basket to collect my share. When I came out of our alleyway, I saw a scene that has been forever frozen in my mind. Under the yellow streetlight, people from my team stood by a pile of potatoes. They were shivering in the cold wind in their shabby clothes. How they resembled a group sculpture of beggars! It was as though I was seeing my fellow team members for the first time. I now knew the face of poverty....

SOURCE: Ye Weili and Ma Xiaodong, *Growing Up in the People's Republic: Conversations Between Two Daughters of China's Revolution* (New York: Palgrave Macmillan, 2005) 115.

 Go to **www.chinasince1644.com** for the full text of Document 14.7.

DOCUMENT 14.8: "Singing Our Turbulent Youth," an excerpt from *Growing Up in the People's Republic: Conversations Between Two Daughters of China's Revolution* by Ye Weili and Ma Xiaodong, 2005

With or without books, people continued their pursuit of knowledge. One boy was a physics nut. He often adjusted the angle of his hoe at the end of the day, applying his knowledge of mechanics to make his hoe more labor efficient. Another boy was interested in international affairs. His hobby was to gather every piece of information he could find about a foreign country; climate, geography, population, and so on. The data primarily came from *The People's Daily*—the only paper available to us. His newspaper clippings eventually filled several thick columns of used magazines. He liked to challenge us to test him about any country in the world, the more obscure the better.

There was no electricity when we first arrived in the village. In the third year the area was connected to a power plant. By then we had become accustomed to physical labor and we needed release for our surplus energy, especially during the long winter months when there was little work in the field. Some of us began to make systematic study plans. My brother finished studying senior high math and physics on his own. Nobody knew if colleges would ever be open again, but the desire for learning was too strong for us to care about its practical value. Several people decided to study English and it was fun to join them. Many of us had short-wave radios. It was amazing how easily we could receive foreign broadcasts such a VOA (Voice of America), BBC [British Broadcasting Corporation], and Radio Moscow in this remote region....

SOURCE: Ye Weili and Ma Xiaodong, *Growing Up in the People's Republic: Conversations Between Two Daughters of China's Revolution* (New York: Palgrave Macmillan, 2005) 122.

 Go to **www.chinasince1644.com** for the full text of Document 14.8.

DOCUMENT 14.9: Excerpts describing the personal experiences of Nathan Hu as a "sent-down youth," written in 2007

The majority of us were happy to go to the countryside because we thought that it was a test to our generation—the leaders of the People's Republic of China in the future. First of all, we really believed what Mao said. He said the world belonged to us, also, the world belongs to you—the youth. You're like the morning sun; the future will be created in your hands. We saw it as Mao offering us a chance to go to the countryside to be re-educated. The education we received before in school was a *bourgeoisie* education and now we needed to go to the countryside to get a farmer's education. This would be a good education. So we said, "OK, yes, why not? We'll go there."

In some ways we felt very superior to the farmers. They were considered the bottom [of the social hierarchy]. We were from the city; naturally we felt superior. Even though we were supposed to receive an education from the farmers, mentally, psychologically we felt higher than them. We were cheerful, optimistic about going to the countryside. We were excited about going to a new environment. We felt it was like a test that we needed to pass. We would gain strength....

In 1991, forty-year-old Nathan Hu came to the United States to continue his studies. After completing his course work toward a doctorate, he worked full time while he wrote his dissertation. In 2005, he received his Ph.D. from the University of Massachusetts Amherst.

SOURCE: Nathan Hu, unpublished memoir; interview with Liz Nelson, June 2007.

Go to **www.chinasince1644.com** for the full text of **Document 14.9**.

DOCUMENT 14.10: Descriptions of two women's reactions to the Cultural Revolution, an excerpt from *Growing Up in the People's Republic: Conversations Between Two Daughters of China's Revolution* by Ye Weili and Ma Xiaodong, 2005

MA XIAODONG: My enthusiasm at the beginning of the Cultural Revolution also reflected my yearning for more thrills in life. I had always wished to be born during the time of war. Now my turn had finally come. My spirits were very high. I was busy making revolution and often didn't go home for days. At night we put a few desks together as beds and slept in the classroom. I was so excited that I didn't need much sleep.

YE WEILI: I shared some of your excitement. I was captivated by the full name of the Cultural Revolution: the Historically Unprecedented Great Proletarian Cultural Revolution. It sounded galvanizing. I felt I was participating in the making of history. It was a grand feeling. I was in this mood when we marched in a parade hailing the launch of the Cultural Revolution after the publication of *The People's Daily* editorial. We just walked around the school campus, shouting slogans and so forth. The parade was led by school administration even though the campus was now covered with posters denouncing them....

SOURCE: Ye Weili and Ma Xiaodong, *Growing Up in the People's Republic: Conversations Between Two Daughters of China's Revolution* (New York: Palgrave Macmillan, 2005) 73.

Go to **www.chinasince1644.com** for the full text of **Document 14.10**.

DOCUMENT 14.11: A peasant's reflection on Mao Zedong, from an interview conducted in the early 1980s

Fifty-four-year-old Zhang Yuxi lived in a village in Shandong Province at the time of this interview. He described the effects of the frequently changing policies under Mao, spoke of how "things were going wrong" under the co-op system, and of how hard he cried when in 1964 he was forced to cut down an orchard of peach trees he had grown from scratch because it was a "capitalist activity." "Life got harder and harder after that," he continued. "It was so hard to get by those days that…I can't find the words." Nevertheless, he had the following to say about Mao Zedong:

Life has been better the last couple of years. I'm still hoping to get the money together for a trip to Beijing to have a look round. Before I die, I want to see what Chairman Mao really looked like. I know about the mistakes in his last years. But they weren't his mistakes. Sitting there in his dragon palace, he couldn't possibly have known what was happening to us peasants. It was the people under him who were bad. They kept him in the dark and did all sorts of terrible things in his name. Chairman Mao had wealth and greatness written all over his face. He had the look of a real emperor, but he was better than an emperor. No emperor ever saved the poor. Chairman Mao was the savior of the poor from the moment he was born. If he hadn't been, would we be missing him now?

SOURCE: Zhang Xinxin and Sang Ye, *Chinese Lives: An Oral History of Contemporary China*, ed. W. J. F. Jenner and Delia Davin (New York: Pantheon, 1987) 117.

Go to **www.chinasince1644.com** for the text of **Document 14.11**.

DOCUMENT 14.12: Poster depicting people swimming across the Yangzi River, emulating Mao's crossing ten years earlier, 1976

万里长江横渡

Mao Zedong was a strong proponent of swimming as a form of exercise. In 1966 (at age 73), he swam in the Yangzi ostensibly to promote the sport but also to show his own well-being. The event was covered extensively by the Chinese press. This poster by Wei Yang was created to commemorate that event. The words at the bottom read: "Crossing the 10,000 li Yangzi River, 1976." (*Collection Stephan R. Landsberger at the International Institute for Social History, Amsterdam, the Netherlands. http://www.chineseposters.net*)

 Go to **www.chinasince1644.com** for the color poster in **Document 14.12**.

DOCUMENT 14.13: Photograph of people waiting to visit Mao Zedong's mausoleum, Beijing, April 2011

Even on extremely hot and humid summer days, hundreds of people still wait in line for the opportunity to go inside the mausoleum and to walk past Mao Zedong's coffin. (*Photo by Liz Gray*)

 Go to **www.chinasince1644.com** for the color photograph in **Document 14.13**.

Activities

ACTIVITY 1:
Assessing Student Goals during the Cultural Revolution

After reading the introductory essay, examine the "One Hundred Items for Destroying the Old and Establishing the New" (14.1). Consider the following questions:

1. Who wrote the rules?
2. What is the overarching tone of the rules and regulations?
3. What language or phrases are particularly striking and why?
4. As a list of rules, how does this compare to other lists or sets of rules that you may have encountered? What are the similarities? The differences?
5. What would it be like to live under rules of this sort?

ACTIVITY 2:
Examining Individual Experiences of the Cultural Revolution

Part 1: Respond to Reading

You will be assigned to a small group to read one of the documents describing experiences during the Cultural Revolution (14.2–14.5). In your group, discuss the reading and then take notes in response to the following questions:

1. What is the tone of the excerpt you read?
2. In what format has the author chosen to tell of his or her experiences? How does it affect what you learn from the writing?
3. How would you summarize the author's experiences?
4. What did you find most striking about the document? What surprised you?
5. From the account you read, what can be concluded about the state of affairs in China during the mid-1960s?
6. In what ways could individuals respond to the events unfolding around them? What were the likely consequences to the choices they had?

Part 2: Summarize

Groups will then present a summary of their excerpt and their discussion. You will then discuss the following questions as a class. (The discussion might be done in a Socratic Seminar with directions provided by your teacher.)

1. What do these accounts tell us about the Cultural Revolution?
2. What were some of the effects of the Cultural Revolution on children, adults, and families?
3. How are the accounts similar and different?
4. What role did justice play?

5. How does the span of time between when the experiences took place and when the individual wrote or spoke about them affect the document?

ACTIVITY 3: **Analyzing Propaganda Posters**

With a partner look at the two posters (14.6a & b) on the companion website, where they are in color. For 14.6a, discuss:

1. What is the overall impression you get from this poster?
2. What is the primary color? Why? What is the significance of this color in traditional Chinese culture?
3. What aspect or aspects of the Cultural Revolution does the poster capture?

For 14.6b, discuss:

4. What do you see in the poster?
5. What is your general impression of the poster?
6. How does this poster express propaganda? What is it trying to say?
7. Given what you read in the introductory essay and additional primary sources, what strikes you about the poster?
8. How do you think people reconciled the discrepancies between the imagery of Dazhai and what, in fact, was actually unfolding throughout China?

Extension Activity: Interview

With appropriate permission, interview an adult about his or her views on a revolutionary movement that occurred in his or her country. Compare and contrast your subject's comments to those of any one of the accounts in this chapter (14.2– 14.5). Write a short essay that analyzes the most salient points of similarity and difference. What influences the interviewee's recollections the most?

ACTIVITY 4: **Jigsaw: From the City to the Countryside**

You will work in a small group to read and discuss one of these documents (14.7– 14.9) so that each group is reading one account. Discuss in your group:

1. How does the individual feel about his or her experience as a sent-down youth?
2. How does the account match the image on the poster (14.6a)?
3. Why did Mao put this huge program into action?
4. What did the individual gain from the experience? What did he or she lose?

You will reconvene in groups that include readers of each document. Share what you learned and discuss the varied experiences.

1. What stands out the most?
2. What would your reaction be if you were told you had to move to a distant rural part of the country to work on a farm? How did these three individuals react? Why?

3. What might be the lasting effects of millions of teens having lived and worked with peasants in rural China? (These individuals are now in their early- to mid-50s.)

ACTIVITY 5: Reflecting on the Chaos and Violence

Read document 14.10, in which Ye Weili and Ma Xiaodong reflect on the Cultural Revolution. Discuss:

1. How do the two authors compare in their views of the Cultural Revolution?
2. What explains the differences in the authors' accounts?
3. Why do both authors express a degree of excitement they felt during this turbulent time in China?
4. What specific factors most strongly affected the authors' opinions of the Cultural Revolution? Cite evidence from the text.
5. What accounts for the complex emotions the authors experienced during the Cultural Revolution?
6. As middle-aged adults, how might the authors' feelings about what they experienced have evolved or changed since the 1960s?

Creative Extension:

■ In response to all that you've learned about people's experiences during this very difficult period, create a piece of visual art (such as a sculpture, collage, poster, painting, or cartoon strip.) Write a brief caption to go with your work.

■ Write a poem in response to any one of the experiences about which you read.

■ Explore posters and other propaganda from the Soviet Union, especially under Joseph Stalin. Write a short essay that describes parallels and differences between Russian propaganda and that of the Cultural Revolution. Evaluate the similarities and try to determine what themes and issues are consistent and why this might be the case. Explain what might account for the differences.

ACTIVITY 6: Exploring Mao Zedong's Legacy

Read the excerpt from the interview with a peasant (14.11) and the final paragraph of the introductory essay. Next, look at the poster on the companion website (14.12) and the photograph taken in Beijing (14.13).

Interview:

1. Why might the man hold these opinions about Mao?
2. What does the excerpt teach us generally about the impact of Mao Zedong?
3. What does the excerpt teach us about Mao's "cult of personality"?
4. How does the man's view of Mao Zedong fit with the official's statement?

Poster:

1. What is the overriding color in the poster? Why?
2. What emotions does the poster convey?
3. How does this poster depict Mao's "cult of personality"?
4. How does this poster help explain the far-reaching impact of Mao on many Chinese people?

Photograph:

1. What surprises you about the photograph?
2. How long does this queue appear to be?
3. Why do thousands of Chinese citizens stand in line for hours to see the mausoleum?
4. How does this contribute to your understanding of Mao Zedong's legacy?

EXTENDED RESEARCH:

Conduct further research on one of the following:

- Write an essay in which you assess the effectiveness of Mao Zedong's leadership. Did he change China for the better or were the costs too high? Support any claims with evidence drawn from both primary and secondary sources.
- Assess the above question in the form of an in-class debate.
- Write an essay in which you assess the consequences of the Cultural Revolution.
- Write an essay in which you analyze and compare the views of three different firsthand accounts of the Cultural Revolution. What are the common threads? What aspects stand out as being markedly different? What could account for these similarities and differences?
- Write an essay comparing China's Cultural Revolution to periods of social and political upheaval elsewhere in the world in the twentieth century (e.g. to the McCarthy Era in the United States or to Stalin's purges in the 1930s). Where do the similarities begin and end? What accounts for the similarities and differences?
- Research the Khmer Rouge regime and its impact on the people of Cambodia in the 1970s. This government claimed to be heavily influenced and supported by Maoist communism. Write an essay that evaluates the impact of Maoist China in Cambodia. Alternatively, write an essay comparing the ideas and actions of the Khmer Rouge with those of the Red Guards during the Cultural Revolution.

Suggested Resources

Books

Cheek, Timothy. *Mao Zedong and China's Revolutions: A Brief History with Documents*. Boston: Bedford/ St. Martin's, 2002.
A collection of essays on Mao and the Chairman's own writing and speeches.

Cheng, Nien. *Life and Death in Shanghai*. New York: Grove Press, 1987.

Dai Sijie. *Balzac and the Little Chinese Seamstress*. Translated by Ina Rilke. New York: Alfred A. Knopf, 2001.
A novel about two teenage boys' time as "sent-down" youth being re-educated in a Sichuan mountain village. Highly recommended for teens and adults. This book was adapted as a feature film in 2005.

Francis, Gregory and Stefanie Lamb. *China's Cultural Revolution*. Stanford: Stanford Program on International and Cross-Cultural Education (SPICE), 2005.
A high school curriculum unit about the Cultural Revolution.

Ha Jin. *Under the Red Flag: Stories*. Athens: University of Georgia Press, 1997.

Jiang, Yarong and David Ashley. *Mao's Children in the New China: Voices from the Red Guard Generation*. New York: Routledge, 2000.
A collection of interviews with former Red Guard members who talk about the effects of the Cultural Revolution on themselves and their experiences in the "New China" of the late twentieth century.

Kissinger, Henry. "China Confronts Both Superpowers." *On China*. New York: Penguin Press, 2011.
This chapter describes China's relationships with the United States and the Soviet Union including the Sino-Soviet split.

Landsberger, Stefan. *Chinese Propaganda Posters: From Revolution to Modernization*. Amsterdam: The Pepin Press, 1998.
Text and images detail the role of posters in the People's Republic of China.

Liang Heng and Judith Shapiro. *Son of the Revolution*. New York: Alfred A. Knopf, 1983.
Liang Heng engages young adults in his own and his family's experiences living with the erratic policies of Mao Zedong.

Luthi, Lorenz M. *The Sino-Soviet Split: Cold War in the Communist World*. Princeton: Princeton University Press, 2008.

MacFarquhar, Roderick and Michael Schoenhals. *Mao's Last Revolution*. Cambridge: Belknap Press of Harvard University, 2006.

Mao Zedong. *Quotations from Chairman Mao Tsetung*. Peking: Foreign Language Press, 1966.
Also known as Mao's *Little Red Book*.

Spence, Jonathan D. *Mao Zedong*. New York: Viking, 1999.
A short biography by one of the most well-known China scholars.

Ye Weili and Ma Xiaodong. *Growing Up in the People's Republic: Conversations Between Two Daughters of China's Revolution*. New York: Palgrave Macmillan, 2005.
A highly readable and thoughtful exploration of the two women's experiences and the legacy of the Cultural Revolution.

Yu, Chun. *Little Green: Growing Up During the Chinese Cultural Revolution*. New York: Simon & Schuster, 2005.
Written in poetic form from a child's perspective, a poignant account of the experiences of one family.

Websites

Bibliography of the Cultural Revolution, University of Maine at Farmington
http://hua.umf.maine.edu/China/culturr.html
A bibliography of resources about the Cultural Revolution compiled by Marilyn Shea, Department of Psychology.

Chinese Posters: Propaganda, Politics, History, Art
http://chineseposters.net
Digitized posters from the collections of the International Institute of Social History, Amsterdam, and Stefan R. Landsberger.

Cultural Revolution, A Visual Sourcebook for Chinese Civilization
http://depts.washington.edu/chinaciv/graph/9wenge.htm
Information and posters from the Cultural Revolution.

Morning Sun: A Film and Website about Cultural Revolution
http://www.morningsun.org/
A site created by the Long Bow Group as a companion to the documentary *Morning Sun*. The site includes articles, images, and multimedia about the Cultural Revolution with the full-text of Mao's *Little Red Book*.

■ **A CLOSER LOOK**

Lei Feng and His Diary

The 22-year-old PLA soldier died helping a comrade in trouble, the public was told. And he left behind a diary. *The Diary of Lei Feng,* published in 1963, expressed the young man's love for the revolution, his country, his comrades, and especially Chairman Mao. Lei had written in his diary that he worked to "make the world more beautiful every day."

In the 1960s, Lei Feng became a household name, and his face was instantly recognized on multiple posters that soon appeared across China. Study of his diary became standard practice in Chinese schools, and Mao himself endorsed the book by adding his calligraphy to the title page. The journal suggested that young people "learn from

Comrade Lei Feng," and included an honor code and list of duties not unlike that of the Boy Scouts. Lei Feng "spent all his spare time and money helping the needy," wrote the *People's Daily* on the fortieth anniversary of his death. The diary was meant to inspire thousands to follow in Lei's selfless footsteps, to live simple, honest lives.

The diary, however, was a work of fiction, created by PLA writers, though there had been a real Lei Feng. Orphaned when he was seven, he joined the PLA at age twenty as a soldier in a transportation unit. He had been killed by a falling telephone pole, which had been accidentally hit by a truck, but that fact came to light years later. Lei Feng's image is still common throughout China, his

picture sometimes found at the entrance to primary schools. March 5 has been designated "Learn from Lei Feng Day," a time for students to engage in community service. According to the People's Daily Online, the Lei Feng Memorial Hall in Fushun has been visited by 64 million people since it opened in 1964.

■ *To see the many posters of Lei Feng, go to the companion website. Discuss why Lei Feng's diary and his story became so inspirational. What stories of everyday good deeds are part of the histories of other countries? How and why do some stories, such as the one about George Washington and the cherry tree, take on a life of their own?*

Songs of China's Cultural Revolution
   http://www.wellesley.edu/Polisci/wj/China/ CRSongs/crsongs.htm
   A collection of songs from the Cultural Revolution compiled by William A. Joseph, Department of Political Science, Wellesley College.

Films

Balzac and the Little Chinese Seamstress (111 mins; 2005)
   A feature film adaptation of Dai Sijie's novel. In Mandarin with subtitles.

The Blue Kite (138 mins; 1993)
   The film captures how the turbulent political times affected the lives of citizens. In Mandarin with subtitles.

Morning Sun (120 mins; 2003)
   This documentary provides a multi-perspective view of a tumultuous period as seen through the eyes of a generation born at the time the People's Republic of China was founded.

To Live (133 mins; 1994)
   This film spans four decades of the twentieth century in China. It tells the story of a couple and their two children as they struggle to survive the constantly changing political climate. In Mandarin with subtitles.

CHAPTER RESOURCES

 Excerpts of these primary source documents appear in this chapter. Go to **www.chinasince1644.com** for the full version of these documents and for the Supplementary Materials.

CHAPTER 15

Overtures Between East and West

By Liz Nelson

Chapter Contents

The Sino-Soviet Rift

China and the United States in the 1950s and 1960s

Steps Toward Diplomatic Relations

Key Idea

Complex relations among the United States, China, and the Soviet Union set the stage for U.S. President Richard Nixon's groundbreaking visit to China in 1972. The presidential visit led to significantly increased contact between China and the United States.

Guiding Questions

What were the relationships like among China, the Soviet Union, and the United States in the period leading up to President Richard Nixon's visit to China?

Why did the United States and China want to establish diplomatic relations?

What were the most important impediments to resuming relations?

What were the results of President Nixon's visit?

Terms to Know

diplomacy

hegemony

"Ping-Pong diplomacy"

Essay

With the founding of the People's Republic of China (PRC) (*Zhonghua Renmin Gongheguo* 中华人民共和国), the Chinese Communist Party (*Zhongguo Gongchandang* 中国共产党) leadership and the majority of the Chinese populace wanted to re-establish their international prestige. Premier Zhou Enlai (周恩来), a skilled and experienced negotiator, directed the government's foreign policy (see A Closer Look at the end of the chapter). By the mid-1950s, he had established warm relations with India's fledgling government, though that relationship deteriorated into a short but sharp border war in 1962. He also sought ties with twenty-nine Asian and African nations whose delegates attended the Bandung Conference in Indonesia in 1955. The most critical relationships that Chinese leaders needed to manage, however, were those with the two world superpowers at the time: the Soviet Union and the United States.

China and the United States in the 1950s and 1960s

The relationship between China and the United States turned frigid during and after the Korean War (*Chaoxian Zhanzheng* 朝鲜战争). The U.S. government was extremely suspicious of China's intentions and fearful of the ability of China's leadership—as demonstrated in that war—to mobilize hundreds of thousands of men to fight as needed. Although managing the Cold War with the Soviet Union dominated U.S. foreign policy, its approach to China consisted of isolating, demonizing, and containing the Communist regime. McCarthyism raged in the United States in the 1950s, further escalating anti-Communist sentiment.[1] The Chinese government, on the other hand, saw U.S. involvement in Korea (and later Vietnam) as proof of Washington's intent to dominate Asia.

By the early 1960s, China's relationship with the Soviet Union was in shambles, as Khrushchev withdrew Soviet advisors and bitter polemics broke out. China's relationship with the United States remained hostile through the 1960s as the war in Vietnam raged. Despite Zhou Enlai's early efforts to partner with other developing nations, anti-Chinese riots broke out in Indonesia in 1965. With the outbreak of the Cultural Revolution (*Wenhua Dageming* 文化大革命) in 1966 (see Chapter 14), the PRC began a decade of near isolation. When the Soviet Union invaded Czechoslovakia in 1968 to prevent its withdrawal from the Warsaw Pact, Chinese leaders feared China might be next. In March 1969, two incidents on the border between the two countries resulted in heavy casualties and added to the tension between the former allies.

"We Must Have Relations with Communist China"

In November 1968, U.S. citizens had elected Richard Nixon to be their next president. The following summer, the Nixon administration eased some travel and trade restrictions with China and stopped U.S. Navy patrols of the Taiwan Straits (*Taiwan Haixia* 台湾海峡), sending signals that the United States wished to improve relations. On the other side of the Pacific, members of the Chinese leadership, recognizing China's need for Western technology in order to move the economy forward, advocated a more pragmatic approach to foreign policy. The Chinese and U.S. diplomatic talks that had started in 1955 in Geneva but stalled, were resumed in Warsaw, Poland in early 1970.[2] As the year progressed, the ways in which the government-controlled Chinese

---

[1] Senator Joseph McCarthy launched the second Red Scare in the early 1950s. Thousands of individuals were accused of being Communists or Communist-sympathizers, and many were investigated by the House Committee on Un-American Activities.

[2] High-level diplomats from China and the United States had been quietly meeting since August 1, 1955. At first they met in Geneva, Switzerland; after 1958, the periodic meetings took place in Warsaw. It was the only contact between the two countries for sixteen years.

press wrote about the United States began to change. At the end of the year, President Nixon announced at a press conference that the United States "must have relations with Communist China," and Mao Zedong told Edgar Snow (see Chapter 11) that he would be happy to talk to Nixon.[3]

One cautious step after another brought Washington and Beijing closer to some kind of formal relations. In July 1971, following National Security Advisor Henry Kissinger's secret meeting with Premier Zhou Enlai in Beijing (北京), Nixon announced he would soon visit China. Later that year, the United States withdrew its opposition to China's joining the United Nations, and on October 25, 1971, the General Assembly gave the "China seat" to the People's Republic of China, concurrently taking it away from Taiwan (台湾). Finally, after months of careful maneuvering, in February 1972 President Nixon flew to Beijing and met with Zhou Enlai and Mao Zedong (毛泽东). China and the United States signed a Joint Communiqué (*Lianhe Gongbao* 联合公报), also known as the Shanghai Communiqué. Here they stated their views frankly, agreed that there should be "one China" (without defining what that meant), and pledged to eventually normalize relations.

Domestic issues in the United States (including the Watergate scandal), and the deaths of Zhou Enlai in January 1976 and Mao Zedong in September that same year, delayed the normalization process. As Deng Xiaoping (邓小平) moved to assume ultimate power (see Chapter 16), the two nations finally extended formal diplomatic relations to each other on January 1, 1979. At the same time, the United States ended its formal ties with Taiwan, though keeping commercial and other ties which have continued to expand. As Deng implemented his policy of "reform and opening up," he moved to create a peaceful international environment in which China could pursue economic development. A new era began.

---

[3] Cohen, Warren I., *America's Response to China: A History of Sino-American Relations* (New York: Columbia University Press, 2000) 197.

Societal Interactions

Although people usually think of the inauguration of Sino-U.S. relations as a government-to-government affair, societal factors, at least on the U.S. side, played an important role. In the mid-1960s, a number of scholars, policy experts, religious leaders, and business people began a series of conferences with the intention of educating the public about China. These efforts soon resulted in the formation of the National Committee on U.S.-China Relations, established in 1966, which soon co-hosted the Chinese ping-pong team when it toured the United States in 1972. Diplomatic breakthroughs led to cultural exchanges—for instance, the Philadelphia Orchestra toured China in 1973.

For the most part, however, cultural exchanges had to wait until after diplomatic relations were established at the beginning of 1979 and an agreement on cultural exchanges signed in January of that year. Famous violinist Isaac Stern toured China in 1979, and in 1981, the State Department organized an exhibition of American paintings drawn from the Boston Museum of Fine Arts that went first to Beijing and then to Shanghai. It arrived at a time of ferment in the Chinese art world. In 1979, the "Stars" exhibit of avant-garde art was the first independent art exhibit in China.

Such humble beginnings presaged the surge of intercultural exchange that occurs today. In 2010, some 2 million Americans visited China, and about 800,000 Chinese came to the United States. About 150,000 Chinese now study in the United States, while about 15,000 Americans study in China.

Hong Kong and Macao

As China began to develop economically and play a role on the world stage, it moved to address the legacy of the "century of humiliation." In 1898 Kowloon and the New Territories, on China's coast across from the island of Hong Kong, were leased to Britain for 99 years, a period that came to an end in 1997. Beginning in the 1980s, China entered into a series of negotiations with Great Britain that culminated in the signing of the "Basic Law," a sort of constitution that would guide the governance of Hong Kong and the return of Hong Kong to China. The Basic Law provides that Hong Kong will be a "Special Administrative Region" with its own government and law, though sovereignty belongs with China.

Similarly Macao, a small enclave on the Chinese coast near Hong Kong that had been a trade base established by the Portuguese in the sixteenth century and later colonized, was returned to China in 1999, also as a Special Administrative Region. Like Hong Kong, Macao is administered separately from the PRC. It has emerged as a major hub of gambling, attracting tourists from all over the world.

Primary Sources

DOCUMENT 15.1: Excerpts from the Joint Communiqué of the United States of America and the People's Republic of China, February 28, 1972

1. [T]he two sides stated that: Progress toward the normalization of relations between China and the United States is in the interests of all countries. Both wish to reduce the danger of international military conflict. Neither should seek hegemony in the Asia-Pacific region and each is opposed to efforts by any other country or group of countries to establish such hegemony. Neither is prepared to negotiate on behalf of any third party or to enter into agreements or understandings with the other directed at other states....

2. The two sides reviewed the long-standing serious disputes between China and the United States. The Chinese side reaffirmed its position: the Taiwan question is the crucial question obstructing the normalization of relations between China and the United States; the Government of the People's Republic of China is the sole legal government of China; Taiwan is a province of China which has long been returned to the motherland; the liberation of Taiwan is China's internal affair in which no other country has the right to interfere; and all U.S. forces and military installations must be withdrawn from Taiwan. The Chinese Government firmly opposes any activities which aim at the creation of "one China, one Taiwan," "one China, two governments," "two Chinas," an "independent Taiwan," or advocate that "the status of Taiwan remains to be determined."

3. *The U.S. side declared*: The United States acknowledges that all Chinese on either side of the Taiwan Strait maintain there is but one China and that Taiwan is a part of China. The United States Government does not challenge that position. It reaffirms its interest in a peaceful settlement of the Taiwan question by the Chinese themselves. With this prospect in mind, it affirms the ultimate objective of the withdrawal of all U.S. forces and military installations from Taiwan....

SOURCE: American Institute in Taiwan

Go to **www.chinasince1644.com** for the link to **Document 15.1**.

DOCUMENT 15.2: Excerpts from the 1979 "U.S.-PRC Joint Communiqué on the Establishment of Diplomatic Relations" and the Taiwan Relations Act of 1979

....

Joint Communiqué

1. The United States of America and the People's Republic of China have agreed to recognize each other and to establish diplomatic relations as of January 1, 1979.
2. The United States recognizes the government of the People's Republic of China as the sole legal government of China....

Separately, the United States issued a statement on Taiwan.

Taiwan Relations Act

1. On that same date, January 1, 1979, the United States will notify Taiwan that it is terminating diplomatic relations and that the Mutual Defense Treaty between the United States and the Republic of China is being terminated in accordance with the provisions of the Treaty. The United States also states that it will be withdrawing its remaining military personnel from Taiwan within four months.
2. In the future, the American people and the people of Taiwan will maintain commercial, cultural, and other relations without official government representation and without diplomatic relations.
3. The United States is confident that the people of Taiwan face a peaceful and prosperous future. The United States continues to have an interest in the peaceful resolution of the Taiwan issue and expects that the Taiwan issue will be settled peacefully by the Chinese themselves.

SOURCE: The American Institute in Taiwan

Go to **www.chinasince1644.com** for the full text of Document 15.2.

Activities

ACTIVITY 1: Interpreting the Motives of the Key Players
....

Read the introduction to the lesson. Then check your textbook and online resources to get a detailed sense of the foreign policy goals of the United States, the People's Republic of China, and the Soviet Union during the late 1960s and early 1970s. See Chapter 15 Activity Websites on the companion website for a link to "Nixon's China Game." Create a diagram (or a cartoon or comic strip) that demonstrates the relationships among the three countries. Be prepared to share your diagram in a small group and to discuss as a class which country wanted to accomplish what goals and why.

ACTIVITY 2: Examining "Ping-Pong Diplomacy" and the Role of Sports and Cultural Exchanges

Research online to learn more about the Ping-Pong diplomacy that took place in April 1971. See Chapter 15 Activity Websites on the companion website for more related resources.

In small groups you will:

1. Compare the Chinese and U.S. accounts of the opening of relations between China and the United States, and the accounts of how the U.S. Table Tennis Team came to play in China. Are the differences between the accounts significant? Why?

2. Why would the Chinese government choose to invite Ping-Pong players as the first group of Americans to enter China since 1949?

3. What kind of sports and cultural exchanges come to mind when you think of international relations? What role do these events play?

ACTIVITY 3: Synthesizing: Stories in Photographs

View a collection of photographs of President Nixon's visit to China. See Chapter 15 Activity Websites on the companion website for a link to this collection and other resources.

Choose among the following options:

- Write a letter from President Nixon to Premier Zhou Enlai as a follow-up to the visit.

- Prepare to assume the role of a Chinese leader in charge of Nixon's visit. Write a proposal for the particular destinations and events planned for Nixon's visit. Explain why you chose them. You will share your proposal in a small group representing the government. Combining the ideas agreed upon, your group will create a proposal to present to the class.

- Take on the role of a reporter traveling with the president, and write a diary based on the photographs.

Prepare to discuss in class what your overall impressions are of this presidential visit. Use specific details from the photographs to make your points.

ACTIVITY 4: Analyzing a Formal Agreement

After reading the Joint Communiqué between the United States and China (15.1), you will work in a small group. Go through the Communiqué again and highlight adjectives and other descriptive words. Then fill in the chart (Item 15.A on the companion website), which will identify China's and the United States' views of themselves and each other, the issues at stake, and each country's goals.

Prepare to discuss as a class:

1. On which issues did China and the United States agree? On which issues did they disagree?

2. What was the most important point in the Communiqué? Why?

Note: for an overview of Taiwan's history see "A Brief History of Taiwan" on the companion website (found as Item 15.C in Supplementary Materials). Chapters 16 and 20 include further information on U.S.-Taiwan-China relations and the "one China" issue.

ACTIVITY 5:
Persuasive Essay: Did the Visit Change the World?

After his visit to China in 1972, Richard Nixon said, "This is the week that changed the world." Write an essay in which you take a stand: the visit did or did not "change the world."

ACTIVITY 6:
Examining Ambiguity in International Relationships

First, read "A Brief History of Taiwan" on the companion website (found as Item 15.C in Supplementary Materials) to understand the context of these diplomatic documents. Then read excerpts from the communiqué (15.2). Take notes on the following questions:

1. What is clear and what is ambiguous in this document?
2. What do the two parties agree to do?
3. What is meant by the phrase "there is but one China and Taiwan is part of China"?

Then read the Taiwan Relations Act (15.2), which the U.S. Congress enacted the following year. Take notes:

1. What is the United States obligated to do for Taiwan under this Act?
2. Why might the U.S. government have proposed and passed this legislation?

Write briefly about how these two documents contradict each other. You will join one of three groups. One group represents the PRC, the second represents the U.S. Congress, and the third represents Taiwan. The "PRC" should describe its response to the Taiwan Relations Act. "Congress" then states why it is in favor of this act. "Taiwan" should then present its position. As a class you will see if you can resolve the differences. Then you will write about the benefits of ambiguity in international politics. Does it help or hurt a delicate diplomatic situation to be vague? Explain.

EXTENDED RESEARCH

Write a paper, create a digital presentation, or work with a partner to write and perform an interview on one of the following topics:

- Richard Nixon
- Henry Kissinger

- *Nixon in China*, the opera by John Adams
- Present-day relations between China and Russia
- The role of China in the Vietnam War
- The Chinese invasion of Vietnam in 1979
- An American or Chinese musician, dancer, or artist who participated in an exchange or visit.
- A Chinese exchange student at the university level

Suggested Resources

Books

Chen Jian. *Mao's China and the Cold War*. Chapel Hill: University of North Carolina Press, 2001.

Clayton, Cathryn H. *Sovereignty at the Edge: Macau and the Question of Chineseness*. Cambridge: Harvard University Press, 2009.

Cohen, Warren I. *America's Response to China: A History of Sino-American Relations*. New York: Columbia University Press, 2010.

Gao Wenqian. *Zhou Enlai: The Last Perfect Revolutionary*. New York: PublicAffairs, 2007.

Kissinger, Henry. *On China*. New York: Penguin, 2011.
Nixon's former Secretary of State examines China's foreign policy and relationships with Western powers and other East Asian countries in the second half of the twentieth century.

Li Cunxin. *Mao's Last Dancer*. New York: Putnam, 2003.
The biography of a man chosen as a young boy to study ballet at the Beijing Dance Academy.

MacMillan, Margaret. *Nixon and Mao: The Week that Changed the World*. New York: Random House, 2007.
An accessible history of Nixon's visit to China, including archival documents and photographs that help shed light on the complex events leading up to the Joint Communiqué.

Tsang, Steve. *A Modern History of Hong Kong*. New York: I.B. Tauris, 2007.

Websites

China's Political System: Special Administrative Regions
http://www.china.org.cn/english/Political/26312.htm
An overview of the legal status of Hong Kong and Macao as Special Administrative Regions of China.

McCarthyism, PBS
http://www.pbs.org/wnet/americanmasters/episodes/arthur-miller/mccarthyism/484/
A brief overview of McCarthyism and the political climate in the United States during the 1950s.

Nixon's China Game, PBS
http://www.pbs.org/wgbh/amex/china/
An American Experience website with background information, timelines, teacher resources, and an interview with Henry Kissinger.

Nixon's Trip to China, The National Security Archive, The George Washington University
http://www.gwu.edu/~nsarchiv/NSAEBB/NSAEBB106/index.htm
Declassified documents of Nixon's visit to China including conversations with Zhou Enlai.

Ping Pong Diplomacy: Nixon's Trip to China, February 21–28, 1972
http://www.presidentialtimeline.org/timeline/bin/
An online exhibition that includes photos, documents, and background information about Nixon's historic 1972 trip. Select Exhibits—Richard Nixon—Ping Pong Diplomacy to open exhibit.

President Nixon in China, February 28, 1972, C-SPAN
http://www.c-spanvideo.org/program/107545-1
Video footage of Nixon's visit to China recorded by a crew hired by the President to document the trip.

■ **A CLOSER LOOK**

Zhou Enlai: Dedicated Communist

Virtually no one in the top tier of the PRC government emerged from the first quarter century of brutal politics unscathed. However, Zhou Enlai did. Most Chinese adults continue to speak of him with great admiration and affection.

Zhou was born in 1898 in Jiangsu Province to a poor gentry family. Since he was the eldest son and eldest grandson, his extended family ensured that he would receive an excellent education. After graduating from a prestigious school in Tianjin (funded by American missionaries), he continued his education in Japan. In 1920, he returned briefly to China, where he became involved in student activism. Later that year, Zhou left for France to participate in a work-study program. It was there that he dedicated himself to the communist cause.

In the summer of 1924, Zhou Enlai returned to China and quickly assumed leadership positions in the as yet nascent Chinese Communist Party. Three years later, he was elected to the CCP Central Committee and its Politburo. Throughout the 1930s, Zhou would be the Party member who skillfully tackled delicate negotiations, chief among them forming the United Front against Japan with the Guomindang, and as the CCP's chief representative to the hostile Guomindang government in Chongqing (see Chapter 11).

With the founding of the PRC, Zhou Enlai became the nation's premier (or prime minister), a position he held until his death. As premier, he managed the immense bureaucracy, but he was also the architect of China's foreign policy, where he became renowned the world over for his diplomatic skills. Though his power was curtailed by Mao Zedong and the Gang of Four during the chaotic years of the Cultural Revolution (see Chapter 14), he was a moderating influence on its worst excesses. It is widely believed that he protected some of the oldest historic sites from destruction by Red Guards and several military and government leaders from recurring purges. Deeply devoted to communist ideals, Zhou was a pragmatic statesman. In the mid 1970s, well aware of Mao Zedong's failing health as well as his own, Zhou helped maneuver Deng Xiaoping into position to take over leadership.

Zhou Enlai's death in January 1976 brought an outpouring of grief by a people desperate for the balance, moderation, and ethics the premier had come to represent.

■ *You can read some of Zhou Enlai's writing, including "Guides for Myself," (1943) on the companion website. Discuss: What characteristics should a statesman have?*

United States-China Accord for Cultural Exchange
http://china.usc.edu/ShowArticle.aspx?articleID=520
The text of the 1984 United States and China agreement to enhance relations and "strengthen cultural cooperation."

Zhou Enlai Posters
http://chineseposters.net/themes/zhouenlai.php
Digitized posters from the collection of the International Institute of Social History, Amsterdam, and Stefan R. Landsberger.

Films

Mao's Last Dancer (113 mins; 2010)
A feature film about Li Cunxin, who was chosen as a young boy to study at the Beijing Dance Academy.

CHAPTER RESOURCES

 Excerpts of these primary source documents appear in this chapter. Go to **www.chinasince1644.com** for the full version of these documents and for the Supplementary Materials.

CHAPTER 16

Socialism with Chinese Characteristics

By Todd Whitten

Chapter Contents

Key Idea

During the 1980s, Deng Xiaoping began to move China out of the rubble of the Cultural Revolution and Mao's economic policies toward modernization. This process rapidly moved into realms beyond the economic. The Party began to confront the social and political consequences of liberalization, which culminated in the events in and around Tiananmen Square in 1989.

Guiding Questions

What is the relationship between economic liberalization and political freedom? Does one necessitate the other?

If an organization of people (a nation, a political party, or another group) is to grow and advance, is dissent useful or distracting? Why? How should a ruling group manage different perspectives and opinions?

Under what circumstances can a revolutionary regime transition into an authoritarian but stable system and ultimately into a democracy?

How did Deng Xiaoping's leadership differ from that of Mao Zedong?

What happened in and around Tiananmen Square between April and June 1989, and why did the government eventually respond with violence? Was this response inevitable?

How did the relationships among the People's Republic of China, the United States, and Taiwan change during this period?

Terms to Know

big character poster	dissent	pension
capitalism	GNP	Politburo
communism	*hukou* system	socialism
Democracy Wall		

Essay

When Mao Zedong died in September 1976, power passed to Hua Guofeng (华国锋), then a 55-year-old former party secretary of Hunan, Mao's home province. Only a month later the "Gang of Four" was arrested, ushering in a more moderate atmosphere that would allow the leadership to begin to focus on economic development. Just two years later, Deng Xiaoping (邓小平) emerged as paramount leader, though he only took the modest title of "vice premier," eschewing the grander title of chairman (which was subsequently eliminated). Assisted by his protégés Hu Yaobang (胡耀邦), who became general secretary of the CCP, and Zhao Ziyang (赵紫阳), who became premier, Deng pushed ahead with a dramatic reform program. The China Deng inherited was extremely poor, with its economy unbalanced, its populace deeply traumatized by the Cultural Revolution, and its relationship with the Soviet Union fractured. The establishment of diplomatic relations with the United States just as Deng took office provided powerful support for Deng's new direction.

The Four Modernizations

Taking power, Deng launched the "Four Modernizations," first proposed by Zhou Enlai in 1975. Focusing on industry, agriculture, science and technology, and national defense, Deng hoped to use economic development to end the ideological contention that had torn China apart in the Mao era and to secure China's place as one of the great powers of the world. To this end, Deng launched a diplomatic offensive, visiting the United States, Japan, and Southeast Asia to create an environment that would allow him to reduce military expenditures, bring in foreign investment, and open up export markets. He also moved quickly to reopen China's universities and strengthen education.

Deng compiled a comprehensive financial plan that included significant foreign investment. He set a goal of quadrupling the Gross National Product (GNP) by the end of the century from $250 billion to $1 trillion (which was achieved two years early). One result of such a leap in GNP would be that more money would be available for re-investment. Deng reached out to other nations for technology assistance, and he made it easier for Chinese college students to study abroad, intending that they would then return to China with the knowledge and skills needed to move agriculture, technology, and industry forward.

Deng was no liberal, and he hoped to separate economics and opening to the outside world by cracking down on liberal intellectual trends. Thus he supported, at least briefly, the "campaign against spiritual pollution" in 1983 and the "campaign against bourgeois liberalization" in 1987, launched when Deng decided that his protégé Hu Yaobang was too liberal and removed him from office.

Rural Reform

Although the Four Modernizations listed industry as China's first priority, reform first took hold in the countryside. New incentives for rural Chinese freed them from the constraints of the commune system (the People's Commune; see Chapter 13) and opened up new markets. The Household Responsibility System (*Jiating Lianchan Chengbao Zerenzhi* 家庭联产承包责任制), under which farmers contracted a specific piece of land, was introduced and in 1983 communes were abolished. Farm production soared—by 1987 rice and wheat yields had risen 50% over that of years under the commune system.[1] At the same time, the state began to transition toward a more market-oriented economy by permitting the development of small-scale rural industries known as Township and Village Enterprises. With more local control over decisions and assets, the new enterprises rapidly multiplied, drawing many farmers off the land.

---

[1] Immanuel Hsü, *The Rise of Modern China*, 4th Ed. (New York: Oxford University Press, 1990) 845.

By the end of the 1980s some 130 million rural Chinese had taken such jobs. Many of the early reforms were propelled from below, especially in the least urbanized parts of China.

Education

The Chinese government simultaneously embarked on a campaign to improve and expand its education system. It established eighty-eight universities throughout China, increased the number of technical colleges, and issued more visas, inviting foreign experts to China and permitting students to leave China to study at top universities in Japan and the United States. Chinese students abroad mostly studied the hard sciences and agriculture, though more and more went to learn languages—essential for work with foreign businesses that would be vital for the much-needed infusion of capital.

Special Economic Zones

In March 1978, Deng oversaw a revision of the Chinese Constitution that allowed for the establishment of four Special Economic Zones (Jīngjì Tèqu 经济特区) the following year (in Shenzhen, Zhuhai, Shantou, and Xiamen). In these zones, foreign companies like Yamaha and Motorola could build factories and conduct business in a "capitalist fashion" and take advantage of China's inexpensive labor. To further joint business ventures, fourteen coastal cities opened to foreign investment in 1984.

The One-Child Policy

Mao Zedong had paid little attention to the potential negative impact of population growth and had encouraged couples to have large families. This approach, together with a dramatic decline in infant mortality and rise in life expectancy, caused China's population to significantly increase. The Chinese population was 594 million in 1953, 695 million in 1964, and 1 billion by 1982.[2] In addition, the population was very young, with a huge number of young women entering their childbearing years. Chinese leaders in the late 1970s faced a formidable challenge: without some kind of controls, the sheer number of people would cancel any material gains in the country's economy and standard of living.

Initially, the CCP encouraged later marriage and child-bearing, longer spacing between children, and fewer children. But when the ambitious goals of the Four Modernizations were announced, officials decided that stronger measures had to be taken and in 1979 they began to implement the One-Child Policy (Jihua Shengyu Zhengce 计划生育政策), which made it illegal for a married couple to have more than one child. This policy ran directly counter to Chinese tradition, whereby large families of children led by sons cared for their parents as they aged. Program workers and village cadres were under pressure to enforce the policy, and forced sterilizations and abortions were widely reported. However, according to official accounts, without this policy in place, it is estimated that China's population today would be even larger, by approximately 400 million people.[3] In recent years, the policy has been loosened—rural families whose first-born child is a girl are allowed to have a second child and two single children who get married are allowed to have two children—but overall the policy is still enforced vigorously.

The Fifth Modernization

The process of economic "liberalization" was not without its critics. Many in China worried at the apparent destruction of both Communist and traditional Chinese values. Others insisted

---

[3] A number of experts believe the effect of the One-Child Policy is exaggerated. They argue that modernization has also played a significant role in reducing the birth rate, as it has in other countries.

that Deng Xiaoping was not doing enough. Almost immediately after Deng launched the Four Modernizations, Wei Jingsheng (魏京生), a young electrician, posted a big character poster proposing a Fifth Modernization: democracy. Students, intellectuals, and eventually workers soon pushed for greater freedoms and a voice in the nation's decision making, echoing the energy of the May Fourth Movement (see Chapter 8). At first, Deng tolerated and even encouraged the Democracy Wall (*Xidan Minzhu Qiang* 西单民主墙) movement as he tried to win popular support for post-Mao reforms, only to crack down on it after he was securely in power. In March 1979, officials arrested Wei on the grounds that he had leaked state secrets and sentenced him to fifteen years in prison.

Tiananmen Square Confrontation

Student discontent sparked again in 1986 and then grew increasingly vocal in the spring of 1989. College students organized protests in support of increased democratic participation, an end to corruption, and improved university buildings. They used the death of Hu Yaobang to stage demonstrations of mourning similar to those that had occurred when Zhou Enlai passed away thirteen years earlier. The government responded by accusing the students of being guided by a "planned conspiracy" seeking to oppose socialism and the CCP. Students reacted by gathering in yet greater numbers and occupying Tiananmen Square in Beijing. Zhao Ziyang tried, with some success, to cool the movement in a speech on May 4, but then a hunger strike re-energized the students on the eve of Soviet Union leader Mikhail Gorbachev's first visit to China. Gorbachev's visit marked the restoration of party ties between the CCP and the CPSU and a significant improvement in relations between China and the Soviet Union.

At first it seemed that the government was going to tolerate the students' actions, but as time went on, the original protesters left, other students took their place, and then the movement began to spread to other sectors of Chinese society. While groups of workers and even writers for the official newspaper People's Daily joined the protests, members of the Politburo sharply disagreed about how to respond. Many who had witnessed the chaos of the Cultural Revolution argued for shutting down the protests. Eventually, the liberal faction that favored allowing the protest, led by Zhao Ziyang, lost the debate to hard-liners like premier Li Peng (李鹏), and the decision was made to have the People's Liberation Army quell the uprising by whatever means necessary. On the night of June 3–4, 1989, they did just that, and Beijing crackled with sounds of gunfire. In the aftermath, protesters were arrested, tried, and sentenced to prison or executed. Several of the organizers of the movement managed to flee to Hong Kong and beyond, some surfacing in the United States. The severe response confirmed that Chinese leaders would not allow economic liberalization to jeopardize the power of the ruling party and social stability.

Since Tiananmen

In the more than twenty years since the Tiananmen Square confrontation, China's economy has grown approximately 10 percent per year, rising from about $450 billion in 1989 to about $7 trillion dollars in 2011.[4] With this growth, China's per capita income has reached about $3,000 a year, making China a middle-income country. Its modern cities seem to reflect modernity and prosperity, but income is distributed quite unevenly. The ratio of urban to

---

[4] There are different ways of comparing Gross Domestic Product (GDP). The figures used here are based on the exchange rate, that is translating Chinese yuan into U.S. dollars. One can also use Purchasing Power Parity (PPP), which tries to measure what a comparable basket of goods would cost in different countries and thus compare living standards. PPP estimates of China's GDP yield a figure of $11.3 trillion and per capita income at about $8,400. There are advantages and disadvantages of both methods of calculation.

rural income is about 3.3:1, extremely high by world standards. The household registration (*hukou* 户口) system makes it difficult for migrants from the countryside to settle in cities and send their children to school there. There have been recent efforts to improve the delivery of healthcare in the countryside, but it remains inadequate, as do pension systems and education.

As the economy has expanded, so have China's military capabilities. Although still far behind the U.S. military, China is becoming a more formidable regional actor. With disputed claims in the Yellow Sea, East China Sea, and South China Sea, there is significant potential for friction and even conflict. Although China has tried to reassure its neighbors and the world that its "peaceful development" would not threaten anyone, a more assertive tone and a series of incidents in 2009–2010 set regional nerves on edge. China has since begun to exert influence through the projection of "soft power"—cultural influence—but such efforts at reassurance will likely have little success until boundary issues can be worked out.

Deng Xiaoping was able to exert a stabilizing hand on elite politics, even after his passing. It was Deng who picked Jiang Zemin (江泽民) in the wake of the Tiananmen incident as well as Jiang's successor, Hu Jintao (胡锦涛). China held its Eighteenth Party Congress in the fall of 2012, and an unusually large number of top leaders were forced to retire because of age. This caused an unusual amount of elite contention, including the scandal-ridden removal of one major leader, Bo Xilai (薄熙来), party secretary of Chongqing, in the spring of 2012. Whether the PRC can maintain the political stability that has allowed it to develop so rapidly thus remains a question.

Primary Sources

DOCUMENT 16.1:
Quotations from Karl Marx, Mao Zedong, and Deng Xiaoping

Karl Marx:

(1848): When, in the course of development, class distinctions have disappeared, and all production has been concentrated in the hands of a vast association of the whole nation, the public power will lose its political character. Political power, properly so called, is merely the organized power of one class for oppressing another. If the proletariat during its contest with the bourgeoisie is compelled, by the force of circumstances, to organize itself as a class; if, by means of a revolution, it makes itself the ruling class, and, as such, sweeps away by force the old conditions of production, then it will, along with these conditions, have swept away the conditions for the existence of class antagonisms and of classes generally, and will thereby have abolished its own supremacy as a class.

In place of the old bourgeois society, with its classes and class antagonisms, we shall have an association in which the free development of each is the condition for the free development of all.

(1938) From each according to his ability, to each according to his needs!

Sources: Karl Marx and Friedrich Engels, *The Communist Manifesto*, trans. Eric Hobsbawm (London: Verso, 1998); Karl Marx, *The Critique of the Gotha Programme*, Ed. C.P. Dutt (New York: International Publishers, 1938) 10.

Mao Zedong:

(November 1938) Every Communist must grasp the truth: Power grows out of the barrel of a gun.

(1955) In order to build a great socialist society it is of the utmost importance to arouse the broad masses of women to join in productive activity. Men and women must receive equal pay for equal work in production.

SOURCES: Mao Zedong, "Problems of War and Strategy," in *Selected Works, Volume 1* (Beijing: Foreign Languages Press, 1965) 224.

Mao Zedong, "Women Have Gone to the Labour Front" 1955 in *The Socialist Upsurge in China's Countryside*, Vol. 1 (Beijing: Foreign Languages Press, 1965).

Deng Xiaoping:

It doesn't matter if the cat is black or white as long as it catches mice.

Poverty is not socialism. To get rich is glorious.

Reform is China's second revolution.

SOURCES: "Cat" qtd. in William R. Doerner "The Comeback Comrade," *Time*, January 6, 1986. "Poverty" from a speech in 1978; "Reform" from "Reform is China's Second Revolution," a speech in March 1985.

 Go to **www.chinasince1644.com** for the text of **Document 16.1**.

DOCUMENT 16.2: Excerpts from Deng Xiaoping's speech "Emancipate the Mind, Seek Truth from Facts and Unite as One in Looking to the Future," December 13, 1978

When people's minds aren't yet emancipated and their thinking remains rigid, curious phenomena emerge....

People whose thinking has become rigid tend to veer with the wind. They are not guided by Party spirit and Party principles, but go along with whatever has the backing of the authorities and adjust their words and actions according to whichever way the wind is blowing. They think that they will thus avoid mistakes. In fact, however, veering with the wind is in itself a grave mistake, a contravention of the Party spirit which all Communists should cherish. It is true that people who think independently and dare to speak out and act can't avoid making mistakes, but their mistakes are out in the open and are therefore more easily rectified.

Once people's thinking becomes rigid, book worship, divorced from reality, becomes a grave malady. Those who suffer from it dare not say a word or take a step that isn't mentioned in books, documents or the speeches of leaders: everything has to be copied....

SOURCE: Pei-kai Cheng, Michael Lestz, and Jonathan D. Spence, *The Search for Modern China: A Documentary Collection* (New York: W. W. Norton, 1999) 448–451.

 Go to **www.chinasince1644.com** for the full text of **Document 16.2**.

DOCUMENT 16.3: **Excerpts related to the "Pan Xiao" discussion on the meaning of life, from** China Youth **magazine, May 1980– December 1980**

"The Path of Life: Why Is It More Narrow?" Pan Xiao's first letter

I turned 23 this year. You could say that my life has only just begun, and yet all of life's mysteries and attractions don't appeal to me anymore. It seems like I've already reached the end. When I look back upon the path I've already taken, the road changes from red-violet into grey, from hope to disappointment. It is a path of despair. It is a river flowing from a source of selflessness and purity into a self-centered end.

In the past, I cherished high hopes and fantasies about life. In elementary school, I had heard stories like "How to Build Iron and Steel" and *The Diary of Lei Feng*.[5] Although I didn't completely grasp the concepts, the heroic adventures excited me so much that night after night I couldn't sleep a wink. I thought, "My father, my mother, and my grandfather are all good Communists. Of course I am a Communist, too, and in the future, I want to be a member of the Party—no doubt about it."

After I had enrolled in elementary school for some time, the Cultural Revolution began and the currents grew increasingly fierce. I was a bit confused, and I began to think that perhaps life around me wasn't as attractive as it was described in the books. I asked myself, "Should I believe what these books tell me or what I see with my own eyes?"…

SOURCE: *China Youth*, May–December 1980. Trans. Diana Lin.

 Go to **www.chinasince1644.com** for the full text of **Document 16.3**.

DOCUMENT 16.4:
Description of a visit to a rural school in the 1980s by Ma Xiaodong

This was the only middle school in the region, and the majority of the students were children of local peasants…. They were shy in front of a stranger and they looked at me with curiosity. To make conversation, I asked to see where they slept and they took me into their dorm, which was a deep cave room. It was already dark and there was no electricity. Under the dim light I saw a long *kang* from one end of the cave to the other. It must have been very crowded at night for the many boys. In the dorm, each boy kept a small box for cooked food. I asked them what food their parents had prepared for them. By now it was completely dark and I was unable to see anything. The kids competed with each other to invite me to feel their food. So I used my hand to touch. I didn't think I touched anything better than bread made of corn and millet.

SOURCE: Ye Weili and Ma Xiaodong, *Growing Up in The People's Republic: Conversations Between Two Daughters of China's Revolution* (New York: Palgrave Macmillan, 2005) 145–146.

Go to **www.chinasince1644.com** for the full text of **Document 16.4**.

---

[5] See A Closer Look in Chapter 14 for the story of *The Diary of Lei Feng*.

DOCUMENT 16.5: Excerpt from "The Fifth Modernization" by Wei Jingsheng, December 5, 1978

Wei Jingsheng was born in 1950 to a family with prominent connections to the Party. (His father worked in the foreign ministry.) Wei enjoyed an early life of relative privilege, attending the best schools. During the Cultural Revolution, he traveled in the countryside and became disenchanted with Communism. When he returned to Beijing he was assigned to a job as an electrician in the Beijing Zoo. In December 1978, he posted his essay "The Fifth Modernization" on what became known as the Democracy Wall in Beijing. After publishing an essay in which he identified Deng Xiaoping as a dictator, Wei was arrested, and charged with passing secret information to "the enemy" and for engaging in "counter-revolutionary propaganda and agitation." He was sentenced to fifteen years in prison, five in solitary confinement and several more years in forced labor camps. Authorities released him briefly in 1993, then arrested him again and convicted him of being a counter-revolutionary. He was sentenced to another fourteen years. He was released in 1997, as the result of U.S. pressure, and exiled to live in the United States, where he continues to agitate for Chinese democracy.

People should have democracy. When they ask for democracy, they are only demanding what is rightfully theirs. Anyone refusing to give it to them is a shameless bandit no better than a capitalist who robs workers of their money earned with their sweat and blood. Do the people have democracy now? No. Do they want to be masters of their own destiny? Definitely, yes. This was the reason for the Communist Party's victory over [the] Guomindang. But what then happened to the promise of democracy? The slogan "people's democratic dictatorship" was replaced by the "dictatorship of the proletariat." Even the "democracy" enjoyed by the infinitesimal portion—one among tens of millions—was abolished and replaced by the autocracy of the "Great Leader"....

SOURCE: The Fifth Modernization by Wei Jingsheng

Go to **www.chinasince1644.com** for the link to **Document 16.5**.

DOCUMENT 16.6: Excerpts from Fang Lizhi and Liu Binyan, two Chinese activists, writing about democracy, 1990

Evidently, these bloodthirsty rulers stake everything on the force of arms. They have lost all ability to understand the people, whom they fear and despise at the same time. They assume that the people, in the eighties, are just as submissive as they were in the twenties and thirties to the bloody rule of the warlords of the time, or just as responsive to the rallying calls and lying propaganda of the Communist Party as they were in the fifties and sixties.

On the surface, the rulers have attained their objective. Under the all-encompassing terrorism, China seems to have been cowed into silent submission. But this will actually create a bigger nightmare for them than if they had made some compromise.

The peaceful demonstration at Tiananmen Square was crushed, but it lit a flame in the hearts of countless people. The long-suffering Chinese people, after repeatedly being bullied and cheated, have finally given up their last illusions about the Chinese Communist Party....

I gave up my youth for the Communist Party in its struggle to seize state power. And now a handful of tyrants have betrayed the Party, turning themselves into enemies of the people in the real sense of the word. My generation has thrown itself into the struggle led by the Communist Party in the hope that our children will lead a better life, and now it is precisely the best and brightest of their generation who have died at the butchers' hands, or are fugitives fleeing from arrest.

SOURCE: Liu Binyan, *A Higher Kind of Loyalty: A Memoir by China's Foremost Journalist,* trans. Hong Zhu (New York: Pantheon, 1990) 282.

 Go to **www.chinasince1644.com** for the full text of **Document 16.6**.

DOCUMENT 16.7:
Excerpts from *Deng Xiaoping: My Father* by Deng Maomao, 1995

Deng Xiaoping was already seventy-five years old [in 1977] when he was reinstated the third time. He did not change his tenacious work style, which he had had for decades, his bold way of thinking, or his firm convictions. His conviction was that a new path of development, suited to China, could be blazed by taking a realistic and scientific approach and by making use of a multitude of assets and strengths, both ancient and modern, both Chinese and foreign. His conviction was that the Chinese people could lead a prosperous life and that China could become a strong and prosperous country....

Deng Xiaoping has held that the Chinese should build socialism with Chinese characteristics. Under his guidance, China has been trying to discover its own path of development and marching forward steadily. More than fifteen years have elapsed since 1978. China has made progress and achievements that are universally acknowledged. There is a popular view that the next century will be the century of the Asia-Pacific countries, and that among them China will attract the greatest attention. China is proud of this expectation....

In 1989 Deng Xiaoping resigned and retired. He retired so as to abolish the feudal life tenure system in China and to promote younger people to the leading posts.... At the advanced age of eighty-eight, he still goes around calling for further development of China.

SOURCE: Deng Maomao, *Deng Xiaoping: My Father* (New York: Basic Books, 1995) 469–470.

 Go to **www.chinasince1644.com** for the text of **Document 16.7**.

DOCUMENT 16.8: Excerpts from "Deng Xiaoping" by George J. Church, *Time*, January 6, 1986

Politically and culturally, that fight [over how much to engage in trade with the West] has waxed and waned. China is still a one-party dictatorship and Deng has no intention of letting it become anything else. Rights taken for granted in the U.S., such as freedom of speech and assembly, are strictly controlled; some limited freedom of religion has been granted. Even so, a revised constitution adopted in 1982 marked a step toward making China a society governed by law rather than the whim of party officials.

In other ways, too, the dictatorship is less oppressive. Deng has permitted a popular press to spring up. Hundreds of new publications have appeared all over China; they cannot criticize policy, but they print lurid exposes of prostitution, pornography, corruption and black-marketeering by party officials (indeed, they sometimes seem to report little else). Culturally, Deng in 1983 permitted officials to start a crackdown on writers and artists, in the guise of a campaign against "spiritual pollution," probably as a gesture toward conservatives concerned that the pace of change was too rapid. But Deng speedily announced that the campaign had gone too far and called it off, leaving citizens and party officials alike in a quandary over just what is permitted and what is not.

SOURCE: George J. Church, "Deng Xiaoping," *Time*, 6 January 1986.

Go to **www.chinasince1644.com** for the text of **Document 16.8**.

Activities

Preliminary Activities: Read the unit overview and the introduction to the lesson. To get a sense of how interconnected the government and the Communist Party are, you may also want to check the *CIA World Factbook* under Chapter 16 Activity Websites on the companion website.

ACTIVITY 1: Comparing the Ideas of Marx, Mao, and Deng

Read Document 16.1, and paraphrase each quote. Then compare each man's viewpoints on the following questions:

1. What problem or issue is the author addressing?
2. What vision of society does the author put forward, and what are his ideas for getting there?
3. How is power obtained to change society?
4. What does socialism mean?
5. Attending to the date of each quote, consider how the historical context has influenced the author's ideas.

As a class, you will discuss your answers, noting points of similarity and difference between each thinker.

Creative Extension:

To deepen your answers to the questions above, read more extensive writings or speeches by each thinker, or consult websites that include additional famous quotations from each man.

ACTIVITY 2: Analyzing Deng Xiaoping's Proposals

Read and prepare to discuss the speech by Deng Xiaoping (16.2), focusing on the following questions:

1. What is your overall impression of the speech?
2. Deng Xiaoping was walking a thin line in his speech. What pitfalls did he appear to be avoiding?
3. What problems did Deng highlight?
4. What criticisms were implied in the speech? Why were they implied and not stated openly?
5. What changes did he insist had to happen?
6. What general impression does this 1978 speech give regarding China's future?
7. If you were a Chinese person hearing this speech, how would you react to it?
8. If the president of the United States were to give a speech like this today, how might it be received by the public, Congress, the press, or other countries?
9. Given the trends in the history of the Communist Party, how big a risk was this speech for Deng? What if it had not been well received?

ACTIVITY 3: Examining the Impact of Change

Read the letter by Pan Xiao (16.3).

1. List the points that Pan Xiao is trying to make.
2. What does Pan Xiao's letter have to do with the economic and social changes taking place in China during this time?
3. Write a response to Pan Xiao. Identify places in her letter where you sympathize with her and/or do not feel the same way.

Next, you will be assigned to a group of four where you will read each other's responses to Pan Xiao's letter and discuss the contents.

1. What is the tone of these letters?
2. Do they offer any practical suggestions to Pan Xiao? If so, what?
3. Pan Xiao's letter generated an extraordinary response. What does her influence tell us about the impact of change on individuals?

4. Examine copies of advice columns from current newspapers and blogs. Compare these samples to the Pan Xiao series. What is similar and what is different in tone and content?

Creative Extension:

Read the selection from Ma Xiaodong's article about a school in rural China (16.4). Compose a series of three journal entries as though you are a child in the middle school described by Ma Xiaodong. Working in groups of three, discuss the entries, then report to the class:

1. What are the recurrent or common themes in the journals?
2. How do you feel about life in rural China after reading this account and creating the diary entries?
3. Do you agree with Deng Xiaoping that modernization was needed in the areas he stressed? (See Document 16.2.) Why or why not?
4. Do you think it is possible to modernize a society rapidly enough to reach these children during their school years? Why or why not?
5. Do you think Ma Xiaodong's article is a typical or atypical report of a rural Chinese school? Why?

For further research, read related segments in Chapter 19 and research the current status of rural education in China. Did Deng's reforms reach the rural areas? What has changed in rural China in the past twenty-five years, and what has remained the same?

ACTIVITY 4: The One-Child Policy: A Debate

Examine population statistics for China (see Chapter 16 Activity Websites on the companion website) and conduct research to learn more about the One-Child Policy and the way it was implemented. You will join one of two teams. One team will take the position that the One-Child Policy is a necessary and proper policy for China to continue to pursue. The other will take the opposite stand. As you conduct your research, be aware that government policies have changed in recent years. Take those changes into account as you plan the debate.

To prepare for the debate, research:

- What are the traditional views regarding children in Chinese society?
- What is the current ratio of males to females in China?
- How popular are ultrasound machines?
- How widely available are abortions in China?
- What were the penalties for having more than one child? Was the policy enforced uniformly across China? Why?
- What, if anything, has changed in the ways the One-Child Policy is enforced?
- What was the rate of growth of China's population at ten-year intervals from 1950 to the present? Compare these rates to those in countries around the world.

■ What are the consequences of spiraling population growth?

ACTIVITY 5:
Essay Evaluating Wei Jingsheng's "Fifth Modernization"

Review the Four Modernizations Deng Xiaoping proposed and his speech "Emancipate the Mind" (16.2). Discuss as a class whether or not democracy is needed to make these four changes happen. What rights need to be protected in order for individuals to be able to "emancipate [their] minds"? Then read Wei Jingsheng's "The Fifth Modernization" (16.5). Address in an essay: Given the nature of power in Chinese politics, is Wei's text threatening to the Chinese government? Why or why not, and what would you do about it if you were the government in charge? For example, from a position of power, is it better to bring your adversary in, or to marginalize or arrest him or her?

ACTIVITY 6: Writing about Dissent and Intellectuals

The intellectual class of China has often been at the forefront of calls for reform. Read the selections by Fang Lizhi and Liu Binyan (16.6).

Part 1: Compose a Dialogue

Role-play or compose a dialogue between the two writers in which Fang and Liu are accused of counter-revolutionary activity and have to defend themselves.

Part 2: Write

In an essay, compare Fang Lizhi's and Liu Binyan's actions and words with those of the intellectuals of the May Fourth Movement (see Chapter 8). Are their actions in keeping with this tradition? Why?

Alternatively, compose an essay about the proper role of the intellectual in fostering change in a nation. Should scientists stick to science, for example, or should they become involved in public affairs? Are these intellectuals qualified to talk about what political changes are needed? What are the benefits and/or drawbacks to society of their political involvement?

ACTIVITY 7: Tiananmen Square

Access online the picture of the civilian halting the line of tanks, or watch the prologue to *The Tank Man* (see Suggested Resources). Write a response to what you see happening, and imagine what could be going through the heads of both the civilian and the driver of the tank. Role-play, add thought balloons, or compose a dialogue to articulate this situation.

1. Who do you think the civilian was? Was he the type of person you would expect to take a stand? Why?
2. What role can an individual play to bring about change?

3. Why do some individuals take a stand and others not?

4. Argue one side: was what this man did effective? How? Why?

5. What has this photo come to represent?

ACTIVITY 8:
Evaluating: Will the Real Deng Xiaoping Please Stand Up?

Deng Xiaoping was an authoritarian leader, an economic liberalizer, and *Time* magazine's "Man of the Year" in 1985. He charmed the American public when he wore a ten-gallon hat and delighted the business community when he opened up the Chinese market to foreign investors. At the same time, he ruled the Party with a combination of political savvy and defensiveness. Read Documents 16.7 and 16.8 and research the many facets of Deng through his own words and the descriptions of his biographers. You will work in a group of three to create a presentation in which you a) present Deng Xiaoping as having had a negative influence on China, b) present Deng Xiaoping as having had a positive influence on China, or c) illustrate the complexity of being the leader of China. After the class views each other's presentations, you will discuss as a class what choices you had to make in order to meet the terms of the assignment. Do documentarians, biographers, and journalists make similar choices? What is the significance of these choices?

EXTENDED ACTIVITIES:

- Watch the film *All Under Heaven* (see Suggested Resources) about the economic life of one small village north of Beijing. Capture the essence of the documentary in a poster, collage, sketch, poem, or sculpture.

- Explore how Deng Xiaoping and the Politburo approached the topic of Mao Zedong's legacy.

- Learn about how the Chinese government dealt with the aftermath of the Cultural Revolution. What was the "literature of the wounded" or "scar literature"? What purposes did it serve?

- Compare and contrast the Chinese leadership's approach to addressing the horrors and tragedies of the Cultural Revolution to the way other nations have confronted tragedies in their recent history (for example: South Africa, Rwanda, Cambodia, Serbia, Brazil, or Chile).

- Compare China's original constitution of 1954 to the revised one it adopted in 1982 (see Suggested Resources).

- Research information about Wei Jingsheng. Read opinions regarding the justice (or lack thereof) of his first imprisonment. What is Wei Jingsheng doing today? Consider: did he inherit the legacy of the May Fourth Movement, or was he an innovator?

- Learn about one of the major figures of the democracy movement in 1989: Chai Ling, Wu'erkaixi, Wang Dan, Cui Jian, or Feng Congde. Make a poster representing his or her ideas. For a follow-up discussion, research the post-1989 lives of these individuals and discuss where they are now, what they are doing, and whether they have come close to attaining their goals.

- Watch Frontline's documentary *The Tank Man* and Carma Hinton's documentary *The Gate of Heavenly Peace,* both of which examine the Tiananmen Square confrontation (see Suggested Resources). Compare and contrast the two documentaries.

- After watching *The Gate of Heavenly Peace,* be prepared to lead a class discussion. Consider how the protest and leadership changed over the two-month period, why tensions escalated, and why the Chinese government responded with violence. What other options were there? Why were they not pursued?

- Write an essay addressing how China's turbulent twentieth-century history and the leaders' experiences during the Cultural Revolution might have affected the response of the government to the protests.

Suggested Resources

Books

Fong, Vanessa L. *Only Hope: Coming of Age Under China's One-Child Policy.* Stanford: Stanford University Press, 2004.

This book by an anthropologist is the first in-depth study of the experiences of the first generation of children born under China's One-Child Policy.

Link, Perry. *Evening Chats in Beijing.* New York: W.W. Norton, 1992.

A compilation of discussions with Chinese citizens about the reform activities happening throughout China in the 1980s.

Lord, Betty Bao. *Legacies: A Chinese Mosaic.* New York: Alfred A. Knopf, 1990.

In this memoir, the wife of a former U.S. ambassador to China interweaves news headlines with her perspectives on Chinese society and culture during the demonstrations of 1989.

Schell, Orville. *The Mandate of Heaven: The Legacy of Tiananmen Square and the Next Generation of China's Leaders.* New York: Simon & Schuster, 1994.

A comprehensive overview of the events surrounding and including the Tiananmen Square incident of 1989.

Shambaugh, David. *Deng Xiaoping: Portrait of a Chinese Statesman.* New York: Oxford University Press, 2006.

A collection of essays that shows many different parts of Deng's life and work.

Vogel, Ezra F. *Deng Xiaoping and the Transformation of China.* Cambridge: Belknap Press of Harvard University Press, 2011.

An exhaustive biography of Deng Xiaoping.

Zhang Xinxin and Sang Ye. *Chinese Lives: An Oral History of Contemporary China.* New York: Pantheon Books, 1987.

A collection of interviews with people from all walks of life. All were facing the challenges of the changes Deng Xiaoping had put in motion, and many were taking advantage of the opportunities.

Websites

China Social Indicators, United Nations
**http://data.un.org/CountryProfile.aspx?cr
Name=CHINA#Social**
Statistics on population growth rate, urban
population, and life expectancy in China.

China Statistics, UNICEF
**http://www.unicef.org/infobycountry/china_
statistics.html**
Basic indicators such as mortality rates, population, life expectancy, and annual births as well as
education data and economic indicators.

China Statistics, The World Bank
http://data.worldbank.org/country/china
Population data, financial statistics, and World
Development Indicators.

Constitution of the People's Republic of China
**http://www.npc.gov.cn/englishnpc/
Constitution/node_2824.htm**
The Chinese Constitution adopted December 4,
1982, and amendments since 1982.

Deng Xiaoping Profile, CNN In-Depth Specials,
Visions of China
**http://www.cnn.com/SPECIALS/1999/
china.50/inside.china/profiles/deng.xiaoping/**
A brief biography of Deng Xiaoping from his
childhood to his death in 1997.

The Gate of Heavenly Peace
http://www.tsquare.tv/
The companion website to the documentary
The Gate of Heavenly Peace. The site includes film
excerpts, a chronology of June 1989, and additional readings and resources.

Rural Chinese Education Foundation
http://www.ruralchina.org/
A non-governmental organization that
promotes education for rural Chinese citizens.
The site includes information about present-day
rural education in China with links to current
initiatives and development campaigns.

Tiananmen Square Protests 1989, The Guardian
**http://www.guardian.co.uk/world/tianan-
men-square-protests-1989**
Videos, photo galleries, and articles detail the
events of June 1989.

Films

All Under Heaven (58 mins; 1986)
Part One of the *One Village in China* series.
This documentary captures the various ways in
which the CCP has tackled the challenge of
land reform and gives insight into rural
traditions.

The Gate of Heavenly Peace (189 mins; 1995)
The detailed and balanced account of what led
to the violent confrontation in June 1989 is the
result of six years of research. The documentary
links the student demonstrations to the legacy
of student activism in twentieth-century China
and captures the idealism as well as the confusion within the movement.

Small Happiness (58 mins; 1984)
Produced and directed by Carma Hinton and
Richard Gordon. Another film in the three-part
documentary series *One Village in China*,
examining life in Long Bow, a rural community
400 miles southwest of Beijing. This segment
looks at the lives of women in the village and
also shows how the pace of change in rural
China is different from the pace of change in
urban China.

The Tank Man (90 mins; 2006)
This PBS Frontline episode provides a look at
the events in and around Tiananmen Square on
June 5, 1989.

■ A CLOSER LOOK

Zhao Ziyang: Economic Reformer

Zhao Ziyang was born in 1919 and began his career in Guangdong Province working for agricultural improvement. During the Cultural Revolution, he was purged and ridiculed as a "stinking remnant of the landlord class." He was later rehabilitated by Zhou Enlai and became the governor of Sichuan Province, where he revived the economy by implementing a series of reforms aimed at developing a market-based economy. Deng Xiaoping brought him into the central government, and Zhao became the premier of the Chinese State Council and eventually the secretary general of the Party. He was widely viewed as Deng Xiaoping's successor after the death of Hu Yaobang in March 1989.

Zhao was a reformer and a modernizer, and during the Tiananmen Square protests he attempted to find common ground with the student protesters. He actually appeared in the square and pleaded with the students to leave before it was too late. He then disappeared for a time, and later it was announced that he had been stripped of his titles and placed under house arrest, though he did get out to play golf in Beijing and was never expelled from the Party. He died in January 2005.

■ *Look online to see how Zhao's death was marked in China, and compare that to the death of Hu Yaobang in 1989. Why was Zhao's death dealt with in this way?*

Li Peng: Promoting Social Control

Li Peng was born in 1928 and was just seven when the Guomindang government executed his father for being a Communist sympathizer. A few years later, Zhou Enlai adopted him and in 1948 sent Li to the Soviet Union to study. "He was carefully groomed for leadership," writes Jonathan Spence in *The Search for Modern China*.[6] In 1982, he joined the Central Committee, and in 1987, he became a member of the Politburo.

In 1988, Deng Xiaoping picked Li Peng to become premier, succeeding Zhao Ziyang. Li emphasized stability over reform, and he became one of the leading voices for social control as the economy liberalized. When the student protests broke out, he advocated for a crackdown. Li met with a group of students protesting with a hunger strike and was chastised on television by students who accused him of being out of touch. Some believe that this interaction led Li to orchestrate the PLA action as a response to such insolence. Li held on to the post of premier for a second term before stepping down. He remains a shadowy presence in the government, and his actual authority is unknown at this point.

■ *Watch* The Gate of Heavenly Peace, *directed by Carma Hinton. See Suggested Resources on the companion website. What kind of interactions was Li probably accustomed to as a leader in the CCP? Does this exchange make Li's response acceptable? What other reasons might Li have had for advocating a hard-line approach?*

[6] Jonathan D. Spence, *The Search for Modern China* (New York: W.W. Norton, 1999) 688.

UNIT FIVE

Contemporary China

UNIT OVERVIEW

By Liz Nelson

The words highlighted in this overview are key people, concepts, or movements that appear in the chapters that follow.

China in the first decade of the twenty-first century is a vastly different country than China in the first fifteen years after Mao Zedong founded the People's Republic of China, or even the first decade of Deng Xiaoping's reforms that began in the late 1970s.

China's economy is now the second largest in the world, and since it became a member of the World Trade Organization (WTO) in 2001, its volume of trade has mushroomed. In 1978, foreign direct investment (FDI) in China was $0. By 2010, it had reached a total of $114.7 billion.[1] China is a major player in the global economy, which has benefited both China and the rest of the world.

As "socialism with Chinese characteristics" has unfolded, however, the shift away from state-owned enterprises and virtually guaranteed life-long employment and benefits (the "iron rice bowl") has made many middle-aged workers feel extremely vulnerable. The extraordinary economic growth has also increased disparities. "Today...there are many 'Chinas,'" write the authors of *China: The Balance Sheet*: "rural and urban, wealthy and poor, educated and illiterate, international and isolated. Within this context of diversity and disparity, China's citizens and leadership are grappling with unprecedented domestic dynamism, coming to grips with globalization's challenges, and deliberating different political and economic futures."[2]

Most of the new economic prosperity has happened in coastal cities, while in rural areas approximately 400 million people subsist on less than $2 a day. Although China is the second largest economy in the world, the Gross Domestic Product (GDP) per capita in 2011 was only $8,400 compared to $48,000 in the United States. Even the rudimentary **health-care** available during the first twenty years of the PRC is significantly diminished, leaving rural people to travel considerable distances to access care and forcing them to pay for many

[1] Invest in China, "FDI Stock as of 2010," accessed at http://www.fdi.gov.cn/pub/FDI_EN/Statistics/Annual StatisticsData/AnnualFDIData/FDIStatistics,2010/ t20120207_140890.htm

[2] C. Fred Bergsten et al., *China: The Balance Sheet: What the World Needs to Know Now About the Emerging Superpower* (New York: Public Affairs/Center for Strategic and International Studies/Institute for International Economics, 2006) 16.

services out of pocket. Too often, the rural poor simply go without. These realities notwithstanding, it is important to note overall improvements in healthcare in China. In the 1950s, life expectancy in China was 35 years; in 2010, it was 73. Similarly, the rate of infant mortality has shown dramatic improvement, falling from 300 per 1,000 live births in the early 1950s to about 16 per 1,000 live births in 2011.

As in healthcare, in **education** the disparities between urban and rural China are significant. Well-equipped, challenging "key" schools in the cities prepare students for universities. In many rural areas, on the other hand, students need to board at schools in the closest larger town in order to attend bare-bones middle schools. In 2007 and 2008, the government launched new initiatives to address some of these inequities. Despite the ongoing problems, if one compares education before 1949 to the present, one sees stunning improvements in areas such as basic literacy: the Chinese have cut the number of people who cannot read or write by two-thirds, to 6 percent of the population.[3]

As a result of work opportunities in the cities, poverty in the countryside, and a relaxation of policies regulating people's ability to move, China is experiencing the largest **human migration** in history. More than 140 million people—about 20 percent of the working-age population—have left their homes in search of jobs. This is putting stress on housing and social services in the cities. However, the money those working in the city send home has helped to pull millions above the official poverty line.

The People's Republic of China faces **domestic political challenges**, too. The Chinese Communist Party's top priority is to manage a rapidly changing economy and society without losing political control. Recently, to offset growing consumerism, the Party has not only tolerated but encouraged the practice of traditional Chinese philosophies and religions, as long as the practitioners do not play any political role. Economic reforms and openness

to the outside world have brought with them an exchange of views that was not possible in the 1950s and 1960s. But the government continues to try—with limited success—to control Internet access. Finally, while the "rule of law" is making some inroads in China, civil liberties and protections, as the West knows them, are not something on which Chinese citizens can rely.

One of the gravest challenges Chinese leadership and citizens face is that of creating a sustainable economy, one that will not destroy **the environment**. "China's economic explosion has created an ecological implosion. Severe air and water pollution along with water shortages are threatening human health, industrial production, and crops. Land degradation and deforestation are exacerbating floods and desertification."[4] Though the central government has welcomed help from abroad and passed scores of laws and regulations to address the environmental crisis, much of the responsibility for enforcing these is in the hands of local officials. Too often, their sole concern appears to be immediate profits rather than pollution control.

Long gone are Mao Zedong's antagonistic **foreign relations** with the West. Under Deng Xiaoping and the leaders who have followed, the PRC has moved back into a leadership role regionally but followed a foreign policy of "keeping a low profile" (*taoguang yanghui* 韬光养晦). Since 2007, leaders in Beijing and Taipei have become comfortable maintaining the status quo while promoting economic and cultural exchanges across the Taiwan Strait. China's leaders also seek to dispel concern over their increased military spending;[5] they consistently maintain that their intentions are to coexist in peace.

Beyond Asia, the relationship between China and the United States is becoming

---

[3] The World Bank, "Literacy Rate, Adult Total," accessed at http://data.worldbank.org/indicator/SE.ADT.LITR.ZS

[4] Harry G. Gelber, *The Dragon and the Foreign Devils: China in the World, 1100 B.C. to the Present* (London: Bloomsbury, 2007)

[5] Estimates of how much China is spending vary, but even using the highest number suggested by the U.S. Department of Defense, China's military budget is about one-tenth of that of the United States.

increasingly complex and challenging. Chinese leadership watches the world superpower with few illusions, ever cautious about talk in Washington of "containing" China or in any way interfering in Chinese domestic affairs. On the global stage, as a permanent member of the United Nations Security Council, China's is an important voice in world affairs. China also plays an increasingly significant role in such international governmental organizations as the World Bank, the International Monetary Fund (IMF), the World Trade Organization (WTO), and the World Health Organization (WHO).

China, writes Harry Gelber in *The Dragon and the Foreign Devils*, is "emerging from two centuries of weakness and trauma...to tell the world... 'presume not that I am the thing I was.'"[6]

---

[6] Gelber, 434.

CHAPTER RESOURCES

Primary Sources

DOCUMENT 17.1: Excerpt from a speech by former premier Zhao Ziyang on the purpose of Special Economic Zones, 1984

DOCUMENT 17.2: "Shenzhen: Showcase for China's Economic growth," *China Daily*, February 4, 2002

DOCUMENT 17.3: "The End of Cheap China," *The Economist*, March 10, 2012

DOCUMENT 17.4: "China's WTO Entry of Great Impact," in *China Daily*, December 3, 2006

DOCUMENT 17.5: Excerpt from "China on the Move," by the RAND National Defense Research Institute (U.S.), 2005

DOCUMENT 17.6: Excerpts from "Prime Minister's War Shrine Visits the Issue That Matters, Beijing Tells Tokyo," in *The Australian*, November 2005

DOCUMENT 17.7: Excerpt from "Japanese Investment into China Hits Record High" by David Ibison, *Financial Times*, April 3, 2006 (not available on the companion website)

DOCUMENT 17.8: "Peace Breaking Out," *The Economist*, April 4, 2007

Supplementary Materials

ITEM 17.A: China's Special Economic Zones

ITEM 17.B: Changes in China's economy between December 2001 and December 2011

ITEM 17.C: Top Ten Economies in the World, 2011

 Excerpts of these primary source documents appear in this chapter. Go to **www.chinasince1644.com** for the full version of these documents and for the Supplementary Materials.

CHAPTER 17

China Steps Back onto the World Stage

By Todd Whitten

Chapter Contents

Expanded Special Economic Zones

Regional Relations

WTO Membership

Effects of Economic Globalization

Key Idea

China's emergence as an economic world power since the 1990s has led to significant gains as well as increased tensions—domestically, regionally, and globally.

Guiding Questions

What is the purpose of China's Special Economic Zones? What effects have they had on China's economy and populace?

Why is unification with Taiwan so important to China?

What has been the impact of World Trade Organization (WTO) membership for China?

What has been the impact of China's WTO membership on the global economy?

What have been the sources of tension between China and Japan?

Terms to Know

Foreign Direct Investment (FDI)

Gross Domestic Product (GDP)

infrastructure

iron rice bowl

Special Economic Zones (SEZ)

World Trade Organization (WTO)

Essay

Since 1992, the Chinese economy has been growing annually at a double digit pace. By 2011, China had become the second largest economy in the world, measured in terms of Purchasing Power Parity (PPP), accounting for 13% of the global economy. The three most significant events that symbolized China's global influence were the accession of China into the World Trade Organization (WTO), the 2008 Olympics Games in Beijing, and the 2010 World Expo in Shanghai. The rise of China or, more accurately, the re-emergence of China as a great power on the world stage, is likely to be one of the most important events of the twenty-first century.

Since the death of Deng Xiaoping (邓小平) in 1997, China has experienced several changes in leadership, first under Jiang Zemin (江泽民), then Hu Jintao (胡锦涛) and now Xi Jinping (习近平). Despite the changes, China has by and large continued Deng Xiaoping's policy of "reform and opening up": supporting Special Economic Zones (SEZ) (*Jingji Tequ* 经济特区) and many other types of high-tech and economic development zones inside China, integrating with the global economy, and modernizing the People's Liberation Army, together with carefully monitoring political dissent. The economic reforms begun by Deng Xiaoping in 1978 have over time lifted over 400 million Chinese out of poverty and created conditions for an ever-expanding middle class to emerge.

Meanwhile, China has been pursuing a global strategy of a self-described "peaceful rise" that has deepened China's influence in Africa and Latin America, in addition to Europe and North America. In the past decade, Chinese leaders have reached out to the global community by working with economic organizations such as the Association of Southeast Asian Nations (ASEAN),[1] joining the World Trade Organization (WTO), pursuing a position of leadership in East Asia, and exercising authority as a permanent member of the United Nations Security Council.

One China

In 1997, the British finally returned Hong Kong (*Xianggang* 香港) to China, a political and symbolic victory much celebrated across the country, and in 1999 the Portuguese relinquished Macao (*Aomen* 澳门) as well. Integrating the territories that had been under foreign control (see Chapter 5) into China as "one country, two systems" (*Yiguo liangzhi* 一国两制) has required diplomatic skill. The People's Republic of China (*Zhonghua Renmin Gongheguo* 中华人民共和国) bears the responsibility for defending each territory and managing the foreign affairs of Hong Kong and Macao. However, Hong Kong is responsible for its own monetary, legal, and immigration institutions, and for maintaining its police force and customs structure.

Often at issue is the autonomy of the local governing body of Hong Kong—how independent is it? What are the limits on its decision-making? The questions brought up by the re-integration of Hong Kong and Macao suggest ways in which Taiwan (台湾) may eventually be reunited with mainland China. At present, Taiwan continues to have de facto independence, and both the PRC's and Taiwan's leadership seem willing to preserve the status quo rather than push for immediate reunification or Taiwan's independence, which Beijing has made clear it will not permit.

Regional and Foreign Relations

China has made significant improvements in its relations with the ten member countries of the Association of the Southeast Asian Nations (ASEAN), although the territorial disputes in the potentially resource-rich South China Sea

---

[1] ASEAN's ten member countries are Brunei Darussalam, Cambodia, Indonesia, Laos, Malaysia, Myanmar, Philippines, Singapore, Thailand, and Vietnam.

often put this relationship to test. In January 2010, the Free Trade Agreement (FTA) between China and the ASEAN countries went into force. By the end of 2010, trade volume between China and ASEAN countries had reached $292.8 billion, an increase of 37.5 percent from the year before. China has become the biggest trade partner and the first export destination for ASEAN countries.

China's relationship with Japan has undergone significant changes since Japan's invasion and occupation of China between 1932 and 1945 (see Chapters 9 and 11). Beginning in the early 1990s and continuing for about fifteen years, the relationship was strained. The issues included China's role in East Asia, territorial disputes, the security alliance between the United States and Japan, and the way in which Japan addresses its history with China. Yet at the same time, Japan and China have become increasingly linked economically. China is Japan's largest trading partner; Japan is China's third largest trade partner.[2] Neither country wishes to disrupt this vibrant economic relationship, but the bilateral relations between Beijing and Tokyo remain difficult at best due to unresolved historical, territorial, and political issues.

Beyond East Asia, China's relations with India have been marked by both cooperation and competition. The rivalry between the two Asian giants has also generated heated debate over the advantages of the Chinese model of development vs. India's. The first decade of the twenty-first century also has witnessed a fast-growing outflow of Chinese investment in Africa, Central and Latin America, and the Caribbean. In addition to mines and resources, China's financed projects range from infrastructure (such as airports, roads, bridges, and railways) to schools, hospitals, and office buildings. China's relations with European countries have seen ups and downs, but in recent years, especially since the debt crisis in several member countries of the Euro Zone, China has shown a much-appreciated willingness to help the struggling European economies over the difficulty.

China's relationship with the United States is often viewed as the most important bilateral relationship for China, and perhaps for the United States as well. Despite the fact that the Sino-American economies have become increasingly interdependent, economic and trade issues such as the devaluation of the Chinese currency and intellectual property rights have often generated much controversy. Moreover, as China is not only rising economically, but also militarily, the mutual distrust between Beijing and Washington is expected to grow.

Joining the World Trade Organization

In 2001, China became a member of the World Trade Organization, after a fifteen-year-long process of negotiations. This has caused significant changes in the global economy as well as China's economy. While some politicians in developed countries like to blame trade deficits and economic uncertainty on China's membership in the WTO, most economists argue that the impact has generally been positive. China's factories assemble products—from toys to high-tech—out of parts made elsewhere in the world, and since many of the firms involved are foreign, their stockholders benefit as well. The finished products are sold inexpensively around the world, which benefits anyone who has limited discretionary income. By 2011, China had become the largest exporting country and the second largest importing country in the world.

Effects of Economic Globalization

The Chinese economic success is the result of bold decisions by the Chinese leaders, the hard work of hundreds of millions of Chinese people,

---

[2] After the European Union and the U.S.

and new opportunities created by globalization. While the revolutionary changes in information technologies and the world economy have produced winners and losers, China overall has greatly benefited from globalization.

As China has the largest foreign currency reserves in the world ($3.18 trillion), it has reinvested part of the accumulated wealth into the global economy by lending about $1.3 trillion to the U.S. economy, literally serving as the largest banker for the United States, and about 800 billion Euros to the European economy.

Because the Chinese economy has become increasingly integrated with the global economy, the 2008 global financial crisis that hit many economies hard also affected China. As demand from the United States and Europe for Chinese manufactured goods declined, many Chinese factories in the South China region struggled

and Chinese economic growth slowed to 7 or 8 percent. The worst global financial crisis since the Great Depression of the 1930s has further convinced Chinese policymakers that in order to sustain long-term economic growth, China needs to shift its export-led development strategy to focus on domestic consumption, which accounts for one-third of its economic growth vs. two-thirds of that of the United States.

As China's economic integration has made plain, the bi-polar world that existed in the second half of the twentieth century has transformed into a multi-faceted, interdependent one. China's relationships with its immediate neighbors and position as a member of the global community continue to change, which highlights the need for flexible, thoughtful diplomatic approaches from everyone involved.

Primary Sources

DOCUMENT 17.1: Excerpt from a speech by former premier Zhao Ziyang on the purpose of Special Economic Zones, 1984

The special economic zones…[and open cities] are the bridgeheads in our opening to the outside world, and they should play the role of springboard. *On the one hand*, they should import advanced foreign technology, equipment, and management…absorb and digest them; apply them in innovations; and transfer them to the interior. *On the other hand*, they should send commodities produced in the coastal areas with foreign technology to the interior, and export the latter's raw materials and produce, with added value after processing… to the international market.

SOURCE: Foreign Broadcast Information Services, *Daily Report, China*, 26 December, 1984. Qtd. in Christopher J. Smith, *China: People and Places in the Land of One Billion* (Boulder, CO: Westview Press, 1991) 106.

 Go to **www.chinasince1644.com** for the text of Document 17.1.

DOCUMENT 17.2: "Shenzhen: Showcase for China's Economic Growth," *China Daily*, February 4, 2002

Shenzhen City, one of China's five special economic zones, has had an annual gross domestic product (GDP) growth rate of 25 percent ever since the late Chinese leader Deng Xiaoping's tour to south China's Guangdong Province 10 years ago. On January 19–22, 1992, Deng Xiaoping, the architect general of China's reform and opening policy, visited Shenzhen and called for bold measures to accelerate reform and opening during his fact-finding and inspection tour of the south China city.

According to local sources, Shenzhen's GDP reached 190.82 billion *yuan* (about 23 billion U.S. dollars) last year [2001], compared with 31.73 billion *yuan* (about 3.82 billion U.S. dollars) in 1992. Over the decade the per capita consumption of urban residents in Shenzhen has shot up to over 20,000 *yuan* (about 2,409 U.S. dollars), from less than 5,000 *yuan* (about 602 U.S. dollars).

Shenzhen, which used to be a small town with about 20,000 residents, has grown into a boom city, which is now highly rated throughout the country as one of China's leading exporters and having won the most "garden-like city in the world " award in 2000....

SOURCE: "Shenzhen: Showcase for China's Economic Growth," *China Daily*, 4 February 2002.

Go to **www.chinasince1644.com** for the full text of Document 17.2.

DOCUMENT 17.3:
" The End of Cheap China," *The Economist*, 10 March 2012

TRAVEL by ferry from Hong Kong to Shenzhen, in one of the regions that makes China the workshop of the world, and an enormous billboard greets you: "Time is Money, Efficiency is Life".

China is the world's largest manufacturing power. Its output of televisions, smart-phones, steel pipes and other things you can drop on your foot surpassed America's in 2010. China now accounts for a fifth of global manufacturing. Its factories have made so much, so cheaply that they have curbed inflation in many of its trading partners. But the era of cheap China may be drawing to a close.

Costs are soaring, starting in the coastal provinces where factories have historically clustered (see map). Increases in land prices, environmental and safety regulations and taxes all play a part. The biggest factor, though, is labour.

SOURCE: "The End of Cheap China," *The Economist*, 10 March 2012

Go to **www.chinasince1644.com** for the link to Document 17.3.

DOCUMENT 17.4:
"China's WTO Entry of Great Impact," *China Daily*, December 3, 2006

As the world's most populous nation marks the fifth anniversary of its entry into the global trade body, it is time for both the 1.3 billion Chinese themselves and the rest of the world to take stock of the changes. For the well-heeled resident of Beijing or Shanghai, the advantages of WTO membership are obvious: His imported Mercedes is cheaper; his local Citibank offers more services; his Wal-Mart sells a wider variety of products. But China's entry into the WTO has not just created winners. Reduced tariffs on agricultural produce have threatened the livelihoods of hundreds of millions of farmers.

Beyond affecting the individual lives of the Chinese, the WTO has also profoundly and irreversibly changed the Chinese economy as a whole....

"In this period of expanding trade, every country has to make some adjustments. Some of its industries expand and other industries tend to contract," said Dollar [World Bank country director for China]. "In China, for example, more than 100,000 people have been released from state-owned banks, as the state-owned banks adjust to this more competitive environment."...

China's entry into the WTO has brought about monumental changes in global trade flows that it will take a long time to absorb, according to Cliff Stevenson [a UK-based consultant].... "It's quite hard to predict when the transition will be over, because I don't think the world has ever seen anything like this before," he said.

SOURCE: "China's WTO Entry of Great Impact," *China Daily*, 3 December 2006.

Go to **www.chinasince1644.com** for the full text of **Document 17.4**.

DOCUMENT 17.5: Excerpt from "China on the Move" by the RAND National Defense Research Institute (U.S.), 2005

The changes in the international security environment have had a profound impact on the threat perceptions of the People's Liberation Army (PLA) and its civilian masters, creating bureaucratic and political support for accelerated military modernization. For the PLA, two of the most important perceived changes were the rise of dominant U.S. military power, as evidenced in Gulf Wars I & II, Kosovo, Afghanistan, and Iraq and the evident desire on the part of the sole remaining superpower to use that military power to pursue a global unilateral agenda.

These changes in PLA perceptions have also significantly shaped the trajectory of its military buildup and rapid acceleration of equipment upgrades and doctrinal revision that had heretofore been relatively gradual. Beginning in the early 1990s and accelerating after 1999, PLA modernization was elevated from a relatively low priority to a core element of national policy....

SOURCE: David C. Gompert et al., eds., *China on the Move: A Franco-American Analysis of Emerging Chinese Strategic Policies and their Consequences for Transatlantic Relations* (Santa Monica, CA: RAND Corp., 2005) viii.

Go to **www.chinasince1644.com** for the full text of **Document 17.5**.

DOCUMENT 17.6: Excerpts from "Prime Minister's War Shrine Visits the Issue That Matters, Beijing Tells Tokyo" in *The Australian*, November 2005

Ambassador Wang Yi made it clear yesterday that of all the recent frictions between Japan and China, the "historical problem" symbolized by the Yasukuni visits had done most to poison the bilateral relationship.

"We need to resolve the situation as soon as possible," said Mr. Wang. "This is not a situation we can simply avoid." Though he insisted that anti-Japanese riots that swept China in April were not sanctioned by the Beijing government, Mr. Wang pointedly declined to rule out further trouble....

Mr. Wang, one of China's most senior diplomats, dismissed [the Japanese prime minister] Mr. Koizumi's contention that he and China's top leaders should hold a summit to deal with other differences, while leaving the Yasukuni issue in abeyance. Those problems include a territorial dispute in the East China Sea covering potentially large gas fields, China's objection to Japan gaining a permanent UN Security Council seat, and the two countries' intense competition for influence in the rest of Asia.

SOURCE: Peter Alford, "PM's War Shrine Visits the Issue That Matters, Beijing Tells Tokyo," *The Australian*, 25 Nov. 2005.

Go to **www.chinasince1644.com** for the full text of Document 17.6.

DOCUMENT 17.7: Excerpt from "Japanese Investment into China Hits Record High" by David Ibison, *Financial Times*, April 3, 2006

According to the Japan External Trade Organization, Japanese investment in China rose 19.8 percent to $6.5 billion in 2005. A Japanese official suggested that the business relationship between the two countries was strong enough to withstand political difficulties. He also pointed out that Japan's market is flat and the population is declining, so the Chinese market is very important for Japan. However, the historic issues remain.

Hu Jintao, China's president, said late last week he would only meet with Junichiro Koizumi, Japan's prime minister, if he stopped visiting the Yasukuni shrine in Tokyo, which commemorates Japan's war dead. In response, senior politicians in Japan criticised China and called into question increases in its military spending, saying China was becoming a threat to its Asian neighbours. This prompted Wen Jiabao, the Chinese premier, to say in Australia on Monday that China posed no threat and that its defence policy was "transparent."

SOURCE: David Ibison, "Japanese Investment into China Hits Record High," *Financial Times*, 3 Apr. 2006.

DOCUMENT 17.8:
"Peace Breaking Out," *The Economist*, April 4, 2007

As for the Yasukuni shrine, to which [Prime Minister] Mr Abe has traditionally been a more committed visitor than has Mr Koizumi [his predecessor], the Chinese believe that they have an understanding from him that he will not go while he is prime minister. Afterwards, says one Chinese policymaker, he can even go and live at Yasukuni, for all the Chinese will care.

If this minimum requirement—no prime ministerial visit, or at least no public one, to Yasukuni—is met, then the Chinese government seems determined to build a new "strategic partnership." Japan seems inclined to reciprocate. In a surprisingly short time, a wide range of topics has come up: economic and environmental co-operation; mechanisms to ease territorial disputes in the East China Sea, complicated by possibly large deposits of gas and oil; even confidence-building measures between the two countries' armed forces.

Mr Wen's visit will formalise a new cabinet-level dialogue on economic co-operation. In addition, Japanese firms will be offered the chance to bid for nuclear-power projects, as well as for parts of proposed high-speed railway lines between Beijing and Shanghai, Beijing and Wuhan, and Dalian and Harbin in Manchuria—whose railways imperial Japan once controlled. Japanese investment and know-how will be sought for environmental projects, including on energy efficiency.

SOURCE: "Peace Breaking Out," *The Economist*, 4 Apr. 2007.

Go to **www.chinasince1644.com** for the link to **Document 17.8**.

Activities

ACTIVITY 1: Mapping and Writing an Analysis of the Special Economic Zones

Before reading the introductory essay, on a map of China, place the Special Economic Zones and cities open to foreign trade and investment, established by Deng Xiaoping (Item 17.A on the companion website). Why were these cities chosen and why were the zones set up in these areas? Read Premier Zhao Ziyang's explanation regarding the SEZ and open cities (17.1). Next read the *People's Daily* article "Shenzhen, Showcase for China's Economic Growth" (17.2) and see Chapter 17 Activity Websites on the companion website for more resources about the SEZ. Discuss what might be some of the advantages and disadvantages of placing all the SEZ near the coast. Then read the introductory essay.

Given their definition and purpose, write an essay arguing that the Special Economic Zones and "open cities" are either a positive or negative policy for the Chinese economy. Consider the impact on people of the shift toward capitalism in light of the guarantees of the "iron rice bowl." You will discuss in class the challenges of taking a pro or con stance such as this.

ACTIVITY 2:
Analyzing the Impact and Interests of Foreign Investors

Watch "Chapter 4: The China Connection," an eleven-minute selection from the Frontline documentary "Is Wal-Mart Good for America?" See Chapter 17 Activity Websites on the companion website for a link to the video. As you watch, take notes on the ways that the United States, China, and Wal-Mart benefit or suffer from the relationship. You will need your notes as evidence for the activity.

1. Choose to take the role of the U.S. Secretary of Commerce, the Chinese Minister of Commerce, or the CEO of Wal-Mart and prepare a two- to three-minute speech presenting the pros and cons of Wal-Mart's involvement in China from your perspective. Consider in your speech: Is Wal-Mart helpful or harmful for enhancing relations between the United States and the People's Republic of China? Who benefits and in what ways? Cite specific evidence from the video in your speech.

2. Read "The End of Cheap China" from *The Economist* (17.3). Then as an advisor to the U.S. Chamber of Commerce, craft a two-paragraph memorandum that

   A. Summarizes the challenges faced by U.S. businesses in the face of rising Chinese wages.

   B. Advises the Chamber of Commerce about which types of U.S. firms would most benefit from opening factories in China. Note your criteria.

   C. At the end, list new questions that a business may want to explore before opening a workshop in China.

ACTIVITY 3: Research: China Joins the WTO

See Chapter 17 Activity Websites on the companion website for an introduction about the World Trade Organization (WTO). Note especially "About Us" and "Who We Are." Also examine the statistics comparing China's economy in 2001, 2006, and 2011 (Item 17.B on the companion website) and the statistics about the "Top 10 Economies in the World, 2011" (Item 17.C). Finally, read "China's WTO Entry of Great Impact," (17.4), written on the five-year anniversary of China's becoming a WTO member. Working on your own or with a partner, choose one of the following questions, research it, and prepare a three-minute presentation for a group of your classmates that includes a handout of some kind.

1. Why was China interested in joining the WTO?

2. What was the position of one of the following developed countries on China's accession to the WTO: Australia, Japan, the countries of the European Union, or the United States?

3. Which country was the most involved in the negotiations for including China? Why? What were that country's concerns?

4. In order to join the WTO, China agreed to meet a series of benchmarks. What are the benchmarks? Is China meeting them? What may happen if they are not met?

5. What have been the effects in China of WTO membership?

6. Describe the effects of China's membership on any one of the following: countries in the European Union, Australia, the United States, Japan, India, or countries in Central America.

Listen to the others' presentations and take notes using the handouts from your group. Finally, complete the statement: "The effects of China becoming a member of the World Trade Organization have been _____." Write an essay providing details to support your position.

ACTIVITY 4: Writing a Position Paper on the Modernization of the People's Liberation Army

Read the RAND Corporation analysis of further modernization in the PLA (17.5) and do additional research online to explore a range of views—Chinese and non-Chinese—on the topic of China's armed forces. Compare China's defense budget with those of the United States and Japan. (Note that Japan's post-World War II constitution prohibits it from maintaining armed forces for any purpose other than national defense.) Then write a position paper in which you analyze the PLA's relative strengths and weaknesses, and answer the question: Should China's neighbors feel threatened, or should China's statement that it is "pursuing economic development with peaceful intentions" be taken at face value?

ACTIVITY 5: Examining the Shifting Relationship between China and Japan

Begin by referring to Chapter 11 for information about Japan's eight-year occupation of much of China (1937–1945). Then read the 2005 news report about the Japanese prime minister's annual visits to the Yasukuni war memorial (17.6).

1. According to the article, what have been the issues between China and Japan?

2. Next, read the 2006 article from the *Financial Times* about record high Japanese investments in China (17.7).

3. Note the main points in the report.

4. Finally, read "Peace Breaking Out," reporting on events in 2007 (17.8).

5. What was changing between the two Asian nations and why?

6. What measures were the two countries putting in place, and why were they taking these steps?

7. Check a major international news source to learn what recent developments have taken place between China and Japan.

You will discuss, as a class, what conclusions can be drawn from the shifting relationship and come to a consensus as to the advice diplomats should give to both countries. (A good supplemental article on the subject of regional dominance is "China Influence in Asia Concerns Japan, Ministry Says" by Sachiko Sakimaki. See Chapter 17 Activity Websites on the companion website for the link to this article.)

Creative Extension:

Create a visual piece of art (poster, sculpture, cartoon, drawing, comic strip) that captures the relationship between China and Japan. Write a caption to go with it.

Suggested Resources

Books

Benewick, Robert and Stephanie Hemelryk Donald. *The State of China Atlas: Mapping the World's Fastest-Growing Economy.* Berkeley: University of California Press, 2009.

Bergsten, C. Fred, et al. *China: The Balance Sheet: What the World Needs to Know Now about the Emerging Superpower.* New York: Public Affairs, 2006.
A look at China's extraordinary economic growth and its many implications.

Brownell, Susan. *Beijing's Games: What the Olympics Mean to China.* Lanham, MD: Rowman & Littlefield, 2008.

Chang, Leslie T. *Factory Girls: From Village to City in a Changing China.* New York: Spiegel & Grau, 2008.
Examines the lives of female migrant factory workers in China, focusing on the experiences of two young women and including the author's story of her family's migration within China and to the West.

Fewsmith, Joseph. *China Since Tiananmen: From Deng Xiaoping to Hu Jintao.* New York: Cambridge University Press, 2008.

Gifford, Rob. *China Road: A Journey into the Future of a Rising Power.* New York: Random House, 2007.
Journalist Rob Gifford travels Chinese Route 312 from Shanghai to the border of Kazakhstan where the social and economic changes in the country are apparent all along the 3,000-mile route.

Hessler, Peter. *Country Driving: A Journey through China from Farm to Factory.* New York: Harper, 2010.
A narrative account of how the development and diffusion of cars and roads have changed China.

Hessler, Peter. *Oracle Bones: A Journey Between China's Past and Present.* New York: HarperCollins, 2006.
Chapters 2, 4, 7, 11, 17, and 22 will be of interest to readers wishing to learn about the lives of young Chinese adults in the new economy.

Websites

2008 Olympics Opening Ceremony, The Big Picture, Boston.com
http://www.boston.com/bigpicture/2008/ 08/2008_olympics_opening_ceremony.html
Twenty-four pictures from the four-hour opening ceremony in Beijing.

China Country Profile, BBC News
http://www.bbc.co.uk/news/world-asia- pacific-13017877
Overview of the country, leaders, and history of China with statistics and a timeline.

China as Host Country, NPR
http://www.npr.org/series/92645309/china- as-host-country
Articles, interviews, and reports about China's preparation to host the 2008 Olympics.

China's Special Economic Zones, Beijing Review
http://www.bjreview.com.cn/nation/txt/2009- 05/26/content_197576.htm
Background information about China's Special Economic Zones.

Expo 2010, Shanghai, China
http://www.expo2010.cn/expo/expoenglish/ oe/es/index.html
The official website of the Shanghai Expo.

Hu Jintao, The Chinese Central Government's Official Web Portal
http://english.gov.cn/leaders/hujintao.htm
Articles about President Hu's domestic and foreign diplomacy.

Hung Huang, "The Chinese Do Take It Personally," MSNBC
http://video.msnbc.msn.com/nbc-news/24430088
An interview with Chinese blogger Hung Huang about the controversy in Western countries over the Olympic torch and protests against the Chinese government.

World Trade Organization
http://wto.org/
The official website of the World Trade Organization provides news, briefs, and extensive information about trade topics.

World Trade Organization and China, The U.S.-China Business Council
https://www.uschina.org/public/wto/
The website of the U.S.-China Business Council, an organization of U.S. companies doing business in China, has an archive of all its reports to Congress on the progress the PRC has made or not made in meeting its obligations as laid out in the accession to the WTO agreement.

Films

China Blue (88 mins; 2005)
A powerful documentary capturing the lives of teen girls in a Chinese factory that produces denim jeans. The film provides another perspective on what China's involvement in the global economy means to one segment of the population and the role Western corporations and consumers play.

Young and Restless in China (106 mins; 2008)
A PBS Frontline documentary following the lives of nine Chinese adults in different parts of the country. The episode documents pressures and decisions they face as they try to balance tradition and modernity and work and family.

■ **A CLOSER LOOK**

Shanghai

■ Access the color image on the companion website to view it in greater detail. List twenty details from the photograph. Next, working in small groups, create a master list of details. Compare Shanghai as shown in this photograph to cities you've seen. What does this suggest about China's modernization?

CHAPTER RESOURCES

Primary Sources

DOCUMENT 18.1: Slide show "Contemporary China: A Study in Contrasts," with photographs taken in China, 2004–2012

DOCUMENT 18.2: Four excerpts of individual stories from the "new China," 2005–2006

DOCUMENT 18.3: Stories of their families written by the children of migrant workers living and working in Beijing, 2007

DOCUMENT 18.4: Excerpt from "Bridge over the Digital Divide" by Rong Jiaojiao in *China Daily*, June 2006

DOCUMENT 18.5: Excerpt from "Too Big, Too Fast" by Feng Jianhua in *Beijing Review*, October 27, 2005

DOCUMENT 18.6: "Bigger Net, Better Net" by Yin Pumin in *Beijing Review* February 1, 2012

DOCUMENT 18.7: Excerpt from "The Price of Health" by Tan Wei in *Beijing Review*, February 2, 2006

DOCUMENT 18.8: Excerpt from "Holiday Season" by Zhang Zhiping in *Beijing Review*, January 26, 2006

DOCUMENT 18.9: Excerpt from "Still Brewing" by Lu Ling in *Beijing Review*, January 19, 2006

DOCUMENT 18.10: Excerpt from "Quick, Pass Me a Burger!" by Tang Yuankai in *Beijing Review*, April 14, 2005

DOCUMENT 18.11: Excerpts from "Should a Lack of Filial Piety Be Penalized?" a Forum article in *Beijing Review*, February 23, 2006

DOCUMENT 18.12: "Wedding Bells?" by Lu Lin in *Beijing Review*, May 18, 2006

DOCUMENT 18.13: "Governing Gender" by Lan Xinzhen in *Beijing Review*, March 23, 2006

DOCUMENT 18.14: "Earning Their Keep" by Yuan Yuan in *Beijing Review*, May 16, 2011

Supplementary Materials

ITEM 18.A: Questions for Activity 4, Documents 18.4–18.7

ITEM 18.B: Questions for Activity 5, Documents 18.8–18.10

ITEM 18.C: Questions for Activity 6, Documents 18.11–18.14

 Excerpts of these primary source documents appear in this chapter. Go to **www.chinasince1644.com** for the full version of these documents and for the Supplementary Materials.

CHAPTER 18

The Consequences of Modernization

By Michael Abraham

Chapter Contents

Key Idea

Modernization has affected different segments of China's population in very different ways. The extraordinary pace of economic development is leading people to adapt to dramatically altered living and working patterns.

Guiding Questions

How has the shift to a modern economy led to a rural-urban divide in Chinese society? Is this divide a new phenomenon?

How is the Chinese government responding to the pressures of a modern society?

What benefits and problems do Chinese people face, living in this era of change?

Terms to Know

demographics
floating population
migrant worker
multinational company
state-run economy
yuan

Essay

One of the most interesting consequences of China's rapid pace of modernization has been the changing face of Chinese society. From the style of clothing Chinese people wear, to the increased quantities of food in the countryside, to the influx of foreign-owned companies, China today looks very different than it did a generation ago.

The Changing Face of the Chinese Consumer and Economy

The face of a homogeneous, Maoist society where men and women all wear drab gray or blue tunic jackets, pants, and caps has become as much a remnant of the past as that of a society whose scholar-officials once wore silk robes. In the cities, in particular, increased capitalism and the growth of free enterprise have helped generate an abundance of consumer goods, such as smartphones and designer clothes. Young adults can now choose their own jobs and career paths. In the face of such change and opportunity, it is easy to understand why the generation that came of age under Mao Zedong (毛泽东) (see Chapters 13 and 14) might harbor resentment, particularly when some of those changes no longer guarantee life-long job security and social services.

The faces of China's industrial and market sectors have also changed. Today, private enterprises, foreign companies, and multinationals compete where state-run industries and factories once enjoyed monopolies. One does not have to walk far in a Chinese city before spotting a McDonalds™, KFC™, Starbucks™, or Pizza Hut™. Pedestrian malls and luxury auto dealerships now also dot the urban landscape. In addition, China's quest to modernize has resulted in large-scale investments in infrastructure, which has increased both the quantity and quality of roads, bridges, communications services, and high-rise housing units.

But while the standard of living has risen sharply during the reform era, the rise has been very uneven, especially when urban areas are compared to rural areas. By and large, incomes and social services such as education and health care are better in the cities (see Chapter 19 for information about education disparities). China's Gini ratio, which measures the income gap between the rich and poor, now reaches 0.47, well above the warning level of 0.40 set by the World Bank.[1] According to some reports, China now has 1.11 million millionaires (in U.S. dollars),[2] and yet about 400 million people still subsist on less than $2 a day.[3] Regional as well as urban-rural income disparities have the potential to threaten China's social and political stability.

Changing Demographics

China's total fertility rate dropped dramatically from 5.8 in 1970 to 1.54 in 2010. Experts credit modernization and improved living standards as well as the One-Child Policy.[4] In part as a response to protests charging human rights violations, the Population and Family Planning Law of 2001 called for far more flexibility in implementing the one-child goal and allowed for a number of exceptions to the policy. While the One-Child Policy has met its goal to control

---

[1] Chen Jia, "Country's wealth divide past warning level," *China Daily*, May 12, 2010.

[2] http://www.bloomberg.com/news/2011-05-31/china-s-millionaires-jump-past-one-million-on-savings-growth.html

[3] Bergsten, C. Fred et al., *China: The Balance Sheet: What the World Needs to Know Now About the Emerging Superpower* (New York: PublicAffairs, 2006) 3, 6. Published by the Center for Strategic and International Studies and the Institute for International Economics.

[4] Hao Yan, "Rethinking of China's Population Policy in Line with the Change in China's Development Strategy," Berlin, August 2006

population growth, it has resulted in several challenging side effects. The age distribution in the population is changing dramatically as China's population is graying. In 2010, 178 million people in China were over age 60, representing 12.5% of the total population. By 2030, the number will grow to more than 350 million, larger than the current total population of the United States,[5] a change that China's inadequate pension system is not equipped to handle. How to take care of a rapidly aging population has become a huge challenge for the younger generation, the government, and the whole society.

In addition, a gender gap exists; China's national census of 2010 showed 118.08 males for every 100 females. According to Chinese tradition, a son takes care of his parents in their senior years. Since farmers do not receive pensions, a son is, in effect, a couple's guarantee for security in their old age (see Chapter 16 for additional information about the One-Child Policy).

Another changing demographic in China is the steady rise in the number of migrant laborers. While the great majority of China's population still makes its livelihood in agriculture, the opportunity to make more money in the cities has led to a "floating population" of workers, estimated at 140 million, moving from rural to urban areas. This phenomenon—a trend seen around the world—has put a strain on city services, as well as the fabric of the traditional Chinese family. Grandparents are stepping in for absent parents and raising children, at least for a few years.

[5] "Getting on: The Consequences of an Aging Population," *The Economist*, June 23, 2011. http://www.economist.com/node/18832070

The Changing Face of Religion and Politics

Religion was strongly repressed during the Mao years, but today the practice of religious beliefs is much more evident. Despite the more tolerant attitude, there have been clashes between the government and religious groups of different persuasions including Buddhists in Tibet (*Xizang* 西藏), Muslims in Xinjiang (新疆), and Christians. Any time one of these groups, or one such as Falun Gong (法轮功), is able to organize its followers, the Communist Party becomes wary, fearing possible political activity.

The government continues its efforts to control the pace of political reform, but China in the twenty-first century is a dramatically different society than China in the 1950s and 1960s. While today's calls for greater political openness and less state corruption have yet to match the high profile outcry of the 1989 Tiananmen (天安门) demonstrations (see Chapter 16), dissidents have proved effective at using the Internet to exchange and express their views. As a result, the government now restricts and censors the activities of foreign-owned Internet companies in China. At the same time, however, political reform is moving forward. For example, village self-government has been carried out since 1998. Entrepreneurs are now admitted into the CCP, and formal establishment of Non-Governmental Organizations (NGOs) is permitted. In addition, there is a growing interest in recognizing the importance of the rule of law.

The Chinese government believes that human rights are important but that for developing countries the communal rights to survival and economic development outweigh the rights to personal freedom of thought, expression, religion, and organization. Nevertheless, in 2004, the Party added a new clause to the Constitution stating that "the State respects and protects human rights."

Primary Sources

DOCUMENT 18.1: Photographs taken in China from the slide show "Contemporary China: A Study in Contrasts," 2004–2012

Fruit vendor in
Shanghai
(*Photo by Jim Brown*)

The Conference Center
in Pudong district,
Shanghai
(*Photo by Liz Nelson*)

 Go to **www.chinasince1644.com** for the slide show
"Contemporary China: A Study in Contrasts," **Document 18.1**.

DOCUMENT 18.2:
Excerpts from four individual stories from the "new China," 2005–2006

Zang Jianhe, born in Qingdao, Shandong Province, used to run a snack stall that sold handmade *jiaozi*[6] at the Wanchai Ferry in Hong Kong. In its heyday, customers would queue for more than an hour for a taste of Zang's *jiaozi*. "A competitive product is a must for any business to start with," says Zang. Today, Wanchai Ferry *jiaozi* come frozen in fine packaging at supermarkets and shopping malls in many large cities. Zang sees much growth in the market for frozen *jiaozi* and jokes, "If we are dedicated to the *jiaozi* business, it will prove to be even more profitable than real estate speculation." In 1996, she invested in a 1,200-square-meter workshop of international standards, putting the stamp of quality on her brand.

One feature of Zang's success has been her ability to know "when to say 'no' and when to say 'yes.'" After declining several proposals for joint-venture operations, Zang chose the 100-year-old United States-based Pillsbury Group for its rich experience in modern production, management expertise of Harvard elites and for being the first to adopt the Hazard Analysis Critical Control Points (HACCP) model which embodies a systematic approach to food safety.

SOURCE: Tang Yuankai, "Quick, Pass Me A Burger!" *Beijing Review*, 14 Apr. 2005.

Go to **www.chinasince1644.com** for the full text of **Document 18.2**.

DOCUMENT 18.3: One of two stories of their families written by the children of migrant workers living and working in Beijing, 2007

My mother worried about us a lot, concerned that we wouldn't be able to handle everything ourselves [at home]. Then she brought us to Beijing and wanted us to go to school here. When I first came to Beijing, I couldn't adjust here at all, because everything in Beijing was so strange to me. They made me feel I was so tiny and insignificant and there was no place in the city for me to exist. Seeing my mother working so hard every day, I felt so empty and had no feeling for going to school. I knew the reason mother worked so hard was to support us so we could go to school and live a better life. But I couldn't do well in school; I would only be wasting money. Schools here were not cheap. Maybe mother saw through me. She said, "Just try your best. Don't worry about the rest."

SOURCE: Hu Yan, "Rebirth," 2007. Unpublished essay. Trans. Kongli Liu.

Go to **www.chinasince1644.com** for the full text of **Document 18.3**.

---

[6] *Jiaozi* are dumplings filled with meat and vegetables. Very popular in China, they take a long time to prepare.

DOCUMENT 18.4: Excerpt from "Bridge over the Digital Divide" by Rong Jiaojiao in *China Daily*, June 2006

"The ancient farmers' houses of these Zhuang minority groups have three floors. The first is for raising animals like pigs and hens, the second is for people and the third is for storing grain and corn.

"It's a pretty smart design because it saves space and is very environment-friendly," said 11-year-old Tang Zijun, a fifth-grader at Haizhuzhonglu Elementary School in Guangzhou and one of the provincial capital's 10 million residents.

Tang is talking about the PowerPoint photos she just received from Tong Jingyan, a student of Jingxi Pilot Elementary School of the Guangxi Zhuang Autonomous Region, 688 kilometres west of Guangzhou.

In the county town of Jingxi, where 99 per cent of the population of 580,000 is Zhuang minority, Tong is studying photos of ancient Guangdong farmhouses taken on Tang Zijun's recent school field trip....

This exchange forms just one small link in a United Nations Children's Fund (UNICEF) distance education project launched last year. The project involves fifteen primary schools in Guangxi and Chongqing Municipality, and seven schools in Guangdong and Anhui provinces and Shanghai. Students were divided into groups to conduct research on the same topic, exchange ideas and discuss their findings in a chat room at the project website (http://www.isnet.org.cn).

SOURCE: Rong Jiaojiao, "Bridge over the Digital Divide," *China Daily*, June 2006.

Go to **www.chinasince1644.com** for the full text of **Document 18.4**.

DOCUMENT 18.5: Excerpt from "Too Big, Too Fast" by Feng Jianhua in *Beijing Review*, October 27, 2005

In the 1980s, Shenzhen was supposed to hold 800,000 people. In the city's 10th Five-Year Plan (2001–05), the population capacity was limited to 4.8 million. Today, with 12 million people crowded into the city, crises loom ahead.

A major problem is the water supply. Shenzhen is listed as one of China's seven thirstiest cities, with its per-capita freshwater resources comprising a quarter of the national average. Even if the population decreases to 7.5 million in 2010, the city will still be facing a water shortage of 1.6 billion cubic meters a year. The local government is fully aware of the grave situation and warns Shenzhen's future development will collide with four major crises—diminishing land resources, water and energy shortages, overpopulation and weakening environmental sustainability.

Shenzhen, one of the earliest special economic zones in China, is a test balloon for the country's reform and opening-up policy. What the city is facing now may afflict other cities in the future. If and how Shenzhen will cope with its problems has great meaning to cities around the country.

SOURCE: Feng Jianhua, "Too Big, Too Fast," *Beijing Review*, 27 Oct. 2005.

Go to **www.chinasince1644.com** for the full text of **Document 18.5**.

DOCUMENT 18.6: Excerpt from "Bigger Net, Better Net" from the *Beijing Review*, February 1, 2012

For more than 30 years after the founding of the People's Republic of China in 1949, those living in urban areas were entitled to nearly free medical services.

However, when China began its economic restructuring in the early 1980s, the old system was dismantled as the country attempted to switch to a market-oriented health care system.

But soaring medical bills plunged many into poverty and made medical services less affordable to ordinary citizens.

The Chinese Government admitted in 2005 that the previous reform was "basically unsuccessful," and started a new round of reform in 2009.

In April 2009, China unveiled a blueprint for its health care system reform over the next decade.

The plan's eventual goal is to establish a universal health care system for the country by 2020, giving people access to affordable public hospitals, clinics and other health care facilities as well as extensive coverage from public medical insurance.

SOURCE: Yin Pumin, "Bigger Net, Better Net," *Beijing Review*, 1 February 2012.

Go to **www.chinasince1644.com** for the link to Document 18.6.

DOCUMENT 18.7: Excerpt from "The Price of Health" by Tan Wei in *Beijing Review*, February 2, 2006

Liu is a farmer from Xinxiang, Henan Province, one of the biggest sources of labor in the country. Since 1999, he has been trying his luck in Beijing with several of his friends. A year-long, hard-earned wage from the farmland was about 1,000 yuan ($807)....

Liu lives on site in a temporary structure made of cardboard. Taking up most of the 15-square-meter floor space are six beds, some piled with washbowls, mess tins, bedding and luggage. The room is bitterly cold. According to Liu, most migrants cannot afford the costly medicine and hospitalization when they fall ill. They would rather grin and swallow medicine to help cure common diseases such as a cold. "We can't afford the time off to see a doctor, as we lose money," he complained....

SOURCE: Tan Wei, "The Price of Health," *Beijing Review*, 2 Feb. 2006.

Go to **www.chinasince1644.com** for the full text of Document 18.7.

DOCUMENT 18.8: Excerpt from "Holiday Season" by Zhang Zhiping in *Beijing Review*, January 26, 2006

Christmas is becoming increasingly popular among the Chinese, although originally it was heavily promoted by businesses. For the holiday last month, in the bustling

Xidan commercial district in downtown Beijing, a large shopping mall put up Christmas trees, welcoming visitors to write down their Christmas wishes and hang the notes on the trees. In just one or two days, the trees were filled with all kinds of Christmas messages, such as, "I wish those who love me and whom I love happiness in the next year," "May God bless my parents' health and happiness," or "I hope my girlfriend will be accepted at renowned universities."

Sociologists say the rising popularity of Christmas is due to the cheerful and bright colors associated with the holiday. Red is the most favored holiday color in China, representing harmony and indicating a happy event. On Christmas Day, people may find that Santa Claus and traditional red Chinese lanterns go well together.

SOURCE: Zhang Zhiping, "Holiday Season," *Beijing Review*, 26 Jan. 2006.

Go to **www.chinasince1644.com** for the full text of Document 18.8.

DOCUMENT 18.9: Excerpt from "Still Brewing" by Lu Ling in *Beijing Review*, January 19, 2006

Teahouses in today's China have emerged to become fashionable. The old-style teahouse is becoming trendy, while newly built teahouses are adapting to the needs of modern society. "Tea drinking and tasting tradition was born along with China's folk culture and stamped with Chinese flavor," said Professor Wang Congren at the Shanghai Normal University. "Its recent rejuvenation is a signal showing that city people are searching for the tradition and roots of the nation, by exploring their peculiar social functions and meanings."…

Professor Wang analyzed that contemporary teahouses embrace at least three new functions. First, teahouses not only provide a chance to sip fine teas, but also provide a place for entertainment. Customers regard them as information distribution centers. The second lies in the matter of culture. Although people drink tea to satisfy their taste and thirst, there is also a healthy aspect on a psychological level and the aesthetic manner in which tea is drunk. Third, there are networking opportunities. Valuable business contacts are made in teahouses as they have always maintained the function of being communication hubs.

SOURCE: Lu Ling, "Still Brewing," *Beijing Review*, 19 Jan. 2006.

Go to **www.chinasince1644.com** for the full text of Document 18.9.

DOCUMENT 18.10: Excerpt from "Quick, Pass Me A Burger!" by Tang Yuankai, *Beijing Review*, April 14, 2005

As lifestyles change, Chinese are taking to fast foods in a big way. Unlike earlier times, they too are hankering after speed, efficiency, convenience and taste. "More people, working under tight schedules, have no time for trivialities like cooking and dining," affirms Ying Hua [a lecturer at Beijing University]. Indeed, many a business is thriving on China's "fast food survival." The fact that it is lucrative has only ushered in more competition, leaving the fast food "connoisseur" spoilt for choice. Coming back to Ying and his classmate. They have a pleasant lunch [of frozen *jiaozi*] that took just 20 minutes to put together....

SOURCE: Tang Yuankai, "Quick, Pass Me a Burger!" *Beijing Review*, 14 April 2005.

 Go to **www.chinasince1644.com** for the full text of Document 18.10.

DOCUMENT 18.11: Excerpts from "Should a Lack of Filial Piety Be Penalized?" a Forum article in *Beijing Review*, February 23, 2006

At the end of January, as the Chinese traditional lunar New Year was drawing near, the local community office of Nanjingdonglu in Shanghai issued new rules requiring children to pay regular visits to their parents living in the community. According to the provisions, children must visit their parents or bring them to their own homes to spend a weekend every one or two weeks, and visit them on state stipulated holidays. If they do not have the time, they can send their spouse or children to visit instead.

Under these rules, if children fail to fulfill the requirements for one or two months, they will be given a friendly reminder. If they refuse to visit their parents after three months, however, they will be "blacklisted" by having their name posted on the community bulletin board. The community office also would send a letter to their workplace, detailing and criticizing their un-filial behavior.

SOURCE: Zhang Zhiping, "Should a Lack of Filial Piety Be Penalized?," *Beijing Review*, 23 Feb. 2006.

Go to **www.chinasince1644.com** for the full text of Document 18.11, including samples of responses generated by this regulation.

DOCUMENT 18.12: "Wedding Bells?" by Lu Lin, *Beijing Review*, May 18, 2006.

For Chinese women, marriage has always been a blend of the bitter and the sweet, but as Chinese society advances, women's attitudes toward marriage are undergoing subtle changes. They are being encouraged to develop their own understanding of marriage and to seek a happy life for themselves....

Fan Fang, a senior translator in a foreign-invested company, holds a viewpoint that also is popular among young professional women. "At the age of 27, I still have quite a lot of things to do. I'm eager for opportunities to study further for my master's degree or to improve my work capability abroad, so why should I get married so early? There are many available young men around me, but I'm afraid that marriage and family life will block me from doing better in my work. To be frank, I won't sacrifice too much for marriage, especially when the ideal partner has not come yet."

SOURCE: Lu Lin, "Wedding Bells?," *Beijing Review*, 18 May 2006.

Go to **www.chinasince1644.com** for the full text of Document 18.12.

DOCUMENT 18.13: "Governing Gender" by Lan Xinzhen in *Beijing Review*, March 23, 2006

On March 1, the research institution under the All-China Women's Federation published a green paper on Chinese women, the nation's first-ever paper by a research institution on the advancement of Chinese women and situation of gender equality in China. The paper is a collection of research results, ideas and practical experiences from experts, scholars and people working in fields related to women. It provides a general overview of the situation of women in China, and offers references for enhancing work on their advancement.

The paper points out that despite the increasing influence women have in politics, challenges are ahead. For example, the proportion of female cadres, especially in top government leadership, is still relatively small and most female cadres hold only deputy positions. The paper also notes that the proportion of female members of villagers' affairs committees is dropping.

Apart from the above-mentioned challenges, the shortage of female cadres poses a significant problem. Many female government officials are approaching retirement age, but the next generation of female cadres hasn't yet grown up. "Even organizations which are most obviously suitable for women, such as the All-China Women's Federation and Family Planning Office, face a shortage of female officials," Duan said.

Source: Lan Xinzhen, "Governing Gender," *Beijing Review*, 23 Mar. 2006.

 Go to **www.chinasince1644.com** for the full text of **Document 18.13**.

DOCUMENT 18.14:
"Earning Their Keep" by Yuan Yuan in *Beijing Review*, May 18, 2011

Yi Rongrong, a postgraduate student at the Communication University of China in Beijing, describes her job-hunting process as a "bumpy road," though she has a good record in the university with quite a few scholarships and internship experiences at Xinhua News Agency and People's Daily, two of the leading media organizations in China.

Majoring in journalism, Yi wants to work in a media company. "I sent resumes to major media outlets in Beijing, but for most of them, I didn't even get a chance for a writing test," said Yi.

According to Yi, male students in her class, even some with much worse exam records than her, were more popular and get more offers. "Media outlets like male workers, as media work is very hard and tiring and women are considered to have fewer advantages in this regard," said Yi.

Source: Yuan Yuan, "Earning Their Keep," *Beijing Review*, 18 May 2011

 Go to **www.chinasince1644.com** for the link to **Document 18.14**.

Activities

NOTE: Many of the readings in this lesson mention figures in RMB or Chinese *yuan*. In some cases, the writer has given the dollar "equivalent." However, it is problematic to convert Chinese salaries to salaries in Europe, the United States, and many other countries because the purchasing power of 1 dollar or 1 euro is much higher in China than in most Western countries. Dr. Zheng Shiping, an expert in comparative politics, explains that for a more accurate sense of what an RMB figure represents, one can consider that 6.3 *yuan* are roughly equivalent to a U.S. dollar in terms of what that money can buy. Another way to compare is to consider that an unmarried white-collar worker in his or her early twenties living in a large city in China earns between 5700 and 7800 *yuan* per month, and that this salary places him or her at the lower end of the emerging middle class, but without prospects of ever owning a small apartment unit. See Chapter 18 Activity Websites on the companion website for the "Big Mac Index" periodically published by the *Economist*, an excellent resource to get a sense of comparative purchasing power.

ACTIVITY 1: Writing about China Based on Photographs

View slide show 18.1 of photographs taken in China in the past few years. Also see Chapter 18 Activity Websites on the companion website for photos on "The Great Divide." Choose two images that show contrast. Write a one-paragraph news article about contrasts in China illustrated by your photographs. You will read peers' paragraphs in a small group and then discuss: what are the overall impressions you get of present-day China from the photographs?

NOTE: Chapter 1 includes an additional slide show of China's rural landscape.

ACTIVITY 2: Individual Stories from "the New China"

After reading the introductory essay, you will be assigned to a team of three or four. Divide the four excerpts in Document 18.2 among members of the group. After reading the assigned accounts, report back to the group.

- The name and gender of a key individual(s) from your story.
- A summary of the account as well as an explanation of how economic changes in China have affected the individual in your account.

Discuss in your group how these accounts fit with your image of China. What is the meaning of the phrase "the American dream"? Do any of these stories reflect a "Chinese dream," and how would you define *that* dream? What changes in Chinese society have made this possible? Be prepared to share your group's ideas with the class.

ACTIVITY 3: Reading Teenagers' Narratives

Begin by reading the stories written by children of migrant workers living and working in Beijing (18.3). You will discuss as a class:

"Hard Life"

1. What factors caused the family to split up?

2. Why was the girls' mother reluctant to allow the elder sister to go to school?

3. At one point, the author acknowledges that being on their own allowed the girls to become more independent. What activities did the girls partake in that might be hard to imagine a Western child or teenager taking on?

4. In light of the parents' level of hardship and sacrifice, how can one account for the continued high level of migration within China?

"Rebirth"

1. Why did Hu Yan name her narrative "Rebirth"?

2. The writing demonstrates a good deal of introspection, but some gaps in the story are evident. Identify some of those gaps. Why might the author have left out certain elements?

3. What made the biggest impression on you as you read the two narratives, and why?

Extended Activity:

You will break into teams of three or four and adapt the settings and circumstances of one of the accounts to India, the United States, Mexico, or South Africa by writing a narrative of similar length. After you have finished, discuss with your team what you had to alter and why. What stayed the same, and why? Discuss whether it was easy or hard to adapt the story. How did the new set of narratives differ from each other?

ACTIVITY 4: Taking on the Work of Task Forces

In this activity, you will take on the role of members of municipal task forces responsible for addressing some of the formidable challenges China faces.

Issue #1: The technology gap between rural and urban China

Issue #2: The growth of Chinese cities

Issue #3: Migrant and rural health care

Work in teams of four or five; each team will explore one issue. After reading the assigned documents (18.4–18.7), responding to the questions (Item 18.A on the companion website), doing further research, and discussing the issue, each "task force" will prepare a public statement of approximately one page in length. Choose one person from your team to present your statement to the class.

ACTIVITY 5: The Impact of Westernization on Chinese Culture

Choose one of the three articles to read (18.8–18.10). After you have read and answered questions related to your article (Item 18.B on the companion website), you will share information about the article with your classmates and discuss:

1. Do Chinese traditions or holidays have a place in other cultures—in the United States, for example, or Canada? Explain.

2. Does the article about teahouses provide optimism that China will be able to retain unique aspects of its own culture in the face of rapid change? Explain, citing evidence from the text.

3. How has China adopted the fast food business? What may be some of the consequences? How is this change related to culture?

Creative Extension:

Create a political cartoon or a comic strip portraying an aspect of cultural change in China.

ACTIVITY 6:
Discussing and Writing about Changing Demographics

Choose the topic that interests you most: "Sons' and Daughters' Responsibility to their Parents," "Marriage in the 21st Century," "Women in Leadership," or "Women in the Workplace." Read the articles from *Beijing Review* (18.11–18.14), answer the related questions (Item 18.C on the companion website), and complete the writing assignment.

Finally, "gather in a teahouse" in groups that include representatives from the three topics. Describe the article you read. Keep in mind the demographic changes China is undergoing, along with the increased Westernization portrayed in Activity 4, Documents 18.8–18.10. Discuss how modernization appears to have affected Chinese citizens (children, young adults, the middle-aged, seniors). Identify what appear to be problems and suggest solutions.

ACTIVITY 7: Role-playing: A Television Talk Show

In this culminating activity, you will role-play a television show hosted by your favorite talk-show host. One student will role-play the talk show host, who will pose the question, "Is change coming too quickly to China?" Other students will take on roles as Chinese citizens listed below, while the remainder of the class will act as the audience. In role-playing and devising questions, call upon information in this chapter and any additional research you have done.

Among the guests there will be a:
social worker, city planner, school teacher, migrant worker, child of a migrant worker, CEO of a Chinese auto manufacturer, architect, physician at a public hospital, nurse at a nursing home, university student, owner of a small business, or any individual about whom you have read in the articles.

EXTENDED RESEARCH:

Choose any one of the topics listed below. Working individually or in small groups, conduct research, using the most up-to-date information, and then present your findings to the class in a lecture, a visual display, or a digital presentation using a program such as PowerPoint®.

- Modernization has had an effect upon traditional Chinese architecture. In many cases, traditional buildings have been replaced by modern high-rise buildings.
  - Find out about the *hutong* in Beijing and traditional neighborhoods that are disappearing in many Chinese cities and the arguments for and against preserving them.
  - Discover the role of Western architects in China's cities. Explore the stories behind some of the most spectacular recent modern construction in major cities, such as the Olympic Stadium, the China World Trade Center Tower III, the Galaxy SOHO Complex and the Jian Wai SOHO in Beijing, the Shanghai World Financial Center, and the CITIC Plaza in Guangzhou.
- Explore the issues facing elderly people in rural China.
- Find out about marriage practices in rural China. Which traditions continue and which have changed?
- Find out about government initiatives in the past three years that aim to change the divide between life in urban and rural areas.
- Report on Dayingjie, a village in Yunnan Province that has enjoyed significant success. What factors led to this success?
- How has the Chinese government addressed the needs of the "floating population" in the past three years?
- The Chinese and foreign press have reported on hundreds of protests in China in recent years. What are the main reasons for the protests? How is the government addressing the issues?
- Find out about the degree to which the press in China is free to report.
- Find recent articles in Western and Chinese publications (for example, the *New York Times, Washington Post, Los Angeles Times, Australian Financial Review, Sydney Morning Herald, Guardian, London Times, Daily Telegraph, China Daily, Beijing Review,* etc.) about China's growing economy and consumerism. In a written summary of your reading, compare the way British, U.S., or Australian and Chinese publications report on similar topics and explore what may account for some of the differences.
- The practice of religion in China has increased dramatically in recent years. Find out about the changes and explore reasons why.

Suggested Resources

Books

Chang, Leslie T. *Factory Girls: From Village to City in a Changing China*. New York: Spiegel & Grau, 2008.
Examines the lives of female migrant factory workers in China, focusing on the experiences of two young women and including the author's story of her family's migration within China and to the West.

Chen Guidi and Wu Chuntao. *Will the Boat Sink the Water? The Life of China's Peasants*. New York: Public Affairs, 2006.
A one-sided portrayal of the plight of Chinese farmers. In particular, it focuses on their lack of legal recourse when trying to fight local corruption. In the process, it sheds some light on contemporary village life.

Florini, Ann, Hairong Lai, and Yeling Tan. *China Experiments: From Local Innovations to National Reform*. Washington, D.C.: Brookings Institution Press, 2012.
This publication explores political reform and changes in governance at the local level in China and what implications these reforms could have for the country.

Gifford, Rob. *China Road: Journey into the Future of a Rising Power*. New York: Random House, 2007.
Journalist Rob Gifford travels Chinese Route 312 from Shanghai to the border of Kazakhstan where the social and economic changes in the country are apparent all along the 3,000-mile route.

Hessler, Peter. *Country Driving: A Journey through China from Farm to Factory*. New York: Harper, 2010.
A narrative account of how the development and diffusion of cars and roads have changed China.

Hessler, Peter. *Oracle Bones: A Journey Between China's Past and Present*. New York: HarperCollins, 2006.
Chapters 2, 4, 7, 11, 17, and 22 will be of interest to readers wishing to learn about the lives of young Chinese adults in the new economy.

Watts, Jonathan. *When a Billion Chinese Jump: How China Will Save Mankind—Or Destroy It*. New York: Scribner, 2010.
An exploration of China's struggles with environmental issues and sustainability amid economic growth.

Websites

"All for One: Tracking the Course of China's 'Perfect' Generation," Usable Knowledge, Harvard Graduate School of Education **http://www.gse.harvard.edu/news-impact/2008/05/all-for-one-tracking-the-course-of-chinas-perfect-generation/**
Vanessa Fong's research about the one-child policy and its consequences is presented.

Beijing Review **http://www.bjreview.com.cn/**
The Beijing Review website provides up-to-date news and analysis on both national and international news. It is helpful for anyone interested in the increasing role that China is playing in global affairs.

The China Beat **http://www.thechinabeat.org/**
A blog written from 2008–2012 about contemporary China. Based at the University of California, Irvine, blog contributors from the United States, China, Australia, Japan, Canada, and other countries provided context for and observations about events in China.

China Daily **http://www.chinadaily.com.cn/index.html**
An English language daily newspaper published in China.

"China in the Year 2020: Three Political Scenarios" by Cheng Li **http://www.brookings.edu/research/articles/2007/07/09china**
(PDF download) An article on Asia Policy from the Brookings Institution.

Danwei **http://www.danwei.com/**
A website that tracks and analyzes Chinese state, commercial, and social media.

Moral Landscape in a Sichuan Mountain Village
http://xiakou.uncc.edu/index.htm
The Xiakou Village website hosted at the
University of North Carolina at Charlotte is a
work in progress. It explores the history, beliefs,
folklife, and economy of a village in western
Sichuan Province through long essays, images,
videos, and audio resources.

"One and Only," Ed., The Magazine of Harvard
Graduate School of Education
**http://www.gse.harvard.edu/news-impact/
2010/05/one-and-only/**
An article asking "Now that the first generation
under the one-child policy has come of age, was
modernization worth the price?"

Films

China Blue (88 mins; 2005)
A powerful documentary that captures the lives
of teen girls working in a Chinese factory that
produces denim jeans. The film provides another
perspective on what China's involvement in the
global economy means to one segment of the
population and the role Western corporations
and consumers play.

China From the Inside (3-hour, 4-part series; 2007)
This PBS documentary includes the episodes
"Power and the People," "Women of the
Country," "Shifting Nature," and "Freedom
and Justice."

China Revealed (102 mins; 2006)
A Discovery Atlas documentary that explores
where tradition meets modernity in China
today.

China Rises (208 mins; 2006)
This *Discovery Times* documentary looks at
the monumental changes unfolding in the
People's Republic of China. Video excerpts and
interviews are available on the companion
website at http://www.nytimes.com/specials/
chinarises/intro/index.html.

*To Have and Have Not: Wealth and Poverty in the
New China* (56 mins; 2002)
The dichotomy between rich and poor is
explored in this documentary from PBS's Wide
Angle. Living conditions of migrant workers are
juxtaposed against the new wealth in China's
cities, displaying economic disparities in China's
economic boom.

Up the Yangtze (93 mins; 2008)
As the Three Gorges Dam is completed,
families living along the Yangtze River are
affected in various ways. This film documents
the struggles of one family as their daughter
takes a job on one of the Yangtze River
"Farewell Cruises" and the family is forced to
leave their home for higher ground.

■ **A CLOSER LOOK**

A Pedicab in Suzhou

■ *Access the color image on the companion website to view this photo in greater detail. Discuss: How does this photograph capture the changes in twenty-first century China?*

(Photo by Elizabeth Lewis)

CHAPTER RESOURCES

Primary Sources

DOCUMENT 19.1: "My Chinese High School" by Zhang Chengyan, 2006

DOCUMENT 19.2: "Schools and Students in China," a slide show, 2004-2012

DOCUMENT 19.3: Eye exercise diagram, translated and prepared by Livia Kohn and Kirk Goetchius (only on the companion website)

DOCUMENT 19.4: Excerpts from "The Fight for Education" by Tang Yuankai, in *Beijing Review*, February 2, 2006

DOCUMENT 19.5: Essays by Dandelion School students, Beijing, 2007, 2012

DOCUMENT 19.6: American students' impressions of their stay at the Dandelion School, 2007, 2012

DOCUMENT 19.7: Excerpts from "Youth Under Pressure" by Zhang Xueying, in *China Today*, June 2006

DOCUMENT 19.8: Excerpts from "Growing Expenses" by Lu Rucai, in *China Today*, June 2006

Supplementary Materials

ITEM 19.A: Activity chart for Activity 4

 Excerpts of these primary source documents appear in this chapter. Go to **www.chinasince1644.com** for the full version of these documents and for the Supplementary Materials.

CHAPTER 19

Growing Up in China

By Kongli Liu

Chapter Contents

Key Idea

Children growing up in urban China in the twenty-first century share much with children in developed countries worldwide. However, the experiences vary greatly between children in urban areas and those in the countryside.

Guiding Questions

What are the key features of China's education system?

What are the differences in education and the experience of growing up for students in urban as compared to rural areas of China?

What does the youth culture in China look like?

Terms to Know

Gaokao

hukou system

Essay

What does it mean to be growing up in China today? It means at a very young age being motivated or pressured to study hard in pursuit of a dream for a good life; it means being exposed to unprecedented opportunities and technologies that even the parent-generation could not have imagined; it means growing up during the intersection of Chinese and Western cultures within the global village; it means being a witness and gradually a contributor to the enormous social, economic, and political transformations of one of the oldest civilizations on earth. As in any other country in the world, there is no one experience that captures "growing up in China." Unequal education resources and opportunities make the experiences of rural and urban youth, in particular, very different.

Public Education Overview

The structure of China's education system is similar to that of many other countries. It includes five to six years of primary school, a three-year junior middle school, and three years of senior middle school. Students can continue with their studies at a two- to three-year vocational school or a three- to four-year college/university, followed by post-graduate education. The 1986 Education Law in China mandates nine years of compulsory education, but in recent years it has not always been free. Before 2007, students paid a minimal tuition fee, as well as for their textbooks, school uniform, and activities. All these combined cost a family about 500–1000 *yuan*[1] a year, which may have meant little to an urban family, but could be an insurmountable burden for many rural families, whose children sometimes had to drop out for financial reasons alone. In 2001, the Chinese government began to gradually eliminate primary and junior middle school tuitions and fees in rural areas, and completed the reform at the end of 2007, a change that benefitted 158 million students.[2] In 2008, the State Council extended the elimination of fees for compulsory education to all students in urban areas. However, the primary reason for students in China not continuing education through senior middle school or college is not financial difficulty, but the highly competitive examinations.

One Exam Changes Everything

Most children in China dream of attending college, a goal which may have been deeply rooted in their minds as early as primary school. This is especially true for children in rural China because going to college and finding a job in a city probably is the only way to improve their lives and that of the next generation. One exam changes the fate of most Chinese teenagers: the *Gaokao* (the National College Entrance Examination 高考). Most colleges in China use an applicant's total score on the *Gaokao* as the single criterion in the admission process. As a result, a lot of students cannot go to college just because their scores fall below the admission score, sometimes just by one or half a point. In cities like Beijing or Shanghai, about three out of four students go to college, but in rural areas the numbers are lower, though they vary from region to region.[3] Students must take the exam in their own *hukou* (户口) region where their family is officially resident and permitted to

---

[1] About $60–$120

[2] Wen Jiabao, "Report of the Work of the Government," First Session of Eleventh National People's Congress, March 5, 2008.

[3] For those students who graduate from senior secondary schools, the percentages admitted to higher-education institutions rose from 28.7% in 1991 to 83.3% in 2010, according to statistics released by the Ministry of Education in January of 2012. The number of students enrolled in higher education in 2012 is approximately 6.85 million.

work, and different cut-off scores for university admission exist for different regions.[4]

An applicant can add up to twenty extra points to this total score if he or she falls into one of the following categories: as an award winner in an international or national academic competition, with proven talent in the arts or sports, with the performance of outstanding and recognized community services, or as the son or daughter of a non-Han minority family, an overseas Chinese family, or a family of a veteran who died or was disabled while on active duty.

Recently, changes in several aspects of the *Gaokao* have been adopted. There are now twenty versions of the test in use, with sixteen provinces or municipalities creating their own versions. With the Ministry of Education's consent, 77 universities in China—mostly top universities in the east and central regions—now choose their own modes of examination and enrollment (for fewer than 5% of their new students) rather than rely exclusively on the *Gaokao*. These alternate modes often take the form of additional exams. Some provinces are experimenting with administering more than one test for a subject, and allowing students to submit their best results. Other initiatives provide funding to help poor students from under-developed regions to improve their test scores. The *National Program for Educational Reform and Development* for 2010–2020 devotes a whole chapter to improving the college entrance system so that a single exam no longer determines a teenager's educational fate.

Exams: A Time-Honored System

Advancement through a series of exams dates back centuries in China's history. It formed the basis for China's civil service system that was created fifteen hundred years ago. The present-day version was established in 1950[5] at a time when China was very poor and educational resources limited. The country needed a relatively just system to select the best-performing students to go on to higher levels of education. However, with the fast economic growth and social changes in the past two decades (see Chapters 16–18), both the Chinese government and public have begun to realize that the education system has to be reconfigured and updated to meet the challenges and opportunities presented by globalization and the information age. As a result there is on-going national reform regarding academic standards and teaching approaches that encourage creativity and incorporate critical thinking and problem-solving skills into curricula. Also, school schedules have been restructured to allow students to engage in more extra-curricular activities.

A Curriculum Designed for Success in the Global Economy

Schools in China emphasize academics above all else. Beginning in primary school, teachers specialize in subjects, including Chinese, English, math, natural sciences, art and music, physical education, and moral education. As compared with systems in some other countries, where teachers do not specialize at the elementary level, this structure enables students to develop subject competence at a very young age. In particular, skills in English, math, and the sciences are stressed to ensure that students can compete in the global information age. Many though not all children in urban China start learning English in kindergarten (in bilingual or immersion settings) and continue through college; in vast rural areas, however,

---

[4] Students occasionally try to take advantage of the different regional entrance standards and quotas to attend university, falsifying their *hukou* to appear that they come from a less competitive region.

[5] The entire education system essentially shut down during the Cultural Revolution (see Chapter 14). Shortly after schools re-opened, the college exam was reinstated in 1977.

especially in the west, the teaching of English is limited in primary schools.[6] English is mandatory in all exams required for advancement, most exams for professional licenses/certificates, and a college degree.

Extra Academics

Many students go to after-school classes provided by public schools, individual teachers, and private schools. All the "catch-up" classes, called *buxi ban* (补习班), and private tutoring are relatively expensive, even to some urban families, but most parents want their child to have as much extra help as possible in order to have a better chance of going to college. In rural areas, however, most students have conflicting priorities after school. On the one hand, they want to have enough time to study hard and be better prepared for the *Gaokao*. On the other hand, their parents need them to help with farming and other chores so that the family can make a living and keep supporting their education financially. Therefore, for many rural students, there is simply not enough time to study. After-school classes and private tutoring are a luxury to them. In fact, after-school class providers usually do not service rural areas simply because most families cannot afford them. In addition, many rural children are "left behind" as their parents migrate to urban centers in search of work, partly because of the *hukou* system that requires students to be educated in their parents' official region of work residency—to go to school elsewhere requires them to pay extra fees. This population of "left behind children" (*liushou ertong* 留守儿童) are watched over by grandparents and relatives who often cannot offer the educational support that students need at home.

Beyond the School Day

The life of urban students is comparable to that of children in developed countries. Their activities may include playing sports, watching movies and TV shows, learning music and arts, visiting museums and parks, playing computer games, surfing online, reading books, socializing with friends, going to summer camps, and traveling with family—domestically and internationally. The activities of rural children similarly may include socializing with friends, reading, and watching TV and films. Often, rural children's lives also involve work responsibilities, time spent outdoors, and locally available forms of entertainment such as games and performances.

Urban Youth Culture

The young generation in China today is experiencing and creating an urban youth culture that embodies two of the most important themes in the world today: globalization and information technology. Young Chinese are very curious about the activities of young people in other parts of the world. They watch movies and listen to music from the United States, Hong Kong, South Korea, Japan, Europe and other parts of the world; they closely follow European soccer leagues, U.S. National Basketball Association games, Formula One car races, and tennis tournaments, which are all broadcast live in China. Many of them pay a lot of attention to international relations and world news as well.

In the urban youth culture in China today, new ideas are embraced, individualities are expressed, and personal dreams are pursued. No better example can illustrate this than the sensational *Super Girl* (*Chaoji Nüsheng* 超级女声), a singing contest show similar to *American Idol* launched by a local Hunan TV station in 2004. In 2005 alone, the show attracted more than 150,000 participants and 100 million votes via text messaging. The event even sparked a discussion of democracy and political reform in China. People joked that the winner was the first "democratically" elected public figure in Chinese history.

---

[6] An estimated 240 million students are learning English in China today.

In addition to *Super Girl*, 2011 saw the reality dating show *If You Are the One* (*Feicheng Wurao* 非诚勿扰) become an instant success among college-aged youth and its unique format spread around the world. The show features a male contestant who is questioned by 24 potential dates. As the questioning continues, unimpressed girls tap out of the competition until the man is left with only a few options (or none!). The show aroused censorship from the Chinese government who argued that the contestant's emphasis on wealth as a prerequisite for a potential partner as being detrimental to Chinese culture and the health of relationships. However, many youth now support the idea that love should not be determined by money. This can be seen with the popularity of the TV drama, *Naked Wedding* (*Luo Hun* 裸婚). This show celebrates young couples who forgo the usual prerequisites of owning a house and car before getting married, and instead opt for a life rich in support and love. These two shows demonstrate an ongoing tension between Chinese youth and their aspirations for the future. On one hand, they are seeking material success. On the other hand, they are beginning to reevaluate the values that the generations before them have held.

While youth culture in China today is influenced by Western pop culture, there has also been a revival of and renewed appreciation for traditional Chinese culture among young people and in the society as a whole. A growing number of students go to classes to learn traditional Chinese painting, music, or calligraphy, and many of them are pursuing dreams of being an artist in traditional Chinese arts.

Meanwhile, globalization provides young people with opportunities to see the intersection between Chinese and other cultures. One of the most popular songs in China in 2006 was by Wang Lee Hom, a Chinese-American who expertly mixed together hip-hop music, rap, and elements from traditional Beijing Opera. In 2012, Taiwanese-American NBA player Jeremy Lin became a star in both Taiwan and the PRC, sparking a phenomenon known as "Linsanity." The Chinese are also witnessing the increasing popularity of their native Chinese idols, such as basketball player Yao Ming and actress Zhang Ziyi among young people in other countries.

Information technology plays an increasingly important role in China's urban youth culture today. Chinese youth use a set of social networking tools that parallel those of the United States, including Weibo (like Twitter), RenRen (like Facebook), and QQ (software for instant messaging and social communities). Online social networks allow youth to socialize and find friends in an increasingly mobile world. These virtual communities allow youth to share artwork and music, organize activities, or even start social and business enterprises online. Moreover, smartphones and the use of apps are now becoming prevalent amongst Chinese youth, meaning that they can carry their online communities with them wherever they go.

Primary Sources

DOCUMENT 19.1:
"My Chinese High School," by Zhang Chengyan, 2006

In my grade, there were nearly one thousand students divided into fourteen classes when I was in Grade 10. Every class has sixty to sixty-five students, and we stayed all day long in the same classroom with the same students. We had the same level of courses if we were in the same grade, and there is no AP or Honor courses. Because there were so many students have the same level of courses, schools arranged different schedules for different classes every day, and there are two to three teachers teaching the same subject for different classes.

In China, when we are in Grade 10, we have chance to choose area in which we are more interested, humanities or science. After we choose the area, we have fewer classes on the other area and by 12th grade none at all....

We do not need to run to different classroom for different classes, teachers come into our classroom for each class period. Every class has its own head teacher to not only teach one subject but in charge of daily affairs for the whole class, such as holds assembly for class every Monday, and contacts with parents when students have any problems. The head teacher arranges seats for students at the beginning of the year, so everybody has their own seat and it is unchangeable. It is the same for every class...

 Go to **www.chinasince1644.com** for the full text of **Document 19.1**.

DOCUMENT 19.2: Photograph from the slide show "Schools and Students in China," 2004-2012

(Photo by Jim Brown)

 Go to **www.chinasince1644.com** for the slide show "Schools and Students in China," **Document 19.2**.

DOCUMENT 19.3: Eye Exercise Diagram, translated and prepared by Livia Kohn and Kirk Goetchius

 Go to **www.chinasince1644.com** for the diagram and text of **Document 19.3**.

DOCUMENT 19.4: Excerpts from "The Fight for Education" by Tang Yuankai, in *Beijing Review*, February 2, 2006

As more rural laborers flock into cities in the search for employment–about 100 million[7] are moving between the countryside and cities, making up 10 percent of the country's total population–the education of their children has become a major concern. And it's an issue not only disturbing the parents, but also the government and society at large. According to conservative statistics from relevant departments, 7 million children in this group are at the school age of six to fourteen, and should be engaged in the nine-year compulsory education program.

Due to the current residential registration system, farmers are deprived of the same treatment as urban residents in education opportunities, social welfare and other areas. In recent years, however, changes have begun to take place....

SOURCE: Tang Yuankai, "The Fight for Education," *Beijing Review*, 2 February 2006.

Go to **www.chinasince1644.com** for the full text of **Document 19.4**.

DOCUMENT 19.5: Essays by Dandelion School students, Beijing, 2007, 2012

The Dandelion School is a middle school that serves children of migrant workers.

I'm from Yangou village, Tianshui, Gansu Province. Because my family was poor, my parents left for cities to make a living when I was very young. I was living with my grandparents, who never went to school. They couldn't control me. Nobody asked me about my school day when I was back home after school. Another excuse for my not studying hard was that I had to help with farming and raising cattle for my family. I failed exams and skipped classes sometimes. I was even thinking about dropping out of school and going with my classmates to a city to work. Finally, my grandparents had no choice but to ask my mother for help. With help from relatives, I was brought to Beijing to go to school.

When I entered the gate of the Dandelion School, I saw a lot of kids with similar conditions like mine. I also realized that all of them are not Beijing natives, but from "five lakes and four seas"—all over the country. They just attend school here. At the beginning, I never listened to teachers and didn't concentrate in class. But with teachers' help, I began to realize the importance of study and that studying can actually be a joyful thing. Since then, I have decided to study hard and to not disappoint those people who have helped me....

SOURCE: Yan Zhiheng (student at Dandelion School, Beijing), unpublished essay, 2007. Trans. Kongli Liu.

Go to **www.chinasince1644.com** for the full text of **Document 19.5**.

[7] Current estimates are significantly higher.

DOCUMENT 19.6: An American student's impressions of his stay at the Dandelion School, 2011

"If I do well on the exam, I go to Guangzhou. If I do badly, I go back to Sichuan for high school," Jodie explained. Her calm countenance surprised me as she spoke about two polarizing paths, neither of which were certain. Here in Beijing, Jodie's parents cram themselves into a one room apartment, barely able to support her education with their factory jobs. If Jodie tests into a competitive high school, she might have the chance to pursue a dream that could allow her to transcend the poverty of her daily life. If Jodie moves back to Sichuan, closer to her grandparents, she would most likely be trapped in poverty, unable to fulfill her goal of becoming a nurse. Yet here she was, discussing the dilemma as calmly as if she were talking about the weather. I wasn't sure if I could be as calm if I were faced with the same choices. Despite the age and gender gap, I have learned a lot from her.

SOURCE: Anthony Yu, Winchester, MA, unpublished essay, 2012.

 Go to **www.chinasince1644.com** for the full text on Document 19.6 of Anthony's experience as well as the experiences of other students.

DOCUMENT 19.7: Excerpts from "Youth Under Pressure" by Zhang Xueying, in *China Today*, June 2006

Too much pressure and not enough sleep are common problems among China's primary and middle school students. One out of every three students suffers psychological problems, and 66.6 percent find it hard to fulfill their burden of study, according to a survey of 20,000 students in 500 classes at Beijing's primary and middle schools by the Psychology Institute of the Chinese Academy of Sciences. Educators say that although today is an era of freedom and opportunity for Chinese youth, it is also one of unprecedented pressure, particularly in cities....

SOURCE: Zhang Xueying, "Youth Under Pressure," *China Today*, June 2006.

 Go to **www.chinasince1644.com** for the full text of Document 19.7.

DOCUMENT 19.8: Excerpts from "Growing Expenses" by Lu Rucai, in *China Today*, June 2006

The average urban, middleclass, young Chinese adult would not be seen dead in footwear other than that bearing the Nike, Reebok or Adidas label. Personal gadgetry of no less than digital camera, handset and MP3 is also mandatory for members of this trend-conscious social sector.

The need of young people to be instantly identifiable with their peer group by virtue of garb, hairstyle and accessories is nothing new. But exorbitant price tags on the image enhancers demanded by today's market economy generation set them apart from those of their antecedents....

SOURCE: Lu Rucai, "Growing Expenses," *China Today*, June 2006.

 Go to **www.chinasince1644.com** for the full text of Document 19.8.

Activities

ACTIVITY 1: An Overview of Schools in China

Read the introductory essay up to "Beyond the School Day" and the description of Chinese schools by a teenager from Yunnan Province (19.1), and look at the slide show with photographs of schools (19.2 on the companion website). In small groups, you will share your impressions of the schools and the education system. What surprised you? Where do the strengths lie? What appear to be weaknesses?

ACTIVITY 2: Exercising Your Eyes

Follow the instructions for exercising your eyes (19.3 on the companion website). For the best effect, traditional Chinese music should be playing while you do this. Eye exercises often take place at the beginning or during the middle of the class, since the exercises can also help a person renew his or her concentration. How did you feel during and after you did the exercises? Why do you think every Chinese student does these exercises daily?

ACTIVITY 3:
Exploring Education for Children of Migrant Workers

Part 1: Respond to Reading

Refer to Chapter 18 for more information about the migrant or "floating" population. Read the article about education for children of migrant workers (19.4) and the essays by some of the children themselves (19.5). See Chapter 19 Activity Websites on the companion website for additional resources related to this activity. Identify on a map the provinces from which the Dandelion School students come and their distance from Beijing. You will consider as a class:

1. How is the government responding to the educational needs of the children of migrant workers?

2. What are the obstacles to implementation of existing policies?

3. What stood out for you most about the student essays? What would you like to know more about? Compare each student's life to your own.

4. How do the essays contribute to your understanding of the lives of China's floating population?

Creative Extension:

Write a dialogue between a Chinese migrant student and an immigrant student in the United States. Highlight the challenges they each face along with the similarities and differences.

Part 2: Discuss

Read about the experiences of American students who spent a week at the Dandelion School (19.6). Prepare to discuss with a partner:

1. What is most striking about these accounts?
2. Why do you think the Chinese students were so warm and welcoming?
3. How did the American students react to this experience? Why?
4. What is the impact of this kind of student experience?

ACTIVITY 4: Comparing After-School Activities

Before reading the chapter essay fill in the top row of the Activity Chart (Item 19.A on the companion website) with your typical activities. Next, fill in the second row, writing what you *guess* Chinese students do in their free time. Read the last section of the introductory essay. Working in small groups, divide up Documents 19.7 and 19.8. See Chapter 19 Activity Websites on the companion website for additional resources related to this activity. Exchange what you learned from your reading with others in the group. Based on what you now know, fill in the bottom rows of the chart. Discuss:

1. If your initial guesses regarding Chinese students' activities were different from what you learned, what accounts for the differences?
2. Create a Venn Diagram showing the similarities and differences between students in urban and rural China. Why do these differences exist?
3. Compare your activities to those of many Chinese students. What can you conclude about Chinese education and culture based on this information?

ACTIVITY 5: Debate: Should the *Gaokao* Be Abolished?

You will be in one of three groups: a pro-*Gaokao* group, an anti-*Gaokao* group, or the Ministry of Education. Read "Battling *Gaokao*," linked under Chapter 19 Activity Websites on the companion website. In your group, you will discuss what you've learned about the national exam, and compare it to exams with which you are familiar (e.g. the SAT, the ACT, or A-levels). The pro and con groups will prepare their arguments and debate the question. The Ministry of Education will research recent policy decisions about the *Gaokao*, and then observe the debate. After the debate, the Ministry of Education group must summarize the advantages and disadvantages of the *Gaokao* and come up with a realistic plan for the future of the exam.

ACTIVITY 6: Rural Education Over Time

Refer to Chapter 10, Document 10.3 (James Yen's efforts at rural education in the early 1920s) and Chapter 1, Document 1.2 (Fei Xiaotong's 1936 study *Peasant Life in China*). Compare the details of education in rural China described in those documents to the information you have learned in this chapter. What has changed over time? What challenges remain?

ACTIVITY 7: Design a Combined School

You will work in a small group to design a school that optimizes the benefits of your school and Chinese schools. Consider what the purpose will be of an education a student receives at your school and all the elements that will need to be in place to achieve that goal. You will present your school plan to the rest of the class as if they were the members of the school board with the authority to approve your plan. "Board members" should take notes on all the proposals (in other words, all plans except their own).

NOTE: The activity can be broadened to include such elements as a design for the school campus, a promotional school brochure, or a school theme song.

Writing Extension:

You will choose the strongest school proposal and write a memo from you as a "board member" to the superintendent of the school district explaining why you think it is the best proposal.

Suggested Resources

Books

Fong, Vanessa. *Only Hope: Coming of Age Under China's One-Child Policy*. Stanford: Stanford University Press, 2004.
This book by an anthropologist is the first in-depth study of the experiences of the first generation of children born under China's One-Child Policy.

Ma Yan. *The Diary of Ma Yan: The Daily Life of a Chinese Schoolgirl*. Ed. Pierre Haski. Trans. Lisa Appignanesi. New York: HarperCollins, 2005.
Written by a young teenager from Zhangjiashu village in Ningxia Province. Ma Yan's diary covers September through December 2000 and July through December 2001.

Websites

Battling *Gaokao*, China Daily
http://www.chinadaily.com.cn/china/2011-06/08/content_12658602.htm
A website about National University Entrance Exams. It includes statistics, photos, and articles about *gaokao* preparations.

China Education and Research Network
http://edu.cn/english_1369/index.shtml
A government-supported project that includes statistics, reports, history, laws, and news about China's education system.

China Prep, Wide Angle, PBS
http://www.pbs.org/wnet/wideangle/episodes/china-prep/introduction/810/
A companion website to the documentary *China Prep* with articles, interviews, and further resources about education in China.

Chinese Education: How Do Things Work?
http://www.open.edu/openlearn/languages/chinese/chinese-education-how-do-things-work
An article from The Open University providing insight into the Chinese education system.

Chengdu Youths Discuss Life in China, NPR
http://www.npr.org/templates/story/story.php?storyId=90781897
Eight Chinese young adults talk about their hopes and what they want people to know about their country.

Rural Education Action Project
http://reap.stanford.edu/
A center at Stanford University dedicated to closing the education gap between urban and rural China. The site includes video documentaries, slideshows, reports, and information about education in China.

Films

Children of Hangzhou: Connecting with China (2010)
Four teens from Hangzhou, China, describe their lives and perspectives about what it means to be a teenager in China in the twenty-first century.

China Prep: Shaping the Next Generation of Chinese Leadership (57 mins; 2009)
This documentary follows five Chinese students in their final year at an elite public high school.

Not One Less (106 mins; 1999)
This film tells the true story of Wei Minzhi, a fourteen-year-old girl who is ordered to a remote impoverished village in Hebei Province to work as the substitute teacher.

One Day in Ping Wei (30 mins, 2004)
New Year in Ping Wei (30 mins; 2005)
Return to Ping Wei (30 mins; 2007)
Filmed entirely on location in Ping Wei, a small village on the banks of the Huai He River within the city limits of Huainan. Follow Liu Yen Twin from age ten to fourteen as she goes to school, celebrates Chinese New Year with her family, and participates in the village's spring harvest.

■ **A CLOSER LOOK**

Dandelion Middle School

Dandelion Middle School for children of migrant workers, Beijing, April 2011
(Photo by Carolyn Platt)

■ *Working in small groups, list all the objects in the photograph, all the individuals and details related to them, and the activities taking place. Compare what you see in this photograph to your own middle school experience.*

CHAPTER RESOURCES

Primary Sources

DOCUMENT 20.1: "A Troubled River Mirrors China's Path to Modernity" by Jim Yardley in the *New York Times*, November 19, 2006

DOCUMENT 20.2: "Pollution from Chinese Coal Casts Shadow Around Globe" by Keith Bradsher and David Barboza in the *New York Times*, June 11, 2006

DOCUMENT 20.3: "Riot Police, Villagers Clash in China" from The Associated Press in *The New York Times*, January 19, 2007 (Not available on companion website)

DOCUMENT 20.4: "Over One-Third of Chinese People Using Internet" in Xinhuanet.com, January 2011

DOCUMENT 20.5: Excerpt from *Oracle Bones* by Peter Hessler, describing a nonviolent demonstration by Falun Gong followers in Tiananmen Square, Beijing

DOCUMENT 20.6: Excerpts from "What Has the Qinghai–Tibet Railway Brought to China?" by Zhang Xueying in *China Today*, October 2006

DOCUMENT 20.7: Slide show with photographs of Tibet, 2005

DOCUMENT 20.8: "Profile: Rebiya Kadeer," BBC News report on a Uyghur activist, March 17, 2005

DOCUMENT 20.9: Excerpt from "China-Taiwan Trade Ties Increase," BBC News, January 17, 2007

DOCUMENT 20.10: Excerpt from "China Takes on the World" by Michael Elliott in *Time*, January 22, 2007

DOCUMENT 20.11: "The Chinese in Africa" in *The Economist*, April 20, 2011

DOCUMENT 20.12: "Playing its Due Role" by Chen Xulong in *Beijing Review*, October 19, 2006

Supplementary Materials

ITEM 20.A: Questions for Activity 1, related to Document 20.1

ITEM 20.B: List of characters for Activity 1

ITEM 20.C: Questions for Activity 2, related to Document 20.2

ITEM 20.D: Additional activity examining the Three Gorges Dam

ITEM 20.E: Questions related to Activity 4, Documents 20.3–20.5

ITEM 20.F: Additional activities examining protests in China

ITEM 20.G: "A Brief History of Tibet"

ITEM 20.H: "A Brief History of Xinjiang"

ITEM 20.I: "A Brief History of Taiwan"

 Excerpts of these primary source documents appear in this chapter. Go to **www.chinasince1644.com** for the full version of these documents and for the Supplementary Materials.

CHAPTER 20

The Challenges Ahead

By Michael Abraham

Chapter Contents

China's Economy
Environmental Challenges
Social and Political Unrest
Tibet and Xinjiang
China and the United States

Key Idea

As China's economy continues to grow and increasing numbers of people prosper, the Chinese government faces serious challenges at home and abroad.

Guiding Questions

What challenges have a large population and rapid economic growth placed on China? How does the Chinese government plan to meet these challenges?

What concerns arise from large-scale engineering projects that dramatically alter the environment, such as the Three Gorges Dam and North-South water diversion project?

How has the Internet affected the dissemination of information and the pace of political reform in China?

How does the Chinese government plan to further integrate the autonomous regions into the "new China"?

What is the Chinese government's position regarding reunification with Taiwan? How is it similar to or different from Taiwan's position and the position of the United States?

What are the short-term and long-term implications of China's many growing trade relationships?

Terms to Know

autonomous region	geopolitical	sovereignty
developing nations	human rights	sustainable development
diplomacy	multilateral	unilateral
dissident	Security Council	World Trade Organization (WTO)

Essay

"The Chinese wouldn't put it this way themselves, but in their hearts I think they believe that the 21st century is China's century."

—Kenneth Lieberthal, former director of the National Security Council Asia desk during the Clinton Administration

To make the twenty-first century into China's century will be a difficult task because China faces many challenges in the years to come. China's economic rise has been remarkable; no other country has grown so quickly for such a sustained period of time. This growth has clearly benefited the citizens of the world's most populous nation. In 1978, 250 million Chinese lived below the official poverty line; by 2004, the number had plummeted to 26 million.[1] China's economy has grown approximately 10 percent a year (with ups and downs in between) for three decades now. Japan, South Korea, and Taiwan each had two decades of high-speed economic growth, but then slowed to more sustainable levels (and then to a virtual standstill in the case of Japan). With three decades of high-speed growth already, can China have a fourth or even fifth decade of such growth? Probably not. How its growth slows, and how fast it slows, will be critical factors affecting China in the years ahead. Moreover, China's economic transformation has come at a price, and examining the tradeoffs involved helps in gauging the scope of the coming challenges.

The Economy

China's growth, both in the Maoist and the reform era, has depended primarily on "extensive growth," that is, on increasing inputs rather than on increasing efficiency ("intensive growth").[2] This economic pattern has been shaped by the political structure, which remains at its core a mobilizational system. In the Maoist period, cadres were evaluated on how well they could mobilize people to meet political goals, whether building backyard furnaces in the Great Leap Forward or carrying out political campaigns like the Cultural Revolution. In the reform era, cadres are evaluated on how well they lead economic development. That has meant mobilizing resources and investing in factories.

China's savings rate, both corporate and personal, is remarkably high—over 50 percent of gross domestic product (GDP) in 2008— and this high savings rate has driven investment, which has averaged about 40 percent of GDP in recent years. These figures mean that China's consumption as a percentage of GDP has been low and getting lower. Whereas household consumption stood at about half of GDP throughout the 1980s, in recent years it has fallen, reaching only 35 percent of GDP in 2007.[3] With high investment and low consumption, China has looked to exports to bolster its economic growth, and China has emerged as the "workshop of the world."

China has to rebalance its economy to decrease savings and increase consumption (just as the United States has to rebalance in the opposite direction, reducing consumption and increasing savings). But rebalancing is not easy. Not only does it run counter to the political-economic structure that has driven investment-led growth, but the tools that are normally used

---

[1] C. Fred Bergsten, et al., *China: The Balance Sheet. What the World Needs to Know Now About the Emerging Superpower* (New York: Public Affairs/Center for Strategic and International Studies/Institute for International Economics, 2006) 18. In 2011 China revised its standard for considering people poor. That change is likely to increase the number of people below the poverty line by as many as 100 million. See *Forbes*, April 3, 2011. The statistics are very sensitive to the standard being used.

[2] This does not mean that there has been no improvement in efficiency (there has been), but that China remains an investment-driven economy.

[3] C. Fred Bergsten, et. al., *China's Rise* (Washington, D.C.: Peterson Institute for International Economics and Center for Strategic and International Studies, 2008) 106-109.

to foster consumption are lacking. For instance, individual taxation rates are very low in China, so cutting the tax rate is unlikely to spur consumption. Similarly, raising domestic interest rates would attract "hot money" looking for further appreciation of China's currency while squeezing the profits of state-owned enterprises. The one thing that China can and must do is to increase its expenditures on social welfare by increasing the amount the government spends on health care, pensions, and unemployment compensation.[4] But such outlays are likely to increase only slowly, suggesting that China, and the world, will have to live with imbalances for some time to come.

Energy and the Environment

China's investment-driven pattern of growth has produced remarkable growth but has not been without consequences. The environment has been one area deeply damaged by the headlong rush for economic development. The one natural resource that China has (or had) in abundance is coal, and China has exploited and expended this resource at a rapid rate and at a high cost—China used to lose some 6,000 lives a year to mine accidents, a rate cut in half in recent years through tremendous efforts. China depends on coal for about 70 percent of its energy needs, but it has invested heavily in green energy technology in recent years. It is now the world's largest producer of solar panels and is the world's largest wind energy provider. As the technology improves and costs fall, perhaps such clean energy can displace China's heavy reliance on coal.

One way in which Chinese leadership has tried to offset the heavy reliance on coal is to tap the country's hydroelectric potential. Unfortunately, doing so creates its own problems. Mega-projects such as the Three Gorges Dam (*Sanxia Daba* 三峡大坝) on the upper Yangzi River, which will generate electrical power

equivalent to that of 40 coal-burning plants, required the displacement of some 1.3 million residents and raised environmental concerns about soil erosion, excessive silting, and salinity of the lower Yangzi. Dams on rivers in the southwestern province of Yunnan present threats to wildlife, fragile ecosystems, and, depending on the river, water-flows into neighboring countries.

China's reliance on dirty energy and determined economic growth has given China the dubious distinction of being home to sixteen of the world's twenty most polluted cities. Some 300 hundred million people drink water with chemical contaminants that may not sicken them in the short term but may well do so over the long term. Nearly half of river water cannot be used for agriculture or industry. China's two main river systems—the Yellow River in the north and the Yangzi through the middle of China—are under severe strain. Famous lakes, like Kunming's Dianchi Lake, have become dead lakes—they cannot sustain fish because the pollution has exhausted the oxygen. And China is a rapidly urbanizing country. Over the next 10–15 years, some 300 million people are expected to move into cities—and these people will consume more energy and create greater waste. The challenge of providing clean energy is thus a formidable problem.

Water is China's most severe environmental challenge, not just polluted water but the lack of water. China has about 8 percent of the world's supply of fresh water and 20 percent of the world's population. Rapid industrialization and intensive agriculture are draining the nation's water aquifers faster than rain or river systems can replenish them. Moreover, the bulk of China's water resources are concentrated in the south, but the population of north China— an area encompassing about 400 million people— continues to grow. The solution to this problem has been an enormously expensive project to divert water from the Yangzi River north to the Yellow River. Environmentalists worry about rapid evaporation, lowering the water table in the Yangzi, and pollution, as well as the displacement of hundreds of thousands of people.

---

[4] Bergsten, *China: The Balance Sheet*, 120-128.

Global warming is already affecting China and seems likely to have more dramatic consequences in the future. China is already one-quarter desert, and the country is losing acreage equivalent to the size of Rhode Island to the desert every year. The Gobi Desert is now only 150 miles west of Beijing. Rising temperatures will accelerate this trend. At the same time, the rise of the sea level will threaten coastal areas. Over the second half of the twentieth century, the average global sea level rose by approximately 1.4–3.2 millimeters per year. With many coastal areas only 5 meters above sea level, these changes will affect the salinity of the soil and soil erosion as well as coastal ecosystems.[5]

Global warming will also affect the permafrost and glaciers in the Qinghai-Tibet Plateau, an area that constitutes 25 percent of China's land area. Thawing permafrost will loosen the soil around shallow tree roots, eroding topsoil, and release methane into the atmosphere. Over time, warming in the Tibet plateau will reduce water flow into China's major river systems.

The Quest for Natural Resources

In the early years of Deng Xiaoping's economic reforms, China was able to supply its own energy needs. That is no longer the case. The country's unprecedented economic development has made the safeguarding and purchase of natural resources, especially energy, an increasingly important component of domestic and foreign policy. In part, the government's determination to keep the autonomous region of Xinjiang (新疆) stable is a product of that area's huge reserves of oil and gas.[6] Regional tensions include a dispute with Japan over

reserves of oil in the East China Sea. The Chinese leadership has made overtures to India (itself in need of energy) to avoid the two countries outbidding each other for resources. In order to meet its growing needs for natural resources, the Chinese government has also turned to oil-rich regions such as the Middle East and Africa. Western nations have criticized Chinese officials for doing business with countries such as Sudan, Zimbabwe, and Iran, which are either involved in serious human rights violations or are hostile to Western interests. China has also been criticized for selling weapons and sharing advanced weapons technologies with nations such as these. The Chinese, however, maintain that they will not interfere with any other country's internal affairs, a stand supported by non-Western developing nations.

"Mass Incidents," Legitimacy, and Political Reform

Although China's economic development has been impressive, it has been unequal; inequality is widening and perceived corruption and the abuse of power at the local level is causing considerable discontent. In the 1990s and early twenty-first century, the primary problem was excessive taxation. Local officials routinely taxed rural Chinese more than they were supposed to because the tax system left them with little income to run the local government or develop the local economy. However, overtaxation created opportunities for corruption, which came to be pervasive. In 2006, the central government abolished the agriculture and other local taxes, relieving the burden on the farmers but driving local officials to find new sources of revenue. They chose land. Land in China is owned by "the collective," with the local party and government representing the collective. Under the Household Responsibility System, farmers contract the land from the collective. As land has become more valuable, the temptation to seize the land of farmers for little or no

---

[5] Information Office of the State Council of the People's Republic of China, "China's Policies and Actions for Addressing Climate Change" (Beijing, October 2008) http://www.gov.cn/english/2008-10/29/content_1134544.htm.

[6] Xinjiang is estimated to have 30 billion tons of oil, 1/3 of China's total, and 13 trillion cubic meters of natural gas.

compensation and then sell it to investors has been great. Farmers objected to being taxed excessively, and they objected even more to their land being appropriated. They expressed their discontent through "mass incidents" (*qunti xing shijian* 群体性事件), protests that could be small-scale or involve thousands of people. Mostly such mass incidents were peaceful, but sometimes they became violent, and the authorities responded with force.

Figures are unreliable because the definition of a "mass incident" has never been made clear and may well have changed over time. Local officials are also reluctant to report such incidents, because they reflect poorly on them. Nevertheless, official figures showed that there were 8,700 mass incidents in 1993 and ten times that number in 2005, when the government stopped supplying numbers. One widely publicized but unofficial number for 2010 was 180,000. Whatever the actual number, there is considerable consensus that the number of mass incidents is increasing, the number of people involved is greater, and that the seriousness of such incidents is growing. These incidents erode the legitimacy of local government, increasing the probability that there will be yet more incidents. The need for political reform of some sort is apparent.

This is not to say that people are likely to rise up and overthrow the party as in the former Soviet Union or Eastern Europe. The mass incidents that occur with some frequency tend to be very local affairs; what happens in one village or township does not affect people in another village or township. It is extremely difficult for rural people to organize across townships, much less counties. Moreover, the resources—finances, organization, and people—that the Chinese Communist Party can command remain extensive, so the party remains firmly in place. But the economic, environmental, demographic, and socio-political challenges the party faces over the coming years are very great indeed.

Xinjiang and Tibet

China's major minority areas of Tibet (西藏) and Xinjiang (新疆) are perhaps unique in that they constitute such a large percentage of China's territory. If one draws a line from Harbin (哈尔滨), the capital of China's northeast province of Heilongjiang, to Kunming, the capital of the southwestern province of Yunnan, some 92 percent of the population lies to the east of the line. The 8 percent of the population that lies to the west of the line is where Tibetans and Uyghurs (*weiwu'er* 维吾尔) (one of the major Turkish populations that live in Xinjiang) are concentrated, although many Han Chinese have moved into both of these areas in recent years. The culture and identity of these and other minority populations in these areas is quite different than that of the majority population, and that has bred conflict.

The Chinese government's control over culturally distinct minority areas is at once a domestic and international concern. Despite being integral to what China now regards as its national borders, and despite efforts to increase the presence of Han Chinese in these regions, China's rule over minority areas—especially Tibet and Xinjiang—still appears harsh to parts of the world that are sympathetic to the Tibetan cause and to Muslim nations who sympathize with Xinjiang's large Muslim population. When protests erupt, such as in March 2008 when the Olympic torch was being carried around the world, Chinese leaders claim these issues are domestic affairs that do not warrant outside interference.

China and the United States

The Chinese government has a complex relationship with the United States. The two have differed over issues such as trade imbalance, protections for intellectual property rights, valuation of the *yuan* (元), political reform, and human rights, but China's importance as a trade partner tends to prevent serious disruptions occurring. For the most part, the United States has exhibited patience with China's continued authoritarian rule, understanding how difficult it would be for that nation to move quickly toward democracy. As experts at the Center for Strategic and International Studies put it, "some research suggests that at present, there is not widespread support within the general Chinese population for Western-style democracy, and that other 'preliminary steps' are more pressing: economic opportunity, clean government, and social stability."[7] Whether this will change in the face of continuing crackdowns on democracy activists like Nobel Peace Prize winner Liu Xiaobo, artists like Ai Weiwei, and numerous "rights protection" lawyers (those who try to help the downtrodden defend against abuses of power) remains to be seen.

Although Sino-U.S. relations improved after the Bush administration's "War on Terror" began, the underlying "strategic mistrust" between the two nations continued and has grown in recent years. Incidences in 2010, such as arms sales to Taiwan and President Obama's meeting the Dalai Lama have only added to the tension between the two countries.

Assuming China's and the United States' current economic growth rates continue, China will become the world's largest economy and by far the largest trading country around 2035.[8] Since it became a member of the World Trade Organization (see Chapter 17), its booming economy has become tightly woven with that of the European Union, the United States, and Japan. Moreover, China has increasingly combined its economic leverage with its position as a permanent member of the United Nations Security Council to lend weight to global issues in which it has an interest.

Conclusion

The list of challenges China faces in the coming years is long. What this list suggests is not that China will fail to meet them but rather that it will need to change in ways that are difficult to imagine at the moment. But China has changed dramatically before, including in 1978 when Deng Xiaoping came to power. It is unlikely that a single leader like Deng can bring about the changes that are necessary, but there is no reason that intelligent leadership at various levels cannot bring about the social and political changes that are needed to meet the challenges ahead. Whether and how China deals with the various challenges will matter not only to the 1.4 billion people of China but also to the rest of the world.

---

[7] Bergsten, *China: The Balance Sheet*, 71.

[8] Bergsten, *China: The Balance Sheet*, 9.

Primary Sources

DOCUMENT 20.1: "A Troubled River Mirrors China's Path to Modernity" by Jim Yardley in the *New York Times*, November 19, 2006

For centuries, the Yellow River symbolized the greatness and sorrows of China's ancient civilization, as emperors equated controlling the river and taming its catastrophic floods with controlling China. Now, the river is a very different symbol —of the dire state of China's limited resources at a time when the country's soaring economic growth needs more of everything.

"The Yellow River flows through all these densely populated parts of northern China," said Liu Shiyin, a scientist with the Chinese Academy of Sciences. "Without water in northern China, people can't survive. And the economic development that has been going on cannot continue."

China's dynamic economic engine, still roaring at record levels, is at a corrosive crossroads. Pollution is widespread, and a nationwide construction spree, tainted by corruption, is threatening to overheat the economy. China's leaders, worried about the unbridled growth, are trying to emphasize "sustainable development" even as questions remain about whether the party's rank and file can carry out priorities like curbing pollution and conserving energy.

The Yellow River, curving through regions only intermittently touched by the country's boom, offers a tour of the pressures and contradictions bearing down on China, and of the government's efforts to address them.

SOURCE: Jim Yardley, "A Troubled River Mirrors China's Path to Modernity," *New York Times*, 19 Nov. 2006.

Go to **www.chinasince1644.com** for the link to Document 20.1.

DOCUMENT 20.2: "Pollution from Chinese Coal Casts Shadow Around Globe" by Keith Bradsher and David Barboza in *The New York Times*, June 11, 2006

The [Chinese] government has set one of the world's most ambitious targets for energy conservation: to cut the average amount of energy needed to produce each good or service by 20 percent over the next five years.... All new cars, minivans and sport utility vehicles sold in China starting July 1 will have to meet fuel-economy standards stricter than those in the United States. New construction codes encourage the use of double-glazed windows to reduce air-conditioning and heating costs and high-tech light bulbs that produce more light with fewer watts....

For the past three years, China has also been trying harder to develop other alternatives. State-owned power companies have been building enormous wind turbines up and down the coast. Chinese companies are also trying to develop geothermal energy, tapping the heat of underground rocks, and are researching solar power and ways to turn coal into diesel fuel. But all of these measures fall well short. Coal remains the obvious choice to continue supplying almost two-thirds of China's energy needs.

China must make some difficult choices. So far, the nation has been making decisions that it hopes will lessen the health-damaging impact on its own country while sustaining economic growth as cheaply as possible....

Source: Keith Bradsher and David Barboza, "Pollution from Chinese Coal Casts Shadow Around Globe," *New York Times*, 11 Jun. 2006.

 Go to **www.chinasince1644.com** for the link to **Document 20.2**.

DOCUMENT 20.3: "Riot Police, Villagers Clash in China" from The Associated Press in *The New York Times*, January 19, 2007

Hundreds of riot police clashed with villagers protesting against an alleged land grab by officials in the southern Chinese province of Guangdong, a lawyer and Hong Kong newspapers reported Friday.

"Scores of villagers, even elderly ones, were taken away by police after being beaten," said Yang Zaixin, an activist lawyer who represents farmers in land disputes. The lawyer told The Associated Press that local officials in Chongyuan village illegally seized the farmers' land without approval from the provincial and central governments. Such allegations are common in booming Guangdong Province, one of China's biggest manufacturing centers. Officials are frequently accused of forcing farmers off land, which is later sold to developers who get rich building factories and other projects.

The *South China Morning Post* reported that hundreds of police armed with rifles, shields and electric batons broke up the sit-in protest Thursday in Chongyuan, part of the Nanhai district in Foshan city. After rounding up the large group of protesters, police released most of them late Thursday afternoon, Yang said. But five were still being detained, he added. Police withdrew after clearing away the protesters, but dozens of plain-clothes officials were watching the site, the *Post* quoted a protester, Chen Huiying, as saying.

The protest site, 66 acres of farmland, was first taken over by local government in 2005. Officials claimed the site was sold to a company that planned to build a warehouse complex, the *Post* reported. A spokesman for the local government, who only gave his surname, Chen, said he "did not know about the case" and declined to provide further information.

Hong Kong's *Ming Pao Daily News* quoted one villager as saying tensions have been simmering since 1992, when local officials began seizing large tracts of land. The villager, identified only by his surname, Tang, said officials never delivered on promises to compensate villagers with monthly deliveries of rice.

Source: Associated Press, "Riot Police, Villagers Clash in China," *New York Times*, 19 Jan. 2007.

DOCUMENT 20.4: "Over One-Third of Chinese People Using Internet" in Xinhuanet.com, January 2011

BEIJING, Jan. 19 (Xinhua): The number of people using the Internet in China rose to 457 million at the end of 2010, up 73.3 million from a year earlier, the China Internet Network Information Center (CNNIC) announced Wednesday.

This meant over one-third, or 34.3 percent, of China's population was using the Internet at the end of last year.

Chinese netizens spent about 18.3 hours online every week or 2.61 hours each day, the report said.

The number of Internet users in China's rural areas totalled 125 million last year, up 16.9 percent from the previous year, thanks to improved Internet-related infrastructure.

The number of people shopping online climbed the most compared to other online services, up 48.6 percent year on year, followed by people using e-banking and online payment services, up 48.2 percent and 45.8 percent respectively.

"The traditional sectors have underpinned Internet growth over the past 10 years, and in the next 10 years the Internet will feed the traditional sectors," predicted Lu Benfu, an expert on the Internet economy at the School of Management, the Chinese Academy of Sciences.

SOURCE: "Over One-Third of Chinese People Using Internet," Xinhuanet.com, January 2011

Go to **www.chinasince1644.com** for the link to **Document 20.4**.

DOCUMENT 20.5: Excerpt from *Oracle Bones* by Peter Hessler, describing a nonviolent demonstration by Falun Gong followers in Tiananmen Square, Beijing

[A] small man directly in front of us drops into the lotus position. Shouts, commands, people running: a half-dozen plainclothes cops. By the time they force the man to his feet, a van is already speeding toward us from a far corner of [Tiananmen] Square. The protestor says nothing. He is about thirty-five years old, and he wears simple peasant clothes of blue cotton. His limbs go slack; they carry him into the van. Sheets have been tied over the windows so nobody can see inside…

[A few minutes later] a middle-aged woman tries to unfurl a banner in front of the flagpole. A plainclothes man tackles her hard. The next protestor is also a woman. She stands to the right of the flagpole and puts both arms over her head; two men run over and force her arms down….

Suddenly, there is a commotion at the flagpole. A dozen at once: men and women, shouting slogans, raising their arms. Another banner. The plainclothes men rush over; punches are thrown; people cry out. A man falls to the ground and gets kicked. Kicked again. Kicked again. One by one, the demonstrators are dragged away.

At the end, a child stands there alone. She is about seven years old, and probably she came with her mother or father, but all the adults have already been forced into the van. The girl wears a green sweater, with matching ribbons in her hair. She hangs her head as the cops march her to the vehicle.

SOURCE: Peter Hessler, *Oracle Bones: A Journey Between China's Past and Present* (New York: HarperCollins, 2006) 126–128.

Go to **www.chinasince1644.com** for the text of **Document 20.5**.

DOCUMENT 20.6: Excerpts from "What Has the Qinghai–Tibet Railway Brought to China?" by Zhang Xueying in *China Today*, October 2006

Tibet is considerably better off now than it was five years ago. Roads in Lhasa are wider and cleaner, ramshackle dwellings have been demolished and replaced with new Tibetan-style buildings and more people can afford private cars. Stores no longer resemble small workshops, and have signboards in Tibetan and Chinese and impressive facades. The post offices and public telephones most commonly seen five years ago are now vastly outnumbered by telecom companies and pharmacies, in front of which sit groups of Tibetan pilgrims. As one pharmacy assistant says, "Tibetan people pay great attention to their health, and in addition to Tibetan medicine also buy Western and traditional Chinese medicine."…

"As a Tibetan, I think the railway will bring a lot of changes that might influence the concepts of the Tibetan people," [a restaurant owner] says, thoughtfully. He cites an example. Ten years ago, Taiyang Island at the center of the Lhasa River was covered with trees, but no more. The island now has row upon row of two-storied buildings and has become the largest entertainment and gourmet center in Lhasa.

Tenzin, [a tour guide] aged 31, believes that such changes are inevitable, and that they cannot solely be attributed to the railway, which merely accelerates changes already underway. Tenzin asserts, "It is impossible to maintain the scenario of a century ago."

SOURCE: Zhang Xueying, "What Has the Qinghai–Tibet Railway Brought to China?," *China Today*, Oct. 2006.

Go to **www.chinasince1644.com** for the full text of **Document 20.6**.

DOCUMENT 20.7: **Photographs of Tibet, 2005**

Barley fields

The Jokhang Temple in Lhasa is the most revered religious building in Tibet. Its origins date back to the seventh century, and over time it has undergone many renovations. The most recent was in 1980 after Red Guards desecrated the temple during the Cultural Revolution. *(Photos by Margaret Harvey)*

 Go to **www.chinasince1644.com** for the slide show **Document 20.7**.

DOCUMENT 20.8: "Profile: Rebiya Kadeer," BBC News report on an Uyghur activist, March 17, 2005

Rebiya Kadeer was a successful businesswoman and philanthropist in China's restive Xinjiang until her arrest in 1999 for allegedly endangering national security. Her crime, the authorities said, was to send local newspaper reports about the activities of Xinjiang's ethnic Turkish-speaking [*sic*] Uighurs to her U.S.-based husband, even though these were freely available. It was a sharp reversal in fortunes for someone whose local achievements the Communist government had until then trumpeted. ...

SOURCE: "Profile: Rebiya Kadeer," BBC News Online, 17 Mar. 2005.

 Go to **www.chinasince1644.com** for the full text of **Document 20.8**.

DOCUMENT 20.9: Excerpt from "China-Taiwan Trade Ties Increase," BBC News, January 17, 2007

China's annual trade with Taiwan grew 18% to $107.8 billion (£54.8 billion) last year [2006], Chinese government figures show. China imported $87 billion worth of goods from Taiwan, up 16.6% on the year before, while Taiwanese firms invested $2.14 billion on the mainland.

Taiwanese firms have invested more than $100 billion in mainland China since the 1990s, with many manufacturers building factories there to take advantage of lower labour costs. China exported $20.7 billion worth of goods to Taiwan last year, a 25% increase on the year before.

Tourism boost

Despite restrictions on travel between the two countries, which requires most people to travel there via Hong Kong or another country, tourism has increased in recent years. According to a Chinese government spokesman, Taiwanese people made more than 4 million visits to China last year while more than 200,000 mainland Chinese visited Taiwan.

SOURCE: "China-Taiwan Trade Ties Increase," BBC News, 17 Jan. 2007.

 Go to **www.chinasince1644.com** for the text of **Document 20.9**.

DOCUMENT 20.10: Excerpt from "China Takes on the World" by Michael Elliott, *Time*, January 22, 2007

China's commitment to nonintervention means that it doesn't inquire closely into the internal arrangements of others. When all those African leaders met in Beijing [President] Hu promised to double aid to the continent by 2009, train 15,000 professionals and provide scholarships to 4,000 students, and help Africa's health-care and farming sectors. But as a 2005 report by the Council on Foreign Relations notes, "China's aid and investments are attractive to Africans precisely because they come with no conditionality related to governance, fiscal probity or other concerns of Western donors." In 2004, when an International Monetary Fund loan to Angola was held up because of suspected corruption, China ponied up $2 billion in credit. Beijing has sent weapons and money to Zimbabwe's President Robert Mugabe, whose government is accused of massive human-rights violations.

SOURCE: Michael Elliott, "China Takes on the World," *Time*, 22 Jan. 2007.

Go to **www.chinasince1644.com** for the full text of **Document 20.10**.

DOCUMENT 20.11:
"The Chinese in Africa" in *The Economist*, April 20, 2011

ZHU LIANGXIU gulps down Kenyan lager in a bar in Nairobi and recites a Chinese aphorism: "One cannot step into the same river twice." Mr Zhu, a shoemaker from Foshan, near Hong Kong, is on his second trip to Africa. Though he says he has come to love the place, you can hear disappointment in his voice.

On his first trip three years ago Mr Zhu filled a whole notebook with orders and was surprised that Africans not only wanted to trade with him but also enjoyed his company. "I have been to many continents and nowhere was the welcome as warm," he says. Strangers congratulated him on his homeland's high-octane engagement with developing countries. China is Africa's biggest trading partner and buys more than one-third of its oil from the continent. Its money has paid for countless new schools and hospitals. Locals proudly told Mr Zhu that China had done more to end poverty than any other country.

He still finds business is good, perhaps even better than last time. But African attitudes have changed. His partners say he is ripping them off. Chinese goods are held up as examples of shoddy work. Politics has crept into encounters. The word "colonial" is bandied about. Children jeer and their parents whisper about street dogs disappearing into cooking pots.

SOURCE: "The Chinese in Africa," *The Economist*, 20 April 2011

Go to **www.chinasince1644.com** for the link to **Document 20.11**.

DOCUMENT 20.12: "Playing its Due Role" by Chen Xulong in *Beijing Review*, October 19, 2006

China has attached great importance to multilateral diplomacy and has strengthened its interaction with the international system. In response to some Western countries' promotion of Western ideology and values in the economic, social and human rights fields, China advocates building a multipolar world and establishing democratic international relations. China holds that all countries should respect the diversity of human civilization and social development models, and should attach importance to the role of the UN and safeguard its authority. ...

China is one of the five permanent members of the UN Security Council, which means that it should shoulder more responsibility than most of the other UN members in maintaining world peace. To achieve world peace and stability, China must pay attention to the coordination among major countries and push forward overall international cooperation. At the same time, as a representative of developing countries, China must consider and maintain the interests of developing countries in dealing with international problems, especially on the issues of development, environmental protection, human rights and humanitarian intervention....

SOURCE: Chen Xulong, "Playing its Due Role," *Beijing Review,* 19 Oct. 2006.

Go to **www.chinasince1644.com** for the full text of **Document 20.12**.

Activities

ACTIVITY 1: Role-Play: The Impact of Rapid Development

Read about the impact of development on China's Yellow River Valley (20.1) and answer the questions (Item 20.A on the companion website). Next, role-play "In the Footsteps of Jim Yardley, Jake Hooker, and Lin Yang." You will retrace the authors' footsteps by setting up mock interviews with the individuals featured in this story (see the list of characters in Item 20.B).

- Take on the roles of Jim Yardley, Jake Hooker, and Lin Yang and the interviewees and prepare questions and responses ahead of time. Check online for up-to-date information using Chapter 20 Activity Websites on the companion website. Conversations may be more extensive than how they originally appeared.

- The "authors" should conclude the oral story by responding to the question: "Has the Yellow River been damaged beyond repair?"

Extension Activities:

1. Create your own storyboard or background scene for the interviews. Download images and create a slide show, or make a video of the story for viewing.

2. Read the sources discussing water diversion in China under Chapter 20 Activity Websites on the companion website, then debate whether China's massive water diversion project is helping or exacerbating environmental problems. Keep in mind the origin of the articles and consider any possible biases.

ACTIVITY 2: Examining the Global Ramifications of China's Reliance on Coal

Read about the problems that come from China's heavy reliance on coal (20.2) and work with a partner to answer the questions (Item 20.C). Check online sources (including some of the general websites in Suggested Resources such as "China at the Crossroads") for the most up-to-date information.

Next, the class will stage a talk show that includes environmental and energy officials from Japan, Korea, the United States, Russia, and India. You will discuss the challenges related to China's dependence on coal. Be prepared to participate in the talk show as one of the officials or as an individual from the readings such as Wu and Cao, as well as those from other readings. In staging the talk show, an anchor person will pose questions such as:

1. What are the reasons behind China's heavy reliance on coal?

2. What are the difficulties involved in implementing pollution controls?

3. What is the potential for change?

ACTIVITY 3: Class Discussion: Solving China's Environmental Problems

Sketch a "balancing scale," with one side holding China's environmental problems and the other side holding potential remedies based on suggestions in the primary sources and your ideas. Prepare to discuss:

1. Has China waited too long to start addressing its environmental problems? Depict which side of the scale is heaviest by utilizing up and down arrows to indicate motion.

2. Is China's environmental damage unique among industrial nations? Are there any positive models that China may want to consider? Is the United States in a position to advise China on its environmental challenges?

3. Would China hold any advantages compared to other nations if it were to follow through on efforts to improve the quality of its environment?

NOTE: An additional activity pertaining to the Three Gorges Dam is on the companion website (Item 20.D).

ACTIVITY 4: Dissent: Writing an Op-Ed Piece

Part 1: Respond to Reading

Documents 20.3-20.5 will be divided among class groups. Read the accounts and answer related questions (Item 20.E). (See also Item 20.F: Additional activities examining protests in China.) You will reconvene as a class and report on your reading and discussions. Then consider:

1. What have you learned about China's political problems and the government's capacity for change?

2. Is China different from any other nation? How? Why?

Part 2: Write

Imagine that you are a journalist for *China Daily* and your editor has instructed you to write a short op-ed on the pace of political reform in China. He or she has given you no indication of what your stance should be. Keep in mind that you are writing for a paper subject to government censorship. Write the op-ed and share it with your classmates.

Extended Activity: **Universal Human Rights**

Research the United Nations Universal Declaration of Human Rights (see Chapter 20 Activity Websites on the companion website). Then compare and contrast the human rights records of the permanent members of the UN Security Council (the United States, Russia, the United Kingdom, China, and France).

ACTIVITY 5: China and Its Ethnic Minorities

Part 1: Analyze: Tibet and the Qinghai–Lhasa Railway

To better understand the issues surrounding Tibet, read "A Brief History of Tibet" on the companion website (Item 20.G in Supplementary Materials). Check online for any recent developments regarding China's policies in Tibet and Tibetan protests. Then read Document 20.6 and complete the following:

1. Locate Golmud, Qinghai, and Lhasa, Tibet on a map that includes both political and physical features of China. Note the topography of the region.
2. Explain how life changed for Rintor, a Tibetan, once he took a job working on the Qinghai-Tibet railway.
3. Provide a direct quote or another piece of evidence that demonstrates the author's support for the railway.

Examine the photographs of Tibet (20.7 on the companion website).

1. What do you find most striking about the images of Tibet?
2. Note six details that you find especially interesting in the photos of Tibetan people. Why did these details stand out to you?
3. Why do you think Tibet deeply stirs many people?

Prepare for a mini-debate around the question: "Is tourism having a positive or negative impact on Lhasa?" Compose an argument that includes two pieces of evidence, paraphrased or quoted directly from the reading, that support your position.

Part 2: Respond to Reading about Xinjiang

Read "A Brief History of Xinjiang" on the companion website (Item 20.H in Supplementary Materials). Then read the profile of Rebiya Kadeer (20.8) and find out more about her activities online.

1. What appear to be the key issues in Xinjiang?
2. Why does the Chinese government appear to be so intent on controlling the region?
3. What changes have taken place among the Uyghur since 2001?

You will work in small teams to:

1. Discuss whether these regions (Tibet and Xinjiang) deserve the title *autonomous*.
2. Identify China's goals in its policies toward Tibet and Xinjiang.
3. Check online for any recent developments.
4. Discuss how Han Chinese and these two ethnic minorities might work toward a mutually beneficial future.

NOTE: See Chapter 1 for more information on China's minority peoples.

ACTIVITY 6: China and Taiwan

Part 1: Research

Read "A Brief History of Taiwan" on the companion website (Item 20.I in Supplementary Materials), information in Chapter 16 related to the relationships among Taiwan, China, and the United States, and Document 20.9 about the increased trade. Also refer to Suggested Resources. Conduct research online to get a clear sense of the current situation.

Be prepared to address the following questions:

1. When and why did Taiwan become known as the Republic of China and begin to function as a separate entity from mainland China?
2. After Chiang Kai-shek and the Guomindang government moved to Taiwan in 1949 (see Chapter 12), why did the United States continue to recognize the Guomindang as the government of all of China rather than recognize the Communist government in Beijing?
3. Why did the People's Republic of China take the place of Taiwan in the United Nations in 1971?
4. Why did the United States shift its diplomatic recognition from Taiwan (the Republic of China) to the People's Republic of China in 1979? What does it mean to "recognize" a country?
5. What are the key provisions of the (U.S.) Taiwan Relations Act of 1979? (See Chapter 16, Document 16.5)
6. What have "trilateral" relations been like among the United States, China, and Taiwan since the late 1970s?

Part 2: Write

Consider each of the options listed below and write out possible reasons for supporting the course of action, as well as concerns regarding the option.

Option 1 – China should set a timetable for reunification with Taiwan.
Option 2 – Taiwan should declare itself independent.
Option 3 – The United States should take a more active role in bringing about a political solution.
Option 4 – Everyone should allow time and increased trade to resolve the issue.
Option 5 – Create your own option.

Choose what you consider to be the best option and draft a one-page statement that outlines your stance and rationale. Your statement should contain two or three specific pieces of evidence from the sources. Moreover, it should demonstrate a broad understanding of the situation.

Part 3: Four-Corner Activity

Report to a corner of the room that has a sign designating your stance. (Undecided students will remain seated.) Once everyone has made an initial choice, begin the discussion. During the discussion, you can move to a different corner at any time. If you are not certain, you may remain seated. Students who are certain of their position need to persuade other students to join them. Once participants have aligned themselves, the facilitator may keep score as to which option wins the most converts or attracts the most undecided voters.

Comparative discussion question: In what ways is China's dilemma over Taiwan similar to and different from President Abraham Lincoln's considerations regarding the secessionist states in the South?

ACTIVITY 7: Trade and Geopolitics

Part 1: Examine

Define the following terms: "geopolitics," "nonintervention," "neocolonialism." Read Documents 20.10 and 20.11 and consider:

1. How has Sino-African trade affected and benefited each region?

2. What are the negative and positive consequences of Chinese officials not attaching political strings to their assistance and investment?

3. Why might trade with China be more appealing for developing nations than trade with Western nations?

Part 2: Mini Debate

You and your classmates as officials from China, the United Kingdom, France, India, and the United States will debate whether China's increased presence in Africa constitutes a form of neocolonialism. Class will end with a discussion on whether China's stance on trade, investment, and non-intervention is fitting for a major world power.

ACTIVITY 8: Is China a Superpower?

Prepare to discuss what it means to be a superpower. Cite historical examples of nations and civilizations that fit your definition. What responsibilities and challenges come with being a superpower?

You will work in a group of six. Read Document 20.12. Each member will then answer a different question below and report back to the group.

1. The author describes four phases of China's involvement with the UN. Summarize China's involvement during the 1970s.

2. How does the author describe China's involvement from the early 1980s to the early 1990s?

3. How does the author characterize the period from the early 1990s to the turn of the twenty-first century? How does the author contrast China's approach to international relations with the approach of some Western nations?

4. How does the author portray China's role in the last of the four phases?

5. Among the different assertions the author makes, which do you find most plausible? Which appear somewhat dubious or less substantiated?

6. Why do you think the author uses the term "multilateral" so often?

In your group identify the events or turning points that led to each new phase of China's involvement with the UN and the global community. Anticipate and discuss future turning points that could conceivably launch China into still another phase of UN and global involvement. What might that phase look like?

Finally, prepare for a class discussion on whether China fits the definition of a superpower. If you conclude that it does not, discuss what any nation must achieve to attain this status.

NOTE: If possible, before the discussion read the full article "China Takes on the World" by Michael Elliott (*Time*, January 22, 2007, available online at **www.time.com**).

EDITOR'S NOTE: The content of this chapter deals with present and future challenges in China, topics where analysts' viewpoints differ. For perspectives not emphasized in this chapter see the section "Perspectives on China's Challenges and Opportunities in the Years Ahead" in Suggested Resources.

Suggested Resources

Books

Bergsten, C. Fred, et al. *China: The Balance Sheet: What the World Needs to Know Now about the Emerging Superpower*. New York: Public Affairs, 2006.
A look at China's extraordinary economic growth and its many implications.

Chetham, Deirdre. *Before the Deluge: The Vanishing World of the Yangtze's Three Gorges*. New York: Palgrave Macmillan, 2002.
An exploration of the impact of the rising water level upriver from the Three Gorges Dam.

Economy, Elizabeth. *The River Runs Black: The Environmental Challenge to China's Future*. Ithaca: Cornell University Press, 2004.

Fishman, Ted C. *China, Inc.: How the Rise of the Next Superpower Challenges America and the World*. New York: Scribner, 2005.

Gifford, Rob. *China Road: Journey into the Future of a Rising Power*. New York: Random House, 2007.
Journalist Rob Gifford travels Chinese Route 312 from Shanghai to the border of Kazakhstan where the social and economic changes in the country are apparent all along the 3,000-mile route.

Gladney, Dru. *Dislocating China: Reflections on Muslims, Minorities, and Other Subaltern Subjects*. Chicago: University of Chicago Press, 2004.

Harrer, Heinrich. *Seven Years in Tibet*. New York: Dutton, 1954.
A true story about two Austrian mountaineers who traveled to India during World War II and instead wound up in the service of the Dalai Lama.

Shakya, Tsering. *The Dragon in the Land of Snows: A History of Modern Tibet Since 1947*. New York: Columbia University Press, 1999.

Steinfeld, Edward S. *Playing Our Game: Why China's Economic Rise Doesn't Threaten the West*. New York: Oxford University Press, 2010.

Wasserstrom, Jeffrey N. *China in the 21st Century: What Everyone Needs to Know*. New York: Oxford University Press, 2010.

Wasserstrom, Jeffrey N. *China's Brave New World: And Other Tales for Global Times*. Bloomington: Indiana University Press, 2007.
An examination of modernization in China in the twenty-first century.

Watts, Jonathan. *When a Billion Chinese Jump: How China Will Save Mankind—Or Destroy It*. New York: Scribner, 2010.
An exploration of China's struggles with environmental issues and sustainability amid economic growth.

Websites

Central Tibetan Administration
http://tibet.net/
The official website of the Government of Tibet in Exile.

China at the Crossroads, *The Guardian*
http://www.guardian.co.uk/world/series/china-at-the-crossroads
This series from *The Guardian* examines life, politics, the economy, and the environment in modern China.

The China Beat
http://www.thechinabeat.org/
A blog written from 2008–2012 about contemporary China. Based at the University of California, Irvine, blog contributors from the United States, China, Australia, Japan, Canada, and other countries provided context and criticism on events in China.

China Daily
http://www.chinadaily.com.cn/index.html
An English language daily newspaper published in China.

Choke Point: China, Circle of Blue Water News
http://www.circleofblue.org/waternews/featured-water-stories/choke-point-china/
Research and articles about China's water challenges.

Constitution of the People's Republic of China
http://www.npc.gov.cn/englishnpc/Constitution/node_2824.htm
The Chinese Constitution adopted December 4, 1982, and amendments since 1982.

Republic of China (Taiwan)
http://www.taiwan.gov.tw/
Government website for Taiwan.

Taiwan Flashpoint, BBC
http://news.bbc.co.uk/2/shared/spl/hi/asia_pac/04/taiwan_flashpoint/html/introduction.stm
This site provides an in-depth understanding of the China-Taiwan conflict over time.

"The World According to China," The New York Times
http://www.nytimes.com/2006/09/03/magazine/03ambassador.html
An article by James Traub published in September 2006 that provides a view of how China approaches international diplomacy.

Xinjiang Territory Profile, BBC
http://www.bbc.co.uk/news/world-asia-pacific-16860974
Overview, facts, and government information about the Xinjiang province of China.

Yellow River Slideshow, The New York Times
http://www.nytimes.com/slideshow/2006/11/17/world/20061119_YELLOW_SLIDESHOW_1.html
Photographs of the Yellow River from 2006.

Films

Beijing Taxi (78 mins; 2010)
The rapid transformation and modernization of Beijing is seen through the perspectives of three taxi drivers.

China Blue (88 mins; 2005)
A powerful documentary that captures the lives of teen girls working in a Chinese factory that produces denim jeans. The film provides another perspective on what China's involvement in the global economy means to one segment of the population and the role Western corporations and consumers play.

China from the Inside (3-hour, 4-part series; 2007)
This PBS documentary includes the episodes "Power and the People," "Women of the Country," "Shifting Nature," and "Freedom and Justice."

China Rises (208 mins; 2006)
This Discovery Times documentary looks at the monumental changes unfolding in the People's Republic of China. Video excerpts and interviews are available on the companion website at http://www.nytimes.com/specials/chinarises/intro/index.html.

Last Train Home (87 mins; 2009)
This documentary examines the consequences of migrant work in China as it follows a migrant couple trying to get back home for the Chinese New Year. Family strife caused by their absence leads their daughter to drop out of school and also become a migrant worker.

Tibet: Cry of the Snow Lion (100 mins; 2003)
This documentary chronicles the dark secrets of Tibet's recent past through interviews, personal stories, and archival images.

To Have and Have Not: Wealth and Poverty in the New China (56 mins; 2002)
The dichotomy between rich and poor is explored in this documentary from PBS's Wide Angle. Living conditions of migrant workers are juxtaposed against the new wealth in China's cities, displaying economic disparities in China's economic boom.

Up the Yangtze (93 mins; 2008)
As the Three Gorges Dam is completed, families living along the Yangtze River are affected in various ways. This film documents the struggles of one family as their daughter takes a job on one of the Yangtze River "Farewell Cruises" and the family is forced to leave their home for higher ground.

Perspectives on China's Challenges and Opportunities in the Years Ahead

Asia Society

http://asiasociety.org/policy/strategic-challenges/china

Blog posts, articles, videos, and op-eds about challenges facing China in the twenty-first century.

BBC News: China

http://www.bbc.co.uk/news/world/asia/china/

Up-to-date reports and news about events and issues in China.

Beijing Review

http://www.bjreview.com.cn/

The Beijing Review website provides up-to-date news and analysis on both national and international news. It is helpful for anyone interested in the increasing role that China is playing in global affairs.

The Bulletin, Newsletter of the China-United States Exchange Foundation

http://www.cusef.org.hk/media/publications/bulletin/

Articles about China's economy, environment, and foreign relations.

China Focus

http://www.chinausfocus.com/

Commentary on China-United States relations and articles about China's foreign policy, economy, environment, and culture.

The China Story

http://www.thechinastory.org

Research and news on contemporary China from the Australian Centre on China in the World.

Danwei

http://www.danwei.com/

A website that tracks and analyzes Chinese state, commercial, and social media.

The New York Times: China

http://topics.nytimes.com/top/news/international/countriesandterritories/china/index.html

The China country news page of The New York Times with articles, videos, multimedia, and links to additional blogs and media about China.

■ **A CLOSER LOOK**

Xi'an: Ancient Wall, Modern City

Street in Xi'an, Shaanxi Province, 2012. In the foreground is the city wall built during the Ming dynasty, 1368–1644.

(Photo by Jim Brown)

■ *Access the photo in color on the companion website. Examine all the details in the photograph, and then discuss how this image captures some of the challenges facing Chinese cities.*

Credits

Glossary

abdication: to step down from the throne

accommodation: the act of negotiating and compromising in relations with foreign countries

agrarian: related to farming

astronomy: the scientific study of the universe through physics and observation

autonomous region: administrative area within China associated with a particular ethnic minority and nominally given rights and controls not extended to the provinces

barbarian: the translation of a term used by Han Chinese to describe anyone non-Chinese, especially someone who did not speak Chinese; a foreigner

big character posters: posters covered with writing that were hung in public places to communicate political messages

biological warfare: germ warfare that causes physical harm through the spread of deadly germs

bourgeoisie: the middle class; according to Marxist doctrine the capitalists who exploit the working class

Boxer Uprising: an uprising in 1900 led by the "Boxers United in Righteousness," a Secret Society that formed in China in 1898, and which gained appeal with the landless, disbanded, and disempowered; during the uprising, foreigners and Chinese Christians were killed in Chinese cities

bureaucracy: the officials or administrators of a government or institution who carry out its rules and functions

cadre: a civil servant of bureaucrat in Communist China; someone who works for the government or Communist Party

Canton: former English name for Guangzhou

capitalism: an economic system based on the private ownership of the means of production of goods, characterized by a free, competitive market and driven by profit

cartography: the making of maps

Chinese Communist Party (CCP): the political party that has governed China since 1949; the CCP was formally organized at its first Congress in 1921

chinoiserie: a style of art and interior design, which reflects Chinese style and influence but was developed overseas

civil service examination system: a system of exams in China that was used to choose appointees to government positions. Chinese civil service exams began around the sixth century and were based on different classical Chinese texts at different times; however, the exams always included the Confucian classics

class struggle: The Marxist concept of struggle for political and economic power between the ruling (bourgeoisie) and working class

collaborator: an individual, a group, an organization, or a country that works with or another individual, group, organization, movement, or country; during wartime, the term has very negative connotations

collective: a group of farms managed as a unit, 1951–1958; farmers pooled their land and worked cooperatively; the product was shared primarily based on the amount of labor one had contributed

commune: a mutually shared community in which property, possessions, and responsibilities are shared; in the "people's communes" organized in 1958 in China, all the land belonged to the government

communism: a system of government in which no individual owns property and wealth is shared in a classless society by the members of the community

concubine: a woman who is the lover of a wealthy married man, but who is not his wife; she has the status of a subordinate "wife"

Confucian hierarchy: a rigid social hierarchy that endured for centuries in China; it placed scholar-officials at the top of society, followed by peasants, artisans, and at the bottom, merchants

Confucianism: philosophy of ethics and morality based on the teachings of Confucius, designed to cultivate a civilized individual and to establish an ordered, civilized society

Confucius: (ca 551 B.C.E.–ca 478 B.C.E.) Chinese philosopher, whose philosophical teachings on ethics and morality became the foundation of the Chinese way of life

connoisseur: a person with expert knowledge and informed taste, especially in the fine arts

conservative: adhering to tradition and cautious about change

coolies: unskilled laborers in China (and India) often doing heavy work for very low wages

counter-revolution: opposing revolution; during the early decades of the People's Republic of China (PRC) "counter-revolutionary" was a term used against individuals who opposed or questioned Party policies

courtesan: royal female attendant who practiced and had talents in the arts, such as music, dancing, and poetry

cult of personality: intense devotion to a person (often a leader) who is portrayed in an idealized, often heroic manner

decentralized: power or rule that is spread out among many regions or individuals

Democracy Wall: a wall near Tiananmen Square where posters with criticisms of society and the government were hung

Democratic League: A liberal party that existed along with the Guomindang and the Chinese Communist Party (CCP) in China; established in 1939, today it is one of eight legally recognized parties in the PRC

demographics: the distribution, density, vital statistics, etc. of a population

diaspora: the dispersion of a people sharing a common origin (in this case Chinese)

dictatorship: absolute power or authority by one individual, gained and/or maintained by force rather than election

diplomacy: skill at managing communication, negotiation, and relationships between nations

dissent: to differ in belief or opinion, to disagree

dissident: an individual who disagrees with an established political or religious system or organization

dynasty: a succession of rulers who are members of the same family

edict: a proclamation

elites: people of the highest class or greatest influence or authority within a larger group

eunuch: a man who has been castrated. In imperial China, eunuchs worked as choral singers, actors, servants, and were the only men permitted in the emperors living quarters or in the vicinity of the emperor's courtesans; some rose to powerful positions

extremist: an individual who holds extreme or radical political beliefs

factionalism: strife and dissent within a party

"factory": the living and business quarters of foreigners trading in Guangzhou (Canton) up to the late 1840s

feudal: a social, economic or political system in which the people working the land do not own it and are often exploited by landowners

feudal Japan: period of Japanese history dominated by regional families and the military rule of warlords from the twelfth to the nineteenth centuries; during this period, the emperor remained but was kept to a figurehead position

floating population: low-paid migrant workers and poor rural laborers, who move to urban areas to fill factory and construction jobs

foot binding: a tradition that lasted some 1,000 years in China in which young girl's feet would be wrapped in tight bandages to dramatically alter the shape and limit the size of the foot; bound feet were considered highly desirable in a young woman; the feet would be so mutilated that a woman could not walk normally

Foreign Direct Investment (FDI): the investment of one nation's funds into another country

Gang of Four: Jiang Qing (Mao Zedong's wife) and three others considered responsible for the worst excesses of the Great Proletarian Cultural Revolution

Gaokao: National Higher Education Entrance Exam, the academic exam that students in China take in hopes of gaining a place at a Chinese undergraduate university

Generalissimo: the supreme commander of a combined military force of the air force, navy, and army; Chiang Kai-shek took on the title

gentry: the class of society who own land; upper class

geopolitical: a worldview approach to looking at politics or a political issue

Gross Domestic Product (GDP): the value of goods and services produced within a country's borders during the course of a given period

Gross National Product (GNP): the value of goods and services produced by a nation's businesses or citizens, whether production occurs within or outside the country itself

gunboat diplomacy: negotiations between nations that involve threats to use military force

Guomindang: also known as the Nationalist Party; the party organized by Sun Yatsen in 1912 and later led by Chiang Kai-shek; formerly spelled Kuomintang (KMT)

Han Chinese: the dominant ethnic group in China who make up more than 90 percent of the population; The name Han stems from the Han dynasty (206 BC–220 AD), considered among the high points in Chinese civilization

hegemony: leadership; dominance

homage: anything given or done to show respect or reverence

hukou **(household registration) system**: Chinese system of assigning each family a residency status (*hukou*) in a particular place and limiting individuals' access to education and healthcare to the place of their family's registration

human rights: the basic rights and freedoms to which each human being is entitled

ideology: an organized system of beliefs, values and ideas that form a political philosophy or program

immigrant: an individual who has migrated to a country from a foreign country

imperial power: power of one country over other countries or colonies

imperialism: the practice of extending rule or authority over other countries or colonies

incursion: a brief, hostile invasion of another country

indentured servitude: a contract which commits an individual to serve a master for a specific time period

indigenous: originating within (native to) a particular place

industrialized: a society in which machine manufactured goods have replaced hand tools; one with large-scale industrial production

inflation: an increase in the supply of currency (money) leading to higher prices; leading to the money being worth less

infrastructure: the facilities or systems that serve a place, such as roads, power plants, and schools

"iron rice bowl": life-time job security in the PRC up until Deng Xiaoping's economic reforms

Jesuit: a Roman Catholic religious order of men known for their scholarship and commitment to education

jia: [in Fei Xiaotong's context] a family unit; individuals related by blood or marriage

kowtow: to kneel and touch the forehead to the ground to show respect to a superior in traditional Chinese culture

li: a traditional Chinese unit of distance about one-third of a mile or 500 meters

literati: intellectuals or the educated class; those involved with literature or the arts

Little Red Book: printed by the millions during the Cultural Revolution, the small book contained quotations from Mao Zedong; red Guards and proper revolutionaries carried it with them all the time, studying and memorizing the words of Chairman Mao

loess: a fine-grained, yellowish-brown, extremely fertile loam deposited by the wind and sometimes by floods

magistrate: a scholar-official in imperial China responsible for provincial affairs, including administering the civil service exams, tax collection, public safety, and administering justice; sometimes used as a synonym for a scholar-official

Manchu: the name a people from what are now China's northeastern provinces gave themselves after they invaded China in the early seventeenth century and established the Qing dynasty (1644–1912)

Manchuria: region of Northeastern China now Liaoning, Heilongjiang, and Jilin provinces

Mandate of Heaven: for millennia, Chinese tradition dictated that a leader/emperor had to have legitimate authority from the gods in order to rule the country; huge natural disasters or civil disorder were seen as signs that a ruler had lost this mandate

manifesto: a public declaration of motives and intentions by a person or group who have some public importance

mausoleum: a large tomb or burial monument

maxim: general rule, principle or truth

Meiji Restoration: a tremendous transformation in Japan in the late nineteenth century; as a result Japan built a powerful militarized and industrialized nation

memorial: a written appeal to a government official

migrant worker: a worker from another region (in the context of this book)

Ming dynasty: ruled China from 1368-1644; the era is known for its remarkable arts and culture and a vibrant commercial and urban life that contributed to great prosperity for some. In the late sixteenth century, however, rural populations were suffering as a result of government mismanagement and natural disasters

mission schools: schools funded by foreign Christians and usually operated by foreign missionaries

missionary: somebody sent to another country by a church to spread its faith or to do social and medical work

modernization: the process of technological, industrial, and intellectual progress or advancement in a country

Mongols: nomadic people of (Inner and Outer) Mongolia, at various points in history, enemies of the Chinese empire

monsoon: a seasonal wind of the Indian Ocean and South Asia, blowing from the southwest from April to October, and from the northeast during the rest of the year, generally bringing heavy rains

multilateral: many-sided; involving more than two countries

multinational company: one that conducts business in two or more countries

nationalism: loyalty and belief in one's country; (can be) excessive narrow patriotism

Nationalist: (in China) a member of the Guomindang, the Chinese Nationalist Party, the party organized by Sun Yatsen in 1912 and later led by Chiang Kai-shek; formerly the Kuomintang (KMT)

occupation: the control of a country or area by enemy or outside forces

party-state: form of government in which one political party controls all political organizations and institutions of the state

Peking: former English name of Beijing, present-day capital of China

pension: a retirement benefit paid from an investment account to which a person or employer has contributed during their working years

"Ping-Pong Diplomacy": In 1971, at the 31st World Table Tennis Championships in Japan, Chinese players invited the American team to visit and play in China, which they did (in both cases with government support). The ping-pong players were the first American group allowed into China since 1949. The United States subsequently announced plans to end the trade embargo with China. Then the Chinese team reciprocated by visiting the United States. These were the first steps in the resumption of Sino–U.S. relations

politburo: one of the highest levels within the Chinese Communist Party made up of between five and nine members, it effectively sets national policy and controls all administrative, legal, and executive appointments

progressive: advocating social, economic or political reform

proletarian: the working class in Communist terminology

propaganda: the use of words, symbols, music, art or any communication specifically to influence people's thinking and behavior; to promote a policy, doctrine or cause

proselytize: to try to convert somebody to a religious faith or political doctrine

province: highest-level administrative division of China

purge: to remove or overthrow opponents, rulers, or people considered undesirable

Qing: the Qing dynasty (1644–1911), also known as the Ch'ing or the Manchu dynasty, was the last dynasty in China

queue: long, braided ponytail worn by the Manchus of central Manchuria, and imposed upon the Han Chinese during the Qing dynasty, as a sign of submission

radical: an individual who favors making sweeping or extreme economic, political, or social changes

reactionary: an opponent to liberal or progressive social and political changes or reforms

"red": Communist (when used in reference to China)

Red Guards: students who participated in the Cultural Revolution and took up Mao Zedong's call to destroy the Four Olds—old customs, old habits, old culture, old thinking; many were involved in extensive violence and destruction

Re-education camp: "re-education through labor" according to the Chinese Ministry of Public Security is a system of reform through compulsory education for those who have committed minor offenses not considered legally criminal; the system was put in place in 1957 and it is not unusual for it to be used for political dissidents; conditions are harsh

reform: social and political changes or improvement enacted by law

reparation: compensation for a wrong-doing given to one group or country by another

Republic of China (ROC): the name for China between 1912 and 1949; also the name of the government Chiang Kai-shek formed on Taiwan after his defeat by the Communists on mainland China in 1949

restoration: the return of something that was removed

revisionist: under Mao, a pejorative term referring to people or ideas that deviated from orthodox Marxist principles

rickshaw: a small two-wheeled carriage with a seat, pulled by a person

rural: agrarian or farming areas; having to do with the countryside

scholar-official: individuals who had passed China's civil service examinations and held government positions; educated in the Confucian classics, they were often amateur artists, and connoisseurs or patrons of the arts

Security Council: the organ of the United Nations comprised of five permanent members (China, the United States, Russia, the United Kingdom, and France) with veto power, and ten temporary members, charged with maintaining international peace and security

sent-down youth: approximately 12 million teenagers sent to the countryside between 1968 and 1975 (during the Cultural Revolution) to live, work, and be re-educated by the peasants

simin: the four classes of people in traditional Chinese society: scholar-officials, peasants, artisans, and merchants

socialism: a political system that promotes government intervention to ensure a more fair distribution of jobs and resources in a society and usually characterized by some public ownership of industries

socialist: an individual who believes in socialism or belongs to a socialist party

sovereignty: authority or rule; independence from others

soviet (as in Jiangxi Soviet, for example): an area under communist control; the Jiangxi Soviet began in 1928 as a hideout for Mao Zedong and a small enclave escaping the Guomindang

Special Economic Zones (SEZ): geographical zones within China established for foreign investment; foreign enterprises receive tax breaks and other incentives

state-run economy: an economic system planned and run by a central government

struggle sessions: meetings during which individuals suspected of harboring "rightist" views that were not in line with communist ideology were forced to confess and "struggle" to rid themselves of their bourgeois ways; these meetings were sometimes violent, especially during the early years of the Cultural Revolution

sustainable development: economic progress that can be maintained over time without damaging the environment

tael: approximately one ounce of silver, formerly used as Chinese currency

tariff: a duty or tax on imported or exported trade

Treaty of Versailles: The 1919 peace treaty that officially ended World War I

treaty: a formal negotiated agreement between countries

tributary relationship: a relationship between two states in which one acknowledged the other to be superior and paid tribute by sending representatives bearing gifts

unilateral: decided or acted upon by only one involved party or nation

vernacular: commonly spoken, everyday language

"victim literature": writings of individuals who experienced or witnessed terrible abuse during the Cultural Revolution; these books were for a while encouraged under Deng Xiaoping as a way for some to express their anguish; some scholars note that these works, as a whole, give a one-dimensional emotional view of that period

warlords: military rulers that had control over regions of China during the Early Republican period

World Trade Organization (WTO): the organization that oversees the rules of trade between nations worldwide

yuan: basic monetary unit of the People's Republic of China

Index

Z

Expand Your Knowledge
with CHENG & TSUI

The Enduring Legacy of Ancient China
By Primary Source, Inc.

The ideal companion to *China Since 1644*, *The Enduring Legacy of Ancient China* introduces students to the history and culture of ancient China through vivid primary sources and classroom activities. Units cover everything from the roots of Chinese language, arts, and philosophy to China's historic relations with its neighbors. Ideal for grades 7-12 and teacher training programs, it is flexible enough for use as a textbook or a teacher's guide. A great resource for learning more about China *before* 1644!

The Secret History of the Mongols
Adapted by Paul Kahn

Before the Manchus established the Qing dynasty in 1644, the Mongols were the only foreigners to conquer all of China and establish their own dynasty—the Yuan—in 1279. This adaptation of the oldest Mongolian text details the Mongols' version of their nation's origins, the life of Chingis Khan, and the creation of their 13th century empire. Rendered in colloquial English, this adaptation of the narrative poem also includes an overview of medieval Asia and maps to help set the stage for another exciting chapter in China's history.

Children of Hangzhou
By Boston Children's Museum

This exciting DVD follows the lives of four teenagers from Hangzhou, China. Through their video diaries, American students experience school days, visit the countryside, see an opera performance, and celebrate birthdays alongside their Chinese counterparts. Includes interactive maps, instructions on making Chinese crafts, and discussion questions, making it perfect for any social studies classroom looking to explore contemporary life in China!

A Dream of Red Mansions
By Hsueh-Chin Tsao, Ngo Kao
Translated by Hsien-Yi Yang, Gladys Yang

One of the greatest Chinese novels ever written, this abridged English translation of the mid-18th century classic is a moving tale of unrequited love and the fall of an aristocratic family. It is also an observant look at daily life during the Qing dynasty, making it an excellent primary source for history classes.

Please Don't Call Me Human
By Wang Shuo
Translated by Howard Goldblatt

At the forefront of contemporary Chinese literature, Wang Shuo's wild novels have formed their own genre—hooligan literature. In this astonishing book, Wang imagines an Olympics where the capacity to humiliate oneself is celebrated instead of athletic prowess. An incisive, satirical look into the rapid transformation of modern Chinese society!

The Field of Life and Death *and* Tales of Hulan River
By Xiao Hong
Translated by Howard Goldblatt

Along with Ding Ling, Xiao Hong was one of China's first feminist writers. This translated collection of two of her most famous accounts of rural China in the early 1900s also contains the original preface by Lu Xun. These works are moving revelations of hardship in the Chinese countryside and life under the Japanese occupation.

Feilong, The China Game
Produced by The Center for Asian Studies,
University of Vermont

Feilong tests what students and teachers know about the history and culture of China, from the Neolithic era to the present. This fun trivia game can be played in teams or individually at three different knowledge levels: beginner, intermediate, and advanced. A great way to test and expand your knowledge about China—at home or in the classroom!